BONJOUR BLANC

Ian Thomson is a writer and journalist living in London.
His biography *Primo Levi* won the W. H. Heinemann Award
2003. He is a Fellow of the Royal Society of Literature.

ALSO BY IAN THOMSON

Primo Levi
Southern Italy

Ian Thomson

BONJOUR BLANC

A Journey through Haiti

With a preface by J. G. Ballard

VINTAGE

Published by Vintage 2004

2 4 6 8 10 9 7 5 3 1

First published in Great Britain in 1992 by
Hutchinson

Vintage
Random House, 20 Vauxhall Bridge Road,
London SW1V 2SA

Random House Australia (Pty) Limited
20 Alfred Street, Milsons Point, Sydney,
New South Wales 2061, Australia

Random House New Zealand Limited
18 Poland Road, Glenfield,
Auckland 10, New Zealand

Random House (Pty) Limited
Endulini, 5A Jubilee Road, Parktown 2193, South Africa

The Random House Group Limited Reg. No. 954009
www.randomhouse.co.uk

A CIP catalogue record for this book
is available from the British Library

ISBN 0 09 9452154

Papers used by Random House are natural, recyclable products made from
wood grown in sustainable forests. The manufacturing processes conform to the
environmental regulations of the country of origin

Typeset by Palimpsest Book Production Limited, Polmont, Stirlingshire
Printed and bound in Great Britain by
Bookmarque Ltd, Croydon, Surrey

For Laura

'Tomorrow I go to Haiti. They say the President is a *Perfect Dear!*'

Ronald Firbank, on a postcard to Osbert Sitwell

'When I told my friends that I was going to
Haiti they raised their eyebrows. "Haiti,"
they said. "But that's the place where they
kill their presidents and eat their babies.
You'd better buy yourself a large-sized gun."'

Alec Waugh, *The Sugar Islands*

Contents

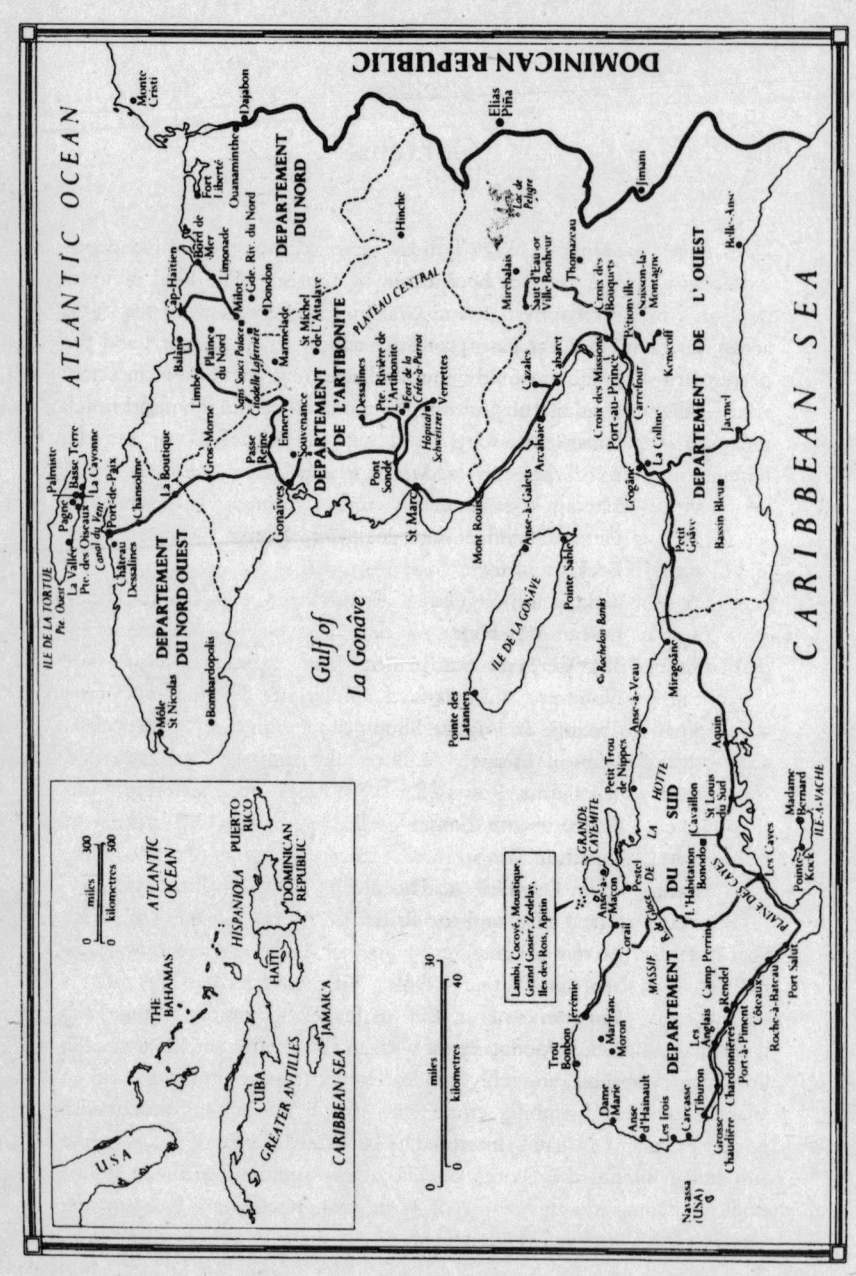

Preface

Does travel, in its pre-package holiday sense, still exist as an independent activity, or has its place been taken by tourism? The kind of journeys on which Evelyn Waugh and Graham Greene set out in the 1930s across Africa and the Far East, protected only by their passports and the nearest British gunboat, would be unthinkable now. Away from the safety zone of the international airport, the car-rental office and the resort hotel, today's unwary traveller is soon faced with disease, civil war and the hostage dungeon. All the more credit, then, to Ian Thomson for his hairraising but entertaining account of his journey through Haiti, which he set out to explore with little more than his toothbrush, a brazen nerve and a truffle-hound's nose for a good story.

Famous for Voodoo, zombis and its late President, 'Papa Doc' Duvalier, Haiti must represent the greatest concentration of misery, cruelty and dashed hopes anywhere on our planet. From the air this one-time Caribbean paradise is a sun-scorched clinker, its forested mountains stripped bare to provide its impoverished people with fuel for their charcoal stoves. Thomson gingerly explores the capital, Port-au-Prince, scarcely more than a shanty town of garbage heaps, open sewers and tin-shack hotels, echoing to the gunfire of the latest coup and roamed by Tontons Macoute, the old Duvalierist thugs eager to hire their killing skills to any brooding general with his eye on the Presidential Palace.

But this small and desperate nation is also an endless parade of jovial, charming and garrulous characters who hail Thomson cheerfully with the *'Bonjour blanc'* (in Haitian Creole, 'Hey, stranger') of his title: a euphoric taxi-driver who never uses his brakes but simply switches the ignition on and off, a Voodoo priest with an IBM computer and a smooth line in psychobabble, an archly condescending teenage prostitute, and an affable, contraband-running crone who prowls the landing-beach with pocket calculator in hand. Interbred, a bewildering mix of black, white and Indian blood, they come on like actors auditioning for an insane tropical sitcom, and the whole of Haiti soon resembles a hallucinating version of the *Black and White Minstrel Show* danced to a tommy-gun beat.

As well as a personal travelogue, *Bonjour Blanc* is an intriguing history of a tragic nation, the world's oldest black republic, founded in 1804 after an uprising against the French led by the former slave, Toussaint L'Ouverture, later betrayed and done to death on the orders of Napoleon. But cruel wars between the black and mulatto factions have been endemic ever since. Ruthless dictators impose their morbid rule, the most weird and grisly being Papa Doc, who deliberately dressed in the black suit and bowler hat of Baron Samedi, chief bogeyman of Voodoo, and devised his own version of the Lord's Prayer: 'Our Doc, who art in the National Palace for life, hallowed be Thy name . . .'

Bravely, Thomson allowed himself to be initiated into a sinister animist cult, which might have turned him into one of the zombis he interviews – victims buried alive after being paralysed by the puffer-fish nerve poison, tetrodotoxin, then resuscitated with damaged brains and set to work in the fields as little more than automatons. The best praise I can give to this superb and pulse-stopping book is to say that I read every page expecting it to end abruptly in mid-paragraph.

J. G. Ballard

A note on spelling

'Voodoo' was the accepted orthography when this book was published in 1992, and I have kept the old spelling rather than replace it with the term 'Vodou' (or even 'Voudoun') favoured today.

I.T.

Prologue

Is there anybody in the National Palace?

'*Eh blanc*, gimme a dollar.' It was the spindle-shanked old man, brandishing as usual an empty bottle of rum.

'Not today, Papa Noir,' I said. 'Not today.'

Every morning in Port-au-Prince the old man was there, busking for alms outside the National Palace. Often he sat crouched over a basket piled with rotted bread-fruit, mischievously hooking any ankles in reach of his stick. I never knew his name; people called him *Papa Noir*. He was half-blind, Black Daddy, with cataracts, the elderly face worn and crumbled. A great moustache like a house-painter's brush lent an air of dignity, but he looked a sight swaddled in shapeless gunny-sacking, his sandals fashioned from a used tyre. One day the old man appeared in a new T-shirt. It bore the sad injunction: 'Shop Till You Drop'.

'Life lasts too long sometimes,' he said sourly, 'even for a white man.' Then he spat – *tfui!* – and added with a faint derisive smile: 'But you will not last very long in Haiti. Nobody does.'

The National Palace stood at the edge of Place des Héros de l'Indépendance, a palm-fringed plaza more popularly known as Place des Zéros. This is the heart of Haitian civic and national life. Numerous public buildings – Headquarters of the Haiti National Guard, the Palais de Justice and the Palais des Ministres – attest to an unwieldy concentration of governance. Beyond the palace loomed the Dessalines Barracks, a vast workshop of horror: in the days of Papa Doc, torture chambers were said to be painted brown so that blood would not mar the walls. Presidential Guard stand at the gates of the palace, shouldering Uzi automatics. They are answerable to His Excellency the President alone and their function is to defend his boundless power, to perpetuate the authoritarian regime. Behind these gates Papa Doc was rumoured to have divined auguries in the entrails of goats. He sought counsel from the gods of Voodoo by sitting in a bathtub wearing a black top hat.

At six every evening the national anthem would sound from the palace – the notes blown from cracked trumpets as the flag jerked slowly up the mast. Often the soldiers waved Black Daddy away with their weapons;

he was known to yell abuse at the President, at the nation, at all the dictators who governed as if never to die. One evening he swung the empty bottle round his head: *'Dérangé!'*, he seemed to exclaim. The presidential chair in the National Palace, that chair was . . . *'– rangé!'* I later understood that this was a term borrowed from Voodoo to describe the curse that supposedly afflicts any man or woman insane enough to sit in the chair: *rangé*, every one of those sedentary despots bewitched.

For three months I tried to secure a visit to the National Palace but was buffeted from the press officer of the City Government to numerous bureaucratic sub-delegates – Minister of Protocol, secretary to the Minister of Foreign Affairs, Director of Culture, several members of the military low command. Part of the problem was that my only contact at the palace had fled the country in the wake of a coup d'état, burning all his personal papers – among them my original letters explaining in careful French why I wished to visit the building. To short-circuit palace inefficiency is quite an achievement but I was determined to see inside that vast depository of power. What lay behind the bedazzlement of its white façade? What spirits lurked? Many Haitian rulers had entered the palace one day, were buried in an unknown grave the next. During the years 1956–57 six presidencies and a military junta followed in succession. Few occupants had died a natural death or survived their term of office. Was this place *rangé*?

One day I reported to the Ministry of Information to see about renewing my papers for a visit. I was ushered into a room with bullet-speckled walls where men in dark glasses sat round a cardboard box containing tins of Mazola Corn Oil, rolls of Élite lavatory paper. 'We are checking the produce for bombs,' one of them explained as he tendered over the table a box full of thick cigars. 'Want one?'

'No thanks. I have an appointment here with the minister.'

'Well, well!' he replied with affected solicitude. 'And do you have an accreditation from the Ministry of Foreign Affairs for this appointment?'

'Yes, hundreds.'

There was a short silence as the official ruminated this information; then, with a scornful curl of the lip: 'Where are these accreditations?'

'Most of them were burned by a previous minister.'

'Burned?' He turned to his colleagues who fell about laughing. 'Why? How? What for?'

'I don't know. As I said, they were burned.'

'But why?'

The conversation might have continued in this circular fashion had I not said: 'I am in Haiti to write. I have permission to come here. Can you please tell me where I might find the Minister of Information?'

'Monsieur the Minister is at the National Palace in conference with the President,' the man said with growing irritation. 'If you have the patience to wait, well and good. Otherwise, goodbye.'

I was led to a room near by, oppressively hot as there was no electricity to power the overhead fans. Minutes turned to an hour and more telephone calls were made, higher officials consulted. The slow tap of typewriters began to annoy after three hours and still no sign of the minister. I had been rebuffed so many times I was determined to wait.

Distant acclamations, words of command could be heard as the Minister of Information finally arrived. He made no apology for the delay and strode past into his office. 'What time is it?' he barked at one of his confidential advisers, a man in white shoes. 'Whatever time Monsieur the Minister says it is,' the minion grinned as he shuffled backwards out of the office bowing.

The minister gave me three minutes. 'And what may I do for you?'

I explained my predicament.

'We apologize for all the trouble you have suffered.' He spoke with studied courtesy, and promised that I should see the palace tomorrow morning. As I left the room he reverted swiftly into Creole to address his secretary: 'Who was that *blanc*?' – adding with apparent irrelevance: 'I see the Communists are trying to overthrow the government again.'

The minister never kept his word, of course, and I despaired of visiting the palace. Again I telephoned one official after another in search of help. 'Call back later': it was always the same. At the National Tourist Board (surely an office without purpose, as there is little tourism in Haiti) I spoke to Mademoiselle Verbil, a gracious Haitian with skin the colour of cinnamon.

'My dear,' she announced, 'how nice of you to look in.'

Once more I explained my problem.

'*Attendez un petit peu*,' and she dialled a number that gave a direct line to the palace.

We were escorted to the building, Mademoiselle Verbil and I, in a black

State Security limousine. Beggars, beggars everywhere around Place des Zéros; in the hills behind the palace, Port-au-Prince had spread like a seeping blot in a vertical sprawl of slums. I held up my press pass at the gates; on mention of Engineer — 's name, a soldier waved us through. Members of the Presidential Guard sat opposite each other in sentry boxes likes passengers in a railway carriage; others lay about in string vests playing cards, or dozing on rattan mats, too lazy to salute.

Inside the National Palace, an officer motioned us to a chaise-longue upholstered in spectacular crimson and tarnished gold threads. 'Wait here a moment.' Then he turned on his heels and marched off. We sat alone in a vast salon with a pompous red carpet and heavy gilt picture frames round the walls. The interior of the palace seemed drowsy in tropical mid-afternoon; a distant peal of cathedral bells was the only sound. Patiently we awaited our tour of the public rooms.

Engineer — came to greet us down a glaring white stairway. He resembled an effete boulevardier with his silken foulard, a carnation in his buttonhole and the Napoleon III beard elegantly trimmed. 'I have been employed here for the last forty years.' The man spoke with pride. 'This restoration is all my own work. I alone was responsible for hanging those drapes.' He pointed to a row of curtains, slightly too ornate, in the Ivory Salon; they were embroidered with elephant tusks.

'Your curtains are quite exquisite,' said Mademoiselle Verbil.

'Do you really think so?' returned the Engineer.

'Absolutely, *chéri*.' She gave me a wink.

Mademoiselle Verbil was playing to the comicality of a man who had clung to the coat-tails of Papa Doc and his son, Jean-Claude. How else had the Engineer managed to stay for so long, if he was not corruptible? For the last forty years Haiti had been a virtual dictatorship; since 1986 ministers and presidents had come and gone, but nothing had changed. 'The new man will differ from the old man only physically,' wrote Joseph Brodsky in his essay on tyranny. 'Mentally and otherwise he is bound to be an exact replica of the corpse.' Engineer — was a symbol of this malaise, a man who had managed to survive through a shrewd transfer of loyalties. Corruption is no respecter of ideology.

'He has his orders,' Mademoiselle Verbil whispered as we made our way through long rococo halls giddy with plush and whorled designs of gold, oriental rugs and gilded *boule* clocks, vases of deep pink roses. Not a single chair, table, sofa or console had been removed since Baby Doc fled the country with his wife Michèle on 7 February 1986. 'Statuettes'

– the Engineer gestured to a row of plaster caryatids in the audience room – 'Jean-Claude simply adored them.'

'And Michèle?' I queried.

'Michèle preferred gold-plated objects,' the Engineer said composedly. 'She was the one with artistic flair.'

On we went, passing the Red Room ('This is for very distinguished guests') and the Yellow Room whose walls were covered with silk imported from the United States. The lengths of fabric were woven throughout with the motto of the Haitian Republic: *L'Union Fait la Force*.

'Strength Through Union', Engineer — felt the need to translate. This motto is the device of the armorial bearing of the Republic. It is a great blazon in honour of the Haitian War of Independence, complete with pikes, drums and cannonballs. Banners unfurl like medieval pennons at the foot of a palm tree topped by the cap of liberty.

We proceeded to the Hall of Busts, lined with bronze heads and torsos of Haitian presidents up to Elie Lescot in 1946. There were no memorials to Papa or Baby Doc: evidently these had been removed.

'You know how it is,' the Engineer said mournfully. 'The political situation has been so volatile in recent years that one president follows another with a rapidity which defeats the Hall of Busts.'

The bust of Papa Doc now lies in what our Engineer called the '*Dépôt de Débris*'. A film of dust had covered the ugly thing. 'We keep it hidden,' he explained. 'Poor François Duvalier,' the Engineer added indulgently. 'He was not such a bad man.' Adjacent to the Debris Depot was a bathroom which the dictator had built in April 1966 to commemorate Emperor Haile Selassie's visit to Haiti. Even the rim of the lavatory bowl was adorned with gold leaf.

'Haitians have always been impatient for eternity,' announced the Engineer as we entered the presidential chapel. A small projector screen hung above the altar, as Baby Doc had a penchant for pornography in technicolour.

'*Cinéma vérité?*' asked Mademoiselle Verbil teasingly.

'Oh yes,' came the innocent reply.

We continued through a great labyrinth of state rooms. The grandeur was beginning to pall on me, stifling as black velvet, but I had yet to see the worst of it. 'This is all due to Michèle' – spring-loaded security doors closed behind us with a heavy clunk as we were ushered into the private apartments of Jean-Claude and his wife. To my knowledge I was the first foreigner allowed inside and I have Mademoiselle Verbil to thank for securing my entrance. 'You can get quite far in Haiti if you pander to authority,' she reasoned.

'As I said, it was Michèle who had the real taste,' the Engineer went on in his worldly voice. There were giant artificial banana trees fashioned from bamboo with mirrored leaves and fronds, huge gold snails in the bathroom, great fluffy footballs behind a Chinese vellum screen, copies of *Vogue* and *Paris Match* neatly piled beside crystal pineapples, and reproduction Ming vases under canopies of Perspex. The bedroom was inlaid, both walls and ceiling, with yet more mirrors reflecting banks of video equipment, plastic cherubs and Dresden figurines perched on a plinth of black marble. There was nothing to disturb the silence save the momentous ticking of a clock. Everything had been preserved in its original place; cut flowers and exotic shrubs were watered by a faithful gardener, his movements monitored by a closed-circuit television.

It has been alleged that Baby Doc, his family and associates embezzled some $120 million. When proceedings to recover this money commenced in July 1986 the defendants denied liability. They claimed it had been a tradition in Haiti for almost two centuries that a new government should take legal action against a previous regime.

The Haitian equivalent of Securicor scanned us with electronic bleepers as we left the National Palace.

My persistence had been answered and I considered the visit a success. Nothing in the building could be described as sinister. There were no gegaws from the mystic lore of Voodoo, no decapitated heads conserved in pails of ice – only a tawdry mediocrity. The National Palace was a purple-lined sanctuary, an empty shrine to the tyranny of father and son.

Papa Doc was distinguished as the only Haitian president to have established a dynasty. The average length of a good tyranny, according to Brodsky, is a decade and a half. Papa Doc had ruled for fourteen years, his son Baby Doc for a further fifteen. François Duvalier had no clear ideology or discernible policy; he was surrounded by a Perónist halo of mystery and magic. His dictatorship, nevertheless, marked the longest period of stability that Haiti has known since independence in 1804. The collapse of this dynasty has been followed by the familiar round of coup d'états, rigged elections, martial law. A recent president, Father Jean-Bertrand Aristide, was overthrown by the military on 30 September 1991. He had been accused of organizing a private police force. There were great hopes for this Catholic priest; he was elected on a wave of popular support just eight months earlier. It remains to be seen whether the incumbent president will prove strong or honest enough to exorcise the ghost of Duvalierism.

Throughout my entire time in Port-au-Prince I never saw anyone emerge from the National Palace. It was an imposing residence, the mountains of Haiti ranged behind its snow-white cupolas. At night a couple of lights would glow like beacons from the windows facing the sea. But nobody, not a soul, was seen to leave. Only Black Daddy was always there.

One night he told me: *'Haïti, m'sieur, Haïti – c'est un pays tête-en-bas'*: a country turned upside down.

The Centaur of the Savannahs

'Let the slave grinding at the mill run out into the field;
Let him look up into the heavens and laugh in the bright air.'

William Blake, *America*

The hero of Haitian independence was sent to die in the Jura mountains of France. His prison is still there. Hewn out of rock, it lies deep within a medieval castle which stands bare on a mountain overlooking the Swiss frontier. On one side, the Fort de Joux defends the approaches to Pontarlier, a dreary town of Tyrolean chalets and municipal rose gardens; on the other, three thousand feet below, flows the icy River Doubs. Ramparts and angular keeps with edges sharp as a knife, the castle must have appeared distant from the tropic warmth of Haiti, its bright exalting sunlight. Records kept in the archives show that the dying prisoner requested his meagre diet be rationed with cane sugar imported from the French colony of Saint Domingue, soon to be declared the independent Republic of Haiti.

In winter, access to the castle is difficult. Climbing the slope on foot you have to lean into the wind to avoid being blown off the narrow ice-bound path. Once inside, a labyrinth of oubliettes and antechambers, damp and glacial, leads to a door with a judas-hole. This opens on to a vaulted dungeon: it is bare with only a rough-hewn deal table, a commode and a primitive pallet. Someone has left a spray of flowers by the single barred window. There is a message – 'In Memory of Toussaint L'Ouverture, First of the Blacks, Bonaparte of the Antilles. You died here of starvation, but the slaves of Haiti were set free.'

The French Revolution of 1789 proclaimed equality among all men. And, in the spirit of the Rights of Man, equality between black and white: slavery was now an intolerable injury to human nature. The refusal of planters in colonial Saint Domingue to recognize this decree led to the only successful slave revolt in history. In 1794, just two years after the composition of the 'Marseillaise' with its clarion-call to 'Live Freely or Die', slavery in Saint Domingue was formally abolished. Yet hostilities continued between the white planters, who rejected the authority of the National Assembly in Paris, and the mulattoes whom they regarded as members of a 'bastard and degenerate race'. It remained for the slaves to take up the tricoloured cockade of the Revolution, and reconcile the warring factions.

Toussaint L'Ouverture, the barely literate grandson of an African chieftain, assumed control of the new slave army. Familiar with the Commentaries of Caesar, and with the polemics of the French abolitionist, Abbé Raynal, he was gifted too in the art of military strategy. Toussaint sat his horse with such ease that he was known as the Centaur of the Savannahs but the origin of his surname – 'the opening' – is a matter of some puzzlement. Whether this referred to his bravery in making a breach among the enemy ranks, or to a gap in his teeth, nobody knows. The French poet Lamartine offers a fanciful explanation in his romantically youthful 1850 play *Toussaint*: the name L'Aurore – 'daybreak' – was awarded the former slave by a Capuchin friar and was later corrupted by his illiterate followers into L'Ouverture.

For Lamartine, as for so many nineteenth-century romantics, Toussaint was the morning star of a new era for Haiti: 'Nothing,' declares the hero of this play, 'can resist the valour of the sansculottes.' Toussaint swore allegiance to the Republic of France, and vowed to defeat its enemies – royalists invading from Spain and England, planters battling for a return of the *ancien régime*. After a prolonged and vicious civil war between black slaves and mulattoes ending in 1800 with victory for the blacks, Toussaint continued to act as the mandatory of France; but in secret he looked to the time when Napoleon would acknowledge an independent republic of Haiti.

In May 1801 Toussaint L'Ouverture, the revolutionary slave, declared himself Governor for Life of the island, with the right to appoint his successor. He still recognized the sovereign rights of France, the seniority of the motherland, but his mimicry of the consular office – the open vaunt that he was the 'Bonaparte of the Antilles' – outraged Napoleon. In the winter of 1801, when he had been master of France for only two years, the First Consul violated the principles of the French Revolution. 'As all men are born equal,' wrote the Baron de Montesquieu, 'slavery must be accounted unnatural.' But the expedition which Napoleon was poised to send to Saint Domingue aimed to bring about a counter-revolution in the state of enfranchised blacks. The former colonists were to be reinstated in their original properties; once more the slaves would submit quietly to the coercion of the cat-whip, branded with the fleur-de-lys. And Toussaint L'Ouverture – in the words of Napoleon 'a gilded African' – would be clapped in irons. Or perhaps carried to Paris in a golden cage and exhibited for the amusement of the public at the newly opened Jardin des Plantes.

The future republic of Haiti was too valuable a colony for Napoleon to lose. Under the *ancien régime*, trade with Saint Domingue had represented more than half the oceanic commerce of France. At a time when the name Australia was unknown, and the United States numbered less than five and a half million people, Saint Domingue was already the most profitable slave colony the world had ever known. The glittering prosperity of Nantes and Bordeaux, of Marseilles and Dieppe, was in part derived from commerce with the Caribbean island in coffee, indigo, cocoa, cotton and, of course, sugar. The sugar plantations alone produced more cane than all the British Caribbean islands together.

Saint Domingue was the pearl of the Antilles: even as the Bastille was stormed, planters across the Atlantic would sate their abundant leisure and boredom with fine food, drink and dice. *Rich as a Creole*, they said in Paris: no small white in Saint Domingue was a servant. An Englishman, visiting the island at that time, remarked on the sartorial finery even of the man who came to shoe his horse:

He had four Slaves at his heels carrying his Tools; and he was dressed in a silk Coat tout à la Mode; his linen fully trimmed and as fine as that of the first Nobleman in Europe; his Gold Snuff-Box, for no man scarcely, whatever his Situation, is without that piece of luxury; his Gold repeating Watch; two gold chains, and Diamond rings on his fingers and every thing in proportion. I say, what would an Englishman think to see his farrier thus equipped?

The slave revolt commanded by Toussaint L'Ouverture, and the prospect of an independent black state, horrified Europe. As Talleyrand wrote to a French general in Washington: 'The existence of a negro people in arms, occupying a country which it has soiled by the most criminal acts, is a horrible spectacle for all white nations.' Four years after the death of Toussaint, in 1807, the German writer Heinrich von Kleist was imprisoned as a Prussian spy in the same cell at Fort de Joux. He later wrote a short story, *Betrothal in Saint Domingue*, which was set in 1803 after revolution; it betrays an almost visceral loathing for the blacks. 'No acts of tyranny perpetrated by the whites,' proclaims a French aristocrat who has lost his wife to the guillotine, 'could ever justify the depths of treachery and degradation of those Negroes.'

Napoleon's expedition, destined to 'destroy the new Algiers being organized in American waters', set sail on 14 December 1801 from the harbours of Brest, Rochefort, Lorient and Toulon. Over in England the November issue of *The Gentleman's Magazine* had reported:

The Consular Government is making preparations for sending a military force of 20,000 men to the island of Saint Domingue for the purpose of reducing General Toussaint L'Ouverture to a due degree of moderation to the mother country, and preventing the erection there of a Negro Republick . . . which would endanger the existence of all the West Indian Colonies, whether French or English.

The French armada comprised 32 French and Spanish ships of the line, together with 31 frigates and troopships.

Abolitionists in London feared the consequences of this massive resort to arms. They suspected Napoleon might use Saint Domingue as a base of operations for the vast colonial dominion he was planning to build in the Americas, to pursue across the Atlantic the mirage of empire that had failed him in Egypt and the East. Such fears were justified: the marble walls round the monolithic tomb of Napoleon at Les Invalides are engraven with consular dictums which proclaim the 'necessity of stifling in every part of the world every kind of disquiet and trouble'. Austerlitz, Marengo, Rivoli, Abukir – Napoleon would have liked to add Saint Domingue to this roll-call of victories. On the eve of the departure of the West Indian expedition, the libertarian MP James Stephen, brother-in-law of William Wilberforce, wrote an open letter to the Chancellor of the Exchequer:

Within a very short period, probably before these sheets which I am now penning can issue from the press, the arrival and first effects of the French armament will be known in Europe. The invasion involves interests more awfully important to the blacks than ever before gave violence and durability to the quarrels of mankind.

Napoleon gravely underestimated the extent to which liberty and equality had become the religion of men enslaved. Since the French Republic had abolished slavery he could not, as yet, openly restore an institution flagrantly opposed to the Rights of Man; he flattered Toussaint L'Ouverture with assurances of his personal esteem and gratitude for the 'great services which you have rendered to the French Republic. If the tricolour floats above Saint Domingue it is due to you and your brave Blacks . . . You need have no doubt about the respect, the fortune and honours that await you.' In secret, Napoleon instructed his commander,

4

General Charles Leclerc, to arrest 'all white women who have prostituted themselves to Negroes', and to ensure that 'all the Blacks or Mulattoes who have behaved badly, no matter what rank, should be sent to the Mediterranean and landed at a port on the island of Corsica'.

Toussaint L'Ouverture was not to be inveigled. He persuaded the blacks of Saint Domingue that the French were about to enslave them once more, quelled any sedition among their ranks, set fire to maritime towns, and awaited invasion in the interior. When the French landed it appeared that the Caribbean island was ablaze. The capital, Cap-Français, was a vast funeral pyre, flames shooting through the roofs of houses and linking in fiery arcs across the streets; everywhere, an awful incendiary. Lady Maria Nugent, the American wife of the British Governor of Jamaica, watched aghast as the conflagration raged four hundred miles to windward of Spanish Town:

It seems that Toussaint's plan [she wrote] is to distress the French as much as possible, by burning the towns, and harassing them from the woods and mountains, where the blacks have already taken refuge. How dreadful a business it is altogether; and indeed, it makes me shudder, to think of the horrible bloodshed and misery that must take place, before any thing can be settled in that wretched island.

By 7 June 1802, however, the trap was set. Despite warnings from allies that General Leclerc was about to arrest him, Toussaint L'Ouverture accepted an invitation to discuss administrative matters with the French at their headquarters in Cap-Français. A betrayal: Toussaint was seized by a squad of grenadiers, hustled to the harbour where he was put aboard a frigate and ferried as prisoner to France. On board ship – it was called *The Hero* – Toussaint prepared a letter to General Bonaparte. 'I will not conceal my faults from you. I have committed some. What man is exempt? But I have too high an idea of the justice of the First Magistrate of the French people, to doubt a moment of his clemency.'

No mercy was shown. 'The fish trusts the water and in the water he is boiled,' runs a Haitian proverb: Toussaint had placed faith in the French Republic and by the French Republic he was deceived. For five long months he languished in the dungeon at Fort de Joux. On Bonaparte's instructions Toussaint was humiliated by his jailers, dressed in convict's clothes, deprived in winter of sufficient firewood. His correspondence to Napoleon – letters left unanswered – makes pitiful reading: 'First Consul, father of all French soldiers, upright judge, defender of the innocent, pronounce a decision as to my destiny: my wound is deep, apply a remedy to it: you are the physician, I rely entirely on your wisdom and skill.'

A remedy had already been devised: as the prisoner lay afflicted with pneumonia, all medical attention was to be abandoned. 'The construction of Negroes,' declared his jailer, 'being totally different to that of Europeans, I have dispensed with his doctor and his surgeon who would be useless to him.' On 7 April 1803 Toussaint L'Ouverture was found dead, propped on a chair by the empty fireplace which is now hung with his portrait. 'The Black Napoleon,' observed a caustic Chateaubriand, 'imitated and killed by the White Napoleon.' Official cause of death: apoplexy. He was fifty-seven and, after ten months in jail, did not live to see the proclamation of the Haitian republic.

The death of Toussaint became the subject of general horror and indignation throughout liberal Europe. 'Perhaps Bonaparte hardly recollects his crime,' complained Madame de Staël, appalled at the guile of the man, 'because he has been less approached with it than others.' News of the black slave's imprisonment had reached William Wordsworth in Calais. The poet was in ill temper, convinced by now that Napoleon's rise to power and the establishment of a consulate based on military force had destroyed any hope of a republican France. His poem 'To Toussaint L'Ouverture' was published in 1803, in the 2nd of February edition of the *Morning Post*:

> Though fallen Thyself, never to rise again,
> Live, and take comfort. Thou hast left behind
> Powers that will work for thee; air, earth and skies;
> There's not a breathing of the common wind
> That will forget thee; thou hast great allies;
> Thy friends are exultations, agonies,
> And love, and Man's unconquerable mind.

Fifteen years later at St Helena Napoleon admitted that his West Indian expedition had been a mistake. He should have ruled Saint Domingue with Toussaint as his envoy. The campaign was in fact a disaster: national resistance led by Henri Christophe and the sanguinary Jean-Jacques Dessalines ('I will have my horse walk in blood up to his breastplate') repulsed the invading French. Yellow fever, that great scourge of the West Indies, soon winnowed the remaining ranks. On 18 May 1803, six weeks after Toussaint died in the Jura, the national flag of Haiti was created when the white band – symbol of colonial supremacy – was ceremonially ripped from the tricolour of France. It was goodbye to the 'Marseillaise'.

On 1 January 1804 Dessalines declared the independence of Haiti, substituting the aboriginal Indian name, meaning 'mountainous land', for the French Saint Domingue. His secretary was said to have threatened on the occasion: 'We will write this act of independence using a white man's skull for an inkwell, his skin for parchment, blood for ink and a bayonet as pen.' Once Dessalines had proclaimed himself Jean-Jacques the First, Emperor of Haiti, he ordered the massacre of most of the whites who had remained on the island. His coronation took place five months after Napoleon's as Emperor of the French.

It was now impossible for Napoleon to maintain his distant territories west of the Mississippi River. His losses in Haiti forced him to sell the French portion of Louisiana to the United States. This put an end to the First Consul's dream of a new world empire in the Caribbean. 'Damn sugar, damn coffee, damn colonies!' he raged.

Little Haiti, Miami: low-income, sprawling, sunbelt America. The filigree mansions of the Caribbean are nowhere to be seen. There is only a Bargain Town awfulness – dingy motels with vibrating waterbeds, fast-food emporiums and coin laundries. Debris everywhere sits uncollected in vacant lots. The Haitian bicolour, its red and blue in tatters, hangs from a Bless the Lord Discount Unisex Salon.

Along 2nd Avenue at the intersection with 62nd Street stands the Toussaint L'Ouverture Elementary School. A classroom bears a large painting of the Haitian hero, the colours garish in mango and guava green. History tells us that his appearance was not very prepossessing: short, thin, gold epaulettes too heavy for the narrow shoulders. 'A maggot in a rag', Napoleon's officers had called Toussaint.

But here in the wasteland of Little Haiti the Centaur of the Savannahs looked fine. 'This man,' a schoolteacher told me, 'was the incarnation of a whole race.' He stood with a cavalry sabre suspended at his side, the uniform coat encrusted with gold buttons, strands of brocade and frog embroidery. A large red cape falling over broad shoulders is stitched with gold chevron; the three-cornered hat adorned with peacock plumes, a powdered wig tied in a graceful queue. His noble black face peers from the top of a high white stock.

Painted beneath Toussaint's feet are the words which he defiantly uttered as they bundled him aboard the frigate bound for France. 'In overthrowing me, you have cut down only the trunk of the Tree of Liberty in Saint Domingue. It will spring up again by the roots for they are numerous and deep.'

Alas, the tree has never flourished. The world's first black republic – seventeen years younger than the United States – has been reduced to a wretched police state. Haiti was destined to be the cradle of liberty for the African race. Now it is the battered pauper of the Americas. Since independence there has only been factious anarchy, a line of illusory presidents who rose to power through successive coups: the midnight court-martial, a fusillade and burial at dawn. Slavery was abolished, but the spirit of slavery remains: a systematic pillaging of public funds by those in office has kept the people in poverty. 'Pluck the chicken as long as it does not squawk,' advised Dessalines, a man in the megalomaniac lineage of Tamburlaine.

The authoritarian fanaticism of President François Duvalier brought him the honorific title 'Lucifer of the Antilles'. His messages to the nation, delivered from the balcony of the National Palace in a peculiar stage-whisper, were nonsensical but chilling: 'I am neither the red nor the white but the indivisible bicolour of the Haitian people. I am already an Immaterial Being.' Duvalier entertained more than an anthropological interest in Voodoo: his habit of always appearing in a black suit, the calcu-latedly nasal voice, a black bowler – all this lent him the aspect, they say, of Baron Samedi, who in Voodoo mythology haunts the cemeteries in topper and tails, smoking a large cheroot. A sort of graveyard Groucho Marx.

The Tontons Macoute, Papa Doc's bogeymen and secret police, displayed a doglike devotion to their president, and efficiency in their hatchetwork. They were still in the woodwork when I arrived in Haiti, though now without the dark glasses and slouch hats. The legacy of François Duvalier and his son Baby Doc remains. A series of political convulsions had followed the overthrow of Duvalier *fils* in 1986: there had been no return to democracy, only a sabotage of elections, more repression and corruption, the awful symbolism of mutilated bodies by the ballot box.

Power in Haiti continued to come from the barrel of a gun: I was about to fly from Miami into a state of siege and felt nervous. 'Man, you gonna lay your *life* on the line out there in Hay-di,' my taxi driver informed me on the way to the airport. 'They're killin' people like *flies*.' As the Chevrolet jounced along I remembered a comment in the current *Fodor's*

Guide to the Caribbean: 'The political instability and street violence in Haiti has escalated to the point where we have suspended review of the properties and attractions of this island until the situation stabilizes.'

'Best of British,' grinned the cabbie.

II

In Cahoots with the Macoutes

'The Foreign Office have apologised to Mr Delorme Mehu,
Haitian Chargé d'Affaires, who was arrested for a short time
last month by the police. A misunderstanding arose, apparently, about the parking of his car outside the Embassy in
Hans Road, London S.W.'

Notice in *The Times*, 16 August 1963

Haiti. It sounds exotic – I still imagined rum punches on the verandah
of some gingerbread villa, delicious in the tropic noontide. The sound
of drums, rumbling in the hills, would reach my hotel at night: a houm-
doum-do from the dread gatherings of Voodoo. The Tontons Macoute,
in crumpled white suits, would call on their victims after dark. Otherwise,
just listless indolence, and Firbankian languor. As in the song by Cole
Porter:

> Katie looked at Haiti
> Feeling rather tired.
> Katie met a natie
> Katie was inspired.

The idyll soon dissolved as the plane banked down towards a landscape
of barren strangeness. When asked by George III for a description of this
island, a British admiral was reported to have scrunched up a sheet of
paper and thrown it on the table. 'Sire,' he said, 'Haiti looks like that.'
From the air Haiti is a harsh conglomeration of mountains slashed by
deep gulches; parched savannahs with not a tree, not a shrub, in sight; a
chaos of rocks and gullies baked by the sun to a dead-leaf drab. I could
see the thin brown ribbon of a river winding through a valley: it seemed
to dwindle in the distance to a mere runnel.

Travellers to Haiti in the days of Toussaint L'Ouverture praised this
country for its greenery and romantic landscapes, for the beauties of
unsullied nature: marshes of wild ginger, plantations of banana and Indian
corn, mahogany, redwood, pine. When Columbus approached the

northern coast in 1492 he marvelled: 'There in that high and mountainous country is the land of God.' Now the topography of Haiti is
desolate like the dried mud-bed of the sea: after independence in 1804
the plantations were dismantled and two hundred years of deforestation,
caused by a ruinous cutting of timber to make charcoal, has destroyed
much of the green.

Flying over this denuded landscape it occurred to me that the obser-
vations on Haitian birdlife, several pages folded in the bottom of my
rucksack, would prove of little use. The field notes had been compiled
in the early 1960s when there was enough forest to accommodate spot-
ted sandpipers, roseate flamingos, long-billed curlews, peregrine falcons
and black-bellied plovers. One would be lucky now to find a single egret,
let alone hummingbird, in the sterile wastes of cacti which loomed to
view beneath my window. I felt privileged, nevertheless, to own these
notes: Gerard Corley Smith had probably spent more hours in the field,
as an amateur ornithologist, than anyone else in Haiti for a generation.
Sadly, his notebooks were left incomplete as he was ordered to leave Haiti
at twenty-four hours' notice . . .

I came across the name of Corley Smith in a document published at
the order of Papa Doc in 1968, entitled: *Graham Greene Démasqué – Finally
Exposed*. Distributed to journalists through Haitian embassies in Europe,
this large and glossy publication sought to discredit Greene for his 1966
novel *The Comedians*, an adventure story about broken-down lives in
Duvalierist Haiti. A 'negrophobic benzedrin addict', 'conceited scribbler',
'chimerical racialist' and – best of all – 'habitué of lazar houses', the
dastardly Greene had apparently 'failed to profit by the lessons of
Wilberforce and still dreams of a bygone era when slavery was the rule
in Saint Domingue'.

Corley Smith, until 1962 Her British Majesty's ambassador in Haiti, is
exposed to a similar drubbing: 'The Haitian Government has made it
known to this famous ambassador that although a plenipotentiary, he
should guard against trespassing the limits of good education and that his
impertinence and haughtiness as a British colonialist would not be toler-
ated.' The document maunders on: 'In fact the ambassador relapsed to
such an extent that the Haitian government . . . deemed it wise to request
the recall of this peculiar individual.' Corley Smith was eventually expelled
for diplomatic protests against the gangsterism of the Tontons Macoute,
long before *The Comedians* was published. 'Haiti President François
Duvalier did not approve of any birdwatcher so spreading his feathers,'

chirped the *Miami Herald* of 16 March 1962. Since that date Great Britain has never appointed an ambassador to Haiti; we have reduced Anglo-Haitian diplomatic relations to the level of chargé d'affaires. Two years later, on the 160th anniversary of Haiti's independence, Queen Elizabeth II did, however, send Papa Doc this cautious telegram: 'I have received the message which you sent to me at the beginning of the New Year in your own name and on behalf of the Haitian people. I reciprocate your good wishes.'

Papa Doc's unfavourable review of *The Comedians* once hung, suitably framed, in Graham Greene's lavatory at Antibes.

I had met Corley Smith a week before my departure for Haiti; he was then a sprightly eighty-one though white-haired and slightly stooped. We spoke in his London club – the Travellers' – over biscuits and tea. 'I liked the Haitians,' he reminisced. 'They were a cheerful lot. Extraordinary, really, their capacity for enduring adversity. Just look at what they did to Napoleon. Terrible mistake, mind you, that invasion: cost Bonaparte more men than Waterloo. I never went to a Voodoo ceremony, though – to be avoided, I'd say. Will you take one lump or two?'

'No sugar, thanks.'

Corley Smith remembered with affection the country-folk who would greet him with a friendly *'Bonjour blanc!'* (a Creole expression which means 'Hi, stranger!' as well as 'Hello, white man!') as he went birding in the hills: 'And I never felt any risk up there on the mountain paths, even though Trollope did say that Englishmen find the Haitians an uncivilized and barbarous lot. Frankly I find it more dangerous just crossing the road to get to my club. The real threat of course came from the Tontons Macoute.'

Heads turned in the Travellers' as Corley Smith repeated those last two words in rather a loud voice. 'As far as I'm aware,' he continued, 'Papa Doc was the *only* Fascist dictator at any time in Latin America. In all its essentials his regime was rightist and completely totalitarian. The Macoutes fulfilled the role of Hitler's Brown Shirts; and the Palace Guard, that of the SS.'

The Duvalierist version of the Lord's Prayer, intended for use in schools, was certainly totalitarian in its supernatural messianism: 'Our Doc, who art in the National Palace for life, hallowed be Thy name by present and future generations. Thy will be done in Port-au-Prince as it is in the provinces. Give us this day our new Haiti and forgive not the trespasses of those anti-patriots who daily spit upon our country . . .' A similar prayer was circulated among groups of Hitlerite girls: 'Adolf Hitler, thou art our Great Leader. Thy name makes thy foes tremble. Thy Third Reich come . . .' In 1962 Doctor Duvalier was excommunicated; this was the first time a Latin American president had been excluded from the communion of the Catholic Church since Juan Perón in 1955.

Corley Smith explained how Tonton Macoute means 'Uncle Knapsack' in Creole patois; this mythological figure appears in Haitian nursery stories as the bugaboo that kidnaps wicked children in his straw bag. Under cover of dark.

'They were not exactly a secret police, the Tontons,' he continued over another pot of Earl Grey. 'There was nothing secret about them except that you weren't allowed to mention their name in public. More precisely they were a party militia, a private army. And through them, Papa Doc was able to terrorize tourists, schools, the university, and the smaller trade unions. But above all, the Catholic Church. In my time Duvalier managed to expel the Archbishop, three bishops, the Pope's personal representative, plus the Anglican bishop.'

Corley Smith smiled: 'Including myself. In fact there was quite a rapid turnover of ambassadors in those days. Needless to say, Papa Doc never supplied me with an airline ticket home.'

What was he like to meet, François Duvalier? 'Oh, the few conversations I had with Papa Doc are of little interest to anyone. There was never very much business to be done in Haiti,' said Corley Smith, adding a third spoonful of sugar to his tea. 'But I will say this: he spoke in a funny sort of whisper, and liked everyone to dress in deepest mourning. Whenever you presented your credentials you were required to wear a black suit and . . . black socks. Most odd. By the way, if anything, Haiti was *worse* than Greene had described it.'

Corley Smith left me with a useful piece of advice. 'You do know the Creole for reverse a car?' I did not. 'Well, it's *faire back*. Remember that. Could prove handy.'

The plane had begun its long descent. A stewardess came round with our landing cards. It was late afternoon: the Haitian mountains looked darkly purple behind the setting sun. I was now three thousand five hundred miles from the Land's End of England; Corley Smith and his club in Pall Mall seemed light years away. I took out a map of the Caribbean.

Haiti is shaped like a lobster's claw. The upper pincer moves in the direction of Cuba; the lower, the longer pincer, juts towards Jamaica. The

Republic of Haiti – I remembered from geography lessons at school – shares with the Dominican Republic an island christened by Columbus as Hispaniola, Little Spain. As far as I know Hispaniola is the sole example in the world today (apart from Cyprus) of an island divided into two independent sovereign states, each of them, moreover, speaking a different language: French and Spanish.

There were only three other whites on the plane – Mormons from Salt Lake City in baseball caps and ties, crew-cut, all-American wholesome. They had been pacing the aisles since take-off, handing out leaflets bemoaning the 'nightmare reign of sorcery and blood known as Voodoo', and mistook me for an American. 'You mean you're British! Wow! That's like coming from Mars or some place. First time to Haiti? Well, transportation's a real dog out there, take it from me. Haven't even got round to building a subway system!'

I offered the Mormon some popcorn. 'Good of you, thank you kindly. Listen, would you like to be a partner in our ministry? The harvest is plentiful but the workers are few. No? OK, but let me give you that leaflet anyway. Have a holy day!'

'You too.'

They reminded me, these Mormons, of Richard Loederer, a Viennese artist who in the early 1930s had sailed on a Dutch West Indian mail steamer to Haiti with the purpose of exposing the 'blood cult of the negro and his orgies'. His lurid publication, *Voodoo Fire in Haiti*, contains such memorable fabrications as: 'According to Haitian connoisseurs, human meat tastes best when boiled with Congo beans.' Congo beans were forbidden at Herr Loederer's table for quite some weeks after.

I had come to Haiti unable to take very seriously the dark conventicles of Voodoo, and considered the religion merely folklore. 'It is what you in England would call a tradition,' said the Haitian chargé d'affaires Mr Delorme Mehu. He was interviewed by the London *Daily Mail* three days after the death of Papa Doc in April 1971. 'Like morris dancing?' inquired the journalist. 'Yes, yes,' replied the diplomat. 'A tourist attraction.' Uppermost in my mind as the plane slanted down towards Port-au-Prince was the current state of siege.

Latin America was reduced to its last three strong men: in Cuba, Fidel Castro; in Chile, the departing General Augusto Pinochet; in Haiti, General Prosper Avril. Avril had faithfully served the Duvaliers, both Papa and Baby Doc, for many years. He was as corrupt as them both, complicit in the trans-shipment of cocaine from Colombia to the United States.

Avril had promised free elections, but nobody believed him. He had imposed the state of siege apparently to 'protect democratic accomplishments against terrorism and the threat of civil war'; but it was obviously an attempt to retain control of the military. The curse of Haiti from independence to the present time has always been the army: despite reducing their number, Avril was in no hurry to change the role of the military in the balance of power. Besides, the United States (expert in the art of coddling dictators) had installed him in the National Palace.

So the Caribbean island was once more in a state of upheaval: the capital was reported to be under curfew, near anarchy in the countryside. The streets of Port-au-Prince were said to be thick with armoured vehicles and marauding Macoutes; shops and schools had closed. 'Shooting as Haiti Mutineers Hold Fast', proclaimed the *Independent*; 'Rebels Routed in Haiti Gunfight', declared *The Times*. Scores of people had been hustled by the soldiery into the National Palace, beaten up, then released by officials who claimed their arrests were a 'mistake'. Haiti's ambassador to the United States had resigned in protest. Members of the opposition had taken to the hills after the deportation of six or so politicians who had dared denounce the military dictatorship. The Foreign Office had left a message on my answer-machine: 'There has been sporadic gunfire and the sound of exploding grenades in the streets,' came the cut-glass voice. 'And heavy shooting has been reported at the airport. Potential visitors to Haiti should consider very carefully whether their trip is absolutely necessary.'

Little Haiti, Miami, had been ablaze with rage; slogans were spray-gunned to walls – 'Avril Is a Drugs Dealer!', 'Down With the Macoutes! Haiti Must Be Clean!'; demonstrations, abusive condemnation of the United States. Outside a church near the Toussaint L'Ouverture Elementary School, a Haitian priest was distributing copies of an open letter to Pope John-Paul II: 'Haitian Catholics and friends of His Holiness call for the downfall of Avril and his thugs. We most humbly beg that they all be put on public trial, like Nicolae Ceauşescu and his Romanian Tontons.' Earlier that day I had tried to reach Hubert de Ronceray, one of the Haitian politicians exiled by General Avril. He was in hiding, protected by friends and difficult to find. I was eventually instructed to leave my telephone number at a seedy little record shop on East 54th; de Ronceray would be in touch. Directions for our rendezvous arrived that night from an anonymous caller; I would have to come alone, with some form of identification. 'Tomorrow Monsieur de Ronceray will have to change his address again,' said the telephone. 'Avril is watching.' Then the line went dead.

No light was on in the house. But the address was surely correct: opposite La Nouvelle Jerusalem Baptist church, round the corner from the Exotic Reality hairdressers. I rang the doorbell again. This time I heard footsteps. 'Have you come to sell life insurance?' asked a voice from behind the door.

'Yes.' (This was part of the necessary procedure.)

'Come in then.' The door opened a crack; a black woman ushered me inside, quickly surveying the street from left to right. I was led along a dark passage to the kitchen.

Hubert de Ronceray rose from the table. *'Comment allez-vous, monsieur?'* he inquired.

I was taken aback by his black eye, and the spectacles which had been Sellotaped at the bridge, missing one lens. The two-hour journey to this part of Miami had been alarming enough: dark avenues lined with strip clubs and mad dogs, cars that I feverishly imagined were following me, headlamps dipped. 'Er, not so bad, thanks.'

De Ronceray explained how he had only escaped death at the hands of Avril because gunmen had mistaken his car for that of a colonel, and opened fire on the wrong man. A friend had intercepted a message relayed by a commando to the National Palace: *'Oh mon Dieu! Nous avons tué Colonel André Neptune! Comment nous avons pu faire une telle catastrophe!'*

Hubert de Ronceray appeared to find this faintly amusing. 'Haiti, *mon cher*, is a comedy, a tragi-comedy. It always has been, and always will be.' Minutes after the bungled assassination, de Ronceray's house was sprayed with bullets. He was then thrown into a cell where guards applied burning cigarettes to his eyelids, beating him with blows from the butt of a rifle, breaking the glasses. Next day, he was shoved at gunpoint on a plane for Miami, hobbling across the tarmac without socks or shoes. 'For as long as Avril is in power I shall never return to Haiti,' said de Ronceray. 'The man is a liar and a cheat, reared in the school of violence. He believes he has the divine right to do whatever he likes, that he has been appointed as the saviour of Haiti. But he was never made for the battlefield, like Toussaint L'Ouverture. He was made only to kill civilians, and to make money. Poor Haiti.

'I strongly recommend that you do not go out in Port-au-Prince after dark. Make your presence known to the British ambassador there,' advised de Ronceray.

'We don't have one.'

'Well find one, *mon cher*, find one.'

As I left, de Ronceray gave me a copy of the anti-Avril paper *Haïti en Marche*. The headline was grim: *'Retour à la Barbare de Papa Doc'*.

Papa Doc was at his most barbarous, perhaps, when he ordered that the bloated corpse of an enemy be tied to a wooden chair beneath a Coca-Cola sign at Port-au-Prince airport: 'Welcome to Haiti' read the sign hung round its neck. But the airport today appeared like any other in the Caribbean. The Mormons from Utah were still dispensing leaflets as the plane rolled smoothly along the tarmac. There was no welcoming corpse.

A group of beggars in tattered straw hats were playing *méringue*, the national dance music of Haiti, at the entrance to immigration. It was a joyful, rackety music of maracas and bongos. *'Bienvenu, blanc!'* they grinned. A young boy approached with trumpery wooden carvings for sale: 'Give me a dollar, *ba'moin un dollar, blanc!'* Customs were perfunctory; a cursory inspection of my passport, a rubber stamp banged on the visa. 'Purpose of visit?'

I hesitated; my interest in Haiti had been inspired by the wonderful chapters written about the country by Patrick Leigh Fermor in *The Traveller's Tree* (a book much consulted by James Bond in his attempt to fathom the mind of that dastardly adept of Voodoo, Mr Big); and subsequent reading of Haitian history had so fascinated that I determined to visit the place. 'Tourism,' I said. To which the official replied: 'Very good, *monsieur*. Tomorrow belongs to Haiti, because Haiti means business.' There seemed an edge of menace to this unusual welcome. A recent article in *The Tablet* told how a missionary priest from Toronto had been detained for twenty-four hours at the airport simply because he bore the surname Greene.

Faded Kodachrome photographs of Haiti – palm trees, sand, naked children with melon-slice grins – adorned the yellowish walls of the concourse. It was a miserable airport. As I waited for my rucksack to come bumping through on the carousel I was badgered by a group of touts yelling: 'Taxi, taxi! Change money. You like hotel . . .?' I followed an old chauffeur who gave his name as Toussaint. This seemed auspicious.

Outside it was already dark; twilight is short in the tropics and the sky over Port-au-Prince was stained with a reddish light, shimmering slightly. It was hot and muggy; there was a strong feral smell in the air

— a fug of sewage, sweat and caramelized sugar. Toussaint's taxi, a Sixty-two Sedan de Ville, was a splendid heap of junk. I don't think he had any brakes: to stop or slow down he ground into bottom gear and switched off the ignition. There was not very much suspension; as we bumped drunkenly over the potholed road I repeatedly knocked my head against the roof. A young boy, Toussaint's grandson, sat in the back of the car, chewing on a ripe shoot of cane. His T-shirt proclaimed in English: 'I Like Your Approach. Now Let's See Your Departure'. In his lap he cradled a fighting cock, shorn of wattle and comb; the bird was tied to the door handle by a length of string.

The road to Port-au-Prince was dimly lit: the only light came from the inside of houses. Black figures stood illuminated in doorways, or huddled in groups around stalls stuck with candles; faces flickered a ghostly yellow. A couple of soldiers, rifles at the slope, stooped to peer at me through the taxi window. It was hot and I was uncomfortable, feeling a little uncertain. I had come to Haiti with a baggage of prejudice and fear: AIDS, Voodoo, black magic, Papa Doc's death squads. My reading of Arthur de Gobineau, the maniacal ethnologist, did not help: 'We are in a different world at once,' the Frenchman wrote in his 1854 *Inequality of Human Races*. 'The manners are as depraved, brutal, and savage as in Dahomey or among the Fellatahs . . . The Haitian ultimately has no serious occupation except chewing tobacco, drinking alcohol, disembowelling his enemies, and conciliating his sorcerers.'

Vehicles careering towards us on the same side of the road swerved across our bows, klaxons blaring. Toussaint would negotiate the pot-holes, and errant mules, in a similar manner. Miserable assemblies of tin shacks, the roofs improvised from plastic sheeting weighted down by bricks, sped by. The roadside was cluttered with cinder-blocks, old jerry-cans, scrap-lumber. A stench of burning tyres and rotted fruit, of urine, overwhelmed. Everywhere, an air of dereliction and decay. A pariah dog lay dead in a gutter, carrion already corrupted into vermin.

Commercial hoardings, the pasteboard torn and tattered, lined the dirt-track road; they seemed curiously antique: *'Tampax! La Femme Connaît Enfin La Liberté'*; *'Fumez Lucky Strike — la Cigarette du Bon Goût'*. There were countless advertisements for Barbancourt rum, reckoned to be the best in the Caribbean. *'Mais oui, c'est notre nectar national,'* enthused Toussaint in strangely classical French.

We stalled at a traffic jam, an infernal congestion of public buses; the weight of human cargo caused these tuppenny jitneys to list perilously to starboard, belching plumes of diesel smoke. Toussaint mopped his brow with a handkerchief smeared in black oil. He turned to look at me. 'We have a saying in Haiti,' he said, flashing a gold bicuspid tooth: *'Qui va lentement, arrive sûrement.'* We crawled past a roadsign punctured with rusted bullet holes; yet there was nowhere any evidence of a state of siege (even though Monsieur Toussaint's windscreen looked as though it had been smashed by a rock the size of a frozen turkey). I wondered whether the British press had not exaggerated the parlous state of affairs in Haiti. Had there been much violence? 'No, no. *Tout OK,'* Toussaint said encouragingly. The thirty-day siege would be lifted tomorrow night, he assured me. This was happy news. Toussaint offered me a Comme il Faut, the Haitian cigarette. It tasted good.

Soon we coasted to a stop at the crest of a hill; Toussaint switched off the ignition and down we rolled. *'C'est le freewheeling, m'sieur,'* he explained. But the engine refused to start once we had regained the flat. It seemed this was a regular occurrence: the grandson hopped from the back of the car, still chewing his cane, and began to push; a sudden jolt, then a lurch, and the motor juddered into life. But not for long; this time Toussaint freewheeled backwards downhill to kick-start: *'Faire back, faire back!'* shouted the grandson. *'Arrêtez! Arrêtez!'* Too late: we had reversed into a tree. In this manner – jolt, lurch, kick-start – we arrived at the Hotel Oloffson.

III

Paris of the Gutter

'Port-au-Prince is an eighteenth-century city like Dublin, where everybody is faced with an audience. Almost everybody figures as a "character", and these characters must put on a play.'

Edmund Wilson, *Red, Black, Blond and Olive*

There was a general air of listlessness, a haphazard South Sea atmosphere, to the Oloffson which conformed very nicely to my filigree mansion of Firbankian charm. Illuminated at night, the hotel was a folly of spires and conical towers. There were sketchy attempts at gingerbread decorations – lacy white grille-work on the eaves and balconies. The façade was so riddled with fretwork that it looked as though a thousand termites had been dining, a needlepoint tracery of arabesques left in the wood. This colonial pavilion appears thinly disguised as the Hotel Trianon in Graham Greene's novel *The Comedians*. There was no hunched body of the Social Welfare Secretary in the swimming pool (although the water was murky enough to be hiding half the Cabinet); otherwise, the hotel was just as Greene had described it: 'You expected a witch to open the door to you or a manic butler, with a bat dangling from the chandelier behind him.' Hurricane lamps burned yellow in the half-light; I could make out white rattan chairs and wicker furniture, Victorian chintz and an upholstered sofa that looked as though it had been purloined from some Regency manor. In the days when there was tourism in Haiti, the Oloffson had been frequented by a gallery of celebrities: Noël Coward, John Gielgud, Malcolm Lowry, the *New Yorker* cartoonist Charles Addams, Mick Jagger even. Now the place appeared more or less abandoned: there was a visible warp in the clapboard ceiling where the Anne Bancroft suite threatened to collapse on to the baby grand, the piano painted gaudily with Caribbean coconut, pomegranate, mango and bread-fruit. Graham Greene had once written an article here entitled 'The Mechanics of Running an Empty Hotel'. I was shown to my room, the Greene Suite; this used to be an operating theatre during the 1915–34 American occupation of Haiti. There was a drain in the middle of the floor, hidden beneath a rug, for sluicing the tiles.

The Oloffson was built at the turn of the century as an elegant residence for the Sam family; on 27 July 1915, however, President Guillaume Sam, of the same Haitian household, was murdered. This is how the London *Times* reported his death:

A mob of infuriated Haitians today removed their President from the French Legation and shot him dead in front of the building . . . According to an official report issued by the State Department the mob at Port-au-Prince, after having shot the President, tore his body to pieces and paraded the town carrying the portions on the end of poles. After being dragged through the streets, the mutilated body was buried by several women in a cemetery outside the capital. The city is quiet.

That was a fairly typical fate for a Haitian president: *'Haïti, Haïti!'* bemoaned Napoleon III. *'Pays de barbares.'* The death of Sam provided the Americans with an excuse to invade Haiti; next day, two companies of Marines and three of sailors marched into the capital, uniformed *blancs* bearing the Stars and Stripes. The Oloffson was commandeered as a hospital for the Marines; it was they who built the maternity wing which is now part of the hotel. After the departure of the Americans in 1934 the Oloffson saw a succession of eccentric proprietors, the most unusual being an American stockbroker named Maurice de Young who raised caymans, a ferocious breed of alligator, in the swimming pool so he could use them as target practice.

A complimentary rum punch awaited me on the wicker table, beneath a large papier-mâché model of Jean-Jacques Dessalines; the general glowered at me from beneath a cockaded hat. My room was still and lonely in the evening quiet; all I could hear was a faint rasp of cicadas, or perhaps a fretting of frogs. I opened my rucksack and removed the grubby bundles of Haitian currency which I had purchased at the airport. They smelt like over-ripe Gouda; some of the notes were so soiled that one could scarcely make out the denomination. I wondered how many cockfights they'd been haggled over, how many bottles of rum.

The Haitian currency is in *gourdes* (it seems that Henri Christophe, ruler of northern Haiti from 1807, had used gourds as a substitute for money ransacked from the Treasury). All these notes bear an image of Toussaint L'Ouverture and Jean-Jacques Dessalines; and one or two of a youthful Jean-Claude Duvalier, flatteringly portrayed without the gimlet eyes and heavy dewlaps. The crisper notes came in higher denominations; the ten-gourde showed Catherine Flon, the goddaughter of Dessalines's wife, stitching together the red and blue bands of the French flag after Dessalines had ripped out the white and trampled it underfoot.

I folded a wad of greasy gourdes and stepped out on to the verandah: not a sound, the hotel seemed quite uninhabited. 'The oddest damn place I ever saw,' wrote John Dos Passos of the Oloffson in 1948. 'Nobody ever stops talking about Voodoo, zombis, possessions, Baron Samedi, etc. . . .' The moon was riding, mysteriously, across the night sky.

'Not much custom tonight.' I drew up a stool at the bar and ordered another rum punch.

The barman was slouched on the mahogany counter fashioned from a pool table left behind by the US Marines, one arm folded beneath his head to serve as a pillow. '*Rien, rien.*' He barely stirred.

I sat sipping under the coolness of the fan blades, wondering whether I should stir out alone in Port-au-Prince, when a sudden howling reached me from outside. The barman looked up, bleary-eyed. 'It's Papa Dog,' he explained. The hound apparently belonged to the hotelier, Richard Morse, who evidently had an unusual sense of the absurd.

Rain began to fall on the wooden roof of the Oloffson; not heavily, but with the carelessness of a leaking basin. I pictured the muddy slough of streets out there, the brimming gutters. I was about to leave when I felt a tap on my shoulder. Behind me stood an elfin figure in a white pongee silk suit and paisley ascot, dapper beyond reality with a silver-topped walking cane. 'I see that you are an *homme d'esprit*,' he trilled. 'And may I ask what brings you to the Pearl of the Antilles? No, don't say. Do you like flamingo meat? It's so exquisite, my dear. Yes, the finest fare.'

The character was like a chocolate soldier, almost as bald as a calabash and with perfect white teeth, a Haitian Sir Fopling Flutter. He warbled on in antique English, flitting from one subject to another: 'It behoves you, my dear, to take it into account that the name for God in ancient Greece is Kronos, or time. So time, my dear, is God. If you are clever you will make time a very good collaborator. Time is my beautiful partner.'

Before I could press the offer of a drink, the gadfly had vanished, leaving behind a waft of after-shave. I was now determined, a little unhinged by the rum, to visit Port-au-Prince by night; the man in white, whoever he was, had disturbed me. It was time to go.

The rain had ceased: only a faint patter as drops fell from the luxuriant foliage, the hibiscus and convolvulus, in the Oloffson gardens. I walked down the Rue Capois towards the National Palace: great craters in the pavement revealed fractured sewage pipes; one could plummet beneath street-level into the ooze and nobody would know. There was a faint miasma in the air: exhaust fumes, burning refuse, the smoke from innumerable charcoal fires. It caught at the back of one's throat, stung the eyes.

Ten o'clock at night and the road was almost deserted. There was only a primitive raving of pariah dogs; the mongrels approached with questing eyes and then scampered off barking into the night. I was fearful of rabies. Halfway down the Capois a large blue and red banner stretched across the street. It was to welcome General Prosper Avril after his state visit to Taiwan: *'Une Absence Rémarquée. Une Présence Rémarquable. Joyeux Retour Président,'* the familiar rhetoric of Duvalierism.

The National Palace, that great lair of power, was flooded with light and the wedding-cake white of the façade dazzled in the dark like an edifice of snow. Dessalines stood near by, wearing a braided military frock coat, his sabre flourished in face of the barracks. The statue was poorly executed; a spindly figure atop a plinth of granite, unremarkable. But history tells otherwise: Dessalines rose through the ranks with a barbarous appetite for command, and a reckless arrogance of hate. One night he ordered his men to erect five hundred gallows and, in full view of the enemy lines, hanged five hundred Frenchmen at dawn. 'Put a little marrow in your bones,' Papa Doc had proclaimed, 'and allow the blood of Dessalines to flow in your veins.'

Only one statue in the Champ de Mars seemed a sculpted work of significance and not just a memorial: *Le Marron Inconnu*, the Unknown Slave. Unveiled by Papa Doc in December 1968, the monument showed a slave paused in mid-flight, legs outstretched, a broken chain from his left ankle and a massive sword resting in his right hand on the ground. His head is thrown back as he sounds a call through an empty conch shell for the slaves to revolt. The mournful music of this shell, heard over the distant crackling of forests and cane plantations set to the torch by the blacks, signalled the first war against colonial France.

The statue of the Unknown Slave stood outside an American Express office, a dead dog at its feet.

I passed a cinema showing two films: *My Stepmother Is an Alien* and *Commando Suicide*. It was a fleapit of a movie house, dimly aglow with an obscure exuberance of life, the windows inhospitable behind chicken wire. A woman outside was roasting cob corn, standing hands on hips over a smoking griddle. I lit a cigarette and glanced nervously at the mandrill-faced young man who had been following me around the Champ de Mars, now crouched beneath a poster advertising the cinematic delights of kung fu. '*Eh bien, mon ami?*' He had been trying to stare me out of countenance. 'So why come to Haiti?' he added in English. I gave an awkward smile. The young man said, 'Think you can just walk around in your fine clothes and make fun of us? Go home, *blanc*. Yankee trash.'

I walked back in the direction of the barracks; it was not promising, that encounter: I half hoped the man was drunk. Billboards, as tattered as those I had seen four hours ago along the road from the airport, passed me on the way to the barracks: '*Guinness Is Good for You – Découvrez Sa Force*'. An equestrian statue of King Henri Christophe, founder of the first monarchy in the New World, loomed into view. And there in Place Toussaint L'Ouverture stood a monument to the Centaur of the Savannahs. Toussaint was without horse, but he appeared regal in Napoleonic dress uniform, silhouetted against the night sky.

I was feeling thirsty. According to my copy of the *South American Handbook* the Champ de Mars is noted for the frequency of its bars. But I could find only the Café Napoli, the 'o' and 'l' fused from the blue neon. I wondered at the Italian name: could there be any Neapolitans in Haiti? I peered through the dirty window pasted with advertisements for Prestige, the Haitian beer: it seemed cramped and fuggy in there, like a Glasgow pub on a Saturday night. I swallowed hard – fearful of my reception as a *blanc* – and opened the door; bleary-eyed men lay slouched over the counter, taking it very easy. Every one of them appeared drunk, huddled in groups around bottles of whisky, arms draped boozily round the shoulders of coffee-skinned women. Coloured photographs of Mount Vesuvius and Sophia Loren, faded to a malarial yellow, were Sellotaped to the wall above a jukebox.

The woman counting money behind the cash till might have been Italian. Heavily made-up, sporting a beehive and a pair of butterfly-winged spectacles, she recalled a madame in some wartime bordello: her lips were smeared with a gash of violent red lipstick. She was probably in her mid-sixties. I sat on the other side of the counter from her, and feigned to inspect the menu: boiled goat, conch shell, guinea hen, dried turkey, congo-bean stew . . . Nothing very much appealed.

'*Da dove viene, signora? Italia?*' I asked the woman in Italian, to chance my hunch.

'*Sì. Sono Italiana,*' she replied, though without surprise, or even the trace of an answering smile.

There was a nice absurdity in meeting an Italian on my first night in Port-au-Prince; I asked the woman from which part of Italy she came and was told she was born in Haiti but of Neapolitan parents. Her name was Aïda, like the heroine, she explained, in the opera by Verdi. Aïda had been running the Café Napoli for twenty-three years; she had returned to Italy several times and seen some changes in Haiti, mostly for the worse. There was real tourism, she remembered, in the days of Club Méditerrané: windsurfing, snorkelling, waterskiing – all gone, sighed Aïda, all gone. We spoke about the traffic in Naples – Aïda reckoned it was much worse in Port-au-Prince; and about the patron saint of Naples, San Gennaro, whose blood is said to liquefy twice a year. '*Madonna mia!*' she exclaimed. '*Che superstizione! Una superstizione di Voodoo!*' I liked Aïda the Neapolitan; it seemed I had broken a little ice with her.

My chicken, a frazzled piece of gristle nestled in a styrofoam take-away box, arrived with a complimentary bottle of Prestige: I was about to risk eating when I heard a voice at my elbow. 'Hey! I'm not a bad guy, you understand. Now listen to me, Mr Yankee, . . .' It was the young man from outside the cinema; he stood contemplating me with an expression that was half amused and half sardonic. I was dreading this. The man was terribly tall and thin, with sharp cheekbones and an aquiline curve to the nose. The eyes were slits. 'So can I sit down with you?' he asked in excellent English: the words across his T-shirt – 'When I Die I'll Go to Heaven Because I've Already Been to Miami' – suggested that he had travelled to the United States. 'The name's Michael.' He extended a hand. 'Remember that. Michael.'

I was irritated by this false assumption of friendship: but I shook the hand. 'Hello, I'm Ian. And I'm English, not American.'

This caused some confusion. 'So you live in New York?' returned Michael.

'No. I live in England.'

Michael appeared to ignore this, and leant over the counter to Aïda: '*Pssst!*' He caught her attention. '*Ba'moin un Prestige, OK?*' I followed the order myself; to slake my thirst and calm the nerves.

'England?' Michael cast me a quizzical glance. 'England where?'

This problem of geography was to nag throughout my five months in Haiti: for most Haitians, the rest of the world consists merely of Miami, New York and Montreal. 'England,' I persisted. 'In Great Britain, you know – Liverpool, the Beatles, Queen Elizabeth the Second.'

'Ah, *Liverpool*,' exclaimed a triumphant Michael. 'Why didn't you tell me! So you are a Danish person. Yes, yes. I know Liverpool. You are a Danish person from Liverpool USA.'

'Why Danish?'

Michael made no reply.

The beers arrived, tepid and chemical to the taste. 'I'm not a bad guy.' He laboured the point. 'I'm just hungry: *moin gin grangou*, as we say in Haiti, a hole in the stomach. So you won't mind if I have some of that chicken, no?' I gave him the lot; anxiety had stolen the appetite.

Aïda was watching this comedy from afar, paring her nails and patting the bouffant. She had probably seen it all, hundreds of times before. 'Listen to me,' said Michael, tearing a wing from the chicken. 'You help me, I help you, eh, *blanc*?' He spat out a piece of bone. 'I'm a guide, see. And you should never – *never* – be walking around Port-au-Prince like that on your own. It's dangerous. There's a state of siege, you understand.'

'But I don't need a guide,' I protested. 'I haven't come to Haiti as a journalist.'

Michael found this hard to believe. 'So what are you?' He took a swig of beer and laughed. 'A Mormon?' (The received wisdom in Haiti, as I later found, is that any foreigner is by definition a missionary, journalist or employee at the American embassy.)

'No, I'm a writer,' it now seemed best to confess.

'Just as I thought – a journalist,' pursued Michael. 'So let me show you Port-au-Prince. You need a guide, understand? How about another beer?'

I told him no; I was feeling unusual enough as it was, what with the rums at the Oloffson.

'*Quant'é in tutto?*' I asked Aïda for the bill. Michael did not pay for his share.

We went out into the tropical night. 'I'll take you to the Roxy.' He offered me a Comme il Faut.

'To the *what*?'

Michael looked at me: 'You'll see.'

We proceeded in the direction of the port, passing Dessalines and

Toussaint L'Ouverture. I had no idea what I was letting myself in for: 'And may I ask what brings you to the Pearl of the Antilles?' – the words from that man in the white suit came back to me. And I thought: What on earth am I doing here? It was eleven thirty; there was only myself and the mad dogs, out at midnight with a guide who described himself as an 'unemployed mailman'. We walked down the Rue Pavée, a street scarcely paved, potholes brimming with rainwater. When the historian James Anthony Froude came to Port-au-Prince in 1886, he bemoaned the capital as 'a Paris of the gutter'; it was, he reckoned, 'the most ridiculous caricature of civilization in the whole world'. I wondered what Mr Froude would make of Port-au-Prince tonight: all that remained of the outward polish of French civilization – at least along the Rue Pavée – was an advertisement for La Vache qui Rit.

We passed a shop, the Dark Lovely Magic Emporium, selling a bewildering array of aphrodisiacs, stimulants, purgatives and astringents; bottles of 'Jinx-Removing Incense', packets of 'Earthly-Vibes Joss-sticks'. There were numerous chromolithographs of saints from the Catholic calendar: St Michael in combat with the Devil, St Patrick driving the serpents into the sea. They were very lurid, these prints – of a fairground gaudiness. 'That's all Voodoo stuff,' said Michael. 'What do you know about *corps cadavres*?' he asked. 'You know, zombis.'

We came to the Avenue Jean-Jacques Dessalines, a great thoroughfare chock-a-block even at this hour with hundreds of public buses. Known colloquially as tap-taps from their vintage engines which emit a tapping sound as they labour over hills, these vehicles – usually Peugeot 404s converted into charabancs – were painted garishly with the gods, angels, saints, demons, numina and genii that people the complicated pantheon of Voodoo. The buses bore attractive, zany names: *Voici Bébé, Merci Toussaint L'Ouverture, Les Vrais Amis Sont Rares*. But they looked uncomfortable; it would be a while before I summoned the courage to board a tap-tap.

'Not far now,' Michael went on. 'Not far to the Roxy.'

We arrived at the port; there was a smell of soggy dock-piling, stale tobacco and bilge. And there, a crumble of white stucco on the corner of Boulevard Harry Truman, stood the Roxy. This turned out to be a miserable clip joint, the façade hung with a miniature neon windmill in imitation of the Moulin Rouge. 'Welcome All Visitors at Casino du Port', proclaimed a sign in ropy English. 'We Open at 10 a.m. We Close at 4 a.m. Jackpots of $15,000. Win a Car at the Roulette. Special Prices. Dice Table.'

A dangerous-looking young man hustled me into the doorway of the club; he obviously procured for customers: 'Nice girlies, sir. They good for you.' Next thing, I was relieved of thirty gourdes, and descending a dark flight of stairs.

'Is this a good idea?' I turned to Michael.

'No problem.' He nudged me down the steps. 'Everything gonna be all right.'

Downstairs, go-go girls in various degrees of undress – sequined body stockings, gold lamé bikinis – were gyrating to *méringue* atop a dais painted with leopardskin spots. 'Dominican ladies,' grinned Michael. 'Cool, eh? Nice colour skin.' Floozies tick-tacked unsteadily on stilettoes, chivvying customers seated round the dance floor, priming them with bottles of sickly wine. A group of Americans, goggle-eyed at the tinsel allure of the place, had found entertainment with a girl naked save for a brief V of black lace and a black sequin star on each breast. 'Awright!' they yelled as she danced for them. 'Cmon. Take it away! Grind baby, grind.' One of them got up and slipped a roll of money – *'L'Union Fait la Force'* – into the elastic of her V. The men flashed a spectral white and blue from the strobe effect of the lighting system.

A huge Haitian in military fatigues sat hunched near by over a bottle of Barbancourt rum, his gun out of its holster on the table.

The Roxy was a nightmare of swirling multicoloured disco lights. 'Let's go.' I tried to reason with Michael. 'I don't feel well.'

My guide lowered his voice, casting a nervous glance over his shoulder. 'But you get good information here. It's a Macoute bar.' Michael had no sooner told me this than the man in military fatigues overturned his table, staggered drunkenly across the dance floor, punched a musician from the *méringue* combo in the face, broke his maracas and yelled *'Vive Président Avril! Vive le Président!'* Screaming broke out from among the Dominican dancers as a power cut failed the lights; it was bedlam generally.

We made our escape to safety tearing up the flight of stairs. '*Now* what?' I pleaded with Michael, panting out of breath.

'More Dominican girls,' he enthused. 'We find more Dominican girls, OK?'

It was curious, this obsession with women from the neighbouring country: Haitian men, explained Michael, preferred the lighter skin of Dominican girls. And this despite the fact that Haitians are generally despised by Dominicans as backward. The hostility has deep and bitter roots: both Toussaint L'Ouverture and Dessalines made no secret of their belief that the Spanish colony of Dominica was a rightful part of their realm; and in 1822 President Boyer of Haiti finally invaded, occupying the country until his fall in 1843. Now the tables have turned: thousands of Haitians every year seek employment in the Dominican sugar industry, working in abysmal conditions for low wages. In October 1937 some 25,000 Haitian immigrants were massacred by the Guardia Nacional of the Dominican president, Rafael Trujillo: a racialist purge of the sugar industry.

Yet girls from the Dominican Republic continue to travel across the border to earn a living in Haiti as prostitutes: *'Dominicaine'* is in fact polite Haitian for whore. Good money is to be made from this business: the black Haitian president Dumarsais Estimé, who came to power in 1946, exhibited such a weakness for Dominican girls that the tan Oldsmobile in which he seduced and pampered them was known as the 'Tomb of Virgins'.

We began to walk, Michael and I, along the Carrefour road – a red-light district which at night apparently teems with thieves and ghouls. 'You need a guide,' wheedled Michael. 'For protection, understand?' The Carrefour is reportedly a seedbed of AIDS; I wondered how many had bought their death in the dingy brothels here: Mon Premier Amour, Club Zodiac, Hotel Harmonie, Copa Cabana. Haitians are now listed with heroin addicts, haemophiliacs and homosexuals – the four H's – as a group at high risk of contracting the virus. The Domaine Idéale, a hotel along the Carrefour offering *'une ambiance folle et variée'*, was a notorious rendezvous for Canadian gays. But the place seemed abandoned tonight.

There was more life at El Caribeño, a brothel run by Dominicans where business hops until four in the morning; it was fabricated from low concrete bungalows painted a distempered hospital green, lined regimentally like bathing cabins at Brighton. There was an air of menace to the place; bow-tied panders were skulking in the shadows. 'Psst. You like good time?' Dominican girls, all of them in a state of semi-undress, were chewing gum, primping a hairdo, adjusting the strap of some Ravish-Me hostess uniform. More *méringue* boomed from a loudspeaker attached to the ceiling above the bar. Michael knew one of the women, Madame Jacqueline Brito. She was black, with giant Fellinian breasts, her face aglow with rouge. Was Jacqueline a Haitian? No, she too was from the Dominican Republic. *'Soy negro,'* she announced in Spanish, *'pero negro blanco.'* Even a black woman from the D.R. is more white than black.

Words were exchanged between Michael and Jacqueline as a girl named

Dominga Sota served me a bottle of Dominican Presidente beer; much better, she reckoned, than the Haitian stuff. Dominga was very beautiful: she reminded me of sketches I had seen of Jeanne Duval, the green-eyed *Vénus Noire* of Baudelaire's sonnets, born herself in the Dominican capital of Santo Domingo:

> . . . the queen of my heart (I recognise those eyes)
> laughing at my pain with all the rest
> and giving me now and then a filthy kiss . . .

Dominga had travelled six days ago to Haiti from the Dominican town of Jimani; her husband had died there in a motorcycle accident, and she needed the money. Dominga earned about $200 a week at the Caribeño – ten times as much as the average Haitian. She was nineteen years old.

The next moment, I was following Dominga, Michael and Jacqueline into bungalow – *habitación* – number 35. The room was cluttered with pairs of shoes, bottles, empty cans of beer, a tin of Hombre hairspray. It was now two in the morning: Dominga opened an armoire and removed a bright red negligée. 'You like Dominga?' grinned Michael. He had already negotiated the price of this woman with Jacqueline, but I had no intention of sleeping with her or anybody else. I said no, let's get back to the Oloffson. Before we left I asked Dominga whether she was not frightened of AIDS. *'Si Señor'*, she hesitated. *'Debe poner la capota.'* You have to wear a condom. Last words, famous last words.

I paid off Michael – we haggled violently over the fee – and walked back footsore in the direction of the Champ de Mars.

Back at the Oloffson, unable to sleep, I tried to read Ronald Firbank's *Sorrow in Sunlight*, published in America in 1924 under the dubious title *Prancing Nigger*. Critics have always claimed that Firbank used Haiti as a background for this novel; but there is no evidence that he ever travelled to the country. A brief passage in the autobiography of Osbert Sitwell is adduced as the single proof: 'Ronald Firbank even managed,' we read, 'to make a considerable stay in the negro Republic of Haiti (which, incorrect though the impression may be, does, nevertheless, sound perilous, as well as very distant, to ordinary English ears) without any untoward incident occurring.' While Firbank often announced travel plans which he never fulfilled, the local colour in this particular novel did seem, as I tipsily turned the pages in the Oloffson, to be realistically Haitian. Besides, Firbank was wildly enamoured of black men; he saw the surface of their blackness as brushed by mauve, dear to him as the colour, he said, of 'decadence'.

I had scarcely begun the tenth chapter – 'Past the Presidency and the public park, the Théâtres Maxime Bush, Eden-Garden, and Apollo . . .' – when a sound of machine-gun fire reached me from outside the hotel. It troubled at first, but one got used to it, like the rattle of musketry in a Hollywood epic.

IV

Sorrow in Sunlight

'. . . the cross and the snake of Haitian Voodoo rites and the
blood of goats whose throats were slit by the *papaloi*'s
machete . . .'

Jorge Luis Borges, *A Universal History of Infamy*

According to the guidebooks, Port-au-Prince was founded in 1749 and
named after a French vessel, *Le Prince*, which anchored in the harbour
there about 1680; and not, as Papa Doc apparently liked to believe, after
The Prince by Machiavelli.

The capital of Haiti lies prostrate across a deep and marshy horseshoe
bay, encircled by high mountains. Beyond these mountains rise others;
there is, they say, an illusion of space – open tropical plains, a fresh and
vital air, the vault of bright blue sky. In bad weather, though, the mountains loom like dark thunderheads; an oppression settles over the city, any
illusion of space dissolved. At such a time one remembers the grim
statistic: Haiti is a land mass of only fifteen thousand square miles inhabited by eight million people. Some two million live huddled together in
the capital. Under rain or burning sun Port-au-Prince is an insalubrious
place; certainly one of the most foul-smelling, dirty and disease-ridden
cities in the world.

The Avenue Dessalines was always a dense bottleneck of human beings
and tap-taps: *Merci Vierge Miracle, L'Aventure Mystérieuse, Qui Sait son Destin?*
– the buses bore their usual crackpot names. One or two were occasionally in Spanish – perhaps the drivers had worked in the Dominican
Republic: *Rapido como un Toro*. These vehicles are painted all over in crude
colours traditional and unvarying like the horse-drawn carts of Sicily, and
the subjects obviously reflect the temperament and tastes of the people.
There is the Haitian flair for pageantry: Masonic pentacles, fantastic flamingos, palm trees – the more flamboyant these decorations, the greater
the driver's status, rather like the number of tattoos on a man's forearm.
There is history, or rather, legend: lurid representations of Jean-Jacques
Dessalines and Toussaint L'Ouverture, their playing card sabres encrusted

with precious stones. And there is the love of a wise and homespun proverb: *Pour mieux connaître les hommes il faut vivre avec eux* – to know men well you have to live with them – is a typical tap-tap slogan. But above all, religion. Many buses are decorated with quotations from the Old Testament, often from the Book of Numbers: 'The one lamb thou shalt offer in the morning; the other lamb shalt thou offer at even . . .' A tap-tap is Haiti in miniature, surreal as a canvas by Dali.

The avenue – too grand a name for what the rain would churn to mud – was busy most days with barefoot men heaving barrows piled with heavy sacks of charcoal, their veins bulged as corded knots and sweat running in rills along legs and arms. I was told that these porters have an average lifespan of seven years from the time they begin to work. Far better to be a vendor of *frescos*, a flavoured ice sold from tiny carts with buckled metal wheels: *'Fresco! Fresco!'* – it is one of the most distinctive cries in all Haiti. The refreshment is concocted from a sickly syrup – lurid green, shocking pink – poured over the scrapings from a large slab of ice, the slab wrapped in dirty burlap. I once made the mistake of buying a *fresco*. I should have known better – the ice is frozen from unpurified water and the carts swarm with wasps.

The Marchée de Fer – a block square of bawling, bargaining Timbuktu – is a great arched iron structure painted a flamboyant red and green. It is not unlike an oriental bazaar, with minaret-cupolas that might have come from Agra or Fatehpur Sikri in India. The din of the place deafens; powerful old *marchandes* – market women – haggle in loud piping voices over pyramids of salted codfish, manioc flour and *biswit*, the staple Haitian bread. Others sell from makeshift stalls meagre supplies of Comme il Faut cigarettes. There is a beetling trade in contraband whisky – Old Smugglers, Ginger Lady – but much of the commerce is craftware: straw hats and baskets, the raffia bags known as *macoutes*.

One is constantly pestered by moneychangers – 'Pssst! Pssst!' – and by hucksters bent double under prodigious loads of contraband. More frequently, though, by ambulatory bootblacks. They sidle up to you like lepers, tinkling a little bell. '*Blanc!* Your shoe very dirty. Gimme shoe!' Never mind if you are wearing plimsolls: the white man is a moneyed man. Young boys would approach with bottles of a saccharine *gaseoso* named Kola-Champagne. 'Hey, mister! You like K'la? You buy one bottle K'la.' This boisterous yelling intensifies the deeper one ventures into the Iron Market. Pedlars suddenly emerge from behind piles of straw hats, waving a shabby panama or plastic topee. It is easy to lose oneself in the maze of merchandise; the swarming, clanging, shouting hell of the market may overwhelm – corridor-like avenues lead to dingy vaults hung with the innards, eyes and ears of pigs or cows, cuts of meat black with flies.

The men carted this meat like the bummarees at London's Smithfield market while women mostly sat behind their goods, puffing on a cob pipe or fanning themselves with a banana leaf. Some, I noticed, were swaddled in what appeared to be lengths of fabric torn from the American flag. In May 1960 *The Times* reported in an article entitled 'Use of the Stars and Stripes for Curtains' how surplus US flags outmoded by the entry of Alaska and Hawaii into the Union had been shipped to Haiti for sale as clothing, curtains or even tablecloths. 'A quick search of the archives in Washington has found no federal law prohibiting such uses of the American flag,' the article concluded. Appropriately, perhaps, the produce which lay at the feet of these *marchandes* had almost certainly arrived from the United States: Clean Boy Deluxe soap, My Dream Stick cologne, Suave bathroom tissue. They sold snowstorms captive in plastic paperweights, 'Make Me Pretty' Barbie dolls, boxes of Pop Secret Microwave Popcorn.

It is just possible, however, that some of this merchandise had been manufactured in Haiti. Since the early 1970s the United States has established some 240 assembly plants – electronics, toys, sporting goods – in the Port-au-Prince area. The labour is cheap and abundant: a minimum daily wage of only three dollars, a non-existent trade-union movement and generous tax concessions offered by the Haitian government. Baby Doc himself was keen on promoting Haiti as the 'Taiwan of the Caribbean' and the island is now the world's largest producer of baseballs. The Rawlings Sporting Goods factory, situated near the airport, maintains a contract for all balls used by the US American and National Leagues. A spokesman there conceded that 'it would cost a fortune' to produce an equivalent number in the United States.

Trinkets and plaster images for use in Voodoo ceremonies may be purchased at the Iron Market. These are mostly sold by a certain old woman whose stall bore the notice: '*Christ est le chef de cette Boutique, Hôte invisible, présent à chaque repas. Auditeur silencieux de chaque conversation*'. Displayed on the wicker tray which hung from her scrawny shoulders was a heap of tiny sugar-candy skulls and skeletons fashioned from pipe-cleaners. There were holy water stoups, pieces of calico stitched with small seeds in the form of a cross, and bright-coloured feathers from tropical humming-birds. One day I asked her about the old-fashioned cavalry sabre, propped like a lost exhibit in a corner of her stall. She took my hand in a claw-like grip – *'C'est pour le papaloi!'* – and pressed it against the amulets pinned to her bosom: a shark's tooth, a coil of snake-skin.

A papaloi, or more commonly *houngan*, is a Voodoo priest. The sword, as I was later to learn, is sometimes used to slit the throats of animals sacrificed in the Haitian rites.

The streets outside the Iron Market are encumbered, for an area of perhaps half a mile square, with globular straw baskets of colossal size, jerry-cans and boxes of Florida Water. With the approach of a tap-tap, the vendors would heave their goods to the edge of the kerb, and the vehicle proceeded until it met with another blockage. It was a sadly comic spectacle – the goods replaced in the middle of the road only to be removed again five minutes later. *'Dèyè mon, gin mon'*, runs a Haitian proverb: 'Beyond mountains there are more mountains' – solve one prob-lem, along comes another.

In the nearby Rue Courbe are several shopfronts with Arabic names: Magasin Hatem, Talamas Store, Chez Walid, Nasri Jiha and Company. Why had these Arabs come to Haiti? The One Stop Market belongs to the Syrian shopkeepers Mr Farah and Mr Samir; the stall was heaped with cheap notebooks and pencils, and great stockpiles of chequered cotton for Haitian school uniforms. Their wives, Fatima and Khaleel, were conducting a fearful row somewhere in the back. Every so often one would hear a slap on the skin followed by a shriek. (Perhaps Evelyn Waugh was right: 'No sound made by mankind is quite so painful as the voices of two Arab women at variance'.) Mr Farah, a wayworn fellow with droopy moustaches, explained how, fleeing persecution from the Turks in the 1890s, his family had set sail for the Americas from their Syrian town of Tartus; the boat took them to Marseilles and thence to Haiti, where they eventually settled as *commerçants*. Both Mr Farah and his colleague were Greek Orthodox.

In 1903 a US minister in Port-au-Prince put the number of Levantine immigrants in Haiti at 15,000. Like the Farahs from Tartus, most of these Arabs had arrived in the Antilles penniless: with only, as they say in Creole, *'boîte nen dos'* – a box on their back. They soon established themselves in Port-au-Prince as successful wholesalers, jobbers, retailers and pedlars – ousting the Haitians from their stalls around the Iron Market. Many of these Arabs now run the *borlette* – Haitian state lottery. Hammered together from the rusting metal of commercial hoardings – Nestlé, Esso, Pepsi –

these gambling boutiques are to be found at every street corner in Port-au-Prince. They provide a steady source of income, as Haitians may lavish their last gourde at the gaming table.

A British visitor to Haiti at the turn of the century reinforced the popular prejudice against the Levantines – contemptuously referred to as *'lezarabs'* – of Haiti: 'They are a race unspeakable, living ten in a room, consummate cheats,' he wrote. 'They are usurers and parasites sucking the blood from the country and in no way enriching their adopted land in return . . .' During the year 1905 a newspaper named *L'Antisyrien* was distributed throughout Port-au-Prince. It lobbied for laws which would restrict the commercial activities of the Levantines, and prevent the arrival in Haiti of more such immigrants. The editorials are ferocious: the Arab is a 'dangerous leper' animated only by 'the greed of Shylock'. Confronted with this racial hatred, it is probable that the Arabs of Haiti conspired with opposition leaders to protect themselves. When President Cincinnatus Leconte was blown up in the National Palace on 8 August 1912, Levantines received the blame.

One of the few Levantines to have participated in the national life of Haiti is the Lebanese doctor Carlo Boulos who had studied medicine at Harvard and was, in 1959, appointed Minister of Health by Papa Doc. I met Dr Boulos, now sixty-eight years old, in his Port-au-Prince office: the Centre Haïtien-Arabe et Complexe Médico-Sociale de la Cité Soleil. Short and wizened, there was an old-world courtesy to Dr Boulos. He had served for only two years under Papa Doc: 'I was obliged in the end to hand in my resignation,' he said behind a cloud of cigar smoke. 'The fellow was quite gaga.'

I asked Dr Boulos about his work in the seafront shanty town of Cité Soleil. 'Just one hour by air from Miami and we are confronted by the most brutal and demoralizing poverty on earth,' he said. 'In early 1974 I opened a small medical dispensary there.' A week before our meeting the *Miami Herald* had enthused about a 'medical miracle amid Haiti's hovels'. The article concluded: 'Thanks to this Haitian physician of Arab origin, diseases in Cité Soleil such as poliomyelitis, tetanus and measles are now almost non-existent. Dr Boulos is a giant in the world of medicine.'

The gravest problem remains tuberculosis from malnutrition: it kills an average of two in ten children before they reach the age of one. 'But we are trying,' said Dr Boulos. 'We are trying to reduce the level of infant mortality.' It is a terrible struggle: almost a third of Haitian children will perish before their fifth birthday. 'You will ask me why I bother. Well, I do it for humanity,' said Dr Boulos. 'And for religion.' He flicked the ash-tip of his cheroot into the palm of his hand. 'My Lebanese grandfather was a Maronite Christian.'

Carlo Boulos arranged for a doctor, another Lebanese, to drive me along the Avenue Dessalines to Cité Soleil. It was a day of stupefying heat. We bumped along in the jeep through great swirls of dust – red bauxite – and grit. 'You'd better wind up your window,' laughed Dr Marzouka. 'You know what they say about the dust in Haiti – it's *la neige locale*.' I had already experienced this 'local snow'; the dust had insinuated deep into my lungs, and caused an infection.

On we drove: past the Iron Market, airing in the sunshine its tatter-demalion suit of harlequin rags; past the only railway line in Haiti – the single-gauge Haitian-American Sugar Company track which shunts cane by night from near the Dominican border. (On several occasions I had tried to gain entry into the giant HASCO sugar mill, only to be met with elaborate stonewalling from the director of publicity. 'It's not that we're a secret operation,' he said. 'It's just that, you know, certain . . . precautions have to be taken.') Past the memorial which marks the spot where Dessalines was murdered at the age of forty-eight by his subalterns. 'You know what they did to *him*,' said Dr Marzouka. 'Hacked the fingers from his hands so they could remove the rings. Slashed the corpse to shreds with swords. Poor Dessalines. He was scarcely recognizable.'

Arriving at Cité Soleil a dreadful stench of humanity brought bile to the mouth. 'Here, have one of these,' the doctor advised. It was a Vick's nasal inhaler (they contain oil of pine needles). 'It'll help with the smell.' It did, probably in much the same way that a pomegranate, stuck with cloves, gave relief to those in the back streets of Restoration London.

Never have I seen such poverty: not even in the slums of Bombay, or the *ciudades perdidas* of Mexico City. One hundred and fifty thousand people live here, crammed into a maze of primitive adobe huts reinforced with abandoned metal sheeting and cardboard packing cases. Swollen-bellied children scramble over great mounds of detritus, sifting the trash for scrap; dogs everywhere snuffle round open sewers. Inside the shacks, all is black from charcoal. There is a Neapolitan adage: 'Where the sun does not enter, the doctor does.'

An emaciated horse, its ribs protruding like the bars of a gridiron, stood fetlock-deep in the mud, covered with flies. Its owner came running up to me: *'Kouman ou ye?'* he asked in Creole – how are you? And then:

'Blanc . . . blanc, ba'moin une gourde, blanc!' One cannot avoid the beggars in Cité Soleil: they creep up to you from behind the decaying mud walls, staring with one hand outheld. Driving in a car, it is impossible to move without endangering their several lives; they swarm about the vehicle in droves.

Cité Soleil is built on landfill at the harbour's edge; even a light rainfall will put the whole area under flood. The water rushes through the shacks in torrents, said Dr Marzouka; mothers have to gather children in their arms lest they be swept away. We have Doctor Duvalier, the so-called Renovator of the Fatherland and Apostle of National Unity, to blame for this misery. The creation of Cité Simone (as the settlement was first named in honour of his wife) was intended to banish the beggars of Port-au-Prince to where they need never be seen again – the city sea-swamps. The slum was rebaptized Cité Soleil as a tribute to the Catholic wireless station, Radio Sunshine, which had played so vital a role in bringing about the downfall of the Duvalier dynasty.

Walking about the slum ankle-deep in refuse, I felt myself a voyeur of misery: it would be so easy now to return to the Oloffson and spend, in a single evening, the equivalent of a year's income for an inhabitant of Cité Soleil.

Religion is the mainstay of Haitian society: Voodoo and Catholicism. It is said that Haitians are eighty per cent Catholic and one hundred per cent Voodooist. Religion is perhaps all that remains for the voiceless poor of Haiti: the spirits of far-away Africa, the cross of Christianity.

The twin-spired pink and white cathedral of Port-au-Prince is quite as ugly as the Mormon Temple at Salt Lake City. It is a turn-of-the-century affair whose Romanesque cupolas vaguely recall those of the Sacré Cœur in Paris, though money apparently ran out before a central dome could be built. Inside, a massive shrine bearing a plaster-cast image of the Virgin, swathed in wreaths of pink tulle and bedded in a nest of palm-tree fronds, stands in the parquet transept. Tasselled standards embroidered with words from the Holy Bible line the aisles. There is everywhere a scent of dying flowers and burial candle-wicks.

Gathered about the Madonna one morning was a crowd of wailing women. Many had prostrated themselves in supplication; they lay prone with faces pressed against the floor, clutching in one hand a lighted candle, a rosary in the other. Some hobbled shrine-wards on their knees; others would kiss the marble pilasters around the Virgin and then genuflect at the four cardinal points with a peculiar shriek. I had witnessed similar ceremonials in southern Italy: 'The Madonnas of Naples,' wrote Norman Douglas in *Siren Land*, 'are sea-queens whose crowns shine with a borrowed lustre . . . they are all reincarnations of antique shapes.' One might say the same for this Haitian Virgin. Some curious votive offerings had been placed at her plaster feet: a small mirror, an old toothbrush, a white silk handkerchief, a plastic necklace, empty bottles of Cinzano and madeira.

These were objects left in honour of Erzulie Freda, an African divinity of Dahomean origin who is mirrored in Catholicism by the Virgin Mary. Erzulie is also identified as the Mater Dolorosa, the Notre-Dame de Grâce and, most reverent, *La Grand Maîtresse*. In the Voodoo cosmology she is a beautiful young mulatta dressed in exquisite raiment, or a creature of beguiling coquetry with a delicate soprano voice. Men flock to escort Erzulie to her boudoir; women placate her with sweet drinks or bottles of perfume. The celebrants wailing before me in the cathedral were respectful then of both Erzulie and the Madonna; Christianity, it seems, has never triumphed over Voodoo for the simple reason that Voodoo itself has always been receptive to elements from Catholicism. I felt sure that all these women, though practised in Voodoo, were in some way conscious of the Cross as an unexplained but potent symbol, that they believed in God – *Le Grand Maître*.

One day I fell asleep in the pews of the cathedral, only to be disturbed by a woman of spectacular girth who introduced herself as Mimi. '*Bonjour, chéri!*' She nudged me awake. 'You have money?' She wore gold hoop earrings, a pair of beaten-up baseball boots and an old alarm clock which dangled from her neck by a length of twine. Her brassière was exposed like part of a bikini combination. Mimi took my five-gourde note with a toothless cackle of delight, rewarding me with a peck on the cheek. I asked her about Erzulie Freda; she widened the whites of her eyes in surprise. '*Gason blanc se vauduisant!*' she whooped in Creole patois – the white boy is a Voodooist. This exclamation was repeated over and again so that soon we were joined by six or so other very portly women, their hair plaited like Mimi's into tight little ropes, all of whom shrilled their applause at my mention of the Dahomean Aphrodite.

'*Mes-z-amis!*' They clapped their hands. And has she spoken to you yet, Erzulie Freda?

Yes, I returned. She even gave me a bottle of Cinzano.

The women howled: '*Tou les jou li sou avè Freda!*' – Every day he's drunk with Freda.

I slipped out of the cathedral before this crazy crowd could gather in size.

A dilapidated sign above the main entrance to the Port-au-Prince cemetery proclaims: *'Souviens Que Tu Es Poussière'*. Remember that you are dust – a happy reminder that the undertaker awaits us all. Here there are no keening angels or draped urns: only giant blocks of chipped concrete painted a mustard yellow or brown. Most of these tombs are choked with weeds and high grass. Broken headstones lie snarled in undergrowth; beer-bottle tops remain trodden into the asphalt paths. Early one morning I watched a *houngan* incanting prayers in the cemetery before the giant cross to Baron Samedi, God of the Dead and chief of the underworld. He sprinkled water over the rood with a hyssop twig in the manner of a Catholic priest. Morsels of food had been left on saucers at the foot of the cross, mingled with strips of black and red cloth – the colours of the Baron.

The Voodoo priest greeted me with quiet courtesy: would I like, he asked, to see the tomb of Papa Doc? He led me to a heap of rubble. Is this it? *'Mais oui, bien sûr,'* came the answer. *'C'est le tombeau de François Duvalier.'* The priest explained how the tomb had been desecrated by a furious mob, soon after the departure of Baby Doc. They broke away tiles from the top of the mausoleum, smashing the reinforced concrete with rocks. The monument was eventually levelled and the vault thrown open. Once inside, however, the crowd found no coffin, nor any trace of Papa Doc. To this day, nobody knows what became of his corpse.

The twenty-fourth of April 1971, the Day of Baron Samedi: Doctor Duvalier's had been a gloomy, solemn funeral. Perhaps the most solemn that Port-au-Prince has ever witnessed – flower-strewn streets, the Requiem Mass, a 101-gun salute. As the crowds filed past the coffin they would have seen the President-for-Life lying in state with a crucifix between his hands, and a red-bound copy of *Memoirs of a Third World Leader* (in which he coined the lugubrious epigram: 'a doctor must sometimes take life in order to save it') resting by his side. The catafalque was guarded by twenty-two soldiers and twenty-two Tontons Macoute: 22 being the despot's lucky number. The three-month period of official mourning caused numerous disruptions in the social world of Port-au-Prince: according to the *Daily Telegraph* it obliged the British chargé d'affaires to cancel the cocktail party held every April in honour of Queen Elizabeth II's birthday.

The *houngan* informed me that Papa Doc had now joined the Voodoo pantheon as 'Loa 22 Os' – Bone Spirit Number 22. Was there a fatality, a sort of superstitious dread, to these numbers? Prosper Avril had declared his state of siege on 22 January; Papa Doc had been elected as president on 22 September 1957 and on 22 November 1963 he celebrated the assassination of John F. Kennedy (an arch-enemy) with a champagne party at the National Palace; there was no room number 22 at the Oloffson.

A portrait of Queen Elizabeth hangs on the wall of a small insurance office along the Rue Pavée, round the corner from the Cèdres du Liban Arabic restaurant. One day the elderly owner of this office told me: 'The Tontons Macoute are a trigger-happy lot. And if you're in the wrong place at the wrong time, God help you.' Rony Chenet is the British vice-consul *ad honorem* in Port-au-Prince. He retired long ago, but still retains his title. The diplomatic power is negligible: 'But I'll hang on until I drop,' he said a little dryly.

Mr Chenet is of Jamaican-English parentage; his family has for decades maintained a commercial interest in both the London and Lancashire Insurance Company and the Guardian Royal Exchange. Slight of build, with silver-rimmed schoolmarm spectacles and a toothbrush moustache, the diplomat reminded me of Ben Kingsley as Mahatma Gandhi. There was the same diffidence of manner, the wry flicker of a smile.

For a week now Port-au-Prince had been suffering from numerous and erratic blackouts. Shopfronts were illuminated at night with naphtha flares or kerosene lamps; those in the slums went about with candles, if they could afford them. Mr Chenet was running his insurance outfit with the help of an auxiliary generator. Queen Elizabeth juddered slightly in her frame as the motor pumped electricity to the light bulbs. 'How can you manage a business like this?' he complained. 'Good grief, electricity is an *essential* of civilization. No, no. The damn country doesn't work any more. If indeed it ever *did* work. Year after year we've suffered the same old problems: nepotism, corruption, rank opportunism. You name it.'

The state of siege had lifted, but there was still political unrest: insurgent Macoutes (Prosper Avril had rechristened them *'Attachés'*) were on the rampage, terrorizing civilians, offering protection in the Chicago sense of the term. Most inhabitants of Port-au-Prince were now loath to venture out of doors once the sun had set. 'Haiti is a powder keg, no bloody fooling. Just one spark and – whoosh! – the whole lot goes up.' Mr Chenet fiddled with the generator: the light bulbs failed for an instant.

And then glowed to life with a whirr from the machine. 'Pardon my French,' he continued. 'But this Avril fellow is a prize bastard. How can we hope to hold elections with a Duvalierist in the National Palace?'

'I should very much like to visit the National Palace.'

'Not a hope. Nobody ever gets in there. And quite a few people never get out alive . . .'

Behind the Oloffson, in the cooler hills of the capital, stands a nine-teenth-century residential area known as Bois Verna. Arcaded and decay-ing, it was probably Bois Verna that Malcolm Lowry described when he journeyed to Port-au-Prince in the winter of 1947, bringing with him the page proofs of *Under the Volcano*: '. . . Strangely beautiful houses of pointed roofs and of seemingly Norwegian design, church spires here and there that rise vaguely in the sun giving it the look of Tewkesbury,' he noted in his journal.

Lowry had encountered some eccentric characters in Haiti – an American editor with a cricket cap carrying a copy of *Moby Dick* in his blazer pocket, a blind man who followed him behind graves, a boy that begged for money from the branches of a trumpet tree; but none so odd as the Cossack whom I met one day in Bois Verna.

He was standing in the garden of his magnificent gingerbread mansion on Rue Lamartinière, pruning a triffid-like profusion of *flamboyants* – flame-thrower flowers. 'From where you come, my friend?' The accent was almost caricature Russian. 'England,' I replied. The old man – tall, thin and rather stooped with the years – put down his garden shears and slowly removed his sunglasses. The eyes were a clouded blue. Nikolai Ivanovich Roude introduced himself as 'the only Cossack in the Caribbean'. He had served as an officer in the Russian Imperial Artillery and had been living in Haiti as a White Russian since, he said, 'oh, not long after the 1917 revolution'. I warmed to him enormously.

'Come inside for the drink.' The *émigré* extended a welcoming hand. 'What you like?'

We sat in low rocking chairs, sipping chilled vodkas on the teakwood planking of the verandah. Flowering creepers scented the air. At my invitation, Nikolai began to relate the story of his remarkable life. Sometimes he would lapse into French, and then into Creole or Russian, but returning always to English. He had the linguistic tic of punctuating his every second sentence with the words: 'That's all right.' The story, occasionally confused in the telling, went something like this . . .

Shortly after April 1922, when Lloyd George – 'that terrible prime minister' – had recognized the Bolsheviks as the *de jure* government of Russia, Nikolai sailed from Yalta to Turkey with a flotilla of 248 boats carrying White Russians. Their journey took them across the Black Sea, and down the Bosphorus to Istanbul. From there they sailed across the Sea of Marmara to the island of Lesbos. 'The largest island after Crete, very famous for the homosexual women, that's all right' – Nikolai gave a salacious cackle, draining his glass of vodka. Looking for sanctuary, the Cossacks returned to Istanbul where Nikolai spent eight months in a prison camp run by the British, French and Italians. A fellow Russian officer helped him escape and for one year Nikolai worked the roads of Istanbul as a labourer. 'I was so poor that I sold my shirt in the local bazaar,' he remembered.

'One morning a man approached me in the market – he spoke very good Russian. Come to my house and live with me, he said, and help sell my merchandise. But on one condition: that you marry my daughter and become a Mussulman. OK, I said. That's all right. (For the daughter was very *magnifique*, and I would do anything for money.) But then I got the cold feet one night and fled the house. My God! I cannot stay in Istanbul much longer. If my boss finds me, I die. So I went to the Bulgarian consulate and obtained a visa to go to Sofia. We are in the year 1923.'

And so the tale continued: one day a White Russian informed Nikolai that a commissar from the Cheka – the Soviet secret police – had arrived in Sofia. He was disguised, apparently, as a member of the Red Cross delegation. 'I thought it prudent to see this man,' Nikolai went on, cool and imperious. 'When I got to his hotel – the *best* hotel in all Sofia! – I was manhandled by two men with revolvers who shoved me into room number 14. "I need your help," said Commissar Tchaikin. "What kind of help you want?" Then the Bolshevik said: "Everyone knows you are Nikolai Ivanovich Roude of the Imperial Russian Artillery. So listen, Comrade, maybe you can furnish us with a little . . . information about White Russian activities in Bulgaria." I said: "I'm not a damned Comrade. I am *Mister* Roude . . . But give me a few days to think it over." After that I went immediately to the French consulate and got a visa for Paris. My Russian friends had told me that Tchaikin was out to kill me.'

It was in Paris that Nikolai met his Haitian wife Estelle, a very *mondaine* mulatta. They sailed to Port-au-Prince from Antwerp; the voyage took one and a half months. 'When I first came to Haiti seventy years ago,' said Nikolai, 'I thought I was a second Christopher Columbus on a voyage of discovery, that's all right.' Their mansion in Bois Verna had been built at the turn of the century by President Tirésias Sam (related to the same Sam who had been murdered prior to the US invasion of Haiti) as a gift for his goddaughter. Nikolai led me on a tour of the house: chandeliers of Bohemian glass, majolica-tiled floors, louvred white doors detailed in gold, an exquisite ceiling with *putti* and fleur-de-lys painted in 1901 by a Parisian artist. The house had been a source of constant delight and exultation, said Nikolai. Sepia pictures of Estelle stood in a leather diptych by a bouquet of tropical anthurium. 'My lovely wife . . .' Nikolai patted the photographs like a tender memory.

His study was a lumber room cluttered with icons from the Russian Orthodox church, broken balalaikas and – most curious – black and white photographs of naked women posed in front of Grecian caryatids. 'My beauty angels, that's all right.' The Cossack grinned. Next to these there hung a portrait of King Alexander of Yugoslavia with his wife Marie, daughter of Ferdinand of Romania. 'He appointed me Yugoslav consul of Haiti and of the Dominican Republic,' said Nikolai. 'But then he was *assassiné*, murdered at Marseilles in . . . 1934 by a Croat.' Nikolai had a remarkable memory for dates. 'And I lost my post.' An old Cossack uniform hung suspended from a coat hanger by a framed quotation of Victor Hugo's: *'Ceux qui vivent ce sont ceux qui luttent.'* Nikolai blew a cloud of dust from the battledress. The tunic had been perforated by bullets – 'four large-calibre ones' – which had left singe damage as they ripped through the cloth.

'How about another vodka, my friend?'

Back at the Oloffson an emaciated she-goat was nosing up morsels of food in the driveway while Papa Dog, a mangy black mongrel, fleaed his rump under a mango tree. I gave the animals a wide berth.

The hotel was in semi-darkness. *'Blackout, m'sieur.'* A porter shook his head. *'Toujours le blackout. Ha ha!'*

The young owner, Richard Morse, was ensconced in his office – a cubbyhole really – reading a book by the light of a storm lantern. He happened to look up as I passed on my way to the bar. 'So what's the word?' he asked wearily.

Richard was a curious sort of hotelier: tall and somewhat lanky, with an expression of terminal ironic bemusement. One had the feeling that he regarded the business of running a hotel in Haiti as a cruel, but nevertheless rather amusing, joke. 'Well, there's not much doing at the Oloffson

tonight.' He raised an eyebrow. 'There's another power cut as you've probably noticed. The telephone lines are down. The switchboards are down.
Same story.'

Richard had studied anthropology at Princeton University. Both his
mother, the glamorous *danseuse* Emérante de Pradines, and his wife Lunise
are Haitian. His father is American, director of Latin American Studies
at the Smithsonian Institution in Washington.

'Tell me, Richard, why do you bother?'

'To run this place? Who knows? Hell, if there's trouble in Haiti we
take care of the people attracted by trouble. If there's peace we're gonna
have a few tourists. Either way I'm ready.' Richard was always noncha-
lant, sometimes even a little glazed with those dolorous eyes. I fancied
him sitting alone in a room smoking his way through a bag of ganja
when there was nothing else to do. Perhaps that was the only way to
survive in Haiti. He had first travelled to Port-au-Prince in 1985, to
explore the *méringue* and other forms of national music. 'And the way I
came to own the Oloffson is really weird.' Richard lifted his hands, grimac-
ing and baffled. 'I was in the back of a taxi with a Voodoo priest, right?
And this priest, he says: "Do you want the hotel?" So I say, "Well I don't
know." So he repeats: "Do you want the hotel?" So I say: "I'm not sure."
So he says, more pointedly: "Tell me you want the hotel." So I say: "OK,
I want the hotel." He says: "Give me twenty dollars."'

'Did you give him the money?'

'Sure I did. And now look at me for chrissakes!' Richard exclaimed,
beaming strangely. 'An American businessman in Haiti!' Then he cried
tremulously: 'I work like a Turk to keep this place shipshape! But you
never know. You never know when it's gonna happen, the coup I mean.
It's those sonsofbitches in the National Palace. They'll come in here one
day and confiscate my hotel. And then what am I supposed to do? Fend
them off with a machine-gun?'

There was more custom at the bar tonight; among the clients was a
group of Salesian nuns, drinking planter's punches. Most of the regulars
here formed a charmed circle of *blancs*, members of a rather exclusive club.
I was not there every evening but the atmosphere was usually convivial.
Morgan Destouches the barman would begin to circulate the punches at
around six thirty. Thereafter it was an endless round of drinks and cigarettes and we would retire to bed comfortably merry. I remember a mousy
sociologist from Montana who had been crusading for the introduction of
birth control in Cité Soleil; and the flaky New Yorker who was seeking

acupuncture at the hands of a Voodoo priest. She was dressed like Blanche Dubois in a flowing silk robe and diamanté choker, enthusing madly about astrology and herbal teas. Hovering most nights around the bar was the bearded Serge Beaulieu, a notorious old Macoute who looked like Dizzy Gillespie wearing a large red beret. Rumoured to have studied criminology in Germany and to have acted as a spy for Papa Doc, he was also – briefly – Haiti's honorary consul in Barbados. A dangerous man, they say: every afternoon he would broadcast Duvalierist propaganda on Radio Liberté. 'There are just four photographs which everyone should have framed on the wall,' came the message on our radios. 'Those of Nelson Mandela, Jean-Jacques Dessalines, Martin Luther King and Serge Beaulieu.'

Friday night in the Oloffson was traditionally the night for a Voodoo extravaganza: carefully choreographed by Emérante de Pradines, the showgirls would cavort to a rhythmic hula-hula, swaying this way and that to a steady rumble of drums. I was observing this spectacle from the bar when a man with thick Bismarckian moustaches leant over to me on his stool and whispered: 'I know where you can get der best German sausage in Port-au-Prince.' He was plainly drunk.

The German, who introduced himself as Rolf, suddenly raised his voice. 'But listen, *mein herr*, to what I have to say: Haiti is a goot, a very goot comedy. Perhaps der finest comedy in the vorld. If you can see zat, you will have a vonderful time here. It all began with Christopher Columbus. Vat could be more comical than discovering both der United States of America *und* Haiti! Yah, he vas a goot one, Columbus. Perhaps der best comedian of them all.'

Rolf had settled in Haiti six years ago. He was the last in a line of countless Germans who had come here after 1888 when Dr Heinrich Goering, father of Hitler's air marshal, was appointed German consul to Haiti. In Port-au-Prince Rolf had set up, he said, an embroidery factory manufacturing Voodoo artefacts for export; he had also worked at the Oloffson as a part-time plumber. But his plumbing, it must be said, was dreadful: the showers gave only a trickle of water and one could never entirely rinse the soap away. I even knew of regular visitors to the Oloffson who would arrive equipped with a spanner with which to adjust the faulty spigots.

The Voodoo extravaganza began to swing a little out of control, the drummers beating feverishly as the dancers whooped their homage to Erzulie Freda. 'Just look at those Voodoo babies.' Rolf stood me another rum. 'I like black vomen, oh how I *love* them. You know vat they say:

Once a black, never go back!' He made a lewd gesture of pushing a finger through a tightly curled fist. There is a drunken old major, similarly gross, in Brian Moore's novel *The Lonely Passion of Judith Heame*: 'I remember in Haiti, it's a nigger republic, you know . . . the pretty little mulattoes. Hot-blooded things, the tropics, the sun does it. Fondle a few round bottoms!' he gloats.

The man in white had arrived. He sat within earshot, sipping iced vin rosé. Tonight he wore blue espadrilles and a pink bow tie. 'Und dere's der liddle Aubelin Jolicœur,' growled Rolf into his moustaches. 'Vatch out for him, Mister Englishman – the serpent beneath der flower!'

Jolicœur appears as the flamboyant gossip columnist Petit Pierre in *The Comedians*. He evidently delights in this fictional counterpart; when Graham Greene died in April 1991, Jolicœur wrote an appreciation of the writer for the London *Guardian*: 'I was grateful to Greene to have enhanced my legend to such an extent that some fans kneel at my feet or kiss my hand in meeting a man living his own legend.'

I watched Jolicœur pluck a buttonhole from the chrysanthemums which stood in a vase on the table. The dandyism of snuffbox and cane . . . at the hotel he had already been rechristened 'Jolifleur', although his name actually translates as Littledawn Prettyheart.

'Oh my darlings, but people simply *love* the way I write.' Jolicœur was impressing upon a group of American women the excellence of his weekly gossip column in the Haitian newspaper *Le Nouvelliste*. 'Mr Graham Greene, whom I shall always love, thought my style was sometimes a little . . . flowery, but he too simply *adored* my prose.' The little popinjay gave a shrewd smile, showing a set of teeth like piano keys. 'Petit Pierre, as you may know,' he went on steadily, 'is the title of an autobiographical work by Anatole France. It's the story of a fellow who was loved and adored in his village. So the celebrated author of *The Power and the Glory* meant to be agreeable, you see, even to flatter me!'

Exclamations from the women of surprise, delight, and Jolicœur raised a hand for silence. 'You may ask how I have survived in Haiti, after all these years of violence. The answer, my dears, is simple. I survived because I am so very famous! Papa Doc would not dare to touch me.' Jolicœur is in fact believed by many to have connections with the Tontons Macoute. He was a Mister Facing-Both-Ways, a man who had clung mollusc-like to the centres of corruption and power, and never allowed himself to be on the side of the losers. For two years Jolicœur was Secretary of State at the Ministry of Information.

He turned his attention to a woman wearing sandals. 'Oh darling! Your toes are unprotected!' Jolicœur tapped her feet with his malacca cane. 'I suffer for your toes. Oh how I suffer. Has anybody told you that you look like Gina Lollobrigida? And did you know that "Gina" means "woman" in Greek? No? O la la, my dear. How very remiss of you! Never mind. I do hope I will have some mangoes for you, my darling!' The tourist giggled like a schoolgirl.

'Vat a silly man,' Rolf whispered bitterly. 'A really *great* comedian, no?'

The Voodoo ceremony had drawn to a close; a *méringue* ensemble came on stage to strike up a lilting version of 'Colonel Bogey', complete with marimbas and maracas. I moved across the dance floor and introduced myself to the widely suspected informant. 'I remember you very well, my dear,' answered Jolicœur. 'A fortnight ago it was, you were sitting over there at the bar on your own. How time flies! She flits from week to week just like a butterfly.'

'I believe we have an acquaintance in common, Monsieur Jolicœur.' Here I mentioned a Haitian psychiatrist whom I had met in London, and who had herself appeared – much to her annoyance – in one of the gadfly's gossip columns.

'Ah, Ginette! How *is* she?' Jolicœur leant forward with his hands locked together over the head of his cane. I told him that Ginette was happy to leave her home in England and return to Haiti should the country ever improve. 'Such a shame,' said Jolicœur, twitching his clothes straight. 'The best of Haitians living abroad.'

Aubelin promised that night to secure me an audience at the National Palace. But it would take another coup d'état before I was eventually allowed inside the building, some three months later.

V

The White Black Men of Europe

'Things have got to change here.'

Pope John-Paul II, 'Address to the Haitian Nation',

March 1983

Dawn was in the sky as we left Port-au-Prince. We were travelling, Enoch and I, in search of a community of Haitians who we understood spoke Polish. They were descendants of the defeated legions of General Leclerc – Napoleon's brother-in-law – who had come to restore slavery to Saint Domingue. Apparently these Polish troops had deserted to the ranks of Dessalines. In a speech to mark John-Paul II's visit to Haiti in 1983, Baby Doc had praised them 'as men who had not hesitated to join the battalions of the revolting blacks'. This was by way of tribute to the Polish origins of the Pope. But it was still a mystery how these Polish-Haitians had come to live as peasants in the mountain village of Cazales, some thirty miles north of Port-au-Prince.

Enoch, a guide who worked at the Oloffson, was sceptical. *'Ah, mon cher,'* he said gravely. 'How can there be any Poles up there? *C'est pas possible!'* I liked Enoch: he was a big man and very black, of great dignity. He had the most infectious grin: everything to Enoch was a joke, even the current political unrest which made it dangerous for me to investigate Cazales on my own. The inhabitants of this village were considered hostile and suspicious. 'But we'll manage.' Enoch laughed behind the wheel of his battered Ford. 'We'll get there in the end.'

I had come prepared with a *laisser-passer* signed by the Secretary-General of the Interior, without which it was now unwise to travel very far in Haiti. It was a curious document:

LIBERTY   EQUALITY   FRATERNITY
Republic of Haiti
Port-au-Prince
22 March 1990

Mr Ian Thomson, British subject, is recommended to the kindness of the authorities. Please attend to his business, and see to it that he be provided with board and lodging wherever and whenever required. He shall be resident in Haiti during the Spring of the 186th year of Independence. *L'UNION FAIT LA FORCE*

'Very useful', Enoch glanced reflectively at the piece of paper. 'That's a very, very useful document'. He was right: the letter would provide a passport, of sorts, into Haitian society. For some time now Port-au-Prince had confused and frustrated me; crowded, violent, infernally noisy, the city had left me jittery with unaccountable bad moods and loss of appetite. Electricity supplies had failed frequently but unpredictably; there were rarely any telephones that worked and the stove-like heat had begun to sap any remaining strength. At least on the surface, Haitians are an affable, happy people, with no apparent animosity to foreigners. However, they are often suspicious. 'What are you doing here?' This was a question I often felt tacitly asked. And again: 'Why come to Haiti if you don't spend money like a tourist?' But I had not come to discover this country as a tourist. I wanted to get beneath the carapace of instant friendliness, the easy salutation *'Bonjour blanc'*.

On our way to Cazales we passed fields of dense canebrake and tumble-weed, gnarled and crabbed clumps of thorny bush. The rough rab-scrab land was barren of trees. Signs put up by the government urged people against cooking with charcoal: *'Non à Charbon à Bois. Haïti a Besoin de Ses Arbres'*. A dry watercourse, the occasional outcrop of stone – this was an unhappy landscape. As early as 1788 a visitor to Haiti, Baron de Wimpffen, remarked sadly on the readiness with which planters cut down every last tree within one hundred yards of a settlement. Noticing a magnificent avocado that had been felled 'for timber', he caustically observed that sufficient ordinary wood was available on an adjacent hill to rebuild the entire French navy. Today the deforestation of Haiti is uncontrolled, and the road to Cazales was often made impassable by a herd of mules labouring under faggots of bush and brake. The scarcity of trees may be judged by the fact that a bag of charcoal sells in Port-au-Prince for three dollars – which is a labourer's daily wage. Worse, there's no practicable alternative to wood fires as canisters of butane are impossible to transport deep into the interior of Haiti where there are few roads.

At the town of Croix des Bouquets stood the remains of the Bon

Repos maternity and paediatric hospital, opened in 1983 by Baby Doc's wealthy mulatta wife Michèle Bennett. The inferior cement had been mixed with sand from Source Puante – Stinking Spring – only metres away. Walls had immediately developed cracks, cisterns and reservoirs leaked and the water was found to pullulate with microbes. After Baby Doc (a man so lumberingly incompetent that he was nicknamed 'Baskethead') fled Haiti in 1986, the government discovered 330 pounds of cocaine stashed in the hospital pharmacy, part of a Bennett cache awaiting transhipment. The Bon Repos was now riddled with a pock-mark of bullets.

Proceeds for the marriage of Baby Doc to Michèle were derived, they say, from traffic in drugs. Held in the cathedral of Port-au-Prince, the wedding cost an estimated $7 million. 'Cheer for My Bride Or Else!' proclaimed the London *Daily Mirror* for 27 May 1980. Unfortunately, festivities were marred somewhat by a torrential downpour which caused the city sewers to overflow.

Our turning for Cazales lay some way after the small village of Cabaret. It was here that François Duvalier practised for a while as a doctor, having spent two terms in 1946 studying public health at Michigan University. Barely four years following his election to presidency in 1957, Papa Doc chose this village as the site of a permanent memorial to himself. The 'flower city' of Duvalierville was to be the architectural equivalent of Brasilia, a striking example of the 'Duvalierist revolution'. As construction got under way, the cement buildings were placarded with DDD signs: '*Dieu*, the Great Worker of the Universe; *Dessalines*, the Supreme Artisan of Liberty; *Duvalier*, Architect of the New Haiti'.

Funds for Duvalierville were exacted illegally from motorists at a toll-booth. Any reluctance to contribute resulted in the ransacking of their premises by the Tontons Macoute. Or in torture during the hours of darkness. The British ambassador, Gerard Corley Smith, was immediately expelled when he dared to protest against these levies.

Duvalierville was a notable failure. It was intended by Papa Doc to be 'a centre where it is always good to live under an ever-blue sky . . . and where every Haitian is master of his own destiny', but there are still no accomplishments to view. A miserable assembly of white one-room boxes, constructed in single file like the dormitories of a shabby motel; a disused *ciné-théâtre* full of pigs and broken benches; a cockfight stadium named Les Eperons Etincelants, the glittering spurs. The roof was tilted upwards like the wings of a toy balsawood aeroplane. It looked about as sturdy.

The stadium has not been used since the departure of Baby Doc in 1986. As we drove away from this wilderness of cement Enoch explained how in February of that year Duvalierville had been ransacked during *'Opération Dechoukaj'*. Operation Uproot was the process whereby Haiti would be rid, once and for ever, of its Duvalierist inheritance. It required the looting and destruction of homes belonging to Macoutes, and the alteration of several street and village names: the Avenue Jean-Claude Duvalier, near the Oloffson, became Avenue Jean-Paul II while Duvalierville itself reverted to its original, unintentionally comic, name of Cabaret.

The road to Cazales is more a bridle path, criss-crossed here and there by streams which churned the route to mud. The wheels of our car began to spin in a rut; then we slid away backwards into a tree bole. *'Oh mon Dieu!'* laughed Enoch. *'C'est formidable!'* He slid a cigarette, nervously, from my packet of Comme il Faut.

A Polish-American priest in Little Haiti, Miami, had warned me that one would really need four-wheel drive to reach Cazales. 'I've never made it,' he had said. Father Thomas Wenski, an amiable man with broad Slavic looks, had for many years been fascinated by the history of Poles in Haiti. 'Dessalines called them the white Negroes of Europe. But you'll probably find that they've intermarried with the blacks now. I dare say they look more or less like mulattoes,' he had told me. 'The folks down in Cabaret talk about the *"moun rouj"*, the red people of Cazales . . .'

We groaned uphill through cane plantations, the sugar plumes waving like soft pampas grass. A bird flapped upwards from the canebrakes and went drifting off into the spacious altitudes – a green heron, perhaps. The further we climbed, the more fresh and vital the air. *'Ah c'est très riant ici!'* Enoch smiled as we scissored this way and that across the mud. *'Très, très riant.'* It was certainly pleasant, as Enoch put it, to have escaped the filth of Port-au-Prince, the rubbish fermenting like compost in the midday heat.

The car finally slid to a halt in a bog. Enoch kicked and thrashed the vehicle, but it was no use: steam began to issue from the bonnet. A woman riding sidesaddle on a mule came splashing along the path towards us. Enoch gestured for her attention and she dismounted, leading the beast down by his rope halter. 'How far to Cazales?'

The woman had high cheekbones, a strong tapering chin and piercing blue eyes. *'Machine en panne?'* she asked in Creole: has your car broken down?

'Yes. But how far to Cazales?'

'Who knows?'

'Is it a town or a village?'

'How can anybody tell?'

Enoch cast me a glance as if to say: this one seems far from sane.

'Merci, chérie,' he thanked her all the same. We decided to walk. The woman rode on downhill, the mule switching away flies with its tail. Her physiognomy suggested European blood. *'Une polonaise,'* reckoned Enoch. *'Mais une polonaise folle.'*

There are only five Polish names in the Haitian telephone directory but earlier in Port-au-Prince I had found a certain Daniel Lovinsky, who ran a funeral parlour on the Rue des Césares opposite the Mr Clean Mini Market. Mr Lovinsky was a little tipsy when I met him. 'Yes, yes. I'm of the same descent as the Pope,' he said with sombre deliberation. 'But don't ask me how I got to Haiti. Just woke up one day and found myself here.' He reached for the bottle of rum by his side, stoppered with a dirty spool of paper, and took an extravagant swig.

Then I asked a silly question: 'Do you get many corpses here?'

Mr Lovinsky burped. 'That depends on the political situation. After a coup d'état business is always good.'

Cazales was ten minutes away from the car by foot. It is a picturesque village. The walls of the houses were fashioned from woven withes caked with mud, the roofs from banana-leaf thatch. These wattle-and-daub dwellings, raised jauntily on groundsills of limestone, are called *cailles-pailles*; they are African in appearance and we might have been somewhere in the Congo, were it not for so many people with blue eyes. Enoch suggested that we report immediately to the *chef de section*, the man who represents the government in all its functions, from tax-collector to policeman. No Haitian village is without this headman.

His office, a thick-walled caserne painted with the red and blue of the national flag, stood at the end of a path shaded by dark-leaved mango trees (their fruit had originally been imported from the East Indies by Captain Bligh, according to Corley Smith). The *chef* was initially suspicious. He affected not to be able to read my *laisser-passer* and complained that the signature looked dubious. Enoch explained that I had come as an anthropologist in search of my Polish roots. This shameless fabrication proved a success. The headman clapped his hands in glee. 'Poland! Poland! My great-great-grandfather's name was . . . Karpinski! Have you been to Warsaw?' he asked delightedly; presently, 'You must both have lunch with me!'

Soon we were honoured with a munificent meal of salted codfish cooked in the Haitian manner with yams, pimentos, oil, garlic and butter, the whole thickened in manioc flour. It was delicious, though I felt some guilt at enjoying this hospitality under the pretence of being a Pole.

'Come and have a look at our cemetery.'

We followed the *chef* to a plot of earth marked with heavy slabs of stone. Many of these tombs bore names which were certainly Polish: Kobylanski, Wilczek, Tarsza . . . Were these the graves of men who had fought for Dessalines? Our host explained how there still existed in Cazales the Creole proverb *'Chajé kon lapologn'*, charge like a Pole, meaning 'raring to go', 'ready for the test'. He believed this referred to the Polish *garde d'honneur* of Dessalines, which apparently inspired awe.

Why had the Poles defected to the insurgent slaves? And how had they managed to remain in Haiti after 1806 when Dessalines proclaimed, in his victorious constitution, that no white man should set foot in the country as a master or proprietor? Consulting the vellum-bound histories of Saint Domingue in the library of the excellent Institut de St Louis de Gonzague, Port-au-Prince, I learned that the Poles were willing to help Napoleon return slavery to his beleaguered colony. This was on the understanding that he would then restore independence to their own country, which in those days was a protectorate of both Prussia and Russia. The Poles worshipped Napoleon: Book IX of *War and Peace* describes how a regiment of Polish lancers plunge like madmen into the waters of the Niemen to meet the Emperor on the other bank. 'They were proud to be swimming and drowning in the river before the eyes of that man sitting on a log and not even looking at what they were doing . . . Hurrah for the Emperor!'

In the summer of 1803 some 2,570 Poles set sail for Saint Domingue from the Italian ports of Livorno and Genoa. All had sworn the French military oath of allegiance, yet how many among them understood the significance of Napoleon's clarion-call to arms: 'Not French, but heavenly citizenship awaits you in Saint Domingue'? One can nevertheless imagine their excitement at the prospect of battling under the tricolour in a foreign land. One Pole wrote home from shipboard to his family in Cracow: 'It seems we are sailing to the Americas, to see many marvels on the islands discovered by Columbus . . . to eat pineapples as abundant as potatoes in Poland, banana, figs, yam . . . to see flying-fish, man-eating sharks, parrots of many colours . . .' But disaster awaited the Poles in Saint Domingue; they were soon to feel themselves betrayed.

The *chef de section* led Enoch and me to an area of Cazales named Belno after the first Pole to have settled there, one Belnovski. A villager volunteered to carry us on his back across the broad stream that divided us from our destination. We must have cut a comic spectacle fording the waters, like the knight errant and erring squire of *Don Quixote*. The villager was probably half my height and I could feel the current swirling coldly round my ankles. A group of women on the other side, beating their washing with wooden paddles, fell about laughing when the portly Enoch tipped over backwards and floundered in the stream, cursing. *'Gwos neg pas capab najé!'* they shrilled – the big boy can't swim. The headman himself remained behind on the opposite bank.

At Belno we met a couple who mistook us for envoys of John-Paul II. The husband sat us down on a wicker chair outside his trash-roofed shanty and feverishly produced a cardboard box containing souvenirs from the Pope's visit to Haiti in March 1983 – a rosary, plastic medallions embossed with the crossed keys of the Vatican. The man was illiterate. 'Read this! Read this!' He handed Enoch a dog-eared transcript of the speech which John-Paul had delivered at François Duvalier International Airport (as it was then known). 'Your country is a beautiful country, rich in human resources' – Enoch read out loud in Creole while the man prostrated himself at our feet and kissed the ground three times as though performing press-ups – 'yet Christians cannot be unaware of the divisions, injustice, the degradation of the quality of life, poverty, hunger and fear suffered by the majority.' The words of this homily would later serve as inspiration for *Opération Dechoukaj*.

Both husband and wife had slate-blue, almond-shaped eyes and sharp aquiline noses. She wore her crinkled white hair much longer than is customary among Haitian women, the carefully plaited pigtails lending her the appearance of a mulatta Heidi or Pippi Longstocking. She gave her maiden name as Dabrowski. But, like her husband, she spoke no Polish. In fact most of the inhabitants of Cazales seemed to have forgotten the language of their ancestors. Like other Haitians, they employed the macaronic jargon of Creole, a mixture of the black tongues of West Africa with the French provincial dialect spoken throughout the maritime regions engaged in the slave trade.

According to the history books, Polish legions in the Haitian war of independence came poorly equipped for the tropics, dressed in heavy uniforms. Ignorant of the French language (let alone Creole), they traversed mountain and forest without maps, unable to adapt to methods of guerrilla warfare as perfected by the former slaves. Yellow fever thinned their ranks and they became dispirited. A Polish lieutenant, Josef Zadera, bitterly remarked in a letter to a friend:

I am writing for the last time before my death in the utmost despair, reproaching myself for the temerity of wanting to go to Saint Domingue, and I do not wish it upon my worst enemy. Far better to be a beggar in Europe than seek a fortune in the Americas where any one of a thousand maladies may strike you down. We are not allowed to resign our commissions; the French compel us to serve and fight . . .

Morale sank further as the Poles realized that the blacks were fighting for the same ideals of freedom and liberty to which they, the Poles, aspired: the expulsion of foreign powers. They were serving, after all, in the ranks of the most brutal of French generals, the Vicomte de Rochambeau.

The American critic Edmund Wilson (who incidentally stayed at the Oloffson in 1949) likened the elaborate horrors of this Rochambeau to 'episodes in Sade's *Juliette*'. One such horror is worth recording, as it may have convinced the Poles that they were battling for a lost and immoral cause. On succeeding General Leclerc in 1802 as commander of Napoleon's West Indian campaign, Rochambeau gave a great ball in Port-au-Prince to which he invited many of the black women of the capital. At midnight Rochambeau called an end to this lavish fête and summoned the women into a neighbouring chamber. The room was illuminated by a single lamp and hung with black draperies stitched with the outline of human skulls. Frenchmen disguised as priests chanted the *Dies Irae* before a row of coffins. Each coffin was then opened to reveal the corpse of a relation of each of the guests. 'You have just assisted at the obsequies of your husbands and your brothers,' announced a contented Rochambeau.

General Rochambeau came to a violent end. One of his last attempts to repulse Dessalines was the importation of 1,500 man-hunting blood-hounds from Spanish Cuba, specially trained to disembowel runaway slaves. After this failed, Rochambeau was taken prisoner by the British in 1803 on board the HMS *Bellerophon* (twelve years later this vessel would ferry Napoleon to St Helena). On 8 October 1813 he was killed at the Battle of Leipzig. Since then no European soldier has trodden the soil of Haiti with hostile intent. Yet Dessalines was to show respect and favour to those

Poles who remained in Haiti after the departure of Rochambeau. With the proclamation of Haitian independence he granted them the right to own property in Cazales. But they would be 'black', not 'white'. Perhaps this was the first time ever that the term 'black' had been employed in an ideological sense. Papa Doc would later esteem Dessalines as a symbol of Black Power.

Today, a small heritage of Poland survives in Cazales through dance and music. An elderly inhabitant of Belno, Amon Fremon, beat on a drum for us the rhythm of a minuet which derives from the polka. It is known up here as the 'Kokoda', a sort of Polish–Haitian half-step. Monsieur Fremon is a Voodoo priest. The entrance to his *hounfour*, or temple, was staked with a couple of denuded casuarinas, what they call locally 'whispering trees'. Chinese chimes, hanging above the porch, chinked in the breeze. Inside, the sanctum was hung with charms against the *mal jok*, evil eye: a goat's skull, objects shaped like twisted red peppers (the same amulets are to be found in Naples), countless plastic dolls like speechless mannequins with lidless eyes. 'I spent eight months in Warsaw,' the priest informed us. 'A Pole came here in search of his relatives. He shared my grandfather's surname – Blokowski. So he said, "Let me take you to the land of your ancestors." That was in 1980 and I'd never been on an aeroplane before.'

'What did you make of Warsaw?'

'Not bad. Wonderful vodka.'

The *houngan* offered us a tumblerful of the pale and ensnaring taffia, a pot-stilled raw rum potent enough to etch out the bottom of a copper cauldron. I had already sampled a bottle of this tropical poteen in Little Haiti: no one but a fire-eater could remain indifferent to its special qualities. Taffia is essential to the ritual lustrations of Voodoo and the stuff now brought tears to our eyes.

The sun was sinking to rest as we walked back downhill towards our abandoned car. The leaves of mango and banana trees glistened in the departing day; the air was pungent with floating field scents. We were in high spirits. At last the Haiti I had come to find seemed to be in reach.

A cockfight – *gaguère* – was about to commence. This is the national sport of Haiti, what the bullfight is to Spain. The spectators, with their familiar blue eyes, had all come down the hill from Cazales. Many of them appeared drunk: one old man staggered about wearing a T-shirt emblazoned with the curious prescription: 'Never Underestimate the

Power of a Woman'. Inside the cockpit there were no women. They all remained on the periphery selling refreshments – bottles of taffia, cobs of maize, chicken wings. In Haiti, the cockfight is very much the province of men.

We were shown to the best ringside positions. The arena was of beaten earth enclosed by a screen of palm-thatch and sheltered from the sun by an overhanging latticework of twigs. There was great excitement round the arena: rolls of gourdes were circulated among the crowd by touts and tipsters as the antagonists – a red cock and a white – were carried squawking into the cockpit. The birds were named after two local tap-taps: Prudence and C'est la Vie. They were cradled lovingly by their seconds, fondled as we might a dog. The Haitian peasant will subject a horse or donkey to unbelievable cruelty, thwacking them across eyes and ears with a cactus club, but not so a gamecock: for weeks the bird is nurtured on a measured diet of millet or grain, and then cleansed in sacrificial water. In Puerto Rico they put steel spurs on the cocks; here the *carcadors* sharpen the natural spurs of their birds to a perfect point with razors. Feathers are clipped, combs cropped and made flush, with meticulous care.

The seconds each took a mouthful of water from a calabash and, pressing the birds to their lips, sucked and sprayed their plumage so that it would adhere flat to their bodies and afford the opponent no hold; this was also, explained Enoch, to keep the birds cool once the sparring commenced. More bets were placed as the men bent down to trace a sign of the cross in the dust; a pinch of this dust was then rubbed over the beaks of each bird, apparently to sharpen the cartilage. For reasons unknown to Enoch the seconds then expectorated three times into the open beaks. This very complicated toilet seemed to last an unconscionable time. Enoch began to yawn. Finally, the man who had been collecting the wagers in a hat blew a tin whistle and the contenders were set down on opposite sides of the ring.

At first they circled cautiously around each other like boxers seeking an opening. Then C'est la Vie tapped as a woodpecker at his enemy's head and there was an almighty flurry of wings. The gamecocks shot up in the air with talons interlocked and seemed to remain there motionless for a while, a heraldic motif. Down they came with feathers tautened into ruffs. The spectators craned forward from their benches to encourage or jeer at the contest, screaming and waving their arms up and down like bedlamites. A hurrah – *'Woaah!'* or cry of dismay – *'Haii!'* – went up whenever Prudence was pecked in the eyes by C'est la Vie. It was evident that Prudence was growing weaker: his breast, rudely torn of plumage, began to bleed under the redoubled and tenacious blows. Increasingly he was forced to take cover from the terrible spurs beneath his tormentor's wing.

Last-minute bets were placed as the man with the tin whistle descended into the cockpit to separate the birds like a referee at a wrestling match. There was by now a pervasive fume of rum, and a rancid onion-smell of sweat. We were far removed from the gracious suavities of the Oloffson; this resembled Saturday night in an Elizabethan bear-pit. The gamecocks closed with each other again. A whirr of wings, and a savage jerk from C'est la Vie – 'Haii!' – sent feathers floating about the cockpit white as the down from a pillow fight. I glanced with a qualm of repulsion at my shirt-front; it was spattered with blood. Prudence spun round and collapsed – 'Woaah!' – like an alcoholic, one wing hanging open. Then he teetered again to his feet, blood streaming from the beak, and with drooping head staggered to fly once more from his foe. To no avail; with a whoop of jubilation from the crowd, Prudence keeled over into the dust. His talons stiffened and relaxed once or twice and then froze. With one bound C'est la Vie was on top of his victim, spurs raking in a frenzy over the dead eyes. Then the victor spread his wings, strained his head to the sky and shrilled a triumphant cockadoodledoo. A moment later C'est la Vie fell dead in the dust beside his conquered enemy. 'Justice is a terrible thing,' sighed Enoch.

Straw hats flew into the air. Money I had won on C'est la Vie sufficed to pay for repairs to the abandoned car.

The inhabitants of Cazales were for the most part mulattoes, and it was they who formed the bulk of spectators at this particular cockfight. This was unusual: generally in Haiti a mulatto would consider the sport beneath his dignity. Tennis is more his line. Haiti, after all, is a country where the mulattoes are the aristocrats – rather like the pale-skinned Brahmins in India. Traditionally it is the *mestisses* who have the money. 'A poor mulatto is a Negro; a rich Negro is a mulatto', according to a Haitian tag. Cazales presents a curious exception to this rule: it is perhaps the only village in Haiti to be populated by poor mulattoes. The reason for this is lost in the mists of antiquity. But it seems that many of the Polish *légionnaires* so generously 'freed' by the blacks were obliged to work as slaves on sugar plantations. Field labour was then in scarce supply; and the Poles were no doubt grateful to be alive.

As I drove home with Enoch the sky above Cazales was thick with rising trails of blue smoke. The unhappy children of the Vistula had found work as charcoal-burners.

The effect was dainty and doily: plastic fruit suspended from the ceiling in wire baskets, curtains of multicoloured plastic beads, an acrylic panda bear on the dressing table. There was also, for some reason, a copy of *The Woman in White* by Wilkie Collins. This was my bedroom in the Church World Service guesthouse on La Gonâve. The beautiful black caretaker, Fifi Nithese, was very proud of these gimcrack decorations; her hospice was certainly the smartest building on the island. There was no lavatory, simply a slop-pail under the bed, or else a hole in a laterite block sheltered beneath a canopy of palm-thatch. But these conveniences were at least clean.

Fifi was furthermore reckoned to be the best cook in Haiti: her goat stew, ladled on to Tupperware plastic plates patterned with a floral motif, was better than anything I had eaten at the Oloffson.

In the days when Haiti was a colony of France, runaway slaves scraped a living on La Gonâve cutting mahogany. Today the island has no trees. There are no longer any *guanavana* – corosol fruit, after which the indigenous Indians named this island. Only a desert of thorn bushes and sand-flats. We are a million miles from what R. L. Stevenson called the 'featherbed of civilization'. No accurate map of the interior has been published. Forty thousand people live here.

On a clear day you can see La Gonâve from Port-au-Prince; it lies like a semi-submerged Leviathan, dolphin-shaped, fifty or more miles north-westward across the bay. Larger than Barbados or Martinique, many mysteries attend La Gonâve, the most primitive of the island dependencies of Haiti. It was on the jagged coral reef of the Rochelois Banks, due south of the island, that the notorious ghost or 'hoodoo' ship *Mary Celeste* was scuttled in January 1884 by an unscrupulous businessman out to recoup on insurance. But the inspiration behind my journey to La Gonâve was a curious book I had read entitled *The White King of La Gonâve*. Published in 1931, this rare volume is the work of a young Polish-American sergeant of the Marines who was appointed civil administrator of the island during the US occupation of Haiti. Formerly a Pennsylvania farmer boy, Sergeant Faustin Wirkus was so adored by the islanders that he was literally crowned their king. 'They believed I was the reincarnated spirit of Faustin Soulouque,' he writes. 'All the people shouted *"Le Roi, le Roi, le Roi!"*, and then my name "Faustin!" . . .'

As for the original Faustin Soulouque, we may be sure that he was made Emperor of Haiti in 1849. His coronation took place three months after the Holy Virgin had appeared to him in a vision, angel-winged, perched atop a royal palm. 'You are destined to rule over Haiti, the Republic of Dominica, and the surrounding islands of the sea,' she declared. His crown, modelled on that of Napoleon III, is now kept in the municipal museum of Port-au-Prince. It is of solid gold, encrusted with white diamonds and turquoise; a spray of gilded palm leaves converges in the centre to support a giant orb of dark blue enamel on which rests a sapphire cross.

On my first night in La Gonâve I was visited by the mayor of the island, inappropriately called Monsieur Joli. He sat down at my table uninvited and asked, *'Vous êtes ici avec quelle mission?'* The tone was peremptory; Joli was an old Duvalierist. He had fled to Canada after the fall of Baby Doc, but was later reinstated as mayor by General Prosper Avril. I told him that I was here to conduct some research into King Faustin II from Pennsylvania. Joli peered at me from beneath lazy, heavy-lidded eyes. It was evident that he had never heard of this trumpery monarch (although he was happy to boast his knowledge of Queen Elizabeth II, 'the Prime Minister of Great Britain'). Joli sat staring at me for a while, a man of enormous girth, stroking his beard and tapping his watch-chain loaded with Masonic insignia.

'Identification?' I handed him my *laisser-passer*. The mayor glanced at this document upside down – he was clearly illiterate – and then produced a heavy automatic pistol, which he placed on the table. Perhaps Joli was entitled to be suspicious. Rumours of an imminent coup d'état had been percolating all week on the mainland; the mayor may have taken me for an emissary of the anti-Avril faction. Monsieur Joli took his leave with the solemn assurance that he would send one of his underlings over as 'guide'. Fifi popped her head round the corner. *'Ça va, chéri?'* Presently the young man sent by Joli arrived.

Isnel Angrand was, in contrast to the mayor, a handsome and very courteous Haitian who spoke excellent French. He bore the deformity of his left hand – it was withered to a stump – with great dignity. I asked Isnel about Joli. *'Il aime le pouvoir,'* he replied. *'Mais il n'est pas méchant.'* In love with power, but not a bad man. In a small, tightly bound community such as exists on La Gonâve, it is important, said Isnel, that everyone should live and work as a family. Isnel himself had been appointed mayor of La Gonâve after Joli had fled to Canada, though he held the post for only a year. He was ousted when Joli returned. The politics of this island might have derived from *Alice in Wonderland*. But this was the comedy that one looked for in Haiti – the comedy of the banana skin.

I warmed to Isnel. For the short time that I was to remain on La Gonâve, we became something like friends and his letters – '*Mon cher et bien aimable ami . . .*' – now reach me in London. Most important, Isnel knew about Sergeant Faustin Wirkus. 'Oh yes,' he laughed. 'The people used to refer to him as *Li té pé vini*, he who was to come. They really did believe he was the reincarnation of Emperor Faustin the First.'

We decided to take a stroll round Fifi's hospice. This was in an area of La Gonâve called Anse-à-Galets, opposite the village of Mont Rouis on the mainland. Wherever we walked, children gathered around to badger for money. 'Give me one dollar . . . Give me your tennis shoes . . . I speak good English. You give me cigarette . . . Good evening mister!' But there was a joshing, merry tone to their entreaties: none of the envy that one occasionally encounters in Port-au-Prince. La Gonâve was an island of unimaginable poverty – subject every year to floods which sweep away livestock and homes – yet the people here were the most gentle and friendly I had met in Haiti. Everyone knew where I was staying: '*M'sieur blanc chez Fifi!*' They seemed to find this amusing.

We came to a shack surrounded by hedges of pineapple and spiky-leaved sisals. This belonged to Commandant Carman, for twenty-two years the island chief of the Volontaires de la Sécurité Nationale, or the Tontons Macoute. Isnel cupped his mouth and shouted '*Honneur!*' outside the front door. This is a traditional salutation in the Haitian countryside; you must wait until the owner of the house replies '*Respect!*' before you may enter. One of the grubby children in the courtyard answered and Commandant Carman emerged, naked except for a towel round his waist. He was a splendid old man with a large ruby-red ring. '*Bonsoir, m'sieur blanc.* I hope you had a good voyage from the Republic.' He spoke of the mainland as though it were on the other side of the world.

'This man,' explained Isnel, 'was such a *good* Macoute that the people called him *Ti Pasteur*, the Little Pastor. He even put the odd Tonton in jail.'

The Commandant gave an awkward laugh. 'It's true. I would never tolerate an injustice.' He claimed the five hundred Macoutes under his jurisdiction were forbidden to wear the familiar uniform of Papa Doc's ragtag militia: denim shirts, blue jeans, red arm-bands and kerchiefs. 'My men dressed as civilians. They were here to keep the peace. To protect the peasants. Nothing more.' One sensed that the Little Pastor was a man of sterling goodness. He had not been ousted from La Gonâve during the days of *dechoukaj*, which suggested he had earned the respect of the islanders as a man of honour. It was seldom that the Tontons Macoute were employed for their original function as a primitive police force. Usually, they were simply a means to extort money.

I asked Commandant Carman about Faustin Wirkus. *'Ah! Le Roi Blanc!'* exclaimed the old Macoute. 'A man after my heart. He never oppressed the people to make himself rich.'

Isnel was sceptical that the marine was a reincarnation of a Haitian emperor. 'The only reason Sergeant Wirkus was crowned king of La Gonâve,' he later told me, 'was that he shared the same surname as Soulouque – Faustin.'

On the way back to Fifi's we passed through the main square of Anse-à-Galets. Old women were selling sweets and sherbets, packets of cigarettes, under naphtha flares. Young girls worked up and down on the handles of the communal water pump. One of the few buildings here which had not been made of mud and straw was the gendarmerie – a stone-concrete bungalow with a big screened porch over which flew the Haitian flag. This, explained Isnel, was where King Faustin II of La Gonâve had kept office some seventy-five years ago. The barrack resembled a Kiplingesque outpost on the edge of jungle. From the photographs I had seen of Wirkus – straw-blond hair, lantern-jawed beneath a tropical pith helmet – it was easy to imagine him ensconced behind his desk in there, dispensing justice under an overhead fan. A regular man from the US Marines: there was nothing very much about his photographs to suggest the living spirit of Soulouque.

The next morning, a group of people gathered round Isnel's house to hear what Madame Atile Altidor had to say about the coronation of Sergeant Faustin Wirkus. We were all drinking tea made from hibiscus, known in Creole patois as *choublac* (after the old English buccaneers who were accustomed to blacking their shoes with a purplish sap from the flowers). Isnel's father, the Justice of Peace, lay swinging in a hammock puffing menthol Comme il Faut. Madame Altidor sat on a wicker chair, fanning herself with a large palmetto fan. Gold earrings dangled from beneath her green madras scarf; round her neck she wore a red coral necklace. Her hair was white and she was barefoot.

Isnel acted as my interpreter: 'Madame Altidor, what was it like, the day they crowned the American?' He asked the question slowly, for the woman had been born on La Gonâve in 1902 (she had never left the island), and her memory was a little unsure. But she remembered discussing with her husband one night how the time was now propitious for Wirkus to become king of the island. And she very clearly recalled the appearance of the crown itself.

'It was made from feathers of every kind of bird,' she smiled. 'Parrot and humming-bird feathers and there were tail plumes of macaws, midnight-blue, stuck to the front of the crown like this.' Madame Altidor gestured vaguely with her hands. 'Also the flame-coloured wing and tail feathers of larger birds . . . flamingos . . . I remember how we sewed sea shells, stained with the juice of red and blue berries . . . around the edge. In double rows like this. There were tiny bits of mirrors and paper flowers and red silk cloth . . . It was a good crown.'

'Isnel, ask her please what she thought of Sergeant Wirkus.'

Madame Altidor nodded. 'He had white skin but the understanding of a *nègre*. He was a nice American man.' She explained how he kept the doors of his office open to children, how he would redress their grievances with the 'patience of a saint'.

This is not the collective memory which Haitians have of the Marines. The nineteen years of American occupation introduced draconian schemes of forced labour which evoked the spectre of slavery before the days of Toussaint L'Ouverture. Any resistance to the Marines from the irregular peasant militias known as *cacos* was ruthlessly quelled. In November 1919 the resistance leader Charlemagne Péralte was executed by the Americans in the town of Grande-Rivière du Nord, his body roped to a door as a warning. The corpse was then photographed – an event which only encouraged the widespread belief that the messianic Péralte had been crucified.

Isnel poured us another round of *choublac*.

It was about two hours short of dawn when I returned to the harbour of Anse-à-Galets. There I stepped on board a sailboat, or *shallop*, bound for the mainland. The sky was still brilliant with stars, a faint drizzle under the cold sheen of the moon. The boat, assembled from planks of wood with a felled tree for a mainmast, was optimistically named *Le Chemin de la Vie*. She was dangerously overloaded with a great hodgepodge of humanity and merchandise: sacks of grain, chickens, and manioc. There was already bilge water in the bottom. This is the sort of leaky vessel in which thousands of Haitians have tried to escape the misery of their lives. Crammed shoulder to shoulder in a filthy hull, they set sail from Port-de-Paix or Jérémie in the hope of a new and remunerative life in Florida or the Bahamas. A Bible is sometimes their only possession, wrapped in plastic to protect it from the water.

On 12 November 1986, two hundred Haitians were drowned when a boat, the *Oke Lele*, sank on its way from Anse-à-Galets to Mont Rouis. The channel of water between these two villages – twenty miles in length – appeared calm enough this morning. But a faint breeze on the port side promised a choppy crossing. By the time I boarded the boat there was scarcely room to sit, no cabin space or canopy. Hung round like a Christmas tree with my rucksack I was eventually shown a niche by the rudderpost. Passengers lay huddled at my feet, trying to sleep.

The roll of the ship was long and slow; her timbers creaked and groaned in the swell like an old door and the patchwork sail flapped madly against the headwind. We were at sea for a good three hours, heeling over a little as we forged ahead. The splash and slap of water against the bows was accompanied throughout by a murmur of voices and laughter. There was a strong spirit of fellowship on board – we were all of us cold and damp with salt water. None of the passengers seemed the least put out when a gust of wind sent a crested roller sploshing over the lip of the gunwale. It was simply an occasion for more jokes and laughter. I did wonder, though, how many among us were able to swim. It had been dark when we left harbour. Faces emerged in the gathering light as the sky slowly cleared to a pink and blue dawn, delicate tints of yellow like the inside of a rare shell. Mont Rouis has no jetty and one has to be ferried to dry land on the shoulders of a porter.

There were about twenty of these porters wading swiftly towards us – stripped to their underclothes, up to their chests in water. The first passengers to descend were the *marchandes*. I watched from the stern as they lowered themselves, gingerly, over the edge of the boat on to a pair of attendant shoulders. Some of these market women were very large and caused the porters who carried them to negotiate with unusual care the stones beneath their feet. How calloused their soles must be – it is hard enough to walk barefoot over shingle without an added weight to carry. Baskets, sacks of rice and millet, chickens and straw hats were passed down to outstretched hands and carried to shore as produce for sale on the mainland.

I was one of the last to leave the *Chemin de la Vie*. The porter told me to place my hands on his head for safety. I clung to the woolly skull and tried to keep my shoes from trailing in the water. I must have looked ridiculous; it was probably twenty-five years ago when I last sat so high on a man's shoulders. As an adult, it also felt precarious to be carried in this fashion.

When we reached dry land the porter stooped low so that my feet could touch the ground, and discreetly withdrew his head from between my legs. This part of the journey had cost me the equivalent of ten British pence.

VI

Marooned in Jacmel

'It is not unusual for a Haitian president to accumulate millions during his term of office, and then retire to Paris with a mistress or two and a large private bank account in Switzerland.'

'The Terror in Haiti,' *New Statesman*, 10 May 1963

The ocean liner moved steadily towards me as I sat for breakfast on the terrace of the Hotel Alexandra. The ship seemed to be white save for a single red funnel. But it was difficult to tell: she was a mere speck, some hundred leagues to sea across the Bay of Jacmel.

Jacmel is a provincial town on the southern coast of Haiti. For six months now it had been busy preparing for the arrival of the *Berlin*, a luxury liner bound from Germany. This morning the Jacmelians were beside themselves with excitement. It was the first time for fifteen years that so splendid a ship had sailed their way. Who knows how much money might be made from the passengers, floating out there on that great white palace?

Port-au-Prince had been very much *en fête* the night I left for Jacmel. The city was placarded with advertisements for Mardi Gras on Shrove Tuesday and high stockades stood round the Champ de Mars festooned in coloured electric bulbs. The dancers, dressed in sequined burlap bags, capered wildly on top of open trucks, bashing on improvised instruments: washboards, saws, cowbells, even automobile springs. Costumes were nightmarish. There were masks shaped as bulls' heads, multicoloured Andy Pandy uniforms with gigantic pom-poms, plastic skulls. Several of the revellers towered ten feet above the carnival on stilts, wearing sets of chattering wooden teeth and cracking a giant whip. These were scare-mongers to excite and frighten the crowd. The Café Napoli was a scrim-mage of drunken Haitians, clamouring round the counter for rum. Aïda stood stalwart behind her till. *'Non mi piace questo periodo di carnevale,'* she complained. It was worse than Naples during the World Cup.

There was little violence and any scuffles were peaceably quelled. In Haiti, as elsewhere in Latin America, the carnival is feared as a time when people might express frustration or discontent with the government. In the past, presidents have been careful to lavish sufficient money on Mardi Gras to ensure that a good time was had by all. Prosper Avril had also taken precautions to police the festivities with a heavy brigade of Presidential Guard and the carnival that year was considered rather tame.

Mardi Gras was still in swing the day I arrived at Jacmel. Place Toussaint L'Ouverture, the main square, was hung with bunting. I had been urged to explore this colonial coffee port by the travel writer Norman Lewis. 'Try to visit Jacmel. It is said to be very charming and quite strange,' he had written. And then – words which were soon to prove prophetic – 'Best of luck in Haiti. I fear you may need it.' Jacmel was founded in 1689 by a French colonist named Jacques de Melo, hence its name. The town had burned down several times, and was substantially rebuilt in 1896 with prefabricated houses from Germany. In that year alone Jacmel exported to Europe some twenty-five thousand sacks of coffee; there was a flourishing trade in both orange peel (destined for use in the distillation of Cointreau) and in cotton.

Jacmel is now in decline. Gone the days when steamships would sail here every month from Southampton, bringing British tweeds to exchange for Haitian coffee. The wooden clapboard houses, brightly painted, still have charm – balconies of elaborate ironwork, shingled mansard roofs; but it is the charm of dilapidation. The cemetery too has fallen into a ragged state of desuetude. Hibiscus has rooted in the shattered tombs, the lead lettering on monuments bored out by marauding weeds. The numerous Europeans laid to rest in this plot of Haitian soil proclaim the days when Jacmel was a bustling and cosmopolitan port. William Henry Webley, for instance, a Protestant pastor from Bristol, died here in 1852: 'Stranger, friend or enemy, the gate that was opened for me, will soon be opened for thee', according to his funerary inscription.

Jacmel is considered the most tranquil of Haitian towns, the least inflamed by violence at times of political unrest. Its prosperity as a port and remoteness from Port-au-Prince meant it enjoyed a certain exemption from the strife and constitutional discord of the capital. Until the French built the Route de l'Amitié ten years ago (a good tarmac road that runs direct from the town of Léogâne), Jacmel was almost inaccessible by land from Port-au-Prince. The old cinder track crossed the River Gosseline some eighty times and during the rainy season the bus would forge upstream like a ferry boat. The Germans on board the pleasure cruiser *Berlin* should find little difficulty settling in Jacmel for a day or two; the population had put up cardboard signs – 'We Welcome Germans People to Pearl of the Antilles' – outside the palm-thatch bars. The beach that morning was cluttered with stalls selling souvenirs for their imminent arrival: straw hats, bits of jewellery, papier-mâché models of Toussaint L'Ouverture. Thirty or so tap-taps had parked three deep across the sand ready to spirit the tourists to Haitian food and drink.

I was the only guest at the Hotel Alexandra and felt a little lone, but the view from the terrace was splendid: houses around the Bay of Jacmel dwindling in size to dice; valleys formed by the spurs of encircling mountains, a luscious green; and the sea a light aquamarine over the reefs – but further out a darkly, deeply beautiful blue. I was about to order another pot of coffee when Gottfried came bounding up the steps towards me out of breath.

'I am afraid the situation is very serious.' He held a small transistor radio to one ear, a furled umbrella in his free hand. 'The report comes through that –' Gottfried turned a dial to reduce the interference – 'that the future of Haiti hangs in the balance.' Gottfried Kraüchi, director of the Collège Suisse, Jacmel, had brought news that was extremely disturbing. Sooner or later it was bound to happen: the country was clamouring for the resignation of General Prosper Avril. 'Yah! It is a mad, mad world, my friend.' Gottfried drew up a chair and ordered a 7 Up. 'It is very dangerous now with this thunderstorm brewing and you must not attempt to leave Jacmel. But Avril, his days are numbered. He must now eat the humble pie.'

'What about the passengers out there on the *Berlin*?'

'They cannot know what is happening,' he said curtly. 'Probably the captain has not even told them that they are sailing – ha ha! – towards Haiti.'

Gottfried gave an inviting, almost conspiratorial wink and a throaty chuckle. This wink was an endearing characteristic, always with the left eye; it punctuated Gottfried's every conversation and indicated that he, too, understood the comedy of Haiti. Yet Gottfried was a man of great warmth and humanity; though he clearly enjoyed his role as minister of information, there was a school-masterly, almost avuncular desire to caution against the danger of leaving Jacmel. Port-au-Prince was in turmoil. Gottfried consulted the clipboard which he carried close to him. 'According to my papers there are five hundred elderly Germans on board that ship,' he said with a wan smile. 'I am afraid they must make the best of a bad bargain and go home. Otherwise the doom for them is sealed. Haiti is most dangerous. The Mayor of Jacmel, he has already barricaded himself within the basement of the Hôtel de Ville. He was a good friend of Avril but now he trembles like the rabbit in fear.'

Gottfried tapped the glass of his watch. 'Time to go.' I followed him from the Alexandra down to the beach. The *Berlin* was anchored some way offshore and a companion-ladder had been let down for the captain who was now lurching towards the jetty in a motor lunch. 'I will have to talk to the fellow,' said Gottfried.

Gottfried Kraüchi had lived in Haiti for seventeen years but was still, at the age of fifty-five, a captain in the Swiss Army. A stocky man of regimental bearing, very spit-and-polish, he marched down to the beach with his umbrella tucked underarm like a swagger stick, wearing white shorts and hygienic sandals. Gottfried had married a Haitian and had four children by her, yet he was still to the core a *Schweiz-Deutsch*: always punctual, very formal and polite. He had graduated from the University of Basle with a degree in physics (Einstein, quantum theory) and then worked for the Swiss pharmaceutical companies Ciba-Geigy and Sandoz before settling in Jacmel. The Collège Suisse itself had been founded one night in 1976 over a game of chess in Jacmel with an Englishman from Enfield named Jack. I had yet to meet Jack; he was still living in Jacmel, but apparently very ill.

Chess remained a passion with Gottfried. In November 1988 he travelled to Macedonia as vice-president of the Haitian Chess Federation. 'Haitians are keen chess-players because there is nothing else to do in their lives,' Gottfried laughed as we approached the beach. 'Only boredom or unemployment!' He was a great admirer of the book *Chess Fundamentals* by the legendary Cuban chess-player and former world champion José Capablanca.

The jetty was in disrepair and some of the planks had rotted or fallen through. Hundreds of Jacmelians had gathered on the sands, shielding their eyes against the sun. They watched as the captain bobbed towards them in his outboard, the air electric with excitement (though there was some consternation lest the jetty prove inadequate). The swell was rolling home as Gottfried strode like a Scoutmaster across the pier to greet the captain of the pleasure cruiser. *'Haben Sie eine Schwimmweste?'* I heard Gottfried joke with the German dressed in nautical white who was now struggling to clamber aboard the jetty. Do you have a life jacket? A few words were exchanged. The captain shook his head and then lowered himself back into the motor launch. Within half an hour the *Berlin* had weighed anchor for Santiago de Cuba.

Her departure was a terrible disappointment for Jacmel, for the vendors of jewellery and wooden carvings. It was like the aftermath of a party which never took place: all the bunting would have to come down. I thought of the money – sorely needed – lost to the Jacmelians because of the rickety jetty that General Avril had built. 'It was unsafe,' Gottfried confirmed. 'The captain could see that. And what with the political situation . . . Well, it was the rain which stopped the play as you say.'

The beach was now littered with empty hemispheres of grapefruit, Coca-Cola tins discarded by the tap-tap drivers. There could be no hope of business now.

'I would be most happy' – Gottfried winked – 'if you could indulge me in a game of chess some time.' We walked back towards the Hotel Alexandra, past the Pharmacie Perpétuel Secours, the Café de la Résurrection and the Shell petrol pump station.

Marooned in Jacmel, I took stock of the news which Gottfried had brought me. The move to expel Avril had been precipitated, it seems, a few days earlier on 6 March when a young girl was killed accidentally by the army in the small village of Petit Goâve. Roseline Vaval had been reading a copy of Dr J. C. Dorsainvil's 1924 *Haitian History Primer* (still widely used in schools) when a stray bullet struck her on the verandah of her parents' house. How appropriate that Roseline should have been killed with that particular book in hand, commented Gottfried. 'The news of her death opens a new leaf in the history of Haiti. If it leads to the downfall of Avril we will have the alpha and omega of Duvalierism.' To which he added, philosophically: 'Mind you, it has taken us Swiss seven hundred years to achieve democracy. The Haitians have much to learn from their history.'

Within hours of Roseline's death five thousand schoolchildren were out on the streets of Gonaïves, a city on the road north of the capital, calling for the dictator Avril to step down. Rioting soon spread to most towns, with mobs sacking government offices and the homes of government supporters. Bonfires of old tyres had left smoke drifting in palls over Port-au-Prince. Most significant, the exiled opposition leader Hubert de Ronceray (whom I had met in Miami, beaten about the face with truncheons) was about to board plane for Haiti. 'For as long as Avril is in power,' he had told me, 'I shall never go home.' Did de Ronceray know something: had Avril already left? Rumour suggested that he had, but news is haphazard in Haiti. Like the verdict given by six or more witnesses to an automobile accident, each account offers a different interpretation. There is often only word-of-mouth information or *teledyòl* – the grapevine, in Creole.

For the time being it was all quiet in Jacmel. But numerous reports would come through from Gottfried ('I bring you the news this morning') that Macoutes had been dragged out of hiding by the vengeful populace in Port-au-Prince, and summarily lynched: hacked to death or burned alive inside a flaming rubber tyre.

The history of this poor, beleaguered country has always been one of cruelty and tyranny. In *Bug-Jargal*, Victor Hugo's youthful romance about the uprising in Saint Domingue, the black slaves ransack the plantations armed with bludgeons and tomahawks, yelling: *'Touyé papa moe, ma touyé quena toué!'* You kill my father, I'll kill yours. Hugo had written this novel at the age of sixteen, to be read aloud at a literary banquet among schoolfriends. André Maurois thought it contained passages quite as poetic as any by Mérimée, but it seemed to me a catalogue of gratuitous Haitian horrors: ritual decapitations, man-eating crocodiles, humans sacrificed to Voodoo. There is a black dwarf named Habibrah who appears as a grisly hybrid of Quasimodo and Dessalines.

Three days after the unhappy departure of the *Berlin*, Gottfried told how he had seen some two hundred troops from the crack Presidential Guard – 'Praetorian Guard' he called them – descend from trucks outside the Jacmel barracks on Avenue Liberté. They were part of reinforcements sent by Avril to quell any disturbance. It was a bad sign.

'Tomorrow a Mass will be held in honour of Roseline Vaval in the cathedral here.' Gottfried looked anxiously over his shoulder as he spoke, glancing at the empty tables in the Alexandra. 'I ask you to keep this a secret. There are many Macoutes and double-cross agents in Jacmel. Trust no one.'

My days in Jacmel began to follow a routine. Breakfast at the Alexandra, an occasional walk along the bay or in the hills near by, then down to Place Toussaint L'Ouverture where I sought news from Gottfried. Transistor radio held to one ear, the Swiss became a familiar sight striding about town, his school closed while the pupils remained on strike. Gottfried would greet me with a broad grin and then gesture us to the shade of a balcony near by. Friends and locals were introduced as they gathered round to listen to the latest news. Gottfried was loved and renowned in Jacmel as a man truly *engagé*, as he described himself. The French radio bulletins were translated first into Creole, and then into English for my benefit. 'The complot against Avril continues . . .'

The Alexandra was run entirely by women. They lived in a sort of outhouse adjoining the main building, so I slept alone in the hotel. You had to climb over a garden wall if you came back after ten o'clock at night. Formerly the home of a prosperous coffee merchant, the Alexandra was cluttered with French antiques, many of them under sheets behind a locked door. There was a plaster-cast.blackamoor which stood, cheeks puffed out like an allegorical wind, at the foot of a rosewood staircase. The proprietor, a diminutive mulatta of fearsome aspect, would affect a certain hauteur towards the black women she employed among the pots and pans in the kitchen, maintaining the aristocracy of skin from colonial times.

Breakfasts were a farce. Each morning the same rather genteel waitress (a mocha-coloured mulatta: blacks were kept behind the scenes) would shuffle up to my table and reel off a tantalizing list of Creole delicacies: '*Aujourd'hui nous avons hareng fumé, patates et bananes frites, confiture de fraises,*' – dreamily counting them on her fingers.

If you asked for a variation on the usual fare, she would sweetly smile and nod, '*Très bien, m'sieur,*' and half an hour later the familiar plate of fried eggs arrived. The terrace sloped at a distinct incline towards the sea below so that one's chair was in danger – it seemed – of slipping backwards over the edge. But I was fortunate to be stranded in Jacmel: Port-au-Prince was, as Gottfried put it, 'taxed to her utmost capacity of violence . . .'

Roadblocks, burning tyres, demonstrations. As tension in the country increased by the hour it became clear that I would need to reassure family and friends in London that I was in fact still alive. The local TELECO – Haitian state telephone – office was chaos.

'I'd like to make a call to London. Collect.'

When I eventually secured a line, a recorded message kept repeating: '*Par suite d'encombrement, votre appel ne peut aboutir. Veuillez rappeler ultérieurement? . . . Par suite d'encomb –'* I had heard that message hundreds of times before in Port-au-Prince and had grown to hate it: 'Because the lines are busy your call cannot get through. Would you like to call later? . . .' *Yes please!* And you bang the telephone down to pick it up again a minute after. *'Par suite d'encomb –'*

Any vehicles outside the TELECO office on the main road to Cap Jacmel had been spray-gunned with slogans, some of them scatological: *'A Bas Caca Avril!', 'Macoute = Merde!'* Windscreens looked as if they had been smashed with rocks. But at least these vehicles had made it – got through the barricades at Port-au-Prince. Others had not, with the result that Jacmel was now seriously depleted of provisions from the capital. The market was almost bare but for a few flyblown cuts of goat or kid.

On the fourth day I saw that a group of schoolchildren had gathered outside the cathedral at the further end of the marketplace for an impromptu carnival. Soon they were leaping up and down waving branches, a traditional symbol in Haiti of *dechoukaj*, or uprooting. 'Down with Avril!' they yelled. 'We want elections!' Their uniforms were red and white – the colours of the Swiss flag.

'Those are my pupils,' explained Gottfried, who was now accompanying me inside the cathedral with his radio held to one ear. 'They will not go back to the Collège Suisse until Avril has left the country.'

But earlier that afternoon I heard through the *teledyòl* that Avril had either escaped across the border to the Dominican Republic or fled to asylum in Switzerland.

Gottfried chortled: 'No, no. The President is still in his palace, fiddling while Port-au-Prince burns.' Then he assumed an expression of grave concern. 'Last night was a night, they say, of terror. The army opened fire on five thousand unarmed demonstrators killing twenty people. Food distribution centres have been looted. The Macoutes are rumoured to have poisoned the city water supply.'

There was now apprehension and panic in Jacmel. This morning the Duvalierist mayor had tried to leave the Hôtel de Ville disguised as a woman. He was caught by a mob on the road to Léogâne. 'We do not know what became of him.' Gottfried shook his head. 'But no Macoute is shown any mercy now. They must *all* eat the humble pie.' The Swiss confessed how impressed he was by the confidence, defiance and unity of the civilian opposition to Avril. But there were fears that the President might resort to violent repression through his coterie of Praetorian Guard . . .

The cathedral was Tropical Gothic. It looked as though it had been transported, brick by pew, from some drowsy churchyard in the English counties. But then you noticed that one of the stained-glass windows framed a graceful coconut tree, that mango, pawpaw and plantains had grown round the plaster-cast figurine of St Michael by the chapterhouse. Monsignor Franz Lichtle, a Spiritain or Holy Ghost priest from France, was about to officiate at Mass in honour of Roseline Vaval. What began as a solemn litany soon amplified into a furious indictment of corruption and Duvalierism. Suddenly, the celebrants stood in the pews linking hands to chant 'Raché manyok! Raché manyok!' – pull up your manioc! This was the rallying cry of *dechoukaj* as coined by Bishop Willy Romélus of Jérémie. It means rid the land of all Macoutes.

Few of those in church had forgotten how the Order of Holy Ghost Fathers had been expelled from Haiti by Papa Doc in 1969 for so-called 'attempts against the security of the state'. Now the Spiritains had returned, evidently with a vengeance. After Mass Gottfried's schoolchildren swarmed on to the streets of Jacmel – '*Raché manyok!*' – to gather in protest outside the barracks. Several began to climb the roof of the Hôtel de Ville to bring down the Haitian flag. 'This is why the government in Haiti has never done much for the education,' said Gottfried. 'More schools mean more revolution. Better to keep the children in ignorance.'

The Collège Suisse was in fact desperate for funds. Any cheques or remittances which Gottfried had begged from Switzerland were usually intercepted by the Haitian postal service (or accidentally directed to Tahiti) and he was forever bemoaning the lack of benches, blackboards and desks. There was no canteen. 'Soon enough, my school will have to close.' Gottfried seemed resigned to this fact although philanthropic townsfolk had often restored the college with a generous donation at the eleventh hour. Education is generally poor in Haiti. At the time of independence in 1804, of course, there were no schools in the country and the colonists sent their children to France for tuition. The illiterate Dessalines, first ruler of the emancipated slaves, failed to recognize the importance of education. Like Papa Doc, he was chiefly anxious to consolidate the authority which he had so violently acquired. Not a single institution was established for the good of the people during the six years of his reign.

In 1816 a Lycée Haïtien was founded in Port-au-Prince with a curriculum of rhetoric, logic, ethics and ancient languages. But it was exclusively for a caste of patrician mulattoes. Little had changed; only the upper classes of Haiti can afford to send children abroad or to the capital for their studies. In rural areas the nearest school may still be miles away. The state provides some meagre primary and secondary education, but the rate of illiteracy in Haiti remains around eighty per cent. 'At least Castro taught the peasants of Cuba to write their own names,' Gottfried had remarked.

Education, both public and private, is chiefly the legacy of the Concordat which President Fabre Geffrard had signed with the Vatican in 1860. From that time, many of the principal schools in Haiti were staffed by French Roman Catholic priests. For years they taught that Toussaint L'Ouverture was a traitor to France. While this francophile prejudice has all but disappeared, there is still an antiquated business in Haiti of learning by rote. Wherever you walk, schoolchildren are to be seen memorizing lessons by heart: mumble, mumble – their lips mechanically follow the printed page. Most nights outside the Alexandra I saw students studying by lamp-light outside the hotel (they had no electricity at home), reciting the facts of Haitian history as though summoned before a Mr Gradgrind.

The Holy Trinity Episcopal School of Port-au-Prince is the largest – and widely regarded as one of the best – private educational establishments in Haiti. It was founded in 1913 as part of the Episcopal mission of James Theodore Holly, a black Bostonian who had responded to Fabre Geffrard's appeal for the emancipated slaves of America to settle in Haiti. 'The Republic calls you,' the President proclaimed. 'The regenerating work that she undertakes will be a formal denial, most eloquent and peremptory, against those detractors of our race who contest our desire and ability to attain a high degree of civilization.'

The Reverend Holly would have been proud of the flag-raising ceremony which now takes place every morning at eight o'clock in the forecourt of his Episcopal school. One thousand four hundred black pupils stand to regimental attention, dressed immaculately in uniforms of green and white. The Haitian flag is raised by one of the Sisters of the Society of St Margaret (most of them *blancs*) who now administer the school. A bell is then rung and the children, all teeth and smiles, give their spirited version of the Haitian national anthem, the 'Dessalinienne':

> *Pour le Pays,*
> *Pour les Ancêtres,*
> *Marchons unis!*

Pour le Drapeau
Pour la Patrie
Mourir est beau!

After this anthem a band of boys and girls moves forward with violins, flutes and clarinets to strike up the 'Slavic Air' by Beethoven (adapted from opus 107), painfully out of tune. 'The Episcopal school brings the children to God,' said Sister Leslie Anne, an American who had worked here for over a decade. 'And the love of God to children.'

'There's nothing we can do about the chanting I'm afraid,' she added as we opened the door to a classroom. *'Bonjour, cher Monsieur le Visiteur!'* – the children automatically stood to attention behind their wooden desks. 'It's an inheritance of French colonialism. But we don't have the money for more staff and smaller classes.' We had intruded upon a history lesson. A portrait of Jean-Jacques Dessalines hung on the wall.

'Did Christopher Columbus discover Haiti by aeroplane?' the teacher asked her pupils (there were some sixty of them, aged between ten and fifteen).

'No he did not!' the children replied in unison, giggling and rocking to and fro in their seats.

'Was it by *camion* that he discovered Haiti?'

'No it was not! Monsieur Columbus discovered Haiti in three *boats* – the *Santa Maria,* the *Niña* and the *Pinta!'*

'Very good. And what is Haiti?'

'Haiti is the Pearl of the Antilles.'

And so it went – a course of question and answer, almost like a catechism. 'Read, learn and inwardly digest,' Gottfried had said. 'That is the formal French system. And we are stuck with it.'

Later that night at the Alexandra, Gottfried moved a castle across the board to challenge my king. 'Now I am afraid you are isolated both externally and internally,' he mused. 'You have no friends – just like General Avril.' I had rather hoped that Gottfried might lose to me out of pity. But, no: his chessmen were lethal. 'Chess is all a question of Euclidian geometrics,' he announced; then, removing his spectacles the better to survey my troops: 'That is a very good move indeed,' he said as I quietly decamped my bishop to where I thought it would not be noticed. 'Capablanca would be proud of you.' But I lost the game.

The hotel was in darkness from a power cut. Insects clamoured zing

zing zing round the hurricane lamp which hung above us on the terrace. Now and again a couple of bugs would detonate against the glass and fall twitching on to the board. 'Ha! There goes another Macoute,' Gottfried flicked away the evidence with a handkerchief. The beach below was a silver-sanded strand by moonlight, the roar of surf broken only by the dim raving of a dog, or a muffled boom in the distance. A grenade? An automobile backfiring? Yeats's *Deirdre* came to mind:

> They knew that there was nothing that could save them,
> And so played chess as they had any night
> For years, and waited for the stroke of sword.

We played to while away the time, and to forget the horror in Port-au-Prince.

Seven days in Jacmel and still no hope of leaving. The roads both north and south were blocked to traffic by barricades of cars and burning tyres. Avril had appeared on television with the announcement: 'I believe that the best way to change a government is through the electoral process. If I left Haiti in a precipitous manner, it would create untold turmoil.' He had apparently resigned as President of Haiti, but refused to leave the country. The General had fled the National Palace under cover of dark and was hiding in his luxurious home at Thomazeau, a small village near the Dominican border where the Haitian-American Sugar Company railway terminates. He was protected by a phalanx of Attachés, or quondam Macoutes. There were rumours that Avril might mobilize these thugs into a private army, and stage a counter-coup. The country was paranoid with fear.

Mornings outside the Alexandra were often interrupted by the Rara bands who celebrate the forty days from Ash Wednesday to Easter-eve. These bands were noisy and sometimes intimidating, with dancers dressed like pearly kings or morris men in huge sombreros and capes sewn with sequins. They whirled batons and blew into long bamboo tubes called *vaccines* that groaned and bellowed with a single four-note song, long and rhythmic like a lowing of cows. The leader of the band would flail a sisal whip at the hapless passer-by and demand money. I kept well away from Rara. There was little to do in the evenings and I would wander along to the Choubouloute, a local bar. The alcohol was pretty uncommendable: bottles of 'Night Train Express Apple Wine' or 'Rum Cocktail

Chateaublond'. But there was a good *méringue* combo, named Les Flamants Noirs.

One afternoon I was about to buy some Comme il Faut from a stall on the Rue de Commerce when I was approached by an ill-shaven and stooped old man. 'Ah Mr Thomson? I hear from Gottfried that you've also been to Albania. Jack's the name.' He extended a hand. 'Jack Carey. Very pleased to meet you, I must say.' I knew at once that this was the Englishman who had helped found the Collège Suisse over a game of chess. According to Gottfried, Jack had been to Albania ten times now; he had also read all the works by the Albanian revolutionary leader Enver Hoxha who died in 1985. I was curious to meet the man, as I had often marvelled at the piquant conjunction of different peoples to be found in Haiti: Poles, Arabs, Germans, other displaced Europeans including Germans, the Cossack whom I had met in Port-au-Prince – all of them swept on to the shores of this island like a flotsam of history.

'. . . dreadful coffee, mind you, the Albtourist stuff. Still, what do you expect from a last bastion of Stalinism? In which part of London do you live? Pimlico – oh yes I know it well. I was born in Enfield myself.' All this from Jack, within the first five minutes of our encounter. He was then seventy-five years old, and clearly unwell – the eyes a little yellow, his lips distempered blue.

We entered his tiny home off Place Toussaint L'Ouverture. The front was of mouldy clapboard, once white. More a lean-to, really, all of one room, and in virtual darkness. Empty tins of food stood on an old iron-ing board; a copy of Hoxha's *The Anglo-American Threat to Albania* lay propped against the wainscot. 'My home's a bit rudimentary,' Jack said ruefully. 'But it does me fine. I've had some good times in Haiti, you know. It's the sun, that's what I like. I came here for the warmth.' Jack had never married, but regulars at the Choubouloute would tell how he was quite a philanderer in early years. He was often to be seen strolling along the beach with a couple of Haitian girls on either side. Jack still wore a gold iden-tity bracelet and a variety of medallions exposed by a manfully open shirt-front. But one sensed that the days of gallantry were over now.

'Can I offer you a drink? I'm afraid I've only got Nesquik. At least it won't give us a hangover.' Jack laughed and then broke into a violent fit of coughing, wheezing in his chair. 'Gracious God.' He caught his breath. 'It's the ticker, you know. The doctors say it's prone to flutter. Don't know why it should make me cough, though. Not like that, all of sudden.' But he soon recovered his composure.

We sat sipping the Nesquiks while Jack told how he had served in the Auxiliary Fire Service during the last war. 'I remember the night St Paul's went up. Dreadful it was, the whole of Wren's chapterhouse destroyed by doodlebugs . . .'

He went on after an instant: 'Mind you, the conflagrations in London were as nothing to what we inflicted on Dresden or Frankfurt. All those incendiary bombs . . . Glad that's over.' Jack had worked as a fireman in Streatham until the age of sixty, when he first left London to travel the world. When he arrived at Jacmel fifteen years ago he became so enamoured of the place that he decided to return there every winter from England. But now, for one reason or another, he was stranded in Haiti.

'I'm just a poor Englishman, see? I'm waiting for death, waiting for death in Jacmel.' He went on with a sigh, 'What with the political situation, I should try and get out of this country while you can. Haiti's never been so bad, take it from me.'

Jack spoke as a Londoner, with a strong hint of cockney. I found it curious that Gottfried should have engaged him at the Collège Suisse to teach the correct pronunciation (though never the grammar) of the English language. 'Yah! Jack was a good one,' enthused the Swiss. 'He delivers the Queen's English.' Occasionally Jack would employ a curiously formal, not to say Latinate turn of phrase. 'Voodoo? Oh yes, it's a rather unusual mode of veneration. I've been to quite a few initiation rites in my time. The participants can get a trifle carried away – eyes rolling, and all that drumming! Racket enough for twenty weddings, dear oh dear. But I think you'll find that the average Haitian, the man, as it were, on the Clapham omnibus, is usually a Voodooist. The mulattoes, on the other hand, they're much more what I'd call cathedral-goers.'

I asked Jack: 'But have you enjoyed them, all these years in Haiti?'

'I should say so, by and large. Certainly makes a change from Enfield,' he humorously declared. 'And while the Haitians are beggars, thieves and liars, they're a good and very accommodating people too. Can't say I've ever had much trouble from them.'

It was time for Jack to walk round the corner to Gottfried's for supper. They were great friends and ate together every evening. Jack was unable to cook very much and Gottfried had taken him under his wing. It began to rain as he put the padlock on his door. 'It's good of you to accompany me to Geoff's' – Jack had anglicized the name – 'but it'll take us half an hour to get there. I run out of breath you see and have to stop now and again to recharge the batteries.' Jack clung to my arm for support. 'Let us go, then.'

He negotiated the slippery road with some difficulty. Far off, a first phrase of thunder warned. Then the drizzle turned to a downpour as Jack faltered further in his step and paused by the sunless vestibule of a house. I wondered whether I should not run for a doctor. A young Haitian approached and asked what was the matter. She looked concerned. *'Je suis malade, chérie,'* Jack gestured for her to go away. 'One of my students.' He turned to me with a feeble sort of smile. 'Taught her English, many years ago. A good girl.'

I helped Jack to his feet and we proceeded in the rain. Presently a young boy came begging for money. *'Eh blanc, blanc!'* He tugged at Jack's shirt. I could have thumped the urchin.

'Go and ask your General bloody Avril for a dollar!' Jack shouted in English. 'I'm just a poor . . .' The boy ran away laughing. Jack laughed too. Then he began to pant again, mopping the rain from his face with a handkerchief:

'Mr Thomson. Would you mind very much if you perhaps left me?' I understood that Jack was ashamed to be seen so ill. 'Perhaps we'll meet in Albania one day,' he said, taking my hand. 'You never know.'

I watched his stooped figure shuffle uphill towards Gottfried's in the rain. Then he turned to me at the top of the hill and gave a sign of impatience: 'Go home!' he cried with sudden passion. 'Get out of this country while you can.'

'While I can?' I mumbled, staring.

'You heard what I said.'

That was the last I saw of Jack from Enfield. But his words would haunt throughout the rest of my journey.

Often I wondered how Jack had steeled himself against the horrors of this country. And in the months that lay ahead he became a sort of symbol of endurance: a man adrift in Haiti, yet nostalgic for the ties of homeland.

The news that Prosper Avril had finally left Haiti came the day I rode horseback from Jacmel to the Bassin Bleu in the hills near by. It was a rough and unfrequented trail to the Blue Pool, winding at times along a steep chasm, fording streams made almost impassable by the rain. The horse was in a wretched condition – mouth lathered with foam, her flanks sore from the guide who kept beating them with a stick. *'Allez! Allez!'*

He bore the unusual name of Mésidor Dieusibon and negotiated the path with light springing steps.

One did not really need a horse to reach the Bassin Bleu. Mésidor had approached me on the terrace of the Alexandra one morning and cajoled me into riding, as he would take a handsome cut from the hire of the horse. Peculiar difficulties are involved with guides in Haiti. They may take you to places which would otherwise prove inaccessible but they will often misinform, only telling of legends: *loups-garous*, or diabolical spirits that fly through the night, zombis working the fields and water nymphs swimming in the waters of the Blue Pool. Now that there is scarcely any tourism in Haiti, these guides are desperate for money. It is a frustration: beyond their welcoming smiles is the inevitable haggling over the fee which has trebled by the end of the day.

In the morning sun, the landscape round the Bassin Bleu glistened with dark groves of coffee and mango trees, a riot of foliage. Jacmel lay far to our right, a pale blot on the lazy line of the bay. On arrival at the Bassin — a series of natural aquifers whose waters are blue-green from dissolved limestone — we found a group of people gathered round a transistor radio wedged in the branches of a tree above a disused cockfight pit. They came running up to us as I dismounted and turned the horse to grass. 'Avril go away! Avril go away!' they cried in Creole.

'*Ki koté l-alé?*' Mésidor returned. Where has he gone to? Nobody knew. The guide was sceptical. Following the news that Baby Doc himself had fled Haiti, the dictator proclaimed from the National Palace: 'There are bad rumours that I have left the country. It's not true. I'm as firm as a monkey's tail.' We sat in the cockpit and listened to bulletins that were broadcast in a French so florid that it required some translation. News came on the hour and we had to wait several hours for confirmation of Avril's departure. In the Haitian countryside, so far from the centres of power, one could well understand the sense of impotence these people must have felt; decisions were being made which they could only guess at. A sudden downpour and we sought shelter in a hut where plates of mashed yam were passed round. We ate the hot, sweet vegetable with our fingers.

After three hours Mésidor threw his baseball cap in the air and yelled '*Haïti libéré!*' News had arrived to confirm that Avril had been flown out of Haiti at dawn to Florida, courtesy of the US Air Force. The deposed president had conceded power to the army chief of staff General Herard Abraham, who now promised to turn the country over to an interim government within seventy-two hours. His voice on the radio was stentorian, military: 'Our mission is clear and the objective is precise. It is to re-establish peace . . . and to hand over power to a provisional civilian council that respects the spirit of the constitution.'

Mésidor translated this message into Creole. The villagers locked their hands in rapture. *'Haïti libéré!'* They grinned and cheered. This was Haiti's fifth change of government since February 1986 when Baby Doc Duvalier escaped to the fleshpots of southern France.

Back in Jacmel, Gottfried was characteristically precise in his specification of the aeroplane which had flown the old president out of Haiti. 'It was a C141 Starlifter Transport. Not a bad jet – better than a tap-tap, yah!' We toasted the dictator's departure. 'Avril is dead!' Gottfried raised his glass. 'He has gone off with a tail between the legs. Long live Haiti!'

VII

Eating Coconuts with Alexandre Dumas

'Nothing can be more laborious, nor more inconvenient and
unpleasant than travelling in Hayti, from the state of the roads,
from the want of inns for accommodation, and from the innumerable rivers and streams over which the traveller has to pass
(to say nothing of being nearly up to his shoulders in water).'
James Franklin, *The Present State of Hayti*,
London, 1828

'*Blanc malade! Blanc malade!*' I had exposed myself to sunstroke. The
women covered my head with eau-de-cologne (or some other aromatic
essence) and fanned me with newspapers. Then I was gestured to lie
down, although there was scarcely the room to stand up. The lower deck
was jammed with faggots of sugar cane, baskets of yams and bananas –
the companionway to the top deck blocked with bundles of wood stoutly
corded for transportation. Some passengers cleared a space amid crates of
piglets (the animals shifted irritably in their quarters) and eased my head
against a pillow of rags. Then the ship began to roll, slightly, and I fell
asleep.

When I came to, the *Neptune* was still berthed in the oily waters of
Port-au-Prince. We should have left for Jérémie a good three hours ago
but, as a tap-tap will never leave until overburdened with passengers, so
the *Neptune* would not weigh anchor until burdened with as much cargo
as she was able physically to bear. Haitians are accustomed to delay and
I had long ago left behind any European ideas of punctuality, of hustle
and haste; so I resigned myself to the vertical sun and awaited the breeze
that would revivify once we had gained the open sea. It was a long wait.
Another two hours, and *marchandes* were still bustling up the passenger
gangway, laden with sacks of charcoal and baskets of Chiclets, packing
cases with bottles of Kola.

By now the ship resembled a sort of floating Iron Market – cluttered
with squawking chickens, their wings pinioned, and with dozens of snuf-
fling, filthy pigs which would defecate now and then under the hatch

tarpaulins. There were no lavatories: women would hitch up their skirts and crouch over a billycan while men simply aimed over the handrail. A couple of lifeboats had been fixed to the gunwales but I looked in vain for any framed instructions on safety drill. She was a terrible crematory oven of a ship: *'Oh mon cher blanc'* – the women would feel my shirt, rubbing the cloth between their fingers like hagglers at a bargain sale. *'Oua mourri sou sole-a.'* You'll die in the sun. They wondered why I had not paid the additional five dollars for a cabin.

The captain had already shown me the only cabin. It was situated directly above the engine room and juddered in the heat as though it might uproot itself from the plankings. I had thought it best to sit on deck with the other passengers. Looking at the peeling white paint of the bulkhead, at the porthole fittings scabbed with verdigris, I wondered whether we should ever arrive at Jérémie: numerous such cargo ships have foundered on the way. *'Eh, blanc.'* A young boy clapped me on the shoulder. *'Ou capab najé?'* Can you swim? In December 1971 the *Celié* sank a mile or so to shore of Jérémie, drowning seven hundred people. To date, this remains one of the worst maritime disasters in the history of Haiti. Few Haitians are able to swim – surprising, perhaps, when they regularly use such unseaworthy vessels to travel from one part of their country to another.

Jérémie is the capital of the province of Grande Anse on the tip of the southern peninsula, one hundred and forty miles west of Port-au-Prince. I wanted to visit this city as it stands near the birthplace of Alexandre Dumas, father of Alexandre Dumas the Elder, author of *The Three Musketeers*, who begat Alexandre Dumas the Younger. (The main square in Jérémie is called Place des Trois Dumas.) 'My father's eyes,' wrote the Elder, 'opened on the most beautiful scenery of that glorious island of Haiti, the queen of the gulf in which it lies, the air of which is so pure that it is said no venomous reptiles can live there.'

There are nevertheless sharks in Haiti: I could see them gliding alongside the *Neptune*, snapping at dead jellyfish or some other piece of flotsam. The predators were particularly attracted to the sugar cane which passengers had champed and chewed then spat into the waters of the harbour. Rolf had already put paid to the idea that there might be a strain of vegetarian shark. 'You go to Jérémie on der ship? My God, you are one crazy Englander!' the German had told me at the Oloffson one night. 'OK, so you can swim. But the sharks vill be waiting for you all der same. They are also part of the comedy.'

* * *

The Oloffson had been milling with American journalists the day I returned from Jacmel. They had come to cover the overthrow of General Avril, and were about to fly back to the States with yet more stories about the horror of Haiti – how they had risked life and limb in their Budget Rent-a-Cars with the bullets whizzing overhead. But they were safe now, cloistered in the Oloffson where meals arrived and where in the end somebody always signed for the drinks.

'All right, there's no police protection in Haiti. But no Haitian's gonna machete a journalist. Leastways not a *blanc*. Not a mighty whitey. No way.'

'You gotta hand it to Avril, though. A pretty smooth article, that guy. I mean, nobody was gonna talk *him* into being peaceable. Hey you there, another rum punch *s'il vous* please!'

'Where have you been?' Richard Morse asked me. 'We thought you were dead.'

'Dead?' I returned. 'Not to my knowledge.'

It was then that I noticed a goat nosing about the hotel, bleating at customers by the bar.

'There's goat curry on the menu tonight,' Richard went on, whimsically. 'It's business as usual.'

Richard in fact had quite a serious problem with goats; the local owners would let them roam and fend for themselves during the day and, as there was plenty of lush vegetation in the hotel gardens, beasts were often to be found eating the flowers. Richard had tried without success to ask the culprits to keep their livestock tethered. 'Now I give five dollars to each of my waiters who manages to catch a goat and let it be known it will end in a stew unless a ransom is paid. And it works,' he added, not without satisfaction. Richard took a certain pride in understanding the priorities of his Haitian neighbours: their respect for business, their concern for money and survival. In Creole: *Lajan fè lòm*, money makes a man.

There was nothing about the Oloffson that night to suggest that Haiti had been on the brink of civil war. Outside the hotel it was another matter. Everywhere stood the remains of barricades, the road to the airport black from pyres of burning tyres, strewn with rocks and trailing telephone wires. Vehicles had been turned over and set ablaze, their windscreens smashed or daubed in paint with *'A Bas Caca Avril!'* Some two thousand Macoutes were reported on the run (Serge Beaulieu himself had escaped into hiding after a mob had ransacked his Duvalierist radio station) and the US embassy had called a provisional curfew for its staff.

Smoke and the corpses had gone from the streets but I felt some apprehension at travelling on my own. Violence here may flare at any moment like a piece of tinder. 'Lift up the Macoutes and smash them down and if that is not enough put a tyre around their necks and burn them' – words from an angry crowd, and they meant it. The supreme punishment of death inside a blazing rubber tyre has come to Haiti from South Africa and is known jovially in Creole as *'Père Lebrun'* after a businessman who sells Korean tyres in Port-au-Prince. The expression *'Nap Père Lebrun ou'*, we're going to Père Lebrun you, is now current throughout Haiti. I had seen burned bodies near the Oloffson and the gorge rose in my throat at the thought of how heaps of cinder and ash, charred bones, could be all that remained of a person.

I immediately decided to escape Port-au-Prince, to leave behind the tension of life in the city.

A faint clanging from the engine room, and a thick rope ripped and roared on the drum end of a winch. Then the engines went astern, slowly and steadily with a plashing of propellers, and the *Neptune* thrummed into life. We were leaving Port-au-Prince. As we cleared the mole, seagulls screamed and mewed over the funnel: like the lucky dollar note which fluttered from the stern on a length of string, these birds would accompany us all the long way to Jérémie. Perhaps they augured well for the *Neptune*. I leant over the rail and watched the water sliding along her hull-plates, hissing and bubbling.

We moved out of harbour passing the giant white and red striped chimney of the HASCO sugar mill, the ugly bulk of the cathedral and the groined dome of the National Palace. The *fauteuil*, presidential chair, was now occupied by Ertha Pascal Trouillot – acting head of state and the first woman president of Haiti. A Supreme Court judge, she was considered incorruptible, with no links to the old regime. Her task was to maintain a caretaker government until such a time as elections could be held.

Cloom-cloom-cloom went the engines, hammering out the same stroke. We were making about five knots, a spout of bilge and refuse splashing from the *Neptune*'s rusty side into the sea as the National Palace diminished to a white dot. Shrieks of laughter went up when a sudden roll overturned crates of livestock. Hours went by and I sat in the mustering darkness of early evening, smoking cigarettes and chatting with the *marchandes*. Was I married? Where did I come from? Why was I in Haiti? As we passed the town of Petit Trou de Nippes a lighthouse flashed short-long, short-long. The *Neptune* herself was probably invisible from the mainland: she was lit only by oil lamps in the bow and stern.

Short-long, short-long. Another lighthouse signalled as we sailed past the archipelago of tiny islands off the Grande Cayemite. I glanced at the luminous dial of my watch: 9.25. The coastwise journey so far had taken almost ten hours. Gulls were still hanging above the stern like toys on invisible wires and I was lulled into boredom by the dreary foaming waves. The monotony of the voyage was broken only once, when a deckhand grabbed a young boy, removed his trousers and dangled him upside down by the ankles over the edge of the boat until he cried for mercy. The passengers laughed and jeered at this unkindness, clapped their hands. A woman who sat by my side atop a box of mangoes explained that the boy had been punished because he was unable to pay the three dollars for his passage to Jérémie.

It was by now almost midnight; we had left Port-au-Prince at midday and I was extremely tired. I tried to huddle asleep on a bundle of goatskins, but the stench of fish, cheap rum and diesel oil kept me awake. There was also the danger of being accidentally urinated upon by men from the deck above. Haitians lay around me swaddled in blankets against the cold, curled on the bottom-boards murmuring or chanting songs.

A terrific jolt, followed by shrieks from passengers thrown headlong against the gunwales, as the *Neptune* ran aground for half her length on the sands at Jérémie. The ship rocked gently in the surf as one by one we went ashore over a plank thrust aside to the jetty. *'Blanc descend! Blanc descend!'* the market women seemed to congratulate me. *'Oui,'* I returned. *'Grâce à Dieu.'*

I took myself to the only possible hotel in Jérémie, a pile of wood by the seafront. *'Ôtel Splendide la lì bon,'* said the owner Madame Lolo as she led me by a torch of tow and resin to a dingy room hammered together from bits of plywood. *'Li fré, epi lì pa tro chè.'* This Hotel Splendide is fine – she'd said – it's nice and cool and it's not too expensive. It was in fact the most verminous hotel I have ever stayed in. An interesting variety of insect spun round the single naked light bulb, crawled round the enamel rim of the slop-pail beneath my bed. By now I was past caring: the Splendide was comfort compared to the *Neptune*. I lit a mosquito coil and fell asleep.

★　★　★

Next day I called on the Bishop of Jérémie in the hope that he could provide alternative accommodation, for the church is usually willing to supply shelter if you leave some donation to cover board and lodging. The Right Reverend Romélus was eating breakfast when I arrived at the presbytery on Avenue Emile Roumer, joined by young seminarians bent over plates of rice. Seated at table in the refectory Willy Romélus appeared almost professorial with his horn-rimmed spectacles, rather mild in manner. He was scarcely the progressive bishop I had expected, not the man who had so fiercely enjoined the Haitians to rid their land – 'Raché manyok!' – of all Duvalierists. Everyone ate in silence as though there were a coffin in the room.

The Bishop knew about the Hotel Splendide ('Yes, it is rather a misnomer') and to my relief offered a room in his residence. Like the seminarians themselves, I was assigned a maid – a young Haitian named Violette from the city of Les Cayes. My window gave on to houses with rust-red roofs, fronting the tranquil bay. Palm trees rose like flagpoles into the tropic sunlight and fishing boats drifted towards the Grande Cayemite with spreading sails. Violette prepared my bed beneath an image of Notre-Dame du Secours Perpétuel, the patron of Haiti borne aloft on clouds stitched in needlework frill. Then she led me to the window where she pointed out the wrecks of doomed vessels exposed by the retreating tide: over there, the rusted container hulks of *Le Dessalines* and *Le Croyant*, Haitian warships which went under in 1912; to the left, the stern rail of *La Valencia*, a Dominican freighter which capsized in 1890. 'Jérémie is a graveyard of ships,' she said, very seriously.

'Well, I got here in one piece.'

Violette gave a clear laugh, and added: 'Please see to it that the Mother of Perpetual Help is known throughout the world.'

The following morning I set off from Place des Trois Dumas for Alexandre Dumas' house – known as L'Habitation Madère – situated seven miles across country in the rural province of Guinaudée. I was soon joined by a mulatto of about middle age who seemed plainly fevered, if not a little unhinged. He introduced himself as President for Life of the United States: 'But there is no sign, my friend, of the helicopter which must take me to Washington.' Then he offered me the roll of bread which he had been chewing and opened a canvas bag to remove a tattered flag, the Stars and Stripes. 'For five years I lived in the United States of the American country where I drove a Pontiac, a Cadillac and a Corvette.'

He unfurled the banner and fingered the material as though it would bring luck. 'And now I would like you to help me write my speech for the White House where my wife is waiting for me. Her name is L'Eternelle Madeleine because she has no beginning and no end.'

The pale-skinned Haitian meant, clearly, as much as he said. He looked preposterous in baggy plus-fours and a pair of parti-coloured brown-and-white shoes, the shaggy white leonine head lending the appearance of an Old Testament prophet. His fine features, the patrician bearing, his almost perfect English all gave the impression that he had seen better days.

Jérémie has been a city traditionally dominated by mulattoes, where the upper-class families refused to contract marital relations with those of a lower social standing (meaning with those of a darker skin). 'It has been repeatedly demonstrated in Haiti that a mixture of aristocratic blood with pure, strong, primitive blood produces fine results,' wrote an American, Mabel Steedman, in her book *Unknown to the World – Haiti* (1939). But the usual aristocracy of skin in Haiti, where mulattoes will only marry with other mestizo-Caribs, may have produced results altogether less fine.

The man began to pace up and down like a peripatetic philosopher, mumbling into the ground: 'You know why all these people are watching me?' He gestured angrily at the urchins who had gathered to laugh and poke fun: 'Gringo! Gringo!' they yelled. 'Because I am a god by destiny.' I learned at the presbytery that his name was Willy St Elmé, a former doctor of medicine who became insane after the Americans had conscripted him to fight in Vietnam, or so rumour held. Born to a family of coffee speculators, he now lived alone with his sister in a village near Jérémie named Moron. *'Willy? Mais oui, il est toujours sur son trente-et-un'* – he's always dressed in his Sunday best, Father Antoine had commented on the mulatto's sartorial finery. Willy extracted a dead cigar stub from the pocket of his herringbone hand-me-down, chewed it, and said: 'Please excuse me, my friend, for having disturbed you.' With that he hurried away in the direction of Place des Trois Dumas.

The rough white marl road to Guinaudée wound through low hills called *mornes*. Deforestation was less in evidence here; the landscape was thick with shrubs like giant green parsley, bread-fruit trees with their soft round loaves, palms and bananas which opened their heavy fans overhead. The tropical foliage seemed to concentrate the Caribbean sunlight, the air was electric with colour.

A crocodile of schoolchildren splashed its way across the shallow waters of the Rivière Grande Anse: *'Bonsoir blanc!'* they greeted me as I waded towards them carrying my socks and shoes. Then they asked if my car had broken down – a question that was repeatedly demanded of me in the countryside: any whites in Haiti drive around in big, high-axled Japanese jeeps with four-wheel drive. *'Moin pas gin machine,'* I don't have a car. 'I just felt like taking some exercise.'

The schoolchildren stared at me and burst out laughing. *'Li anrajé,'* I heard them say. He's barmy.

As I approached the hamlet of Latibolière (little of interest here save a lovely Parisian pissoir) the path became congested with women flocking to market in Jérémie. Men in rural Haiti tend to resist any labour once they have cleared and prepared the fields. The care and sale of the crop, even the raising of poultry and cattle, largely devolves to the women. It is thought that this custom derives from Dahomey, West Africa, home to many of the original slaves; another theory holds that in the years after independence in 1804 governments found it necessary to maintain a large standing army and crop production thus fell to the hands of women who, in those early years, probably outnumbered men by three to two. At any rate, the women of Haiti now hold responsibility for domestic affairs. In an article for *The Times* of 1904, the explorer Sir Harry Johnston remarked how they reminded him of 'certain patient types of ant or termite, who, as fast as you destroy their labour of months or days, hasten to repair it with unslacking energy'.

I saluted the women as they rode past me on my way to Alexandre Dumas's house, a great cavalcade of *marchandes* swaying on the spun cotton cinches of their saddles. At Latibolière I turned left down a steep path which came out as a goat track in the middle of jungle. The rolling *mornes* soon disappeared from view; I had entered a luminous world of tropical creeper and giant tamarinds. Swarms of Hispaniolan Emeralds (humming-birds later identified from Corley Smith's ornithological notes) fluttered upwards from the tangled vegetation. A pregnant woman, borne aloft on a makeshift sedan, was rushed past me along the track by four men. It was a surreal apparition. 'Where are you going?' yelled the bearers as they hurried by. 'Alexandre Dumas's house,' I replied. 'Straight on! Straight on!' Elsewhere directions for L'Habitation Madère were provided by locals whose knowledge of Dumas had been handed down from generation to generation.

With the absence of literacy there is a strong tradition in the Haitian countryside of an 'oral culture'. Every region here has its itinerant *maître-conte*, storyteller – similar to the medieval troubadours of southern France and eastern Spain. The written word forms no part of an ancient slave culture: no theory, for example – not one written line – embraces the cult of Voodoo. The religion is based simply on a mesh of recollected superstitions and folktales, celebrated through song and dance. Yet every one of the farmers I met on my walk from Latibolière knew that Alexandre Dumas was the son of a black woman and a wealthy plantation overseer, also that he later became a French general and father to a famous writer.

The mulatto General Dumas, christened Alexandre de la Pailleterie, was much romanticized in the 1854 autobiography of Alexandre Dumas the Elder ('My father was a true child of the colonies, a child of the seashore and of the Savannahs . . .'), but he merits a biographical note.

He was born on L'Habitation Madère in 1762. His mother, Marie, was a black courtesan and it appears that his aristocratic father changed his own name from Marquis de la Pailleterie to Dumas in the hope of avoiding scandal when he returned to France with his young son. No one knows what became of Marie; it seems she died in penury at Jérémie, having never seen France. At the age of fourteen Alexandre was enrolled in the French dragoons under the name of Dumas. He fought as a general alongside Napoleon in Italy and in Austria, where he earned the soubriquet 'Horatius of the Tyrol'. In 1798 he accompanied Bonaparte on the Egyptian campaign, but his fierce republicanism incurred the wrath of the Corsican. *'Jamais je ne donnerai des épaulettes à un Nègre,'* Napoleon wrote to Dumas. The First Consul neglects to mention Dumas in his memoirs, though the mulatto's name is now engraved on the stones of the Arc de Triomphe as one of the three hundred and eighty-six generals of the French Republic and Empire. The generals Leclerc and Rochambeau also appear on this monument, but Dumas took no part in Napoleon's campaign to reinstate slavery at Saint Domingue. He died in genteel poverty at Villers-Cotterêts, Aisne, in 1806. The General's son was barely four years old at the time.

Alexandre Dumas the Elder never visited Haiti. And nowhere in the twenty-two volumes of his *Mémoires* does he define himself, or indeed his father, as a mestizo. The account Dumas gives of how his father was chased by an alligator maintains the pretence of his being white:

He knew how to run fast but it would seem that the alligator ran or rather jumped still faster than he, and his adventure bid fair to have left me for ever in limbo, had not a nigger, who was sitting aside a wall eating sweet potatoes, noticed what was happening, and cried out to my already breathless father:

'Run to the right, little sah; run to the left, little sah.'

Which, translated, meant: 'Run zigzag, white man,' a style of locomotion entirely repugnant to the alligator's mechanism, who can only run straight ahead of him, or leap lizard-wise.

As far as I know, the only novel by Dumas to treat of racial issues is *Georges*, based on the true story of Ratistante, a rebellious Negro chieftain from Madagascar sold to slavery in present-day Mauritius. Yet after his death most Afro-American visitors to Paris made a point of visiting Dumas's grave in the cemetery of Père Lachaise, and he was lionized by the handful of French-speaking New Orleans blacks who lived in France during the nineteenth century. William Wells Brown, the first coloured American to produce both a full-length play and novel, held Dumas in particular esteem. He saw the Frenchman as a descendant of those Haitians who had brought about the only successful slave revolt in history, as a man in the noble lineage of Toussaint L'Ouverture. Brown relates how he espied 'a light-complexioned mulatto with curly hair dressed in a black coat with white vest and white kids' attending a performance of *Norma* at the Paris Opera one night:

He seemed to be the centre of attention not only in his own circle but in others. So recently from America where caste was injurious to my race, I began to think that it was the woolly head that attracted attention when I was informed that the mulatto before me was no less a person than Alexandre Dumas, the son of a coloured General born in Haiti.

Alexandre Dumas the Elder was not, in fact, a mulatto. His true colour can be determined from the sinister tables of genetic descent as reported by Moreau de Saint-Méry, the French eighteenth-century writer of Saint Domingue. These divide the offspring of black and white and indeterminate shades into some 128 categories. Advancing from black to white, first comes the *Sacatra*, seven-eighths African; then the *Marabout*, five-eighths; and halfway up the scale, the true Mulatto (child of the pure black and the pure white); then the Quadroon, one-quarter; the Octaroon, one-eighth; and finally several varieties of *Sangmêlés*, one-sixteenth.

The author, then, of *The Count of Monte Cristo* and other romantic novels was a quadroon: the child of a mulatto father and a white mother. I mention these racialist tables because they still apply in Haiti. The snobbery of the Haitian élite is in fact a *reductio ad absurdum* of the practice and theory of snobbery. Many mulattoes will insist that they are quite 'untouched' by African blood, ascribing their skin tone to the aboriginal Indians of Hispaniola (although the word 'mulatto' probably derives from the Arab *mouallad*, meaning born of a slave father and a freed mother). Most mulattoes live above Port-au-Prince in the leafy suburb of Pétionville, where Hollywood mansions remain inhospitably padlocked. A small number of these coffee-coloured *herrenvolk* are no darker than, say, Italians; I was curious to find that the more sunburned I became in Haiti the more I was taken for either a mulatto-cum-quadroon or for an Hispanic from across the border in the Dominican Republic.

The canopy of forest and jungle cleared before a stream, the Rivière Petit Guinaudée. *'Koté caille Dumas?'* I asked a young girl seated outside a primitive hut of lath and mud. Directions were precise: cross that bridge over there – the Pont Marie named after General Dumas's mother – and proceed uphill until you come to a field. You can't miss it: patches of yam and cassava plant, tendrils trained up the beanpoles. When I reached this field, there were only the remains of a plantation house: it looked as if it had been destroyed by some great convulsion. Here an iron boiler, half buried in the surface; there an old iron shaft of a mill, or some other part of the apparatus for the production of sugar. The walls of L'Habitation Madère were obscured and overspread by creeper and other weeds. It seems likely that the plantation was set to the torch during the slave revolt. 'The rage of fire consumes what the sword is unable to destroy,' wrote the Englishman Bryan Edwards in his eyewitness account of the revolution. 'And in a few dismal hours, the most fertile and beautiful plains in the world are converted into one last field of carnage – a wilderness of desolation.'

The only evidence of life up here was a teenage boy planting manioc outside his house, a wreck of wood and galvanized sheets of iron. *'Honneur!'* I approached the boy.

'Respect!' He slowly put down his hoe. I asked if that pile of rubble over there marked the spot where General Dumas was born. Yes, he said. And there used to be a cross, with the General's name, but it was stolen years ago. Now there was nothing, no memorial, not even a commemorative slab. My disappointment was acute: were L'Habitation Madère situated in France, one could imagine the three statues: General Alexandre Dumas, 'Horatius of the Tyrol'; Alexandre Dumas *père*, originator of

d'Artagnan, Athos, Porthos and Aramis; Alexandre Dumas *fils*, author of *La Dame aux Camélias*. In Haiti, there are few monuments to history that one might associate with countries in the West, nor is there very much patronage of the past. All is left to rack and ruin.

I settled myself against the bole of a tree which resembled a fantastic banyan, roots like giant boa constrictors. From the straw bags, garments and garlands of flowers which hung suspended from its gnarled branches, I recognized this tree as a mapou. Haitians have deforested much of their country, but they will rarely fell a mapou: it is sacred, inhabited by the Voodoo divinity Papa Legba, known variously as the Old Man at the Gate, Navel of the World and God of the Crossroads. In Dahomey Papa Legba was called *Fa* (Destiny); in Haiti he is sometimes identified with John the Baptist. The boy, Eugène Dorestan, grinned when I told him that I had found a good tree under which to rest. It was peaceful here: a gentle rasp of crickets and grasshoppers, the plaintive wheepling of a bird somewhere.

'*Vous voulez manger les cocos chez Dumas?*' Eugène asked.

Within seconds he was propelling himself up the trunk of a palm tree, knife between his teeth. It gave a sense of vertigo just to watch: Eugène had to scale forty-odd foot of bark to reach the coconuts clustered beneath the fronds. I was concerned lest he fell. But down they came, one after another: thump, thump – the shiny green globes hit the grass. The noise must have alerted the old man who was now lolloping towards me brandishing a machete. '*Eh blanc! Kouman ou ye?*' he asked, panting out of breath. '*Oh, pa pi mal,*' I replied – not too bad. I was somewhat disturbed by his blade: often on my walks around the Haitian countryside men would leave their work in the fields and come running towards me, shouting and waving their sharp machetes in the air. The correct attitude in these circumstances is to affect pleasure at meeting, since you are quite as much an object of curiosity to them as they are to you. No harm is intended. The old man introduced himself as René Bernard.

I began to wonder whether Eugène would come down from the palm, whether he had not chosen to spend the rest of his days there, like Cosimo from Italo Calvino's *The Baron in the Trees*. Thump, thump – more fruit, but no sign of the arboreal acrobat. 'I take it you have snow in your country, monsieur.' René crouched by my side beneath the mapou. 'I should think that snow is much better for one's health than dust. Here in Haiti we have too much dust.'

He wanted to know what snow looked like. 'Well, it floats down from the sky like confetti, like large bits of white dust, very cold . . . or like –' the similes came easily: Haitians are curious about the weather in the North – 'like a storm of millet grains. And when it settles, this snow, it resembles cassava or mashed yams. Sometimes we make men out of the snow, and dress them up—'

'*Oh-oh!*' René interrupted with this very Haitian exclamation: it intends surprise, approval, delight or – in this case – disbelief. 'I'm sorry. *Moin pa konprann.* I don't understand. I just don't see how . . .'

Eugène returned with about a dozen coconuts piled in his folded arms. Both he and René (the old man still shaking his head over the snow) began to slice the top off each fruit to make a hole through which we could drink the milky sap. It was cool and delicious. Soon the grass beneath the mapou was strewn with discarded coconuts, like empty bottles at a picnic. After we had drained all twelve, Eugène and René split the fruit to reveal their pearly flesh. This we scooped into our mouths with a sliver of shell. What we did not eat was thrown to the hens who pecked greedily around us. Nothing, absolutely nothing that can be absorbed by the digestive system is wasted in Haiti. Poverty has forced the people to conserve what we in the West would cast aside. In Haiti children will use the metal frame of a bicycle wheel for a hula-hoop, fashion a toy yacht from a rubber flip-flop, construct a car from a couple of Coca-Cola cans. Fibrous membrane which the hens were unable to eat would later serve as fuel for cooking.

We were having quite a party up here with coconut flesh and milk. Soon we were joined by Eugène's young brother Jean-Rabel, who came running up the hill with school books under-arm. 'Aha!' he broke in mirthfully. 'I see you are eating coconuts with Alexandre Dumas.' The four of us lounged beneath the mapou as the sun began to sink – a melancholy event in the tropics – beyond a green line of distant palms. A strangely meditative conversation ensued, peppered with words which had become current among Haitians since the departure of Baby Doc Duvalier: *justice et réparation, corrompu, malversation* and – most particularly – *magouilleur*, French argot for racketeer or con-man, now applied across the board to politicians.

'Every Haitian is a philosopher, *mon cher*,' Eugène reasoned in an abstract way. 'And I am not talking about those more . . . classical philosophers among us who are unable to lift a machete or climb a tree. I mean –'

'*La misère dérobe le peuple,*' Jean-Rabel silenced his brother with a raised finger. 'Poverty strips bare the people, yet we all know how to survive. The children of slaves are never beaten.'

René, the old man, remarked with some sternness: 'Yes, but there are those in Haiti who would sell their soul to the devil to make money, to exercise power over the people. That *magouilleur* of a dog General Avril has left, but the tail of Duvalierism remains, *la queue reste encore . . .*'

'That's right René.' Eugène lit another Comme il Faut and watched the match burn to his fingertips. 'It's as we say in Haiti: *lefieb la pa nan dra, se nan san li ye.* The fever is not in the sheets, it's in the blood. And sadly there are politicians who want only to change the *sheets* of Duvalierism, not to rid the poison from their blood . . .'

This sad verdict may have applied to Ertha Pascal Trouillot. She had pledged to maintain her duties as provisional president until a new leader was inaugurated. But rumours that Madame Trouillot might be less than honest had already circulated in early July 1990 when she allowed Roger Lafontant to return from exile in the Dominican Republic. Lafontant was a former interior and defence minister under Baby Doc and also unofficial chief of the Tontons Macoute. One of the most feared men in Haiti, he actually staged a coup d'état by kidnapping Ertha Trouillot from her home. Lafontant then took her at gunpoint to the National Palace and held the woman hostage dressed only in her nightgown. That, at any rate, is the version she gave of the events. But nine months later Madame Trouillot was accused of conspiring to overthrow her own government and sent to prison. 'It was pretty shocking,' an American friend in Port-au-Prince told me, 'sort of like tossing Margaret Thatcher into the drunk tank.' Lafontant himself was later murdered during the putsch which overthrew President Aristide in September 1991.

The sun had long since sunk behind the palms at L'Habitation Madère. *'Faire le bien, éviter le mal,'* René Bernard advised as I left for Jérémie.

'Au revoir, m'sieur blanc!' chimed Eugène and Jean-Rabel.

On the road to Jérémie I hopped aboard an open lorry packed with human cargo – workmen, cane-cutters, cowherds. We stood shoulder to shoulder clinging to a metal rail for support, bracing ourselves against the jolts. Strange feathery trees resembling giant asparagus would loom into view, and then disappear into the Haitian night. The headlamps pierced only a few feet of darkness. At one point a ferret-like creature scurried across their beam: a mongoose, I think. The air was heavy with the fall of perfumed dew and I was happy to be free of the discomforts, delays and disappointments that I had weathered in Port-au-Prince; here in the south it seemed that life was more leisurely, that one could pause in a more pensive mood and reflect on the strange variety of the place.

Back in Jérémie, Willy St Elmé was still waiting on a bench in Place des Trois Dumas for the helicopter to take him to the White House. He asked me, almost tenderly, for a dollar.

'My wife in Washington will be very jealous if she knew about this money!' blowing his nose on a silk handkerchief.

I noticed that the plus-fours were now upheld by bicycle clips. 'Somebody in Jérémie is bound to tell her! But thank you very much, my friend. The Vietnamese people are watching me.'

As I walked back to the presbytery I could hear Willy singing 'Delilah' by Tom Jones. Out of tune.

VIII

Back to Africa

'Lord, Our skin is black,
But our sins were blacker.
You have delivered us from sin
And made us white.'

From a booklet published by
the US Baptist Mission in Haiti

The Grande Rue of Jérémie is lined with abandoned coffee warehouses, decayed gingerbread mansions, old tailors' shops cluttered with broken Singer sewing machines. The city has been dead to the world since 1964 when Papa Doc closed its port. Trade with Europe has vanished; Jérémie is no longer the 'shop window of France.' Burgundy bottles are filled with cheap rum, packets of Gauloises replaced by those of Comme il Faut.

At 225 Grande Rue stands the rare warehouse still open for commerce with the rest of Haiti, if no longer with France. A sign outside proclaims: *'Monsieur Guerdes Gaspard. Vente – Gazoline, Gaz-Oil, L'Huile Motor; Achête – Café, Cacoa'*. Gaspard is a dapper man with a pencil-thin moustache, white leather Cuban-heeled cowboy boots, reflector sunglasses and a 'Get Smart' T-shirt. He spoke demotic English, the result of ten years in Brooklyn as a taxi driver. 'Be a guest and take the seat.' We sat opposite each other on great mounds of unground coffee, our chair-legs crunching into the beans. 'Want one?' He offered me a Lucky Strike and produced a large gold cigarette lighter in the shape of the Statue of Liberty. 'Bought that in Manhattan,' he confessed with pride.

Gaspard is a symbol perhaps of the new Jérémien, a black Haitian returned from the United States to rekindle the trade which was once the province of the mulattoes. He seemed head-over-heels in love with the American Dream, the walls of his warehouse pasted with pin-ups from dolly-bird magazines, and with empty proverbs culled from two-a-dime greeting cards: 'When you're over the hill you pick up speed', 'A clean desk is the sign of a blank mind'. Gaspard was still eligible for a Resident Alien's Card in the United States, but had chosen to pitch tent here in Jérémie where his father was born. 'It's as calm as Long Island,' he said. 'No crazy violence.' He even planned to open a video shop in Jérémie, although most Haitians do not possess so much as a radio.

Gaspard had promised to take me to see his *guildive*, taffia distillery, some fifteen miles north of Jérémie in the village of Marfranc. 'Gotta make it a bit more up-to-date,' he said behind the wheel of his silver Pajero, a Japanese jeep usually associated in Haiti with the Tontons Macoute. 'But what the hell, it brings me the bucks.' Gaspard himself would never touch taffia, this Caribbean hooch: instead, he dilutes the liquor and bathes his five children in the stuff, apparently to keep the microbes at bay.

We were accompanied by the most irritating Haitian I had met so far. 'Man, I'm proud to have lived in the US of A. England's so damned insular. I don't trust nothing from Europe,' he said with some asperity. 'Olivetti, Fiat, British Leyland, that's all garbage. You gotta go for IBM, for the Mustang. You gotta realize that –' And so on, all the way to Marfranc, a barrage of pro-Americanism. The youth had spent some time in Chicago, where he attended a course in business studies. One understood that he would rather be taken for an American: 'Barbancourt rum? That's frigging crap. Me, I like Miller Lite. I know where you can get a six-pack for just *five* bucks . . . Aston Martin? Nah, give me the Chevrolet any day.' He was a catalogue of trademarks, if nothing else.

The *guildive* had not changed since the days of slavery in Saint Domingue. 'Sure it could do with some face upliftment,' Gaspard lit a cigarette with the Statue of Liberty. 'But then you could say the same for the whole of Hay-di.' Coopers and carpenters bustled about the distillery, hammering at wooden puncheons; carts drawn by oxen brought bales of Indian corn from the fields. Two men were appointed at the mill: one to heap bundles of ripe green cane into a crushing machine, the other to remove any pulp once the juice had been extracted. The spent cane, or trash, was carried away by a third on his head to serve for fodder, fuel or thatching. The workers were dressed only in loincloths and seemed exhausted. 'Why do you ill-treat your mule in that way?' asked a French colonist of his black slave. 'But when I do not work I am beaten, when he does not work, I beat him – he is my Negro.'

A miserable old horse circled the mill at a pace habit had made mechanical, constantly whipped so that he would turn the great wooden beams which revolved the cogs and rollers for crushing. The cane juice, pale ash in colour, gushed forth in a great stream, white with foam. This travelled along a wooden gutter into the boiling house where it was received into a copper siphon and boiled for eight hours. The resultant syrup is fermented for five days in large oak casks and is then boiled again, the vapours trapped to form taffia – one hundred per cent pure alcohol.

The boiling house resembled a moonshine operation from the days of American prohibition, a great lumber room piled with barrels. There was an overpowering fume of molasses and treacle. Gaspard ladled some taffia into half of a hollow gourd, and put it to my lips. Just one sip, and I felt terrifically inflammable. 'Don't touch that stuff, man. I'd rather have a good bourbon,' the young man interrupted. Four hundred gallons of taffia are produced here a week; each gallon sells at $4. Monsieur Gaspard does not miss his days as a Brooklyn cabbie.

I declined the offer of a lift back to Jérémie and wandered around Marfranc until sunset. It was Wednesday, market day: *marchandes* were ferrying goods across the Grande Rivière on rafts, others were simply wading across the waters, baskets of mangoes balanced on their heads. Marfranc is dominated by the ruins of an English fort. In 1941 the Haitian-American Company for Agricultural Development plundered its stones to build houses for the workers it employed on rubber plantations. (The company survived for just four years, running roughshod over peasant proprietors, bulldozing Voodoo temples, paying in pittance.) Little remains of the fort save the dilapidated tomb of Laurent Ferou, one of the signatories of the Act of Haitian Independence, and a brace of rusted cannon nestled in the undergrowth beneath a blossoming mango tree. These bear the initials 'GR', George Rex.

British military involvement in Haiti opened on 19 September 1793 when a small force of about seven hundred grenadiers was sent from Jamaica to disembark at Jérémie. They were welcomed there by planters who had refused orders from the French government to free their slaves. The colonists declared fidelity to the British king and even made themselves British subjects. (George III had not yet liberated his own slaves over in Jamaica.) A few days later Môle St Nicolas, the great naval base commanding the Windward Passage between Saint Domingue and eastern Cuba, fell to the redcoats amid cries of *'Vive les Anglais!'*. Port-au-Prince surrendered to the British in June 1794. Within the space of nine months Great Britain had captured almost one third of France's richest colony.

To my knowledge the only legacy in Jérémie of the British occupation is an excellent drink, concocted from the skins of pineapple marinated in water, named 'Goodring'. This is reckoned to be a linguistic distortion of the words used by the redcoats on raising a glass of the nectar: 'Good drink'. Violette would occasionally prepare me this draught when I was lodging at the presbytery, laced with taffia for a nightcap. 'Giggle water', she called it.

The Haitians gained their freedom twenty-nine years before Britain freed its slaves and sixty years before the Civil War liberated the slaves in America. Yet there are no memorials in Jérémie to the heroes of Haitian independence. Brother René Gille, a Quebecois teacher at a Catholic school near L'Habitation Madère, told me: 'Nobody has ever heard of Alexandre Dumas in Port-au-Prince. On the other hand, there were many in Jérémie who chose to ignore Toussaint L'Ouverture and Jean-Jacques Dessalines.'

Perhaps this ignorance derives from the mulatto prejudice against these blacks. The nineteenth-century Haitian historian Guy-Joseph Bonnet referred to Toussaint as 'an ensign whose very presence was an incitement to hatred against the mulattoes'; Dessalines himself was merely the harbinger of 'disorder, waste, immorality and violence'. Thus Jérémie, traditional stronghold of the *métisses*, has over the years turned its back on Africa and looked towards France for suitable identity. A leather-bound history of the city – *Annales de la ville de Jérémie* – is now kept under lock and key by the patron of the dilapidated Restaurant Trois Dumas. The pages and cover had been attacked by insects, but the book gives an intriguing account of Jérémie at the turn of the century. The mulatto author, Axel Martineau, notes in exquisite handwriting how the city was once esteemed for her *'cachet de distinction raffinée'*: there was not a single mestizo family without a bottle of good French claret at every Sunday luncheon. Camembert, Roquefort, smoked Breton ham – the produce was shipped from Le Havre and Bordeaux to the 'Athens of Haiti', as the romantic Martineau rechristens his place of birth. Mulatto children were sent to Paris for their studies: boys to the Lycée Stanislas, girls to the Collège des Oiseaux. And during the fifty years before the US occupation of Haiti in 1915, Jérémie was host to consuls from Belgium, Germany, Chile, Colombia, Sweden, America and, of course, France.

A drowsy, paradisal capital of affluence and prosperity, Jérémie was also known in its heyday as the 'City of Poets'. Some of its inhabitants were quite good poets. Chief among them was Edmond La Forest who committed suicide in 1915 on the anniversary of Dessalines's assassination. (He weighted himself with two large Larousse dictionaries and jumped to a watery grave in the Grande Rivière.) La Forest is renowned today for the sonnets he composed in honour of such nineteenth-century deca-dents as Baudelaire (*'La Douleur est ton chat voluptueux et rare'*), Edgar Allan Poe and Arthur Rimbaud. His sonnets betray the influence of Hugo and Lamartine; they are very much *l'art pour l'art*, redolent of lilies, lilacs and lotuses – somewhat etiolated, but not without merit. La Forest was a mulatto of immense erudition, well read in the works of Goethe, Leopardi, Alexandre Dumas, Tennyson and Dostoevsky. The words which occur the most frequently in his sonnets – *'tristesse'*, *'crépuscule'*, *'douceur'* – speak of a Jérémie that is no longer. Of a vanished city.

What has become of the poets? The Reverend Father Pierre La Forest, a black great-grandson of the unfortunate Edmond, shook his head in sorrow: 'The Jérémie poets are all in their graves.' Then he made the sign of the cross after each of their names: Georges Lescouflair, Hamilton Garoute, Timothée Paret, Émile Roumer – all dead, may these poets rest in peace. Chain-smoking and somewhat dispirited, Father La Forest would lament the decline of Jérémie – *'C'est fini, fini, absolument fini'* – in rather theatrical terms: *'Terminé, terminé, complètement terminé.'* Then he would sigh, remove his spectacles and mop his face with an old handkerchief. Most evenings in Jérémie I would call on this elderly priest and we sat on the verandah of his house opposite a rusty petrol pump – one of the old style with a painted bubble head – talking until the sun went down behind the cathedral. Now and again Willy St Elmé would amble past in knickerbockers or a crumpled pinstriped suit, a mess of nerves. 'I loved my mother from the bottom of my heart,' shouting at the air. 'But now she is in paradise where it is good to be alive. Take good care in your life, my friends!'

It emerged that Father La Forest was fiercely against the 'Coca-Cola plague', an expression he used to describe the encroachment of American values in Jérémie. Much of this country, it is true, appears more Yankee than Gallic, the shelves of shops lined with boxes of breakfast cereal – Captain Crunch All Star Baseball Clubs – and plastic bottles of Dream Whip Topping, or Hickory Smoke Barbecue Sauce. La Forest was further saddened by the waning popularity of such *chansonniers* from an earlier generation as Maurice Chevalier, Tino Rossi, Nelson Eddy – even Mireille Mathieu; now there are only kung-fu or pornographic films, he complained. Still worse: Creole, that 'barbarous idiolect', had replaced *'un bon français authentique et littéraire'*.

La Forest blamed Baby Doc for this linguistic regression. In 1979 the dictator decreed that Creole should become the official language in Haitian schools; and he employed philologists from the United States to standardize a synthetic orthography. These men patched together a phonetic system of Creole quite antipathetic to written French, with an ugly proliferation of the letter K. Thus 'Jesus Christ' became *'jezikri'*; 'cœur', *'ke'*; 'bourrique', *'burik'*; 'sucre', *'siki'*. And so forth.

'The Americans have made us infants with no language but a cry,' Father La Forest murmured with indignation. 'Pidgin has become the mother tongue of our community, and this will only render us more insular.' He remarked on how there was little illiteracy in Martinique or Guadeloupe, where French is still the approved language in schools. The American distortion of Creole was apparently motivated by politics: to gain control over the language of a people is to gain control of their country. The lexicographers from the US Evangelical Press who compiled the booklet *Speak Creole in No Time and Get a Little Taste of Haitian Culture!* ask us to translate into Haitian idiom such revealing sentences as 'You are Washington's children' and 'Voodoo is bad. There is only one God.' Indoctrination is perhaps too strong a word – but there is an insidious sort of tutelage at work.

Haitian Creole nevertheless remains a language based on French – albeit a simplified, corrupted and elided French. It incorporates some words of Breton, a scattering of the aboriginal dialects still lingering on Hispaniola at the time of Columbus, a little Spanish, and more than a little English together with a few words of African origin. Despite the American orthography, Creole is still a lively and rumbustious idiom, rich in salty witticisms and homespun proverbs. French is moreover unintelligible to eighty per cent of the Haitian people: away from the principal towns it is no more useful than English. For two months now I had endeavoured to learn Creole: 'He that travelleth into a country before he hath some entrance into the language, goeth to school, and not to travel,' proclaimed Sir Francis Bacon.

Sometimes I felt that the Reverend Father La Forest was a little harsh on his country. He would even curse the boxes of Haitian matches which had long ago replaced the *allumettes* from France. *'Finalement!'* he exclaimed as the unreliable match flared on the tenth scratch. *'C'est fini, fini, absolument fini . . .'*

La Forest was regarded by the younger priests at the presbytery as something of an eccentric. But I felt a twinge of sympathy for his grumblings: one day I noticed a young man reclining Byronically on a tombstone in the cemetery at Jérémie. A poet himself, I had imagined. But no, he was immersed in an American comic strip: 'PLAFF! SPLATTT! UGHHH!' – every page articulated violence. *'Eh blanc!'* He moved aggressively towards me. *'Donnez-moi un smoke, blanc!'* Often I could spend a whole afternoon dispensing Comme il Fauts.

Emile Roumer died in Germany in 1989. Much admired by the American critic Edmund Wilson, Roumer was perhaps the only poet from Jérémie who could lay claim to greatness. Like Edmond La Forest before him, Roumer was influenced by classical French models, although he also came under the spell of surrealism. Far less a francophile than La Forest, Roumer celebrated the 'beauty' of the black women of Haiti and scorned the mannerisms of the mulattoes into whose class he was born. Roumer's *Poèmes d'Haïti et de France*, published in 1925, is a peculiarly sensual collection – and sometimes comic, as in the poem 'A Peasant Declares His Love':

> High-yellow of my heart, with breasts like tangerines,
> you taste better to me than aubergine stuffed with crab,
> you are the tripe in my pepper-pot,
> the dumpling in my peas, my tea of aromatic herbs.
> You are the corned beef whose customhouse is my heart . . .

Roumer came from a Franco-Haitian family of nine brothers. Only one survives and I met him in Jérémie. Antoine Roumer was then an eighty-year-old mestizo almost white in complexion; he lived in a shack behind the presbytery with his mulatta wife, her skin the colour of gall speckled with liver spots. Antoine resembled the late Samuel Beckett, with his crop of spiky, gunmetal-grey hair and sunken cheeks. He wore a white vest and a pair of khaki trousers flecked with paint. Like his brother Emile, Antoine was educated in both France and England. He disliked Port-au-Prince: 'It's more like Port-au-Crime', he echoed the words of the nineteenth-century Haitian president Louis Pierrot. For two years in his late teens Antoine lodged with a family in Birmingham, and still kept the books which they had presented him as gifts: *Maud, and other Poems* by Tennyson, Swinburne's *Songs before Sunrise*, the volumes wrapped in brown paper.

> 'Is it worth a tear, is it worth an hour,
> To think of things that are well outworn . . .?'

Antoine was still able to recite by heart numerous of the roundels, burlesques and ballads by Swinburne. His wife would usually intervene to put an end to these effusions but he blithely ignored her irritation:

> '. . . Of fruitless husk and fugitive flower,
> The dream forgone and the deed forborne . . .?'

The lines were proclaimed with majestic and eloquent gestures of the hands.

As a girl Madame Roumer was sent to the Paris Collège des Oiseaux. She described how the voyage from Jérémie to France took a minimum of twenty days. The ship would call at the Haitian harbours of Saint Marc, Port-de-Paix and Cap-Haïtien, then at Puerto Plata in the Dominican Republic, San Juan in Puerto Rico and finally at Le Havre. Both husband and wife remembered the names of the old shipping lines: the Hamburg-American, Panama and Atlas, the Compagnie Générale Transatlantique. The ships would berth every month at Jérémie laden with English cloth ('Ah yes, *twill* I think it was called,' Antoine said), perfumes, soap, butter and salt meat; they would then weigh anchor with a cargo of coffee, tortoiseshell, beeswax, goatskins and cocoa.

'Gone, all gone.' Monsieur and Madame Roumer sat on their rocking chairs in the deepening twilight. 'Trade with France, gone, all gone. *Jérémie était le jour, maintenant ç'est la nuit.'* Today the Roumers run a threadbare chemist's at 22 Grande Rue, down the road from Guerdes Gaspard. To my knowledge, they were virtually the only mulattoes still living in Jérémie. What had become of the others, in this city of twenty-two thousand inhabitants? I discovered the truth one week later, and it frightened.

In December 1945 André Breton became instrumental in the overthrow of a Haitian dictator. The grand old magus of French surrealism arrived at Port-au-Prince to deliver a series of lectures in praise of African animist religions, and within a fortnight the autocratic regime of the mulatto president Elie Lescot had collapsed. The lectures were attended for the most part by an audience of middle-class blacks affiliated to the intellectual movement known as *Noirisme*. This had been founded during the years of the American occupation as a reaction against the Frenchified pretensions of the mulatto caste, and as a return to the roots of Africa: Senegal, Dahomey, the Congo. Jean-Paul Sartre would later define this movement, somewhat pretentiously, as the 'descent of the black man into the hell of his soul to retrieve his Eurydice'. It was more simply an attempt to return dignity to those millions of Haitians descended from African slaves.

The doyen of the Négritude movement was the Haitian ethnologist Dr Jean Price Mars. In his classic book *Thus Spake the Uncle* (1928), he enjoined his countrymen to *'Plongez vos baquets!'* (Cast down your buckets) into the rich resources of Haitian folklore and celebrate Voodoo as their true religion. No book gives so detailed or eloquent a study of the religious syncretisms of the New World – Candomblé in the Brazilian hinterland, Schango and Yoruba in Trinidad – but Dr Mars concludes with an entreaty to the blacks of Haiti to destroy the cultural and political hegemony of the mulattoes: Papa Doc would later take this message to heart, with horrific effect.

Consulting the yellowing newspaper held in the Institut de St Louis de Gonzague (always a cool haven from the noonday sun in Port-au-Prince), I discovered that André Breton was greeted by Haitian intellectuals as Dr Jean Price Mars resurrected. One paper conducted a solemn interview with the Frenchman – 4 December 1945 – under the banner headline *'GRAND-PRETRE DU SURREALISME CONTRE TOUTES LES FORMES D'IMPERIALISME ET DE BRIGANDAGE BLANCS!'*

The journalist asks: 'Eminent and Distinguished Ambassador of Surrealism, tell us about your first impressions of Haiti.' To which the courteous Breton replies: 'Please take it into account that I have scarcely got off the aeroplane.'

Behind his lectern in face of the assembled *Noiristes*, Breton commended the savage state that Rousseau had sought in the heart of the Alps, and which Chateaubriand had found in the virgin forests of North America, as regions free from the 'pernicious forces of society'. He urged his audience to embrace the aboriginal cult of Voodoo as a means to overcome poverty and political oppression. The result was electric; within hours student demonstrations spilled on to the streets of Port-au-Prince, calling for the overthrow of President Lescot and for the substitution of a black administration. Following a general strike, a committee of public safety was formed and Lescot quietly left the country. It has been said that this was the only political action which Breton's revolutionary pronouncements ever provoked.

Papa Doc was in his late thirties at the time of the Breton affair, a softly spoken and introverted doctor of medicine. He had been a regular contributor to the anti-European, pro-black newspaper *Action Nationale*, and wrote his column under the fanciful pseudonym Abderrahman. Perhaps this was the first sign of grandiose delusion: the pen-name derived from Abd-al-Rahman, eighth emir and first caliph who founded the medical school of Cordoba in the tenth century. The young François Duvalier attacked the mulattoes as a 'useless élite, bloated with pride, stupid and imbecile'. In 1938 he became involved with a movement known as *Les Griots*, a Guinean word meaning praise-singer or magician. The group mingled literary and ethnological interests in honour of Haiti's African past, glorifying Voodoo and the vanished splendours of Sudanese civilizations. In numerous poems, many of them incomprehensible, the future president portrayed the fate of the black man dominated by the values of Europe:

I then remembered the route crossed by my ancestors of distant Africa –
The sons of the jungle
Whose bones during the 'centuries of starry silence'
Have helped to build the pyramids.
And I continued on my way, now with heavy heart,
In the night.
I walked on and on and on
Straight ahead.
And the black of my ebony skin was lost
In the shadows of the night.

When elected President of Haiti in 1957, Abderrahman alias Papa Doc began to incorporate the *Noiriste* values of Dr Mars and others into a political doctrine. This sought to explain the history of Haiti in terms of racial struggle: the heroes of independence were exclusively black; yet the mulattoes, François Duvalier reasoned with some justification, were now the acknowledged rulers of the country. Under Papa Doc, Dessalines therefore became the true symbol of Haiti. Streets and cigarettes were christened after him; a memorial of variegated jasper and polished marble was erected to him in the grounds of the National Palace. His brutalities were forgiven and forgotten: in Papa Doc's 1968 *Bréviaire d'une Révolution*, an imitation of the Little Red Book by Chairman Mao distributed gratis among the illiterate peasants, Dessalines is even upheld as 'the first socialist of Haiti'.

A masterpiece of delirious nonsense in which Papa Doc appears as 'the wild black slave in search of the pure rays of the radiant sun', this collection of political maxims nevertheless shows how unwise it would have been, in those days, to express discontent with the cult of Dessalines. 'You would have been strung from a lamp-post or worse,' the great mulatto historian Alain Tournier told me in Port-au-Prince one day. Monsieur Tournier, a frail man with rimless glasses and fastidious manner, had just published a book – *Quand la Nation Demande des Comptes* – which accused Dessalines of 'tyrannical violence and massive corruption'. He was a little fearful of how it might be received among the surviving *Noiristes*, many of whom were still Duvalierists.

The Bureau of Ethnology at Port-au-Prince was founded in 1941 to preserve the cult of Voodoo. One day I met the Director, Dr Max Paul, in his office there. He was a bearded, enormous Haitian in the middle forties – very black, and built like a heavyweight. 'Who are you?' he asked, his eyes steady and penetrating, the huge flat hands placed next to a Voodoo fetish on the desk in front of him. 'Show me your identification.' I presented my *laisser-passer*.

Dr Paul photocopied the document and threw it across the desk. 'What's your business here?'

'I just want to ask a few questions, about Haiti.'

He seemed extremely suspicious of me and was one of the most difficult men I had so far met in Haiti. In response to whether Voodoo was ever entangled with black magic he said this:

'Voodoo is no more sinister than your cryptic supposition of transubstantiation. White Christians! They only come to Haiti to satisfy a banal curiosity about such matters.'

Dr Paul glanced at a lurid painting of African slaves ironed together by some colonial overseer, and then at the old-fashioned cavalry sabre resting on his desk. Fancifully, I cast him in the role of the dastardly Mr Big, chairman of the Black Widow Voodoo cult in Ian Fleming's *Live and Let Die*. Dr Paul looked a good six foot tall.

Was Papa Doc a racialist? The dictator would often quote the words of Alfred Rosenberg, chief ideologist of the Nazis, when defending the supremacy of black Haitians. And much of his rhetoric in the days when he was a member of the Bureau of Ethnology recalled the European Fascist movement: 'redemption of the black masses', Dessalines as 'saviour of the nation's soul'. Pictures of François Duvalier emblazoned with the Nietzschean words *Ecce Homo* became familiar to those who visited Haiti in the late 1960s.

Dr Paul said, sharply: 'Racialist? I don't know what you mean. This is merely a colonial prejudice on the part of Europeans. We are here to enter into communion with the souls of our distant Mandingo and Bantu ancestors.'

I then asked Dr Paul about the curious titles which Papa Doc had awarded himself in 1964, namely 'Professor of energy and Napoleonic electrifier of souls'.

'So you find this odd?' He hesitated.

'A little odd, yes.'

Then he added quickly, in a different manner: 'You have understood nothing about Haiti.'

As I left the Bureau of Ethnology I noticed a copy of Jean Genet's play *The Blacks* by Dr Paul's desk. It contains lines which might have been written by Papa Doc at the height of his *Noirisme*: 'Dahomey! Dahomey! Negroes from all corners of the earth, negrify yourselves! Sulking Africa, wrought of iron in the fire, I call you back this evening to attend a secret revel.'

Three weeks later I found that Dr Max Paul's office had been ransacked by students in the wake of President Avril's departure. Dr Paul's brother, Colonel Jean-Claude, was himself a notorious Duvalierist and practitioner of *wanga*, or black magic. He was moreover the head of the Dessalines Barracks in Port-au-Prince where Papa Doc tortured enemies. Colonel Jean-Claude Paul died mysteriously early in 1988 after eating pumpkin soup. There was a suspicion that he had been poisoned, as he reportedly ran Haiti's cocaine trans-shipment business and may have crossed swords with General Avril, himself no stranger to the Medellín cocaine cartel. According to the US Drug Enforcement Administration, Colonel Paul was the linchpin connecting the Colombian wholesalers with the jobbers who turned the big brown shipments into the little white packages that retailers in New York and Miami sold for billions. With Paul dead, Avril became the undisputed drugman of Haiti. 'He was one of the most corrupt figures in the entire Haitian armed forces,' the British vice-consul in Port-au-Prince told me, 'and profited from every racket in the country.'

Among the more unusual manifestations of *Noirisme* during the fourteen years of Papa Doc's dictatorship was his transformation of the national flag. The horizontal bands of blue and red were replaced by vertical ones of red and black, the black closest to the mast to symbolize that the Negroes, and not the mulattoes, were now in control of Haiti. In *Graham*

Greene Démasqué – Finally Exposed (that strange pamphlet published by Papa Doc's Department of Foreign Affairs to discredit Greene and his motives for writing *The Comedians*), Haiti is now upheld as 'the promoter of liberty in the New World', a 'proud nation led by the Dessalinian ideal of survival in DIGNITY' whose people 'wrote one of the most beautiful pages in the history of the Negro race'. The country, though, is maligned on all sides by racialists and imperialists – the worst of them being Graham Greene, 'the shame of proud and noble England', no better than a 'colonial slave-driver' harbouring 'some delirious dream of conquest'. The rhetoric is paranoid ('We have been warned that Mr Greene was some sort of private detective'), but one cannot doubt the sincerity of Papa Doc. He clearly believed himself to be a crusader in the battle for black solidarity, and named two streets in Port-au-Prince after his great heroes: Martin Luther King and Haile Selassie.

The day Papa Doc changed the national flag – 22 May 1964 – was the day the last French ship ever sailed to Jérémie. By that time, however, the dictator had ordered the massacre of virtually the entire mulatto population in the city.

A bell was rung every morning at six in the presbytery, to signal that breakfast was ready. I was usually woken an hour before by the hum of seminarians intoning prayers in the chapel beneath my room, or by a baying of mules from the vegetable allotment. Breakfast consisted of bread rolls and peanut butter, coffee, grapefruit juice and boiled eggs. The fare had become less frugal now that Bishop Willy Romélus had departed for the United States on some matter of religious protocol. The conversation in the refectory was also more animated. It often revolved round the subject of the Mormon Church, which has extensive real-estate holdings in Haiti.

'These Mormons, they are racialists!' complained young Father Samedi (no relation to Baron Samedi). 'How dare they claim that Negroes shall only be *servants* when they reach the Celestial Heaven, and not gods as white Mormons are privileged to be.'

Father Antoine said, 'CIA, that's what they are. The Book of Mormon, I am told, is translated from reformed Egyptian hieroglyphics written by the hand of Abraham – can you imagine! – but it is really a cipher for espionage. The Mormons are everywhere.'

That much was true. I would often see Mormons walking in pairs along the Grande Rue of Jérémie, polyester-suited evangelists with cropped hair and Plasti-Coat name cards pinned to their lapels. They did not merge very well with the natives, clutching copies of *The Pearl of Great Price*, the sacred scripture of their religion.

One day I struck up conversation with two Mormons – the Elders Walsh and Cumming – while having my hair cut by Monsieur Célestin Excellent, chief barber to Jérémie since 1962. One after the other we sat on a high, old-fashioned black leather swivel chair, talking as blond hair fell to the floor amid woolly curls shorn from the heads of Haitians.

'Well whaddeya know! So you're gonna write a book about Hay-di, huh? Boy, that's a tough one, real tough. For a start, you got the Voodoo. Man, that can really put the whammy on a guy.'

'The what?'

'Elder Walsh's talking about the evil spirits abroad at night,' explained Elder Cumming from Las Vegas. 'Gotta watch out for them, with the dark-skinned thousands all around you. Yes sir, you gotta watch out for the *spirits*.'

'It was a real shocker, when they told me I was gonna be posted to Hay-di. Didn't even know where the place was, let alone that it was a . . . Black Republic. I figured there might be Red Indians here, or like a variety of Hispanic folk. But *blacks*? No-o sir.'

As missionaries in the Church of Jesus Christ of Latter-Day Saints, Mormons are here to prepare the people for the Grand Millennium. ('You never know when it's gonna happen,' said Elder Walsh. 'The Second Coming, I mean. But we're waiting, we're ready.') Servants of the Lord, they feel it their duty to dress with becoming moderation – 'We are not here to swim or ride motorbikes or drink alcohol' – and are proud to announce that no single convert to Mormonism will ever revert to Voodoo. Anyone foolish enough to believe that Mormons work in concert with the CIA has not, in the words of Elders Walsh and Cumming, 'been converted to the True Faith.'

American missions are to be found everywhere in Haiti: Larry Jones's Hands of God Ministries, Mission to Haiti Inc., Mission Possible . . . There are Baptists, Methodists, Jehovah's Witnesses, Seventh-Day Adventists. All are devoted to the extirpation of Voodoo and scorn this religion in much the way that Dr Johnson scorned the ideal of Rousseu's Noble Savage: 'The savages have no bodily advantages beyond those of civilized men. They have not better health; and as to care or mental uneasiness, they are not above it, but below it, like bears.'

The Eglise Baptiste Conservatrice of Pastor Wallace Turnbull, built half a century ago in the green hills above Port-au-Prince, is particularly virulent in its missionary preachments. 'The Haitian people are caught in Satan's grip,' says pastor Wally in his Middle American twang. 'Voodoo divides with mistrust, requires unnatural acts.'

Two hundred and fifty baptized Haitians work for Pastor Wally and his mission, tilling the fields in return for food, rarely for dollars. This Food-for-Work programme is typical of US missionary endeavour in Haiti. It conserves money for the evangelists and has enabled Pastor Wally to run the Mountain Maid Gift Shop (where one may purchase embroidered garments as well as hamburgers, French fries and peanut-butter cookies). Thus Haitians become dependent on food supplied by Christian aid agencies, usually imported from the United States, and neglect to produce their own. In small, self-sufficient communities such as exist on the islands around Haiti, there is a danger that the land may run to fallow.

Monsieur Excellent's *salon coiffeur* was piled with large boxes of dried milk 'Fortified with Vitamin D and Furnished by the People of the United States of America'. Sellotaped to the wall were faded photographs of the White House and Buckingham Palace, torn no doubt from a travel brochure. It was a miserable barber's. The electric razor kept sparking and glowing luminous green beneath its Bakelite casing; the Mormons told me there had sometimes been electrocutions from a misconducted voltage.

'I'd'a been killed one time,' Elder Cumming dimly smiled. 'Had the Lord not intervened to save me.'

'Five dollars.' Monsieur Excellent wildly exaggerated the fee.

'Five gourdes you mean!' I pointed to the list of prices framed above the White House. Clearly, it read:

BARBE ELECTRONIQUE,	3.50 GOURDES
BARBE SIMPLE,	2.50 GOURDES
CHEVEUX,	5.00 GOURDES

'No, no. It's five gourdes for children,' the barber lied.

'So that list is for children, not for adults?'

'For children only,' he said briskly.

'So there are children in Jérémie with beards who get an electric shave for three gourdes fifty?'

'*Bien sûr, m'sieur.*'

* * *

The Mormons later invited me to church. 'We'd be mighty proud to have you. Whaddeya say?'

'OK.'

'Ian, you're a Christian gentleman.'

I could almost pass for a Mormon now, with my hair shorn close to the skull like an urchin's.

'L'Eglise de Jesus Christ des Saints des Derniers Jours (Salt Lake City, Utah)', proclaimed a placard outside a converted warehouse on the Grande Rue. It was April Fool's Day and the Mormon church was packed with converts to Joseph Smith Junior, the superstitious mystic from Vermont who laid down the rudiments of Mormonism in 1830, before he was shot dead some fourteen years later by a lynch mob in Illinois.

The service was the lectern-pounding share-it-brother stuff of Bible Belt religious communities. For two hours we were required to sing dismal hymns in anticipation of the Second Coming written by Mormons with names like Ebeneezer Beesley and George Careless. Elder Cumming stood on a dais before the assembled Haitians, and drilled them on the evils of marital infidelity. *'TU NE COMMETTRAIS PAS D'ADULTÈRE!'*: he chalked these words from the Book of Exodus on to a blackboard and asked the congregation to repeat them, over and again.

Heads turned in the pews as an old man stumbled into church incapably drunk. I had seen him before, dispensing sweets to children from the back of a battered pick-up. 'Saint-Ange Bontemps, *assassin!*' A woman sitting next to me whispered his name. Father Samedi at the presbytery had told me how this Bontemps was a notorious Macoute, rumoured to have sanctioned the murder of countless mulattoes in 1964.

'Do you think I could talk to him?' I had asked the priest.

'I shouldn't even try,' came the answer.

The drunkard lurched to an empty space in the pews and collapsed there with his head hung low. The congregation ignored him and raised their voices, ever louder, in hymn. As if to say: there will be no Celestial Kingdom for Saint-Ange Bontemps.

Locked in four-wheel drive the jeep gripped the road as it dipped almost vertically into streams and up the other side over bedrock and thick riverine mud. Father Samedi made the sign of the cross as we ploughed like an amphibious tractor through the toad-green waters round a mangrove swamp. There was a nasty stench of marsh gas. 'Nearly there.' The priest was familiar with the road. Arrived at Jérémie airport and the land became quite arid, snarled with gorse and bramble. More a prairie of burnt grass than an airport – lozenged here and there with flat stones. It has been closed to airborne traffic since the massacres of 1964 – *'L'Année Terrible,'* said Father Samedi.

We clambered out of the jeep and walked across the disused runway, my trousers and Father Samedi's cassock spattered with mud. This was hallowed land: some two hundred mulattoes lie buried here, they say, in shallow graves. We had to climb over barbed-wire fencing to reach the monument which Bishop Romélus had established in their memory. It was a simple upright slab of white marble, graced with a vase of wilted flowers. There was no inscription, as the memorial had been erected only a month before with money donated by relatives of the murdered mulattoes. Father Samedi knelt in prayer. Not a sound. Wisps of woodsmoke drifted by: someone was burning charcoal.

These massacres were the horrific outcome of several attempts to overthrow Papa Doc. The night of 28 July 1958 saw the first and most serious of these attempts which, in its buffoonish absurdity, almost succeeded. A group of mulatto former officers, together with several US mercenaries and three ex-deputy sheriffs from Miami and Buffalo, disembarked from a motor launch at Mont Rouis opposite the island of La Gonâve. Posing as tourists, the rebels were offered a variety of straw hats to buy as they quietly began to unload their cache of weapons. A peasant, however, managed to alert the local *chef de section* who soon arrived in a jeep with a patrol of three Macoutes. A skirmish ensued in which the policeman and his party were shot and left for dead. The invaders stole their jeep and sped towards Port-au-Prince. When the vehicle broke down at the town of Arcahaie the rebels commandeered a tap-tap and forced the terrified driver to help transfer their weapons from jeep to bus. Dressed in the khaki uniforms of Haitian soldiers, the invaders drove into the capital where, bluffing their way past military guards, they managed to seize the Dessalines Barracks adjacent to the National Palace.

The army were by now dimly aware of the situation; but they had not expected the invasion to arrive by tap-tap. The bus was painted with the legend: 'In Spite of All, God is the Only Master'.

Having overpowered the sleeping soldiers, the rebels began to make telephone calls from within the barracks, informing various commanders that they had taken control. They then telephoned Papa Doc and told him the game was up. Surrender, or else. The President of the Republic panicked, packed his bags and prepared his exit via the Colombian embassy.

As dawn broke, however, the extent of the invasion became apparent when one of the rebel mulattoes developed a craving for a cigarette and sent a hostage to buy a packet of his favourite brand. A fatal mistake. The captive soldier was grabbed and taken before the Minister of the Interior, who then relayed the news to Papa Doc that there were only eight invaders in the barracks.

The palace issued guns to anyone who would take them, including shoeshine boys. At the height of the fighting, behind a hail of bullets and grenades, one of the hostages accidentally rocked his chair backwards through an open barracks window and fell into the street unscathed. This gave encouragement to the Tontons Macoute who now redoubled their fire and stormed the building. The former Haitian captain, Alix Pasquet, was killed when a grenade blew away the back of his head; the mulatto fell face upward looking towards a photograph of Papa Doc hanging on the wall. The picture was pierced by a bullet hole. Within minutes the farcical invasion was over and all eight were dead, their mutilated bodies paraded triumphantly through the streets of Port-au-Prince and brought before the dictator in the National Palace.

Later that day Papa Doc was photographed by the national press in military fatigues and steel helmet, brandishing a Colt .45. Anti-aircraft guns were installed on the lawn in front of the palace. A neon sign in the Champ de Mars proclaimed: 'I Am the Haitian Flag, One and Indivisible. François Duvalier'.

The plotting, invasions and retribution continued until the summer of 1964 when a group of thirteen mulatto aristocrats invaded the south-western town of Dame Marie, not far from Jérémie, hoping to incite an insurrection. They belonged to a movement called the Camoquins after the name of an anti-malarial pill in Haiti; the rebels hoped to provide an effectual antidote to the disease that was killing the country – Duvalierism. Hitherto, the details of both the invasion and its terrible aftermath have not been fully revealed. What follows is the result of several interviews I conducted with people living in Jérémie at the time of the massacres, many of whom were fearful of talking because of possible retribution from former Tontons Macoute. Father Pierre La Forest kindly lent me the draft of a book which he hoped to publish one day about the events of 1964. It is entitled *Un Bain de Sang* and I am grateful to the priest for his permission to use the information. 'Before I die I'd like to see that *all* the assassins are brought to justice,' La Forest told me one evening. 'The entire mulatto side of my family was massacred.'

The Camoquins fought government forces for eighty-three days, equipped with MI rifles, revolvers and grenades. They held out in the hills around Jérémie near General Dumas's house, paying for food with crisp dollar notes which they had brought with them from exile in America. Any peasants found in possession of this money were summarily executed by the Tontons Macoute – many were garotted. Entire families were arrested simply for having supplied the rebels with cigarettes. Planes and helicopters were flown from Port-au-Prince to land at Jérémie airport, where they disgorged policemen, majors, prefects and paramilitary *chefs de section*. The notorious Duvalierist Colonel Williams Régala, chief of the military academy (his motto: 'Many people don't know when their rights stop'), was among them.

Most of the rebels had been born in Jérémie. Here was the chance for Papa Doc the *Noiriste* to implement what Father La Forest terms the 'final solution against the mulattoes'. He ordered his militia to terrify the mestizo inhabitants of the city – the implication being that all mulattoes in Haiti were set against the government, and blacks were not exempt. Prosper Auguste, now a sixty-year-old black professor of Latin and French, described a nightmare he suffered on the eve of the reprisals. 'I dreamed that Jérémie had become a ghost town. Everything was draped in black, in black shrouds, as though we had been visited by some terrible plague.'

I met Professor Auguste in his shack near the Cathedral of St Louis at Jérémie where he lived alone. The sordid isolation of his lodgings – a rattan mat for a bed on the cold stone floor – was in part the result of his anti-Duvalierism. He had never pandered to the authorities. The professor lit another cigarette with his old liquid-fuel Zippo, 'Then a very beautiful mulatta came to me in my dream, so beautiful that she was known I think as *le bijoux du palais*. She told me to place a bouquet of roses on the tomb of my godmother. When I awoke the next morning I considered this dream rather banal, and thought no more of it.'

The following evening, Professor Auguste had gone for a walk and seen that the streets were overrun by Tontons Macoute. They announced through megaphones that thirteen rebels had disembarked at Dame Marie to bring down the government. Then sirens wailed and soldiers careered round the city in jeeps, yelling *'Couvre feu!'* – curfew! There was a sharp crackle of automatic fire. 'Where to run?' The professor remembered the panic. 'To the tobacconists? To the newsagents? . . . Then I recalled my dream and hurried to the cathedral where I spent two gourdes on roses which I placed on my godmother's tomb in the cemetery here. I don't know why, but I felt that something awful was going to happen in Jérémie that night.'

When Professor Auguste arrived home, his wife confirmed: *'Il y aura une grande carnage ce soir.'* She had heard that Papa Doc had ordered the arrest and execution of all mulatto families related to the rebels. Husband and wife jammed a chest of drawers against their front door and placed a machete beneath the pillow. Over a period of two months some twenty-seven families were exterminated. 'We were not allowed to mourn the deaths,' writes Father La Forest. 'Even if the Pope had given us divine dispensation to do so.' There was complete censorship of news: in Haiti only those who were able to pick up Radio Havana or Radio Moscow had any idea of the massacres. Cultivated, European-educated mulattoes were rounded up at night, stripped naked and forced to walk down the Grande Rue in handcuffs where they endured the jeers of Duvalierists. Herded along to the Jérémie barracks, they were pushed into open trucks and driven to the airport for execution. The Tontons Macoute dispatched their victims with relish: infants and little children were killed first (hurled into the air and skewered on the points of bayonets) to inflame their parents; and then the women, to inflame their husbands. 'It was like the Saint Bartholemew Day Massacres, the Sicilian Vespers,' notes the priest in his manuscript.

Father La Forest gives the names of several families slaughtered in 1964: the Drouins, the Villedrouins, the Guilbauds. He estimates that some four hundred mulattoes died in the massacres; all twelve members of the Sansaricq family – a child of two and a paralysed grandmother among them – were murdered in a single evening. (Madame Pierre Sansaricq's nightgown is now preserved in the presbytery 'like the Turin shroud', a seminarian told me.) From behind the barricaded door of their house, Prosper Auguste and his wife heard the cries of those condemned to death. 'One night we listened in horror as a woman began to chant the hymn they sang as the *Titanic* went down: *"Plus près de toi, mon Dieu"*. It was very distant, borne to us on the breeze. But I knew it was the voice of Madame Victor Villedrouins, for she had sung with me many times in the cathedral choir at St Louis. But now she was on her way to the airport, on the back of a lorry with her children . . . She had a beautiful voice.' I stared at Prosper Auguste. Tears came to his eyes. 'No, no.' The professor gestured for me to sit down as I fumbled to take my leave. 'Stay, a little longer.' He took a deep breath and tamped out his cigarette on a kitchen plate.

'The great houses belonging to the murdered mulattoes were afterwards thrown open to sack,' Prosper Auguste went on, grimly. 'Then the Tontons Macoute moved in to pillage and plunder.' Fine French silver, leather-bound books, clothes, furniture, even photographs were heaped in the market square and sold by *marchandes* – many of them married to the assassins – for a pittance. 'They made great bonfires of private libraries,' said the professor. 'If only I'd had a little money at the time, I would have bought those books and kept them for posterity.' The Sansaricq house, a nineteenth-century gingerbread, was gutted and converted into a *caserne des forces paramilitaires*.

The cycle of revenge came to a gruesome end when two of the rebels were captured alive, and sent to Port-au-Prince. After weeks of torture, they were executed at the National Cemetery in a televised ceremony attended by crowds of children whom Papa Doc had ordered to be brought from the schools. Leaflets were distributed to these children like programmes at a football match: 'Thus will perish the antipatriots who wish once more to submit the Haiti of Jean-Jacques Dessalines to the whip of the colonials. No force will stop the invincible march of the Duvalierist Revolution . . .'

The old Breton priest sat drinking brandy on the verandah of his house by the presbytery, the floorboards creaking like the beams of a ship under his rocking chair. Father Jean Roussel of the Franciscan Order of St Jacques had lived in Jérémie for some thirty-five years. 'I came here on the twelfth of October 1954, just two days before Hurricane Hazel, and I've not left since.' He had seen many changes for the worse. 'Jérémie used to be the most respectable place in all Haiti.' The Breton poured himself another brandy and continued in his guttural dialect. 'Men would be out on the streets sweeping away rubbish at *four* in the morning. So one day I asked a peasant why he didn't sweep away human beings as well. A joke, you understand. And this man replied, *"Non, mon père. Les hommes sont trop sales,"* men are too dirty . . . Now of course the rubbish is everywhere. You can't move for the dirt. Jérémie is finished. The mulattoes left years ago.'

Father Roussel could only walk with the support of aluminium-frame crutches but he was still agile in mind; when I asked about the massacres of 1964 he ceased rocking in his chair and craned towards me, forearms resting on the crutches. 'I am one of those who witnessed *all*. I know everything . . . But there are secrets which must accompany me to the grave. A priest is not made to divide people, but to provide forgiveness.'

He raised a finger heavenwards. 'Only God, *le Bon Dieu*, will decide which of the assassins must pay for their deeds.'

'Did you know just how many mulattoes were being executed?'

'No. I rarely went out at night in those days. Even with a *laisser-passer* it was too dangerous.'

For a moment the priest said nothing; then, with a little suppressed sigh: 'If I had known the terrible extent of the massacres, my conscience would have driven me to implore the President to put an end to them, although it would have meant certain death for me. I did not even know that the airport was the place of execution.'

I found this difficult to believe. Perhaps Father Roussel had been compromised in his duties by the fear of retribution. Then he said, 'The memory of 1964 will never fade. They say women were buried alive in front of their husbands, wrapped screaming in sheets and held down in a shallow grave. But I know everything, the most guilty, everyone.'

'Who?'

The Breton would not be coaxed into revealing names; he was playing games with me. 'It's past my time for bed. I am very tired.' I shook his hand and began to walk back in the direction of the presbytery. *'Monsieur!'* Father Roussel beckoned for me to come back. He had begun rocking in the chair again, under the glow of a storm lantern suspended from his porch.

'What is it?'

'The most guilty . . . I want to tell you that the most guilty are still living. Here, in Jérémie.'

'Saint-Ange Bontemps?'

'I think you already know enough.'

On my last night in Jérémie I took Willy St Elmé for supper at a makeshift canteen near the port. It was a rough location, crammed with stevedores from the *Neptune* who were ladling fried pork and rice out of steaming cauldrons. Willy looked a little conspicuous in plus-fours and bow tie. Professor Auguste confided that Willy's mental instability was as much the result of Vietnam as of those terrible nights in 1964, when half the St Elmé family also disappeared. We ate beneath the eager eyes of urchins who had gathered to laugh at Willy, now rheumy-eyed with rum. 'We are many miles from the White House tonight, my friend, but I have a big appetite,' Willy gnawed hungrily on a piece of fish and spat the bones on to the floor. 'Excuse me.' He blew his nose on a paisley handkerchief and then accidentally flipped the ash-tip of his cheroot into my bowl of rice. 'I will kiss you all the night long, my friend.' Willy had become quite lachrymose. 'I am going to love you in the evening and in the morning too because you are a good singer like Tom Jones.'

'I'm leaving Jérémie tomorrow, Willy.'

'Aha! So let me make you a present of my tie. It is de luxe drip-dry from a very good tailor's in the United States of the American country,' he exclaimed with an odd weariness. 'Then you will remember Willy from the City of Poets where the Vietnamese people are watching him.'

'Goodbye, Willy.'

Saint-Ange Bontemps was lying drunk in the middle of the Grande Rue, outside the Mormon church. I walked back to the presbytery on the other side of the road from his body. In the good old days they say Bontemps kept a direct telephone line to Papa Doc at the National Palace.

Bontemps lived ten minutes away from Father Roussel on Avenue Emile Roumer. Some nights earlier I had called on him armed with a bottle of rum in the cynical belief that alcohol might incite some sort of confession. The old Macoute refused to open his door to me. But he must have understood the purpose of my visit because he later left a document for me at the bishop's residence, pinned to a note which read: 'This will explain everything.' The document was a photocopy of a letter composed by a group of mulatto officers on 16 April 1849 attacking Faustin Soulouque, the black emperor of Haiti. These mulattoes betray a quite rabid racialism: 'The heart of Faustin is as black and filthy as his skin'; Negroes – 'les chiens de sa coleur' – are only 'half-men' and 'savage beasts'. The officers conclude their letter with the line: 'Haiti is our country and does not belong to the dirty Negroes. The sooner they learn that this is Europe and not Africa the better.'

Bontemps's document was no justification: it only explained that there is a colour prejudice in Haiti so deeply entrenched that Noirisme was inevitable. Curiously, both Papa Doc and his son married mulattas. Dessalines never stooped so low – his wife was a black woman.

IX

Talking in Tongues

'The celebrants violently strain their eyeballs inward, half-closing the lids; then, as they sit, they are in a perpetual motion of see-saw . . . perfectly dosed and flustered, like one who drinks too much in a morning.'

Jonathan Swift,
A Discourse on the Mechanical Operation of the Spirit

'I really wouldn't advise you to take one of those sail boats,' Father Samedi fumbled with his knotted scapular. 'If you are not used to them you may be drowned.'

'At least I can swim.'

'That is scarcely the point.'

The fishing port of Pestel some sixty miles north of Jérémie is only accessible by boat. But Father Samedi persisted. 'If there is no wind you will be stranded under the boiling sun for hours, maybe days. If there is too much wind the boat may capsize. Dice with your life or stay here in Jérémie. The choice is yours, *mon cher*.'

I was not to be dissuaded; from Pestel I hoped to visit the archipelago of minuscule islands – some eighty in all – which surround the Grande Cayemite. Most of them are deserted but one or two are inhabited by fishermen, jammed together on a narrow spit of sand in huts of mud and lath. Apparently, they paddle to and from the mainland in dug-outs, and manage to subsist by selling fish. I was curious.

'Bonne chance,' Father Samedi wished me luck. 'Let's hope you won't need it.'

Down by Jérémie harbour, gusts of wind whipped the dust against my face. Blown spume stung the eyes. A woman ran laughing in pursuit of her straw hat which had been swept away. Her skirt billowed upwards to reveal her underwear and she yanked the hem down with a shriek. This was bad news. No boat would take to sea in such foul weather. The *Agoué* rocked and rolled in the swell as sacks of maize were lowered into her hull by Marcel Paul and his son Ivert. 'We must be patient,' the father said as he began to bale out the bilges with a tin can. 'Soon the winds will drop and we shall arrive at Pestel before nightfall.'

It was eleven o'clock in the morning. I was in for a long voyage, no matter the wind. The boat was named after the Voodoo divinity of water, who married a mermaid with hair like seaweed named La Sirène. Agoué is often painted in temples as a naval officer dressed in a blue serge uniform bright with brocade. An initiate of Agoué is apparently able to remain underwater for long periods, although there is widespread belief in Haiti that this deity will carry those he dislikes to a region beneath the sea from where they never return. Such hocus-pocus may distress even the most reasonable mind and throughout my travels in Haiti I had become ever more wary of Voodoo. The boat was painted white and blue, colours which are sacred to Agoué; I was quick to endear myself to both Marcel and his guardian divinity. *'Ça c'est la barque d' Agoué?'* I asked. The man gave a cackle of delight, impressed by this knowledge of Voodoo. 'Will Agoué protect me against the winds?'

To which Marcel replied, 'If you give me another dollar, yes.'

Marcel was a tradesman; every Thursday he sets sail from Jérémie laden with provisions to sell at Pestel. One sack of maize in Jérémie costs fifteen US dollars; in Pestel, it sells for seventeen. There is not a great deal of money to be made in this and the *Agoué* herself was in a dreadful condition from lack of funds and maintenance. The oars had been fashioned from gnarled lengths of wood with triangular sections of metal, cut from an old Esso drum, lashed to each end as primitive paddles; the rowlocks were simply two sticks of wood forming a fulcrum cushioned with rubber from a pair of flip-flops. May Agoué have mercy.

The sea was breaking clean over the jetty and a keen salt wind lashed as I helped Marcel and Ivert lower more sacks of grapefruit and grain into the boat. A sudden roll slewed the barque round and poor Ivert fell into the water. He scrambled over the gunwale grinning. I began to wonder whether I should return to the presbytery and confess my defeat to Father Samedi. Marcel sensed my fear and offered me a swing of taffia – the rum was heady and burning in the throat but it lent courage. 'Soon the winds will drop,' he said doubtfully. 'Soon the winds . . .'

But after two hours the *Agoué* began to loll in slack water, mysteriously becalmed, and the sea towards the Grande Cayemite sparkled with sunlight. We set sail at two o'clock, joined by two urchins in underpants named Gilbert and Jean-Lucien – also the offspring of Marcel. The father began to chant an invocation to Agoué as the boys unfurled sailcloths from the bamboo masts. Translated from Creole, it went something like this:

Agoué, Agoué, protect my children,
Sea shell in hand, care for my little ones.
Agoué, Agoué, there are none who surpass God,
We are here to watch for you, Agoué, Agoué!

No mention to Agoué of the *blanc* on board.

The foresail was hoisted into position with much heaving of ropes and pulleys. The rigging looked precarious, a tangle of tarpaulin, sisal and cork; I trusted to Agoué, the Haitian Neptune, that we should arrive at Pestel without having to swim. Presently Marcel began to skewer a piece of squid to a rusty hook and cast it overboard. The line tautened and trailed in the sea behind the rudder. None of us had eaten lunch; fish would be welcome. For larger creatures we had a harpoon, or rather a kitchen knife bound with twine to a broomstick.

The urchins set about their preparations for cooking. Each took a machete and hacked away at pieces of driftwood stored on board. Empty packets of Comme il Faut served as kindling, the paper scrunched in a tin plate beneath a skillet in the bows somewhere. There was still no wind; the *Agoué* drifted in a great emptiness of quivering slack water and the sun glowed a fierce red-hot. My throat and tongue felt cracked with heat but stupidly I had brought nothing to drink. Only a little food – five wedges of La Vache qui Rit plus a single banana from the presbytery. The cigarette packets took fire and Ivert the eldest son began to fan the flames while his father slit a sack of grain with a knife. For the moment there would be no fish, only Caribbean porridge – millet boiled in sea water and evaporated milk which tastes very faintly of brown paper. Smoke from the skillet wafted against my eyes and made them water but the mush of steaming gruel, handed to me in a dented billycan, soothed the hunger. The cans were afterwards dunked into the sea and scrubbed clean with a clump of sisal torn from the rigging. The millet brought a parching thirst and dryness in the throat.

Ivert and his father took to the oars and began to row while Gilbert and his younger brother – *'le camarade'* – tilled the rudder and scooped out the bilges with the half of a hollow gourd. Still no wind, and three hours at sea. Ivert poured a tin of water over the rowlocks, which would otherwise splinter from the friction of wood on wood. All of a sudden the sails billowed and father and son ceased rowing and pulled the sculls in. For an hour or so we were borne along by an idle breeze. So far, no fish had taken our bait.

'What's this in American?' Marcel produced a piece of fishing tackle.

'That's a hook,' I said.

'Tha-a-ook,' he cocked his head to one side, inquisitive. 'And this?' It was a length of cotton-thin string.

'Line,' I returned.

Gilbert and Jean-Lucien scrambled from their post at the rudder to repeat the words after me. *'Lai-yan,'* they answered. 'And this, this! What's this?' They gave me a piece of lead.

'Sinker, that's a sinker. Hook, line and sinker.'

'Ook, lai-yan, stinker!' came the chorus.

Creak, groan. Marcel and son had taken to rowing again, as the breeze died away into a breathless calm. Dusk was gathering and the sea looked unreal, a stretch of painted cardboard with the odd gleam, waves shiny as tinsel round a milk chocolate. I remembered the packet of butterscotch which I had bought in London, nestled at the bottom of my rucksack. I passed the sweets round to another chorus of *'Ook, lai-yan, stinker!'* and the gold wrappers flew overboard, glinting under the moon-bleached blue of the evening sky.

'I thought we'd arrive at Pestel before dark.'

Marcel replied that he had not anticipated the absence of wind and we would have to leave for Pestel early the next morning. Tonight I would sleep with his family at the village of Corail, ten miles from Pestel. The moon hung suspended in the dark like a luminous ping-pong ball as we ladled more bilge from the plankings. There was in fact a good deal of water sousing about the *Agoué* but for the first time in years I thrilled to a boyish delight in adventure. I thought of Robert Louis Stevenson, who had brightened my bedtime with tales of stowaways at high sea, highwaymen on a moonlit lane. 'The most beautiful adventures,' wrote Stevenson, 'are not those we go to seek.' But this was no adventure for Marcel, Ivert, Gilbert and Jean-Lucien – only hardship, a way to earn a living. The oars sliced the black water and left a trail of silver bubbles in their wake; Jérémie glimmered in the distance, transformed by night into a city of jewels.

Nine o'clock, and the urchins began to kindle more wood beneath the skillet for supper. In the dark their faces glowed a supernatural orange as they poked and fanned the embers; scintillas of burning paper floated upwards into the balmy air. I declined the offer of another bowl of millet and yelled in surprise as a school of silver fish leapt suddenly from the water; Jean-Lucien grabbed our fiercely barbed harpoon and hurled it into the sea. It struck something and he cried in delight, tugging the weapon back into the boat by its length of twine. 'Bonito, my friend,' he grinned. 'Bonito, *bon poisson*. Thank you, my friend.'

I had not heard of this fish, bonito: the size of a giant trout, it wriggled in our boat, skewered to the harpoon. Ivert yanked the jagged kitchen-knife from its side and dealt the bonito a blow. Then he made a slit between its gills and began to pull out the entrails; the viscous black liquid on Ivert's fingers turned my stomach (a smell of blood like damp copper coins) as he scraped with a machete at the silver-green scales. So it was millet and bonito for supper, though by now I had lost all appetite. '*Ook, lai-yan, stinker!*' Everyone laughed as they champed on the flesh.

There was no light other than the stars and it was close to midnight when the *Agoué* nosed her way through a bank of rushes outside Marcel's shack, paddles idle in the water. Inside, five or so young children lay huddled asleep on raffia mats. There was a strong feral smell, as of stables, and a rank odour of molten tallow. A hurricane lamp hung from the rafters above an old trestle table, and burned with a soft glow. Marcel's wife, Madame Facile, emerged in her nightgown from behind a curtain of plastic beads and welcomed me. She wore a straw hat garnished with paper violets.

I never saw Corail by daylight; it is an old colonial village, once a port for coffee speculators but now apparently dilapidated. There was no electricity anywhere in the village and Madame Facile led me to her bed by the light of a candle, the downward sag of her bosom shadowy beneath her gown. 'No, no!' I protested. 'Please, this is where you sleep with Monsieur Marcel. I'll sleep on the floor.'

She was not to be gainsaid; the hospitality of Haitian country-folk is renowned and so it was that, without any demand for money, husband and wife surrendered me their bed for the night. A zinc washing tub full of bloated shirts and sheets stood by the bed, giving an acrid smell of detergent. But the soft murmur of water as it lapped against the shack soon sent me to sleep. At two in the morning, however, Ivert the eldest son crept into bed with me. There was no room to sleep elsewhere, he complained. I did not want to abuse the hospitality already offered, and let him be. The candle guttered; the wick tottered and popped out the flame. Then all was dark.

★ ★ ★

'Blanc! Blanc!' It was Marcel, shaking me awake. 'Time to go!'

I shone an electric torch against my watch: 4.00 a.m. Why so early? He explained that the waters between Corail and Pestel were calm in the early morning; therefore the dug-out would not capsize. I could not fault the reasoning and groped about for shoes and rucksack, disentangling myself from the weight of Ivert. The dugout was a hollowed tree, about fifteen foot in length. Marcel punted us free of the rushes and we drifted out to sea like a couple of contrabandiers, pitching so far to starboard that water lapped over the lip of the canoe. 'Sit in the middle!' Marcel waved an angry paddle.

'Sorry!' The dug-out cut the waters smoothly, hugging close to shore. A single point of light – Venus – blinked low on the hem of sky above the Grande Cayemite, a mass of land which echoed with a houm-doum-do of drums.

'Voodoo?'

'Baron Samedi,' said Marcel, who was the glowing tip of a cigarette in the dark. 'Ceremony for the Baron.' I asked Marcel how many children he had had. Eighteen, came the reply. *Eighteen?* Yes, and only eight survived.

Marcel had done all he could to save his children, even taken them to a *bokor*, witch doctor, for his curative ministrations. But they all died, of hookworm, malaria, tuberculosis. 'Agoué, Agoué, protect my children. Sea shell in hand . . .' Marcel repeated his incantation. The dug-out lurched over waves with collapsing crests of foam as he explained how the *bokor* had concocted a philtre from such diverse ingredients as a dead chicken, some grains of indigo and maize, various amulets and pieces of money, the whole contained in half a calabash. To no avail. Sadly, Haitians like Marcel who live in secluded villages receive practically no medical attention and the witch doctor is often the only resort: disease is thought to be caused either as punishment or a warning from one of the Voodoo spirits.

The *bokor* is quite distinct from the *houngan*, or Voodoo priest, as the witch doctor may practise magic without conducting any religious rites. They are close to sorcerers and can turn anyone into a zombi – a Haitian living abroad, a foreigner. *Bokors* thrive across the Caribbean. In Barbados I once met a man who kept two giant carved wooden masks of Winston Churchill and Lord Nelson which had flared nostrils and thick lips. 'I am the Reverend Doctor Ivan Beckles,' the Barbadian *bokor* had said, taking my hand in a claw-like grip. 'Whom nothing does baffle.' In Haiti, *bokors* are believed to hold mystical communion with *baka*, or malevolent spirits embodied in the form of various animals. But they also trade in herbal simples and medicinal plants, as Marcel had confirmed.

One can usually tell a *bokor*'s house: it is often draped with the black and red flag which Papa Doc had devised in 1964.

After three hours the sky was flushed pink with sunrise and we arrived at Pestel with the first cock's crow. From here I would travel to the Grande Cayemite, and thence to the galaxy of atolls and islets with such fanciful names as Lambi, Cocoyé, Zedelay, Iles des Rois and Apitin. At Pestel a teenage boy wearing a T-shirt with the legend 'Rolling Stones First Tour' led me to the San Salvadorian missionary of the Franciscan order whose name I had been given in Jérémie.

The mission was five minutes away, up a steep path lined with prickly sisals draped with drying laundry. Father Fabian from San Salvador spoke no French, only Spanish. I managed to communicate in Italian, and the young priest took me to a keg of purified water. My tongue was cleaving to the roof of my mouth from thirst and the water glugged from a spigot to make a balloon of my insides. When I explained that I wanted to sleep a night on one of the islets around the Grande Cayemite, the priest exclaimed (more to himself than to me): 'There's nothing to see! Only mosquitoes, sand-flies, sand and heat. And a few fishermen. Nobody knows what goes on there.'

This was precisely what I had hoped to hear and I managed to persuade Father Fabian to assign me two guides for the expedition: Pricien Cangas and his friend Cerdieu Pierre. They made an odd pair: Pricien, his cheerful fascination with Mick Jagger; and Cerdieu, a tall and rangy character with betel-stained teeth and distinctly saturnine manner.

We took a rowboat across the mile or so of sea from Pestel to the Grande Cayemite. It was a safe crossing since the day was clear and calm, with a fresh salt smell in the air and a few gulls planing overhead. Soon I noticed twenty or so human heads floating out to sea near the Grande Cayemite village of Anse-à-Macon. Pricien and Cerdieu explained that these were fishermen laying down traps for lobster.

Anse-à-Macon lay in a landscape of unrelieved desolation: dry red earth blackened here and there by fire, dehydrated patches of cotton and manioc. The village was a derelict assembly of huts stuck like oyster shells on a hill. There is no electricity or potable water on the Grande Cayemite (its two thousand inhabitants are obliged to collect rain in buckets), and no telephones or roads. Mules provide the only form of transport and as we beached the boat against the sands of Anse-à-Macon I saw several of the beasts toiling uphill, festooned with calabash bottles like bunches of gigantic yellow grapes. The mules were followed by a procession of children in single file, each with a tin pail balanced on his head.

Cerdieu and Pricien made inquiries after the hire of a dug-out to visit the archipelago of minuscule islands. Having secured the canoe, they suggested a tour of the Grande Cayemite as there are apparently more *bokors* here than anywhere else in Haiti. 'Good fun to talk to them, no?' Pricien gave his high-pitched laugh.

Two hours on foot across fields of dense canebrake and we arrived at the first of our witch doctors, Dieuseul Fleurant. He was a middle-aged man in a great straw hat, his teeth broken and distempered a nicotinous yellow. He had been a *bokor* since 1957 and said this was the first time he had set eyes on a white man. I had been forewarned that Fleurant *'servi ak dé main'* – serves with both hands, meaning he practised both good and evil. The long-tailed black frock coat, very moth-eaten, which dangled from the branches of a tree outside his shack indicated he was in communion with Baron Samedi, God of the Dead. Near by a baby girl lay very still on a raffia mat under a palm-thatch canopy, her tiny body covered in a white mesh dress like a net; two plates filled with bread and sweet biscuits had been placed at her head; at the feet, fragments of roast maize, potato and yam. Stuck into the soil all round her were lighted candles which guttered from the necks of empty bottles of rum.

Madame Fleurant sat on a wooden chair as a young boy picked lice from the plaited ropes of her hair. She explained that the girl beneath the white dress had been bewitched by a *loup-garou*, French for werewolf. Her husband Dieuseul was now attempting to banish the incantation and return the girl to health.

Most of the children who are diagnosed as suffering from *loup-garous* – female bloodsuckers – are probably infested with intestinal worms which may produce fevers and convulsions. But Voodoo has inherited from Catholicism a terror of the devil and at any moment one might be *'ensorcelé'* – bewitched – by an evil spirit. Dieuseul Fleurant told us how werewolves may sometimes poison the air with clouds of pollen. If so, the most effective antidote will be a decoction of basil, or *ti-baume franc*, castor-oil plant, sesame and a bunch of citronelle, three pinches of earth taken from three crossroads, honey, sugar cane syrup, dry maize boiled and pounded, and one half of seven lemons cut in two. Such a compound, said Fleurant, is guaranteed to restore the *'gros-bon-ange'* (Haitian for spirit or soul) to the poor girl who lay before us on the ground. I thanked the witch doctor for his time.

It was almost midday as we trekked across a vast tundra of burned grass called the Plaine Davide in the direction of Palmiste. This village is reputed to be the crossways, the absolute cynosure of *bokors* on this godforsaken island. On our way, we met a man described to me as both a sorcerer and a *médecin feuille*, or leaf doctor, Charles Jean François. I asked him from where his knowledge of herbal remedies came. 'From the heavens,' the old man grinned. 'From the *mystères*, the *invisibles*, the *racines* – and always in my sleep, when I dream.

All these words – 'the mysteries', 'invisible ones', 'roots' – mean the same: Voodoo divinities, more commonly known as *loas*, perhaps a corruption of the French *les rois*, the kings. These divinities are at the same time angels, saints, demons, numina and succubi; guides, counsellors, judges and protectors. Well over a hundred *loas* hover about the complicated olympiad of Voodoo and most Haitians will entrust their fate to a single chosen divinity, rather as the ancient Romans appointed one of the *lares familiares* – spirits which presided over the cares of house and household – at the domestic hearth on occasions of importance such as a funeral or wedding. Charles Jean François himself worshipped the *loa-racine* of Ogoun Feraille, a spirit of Nigerian origin mirrored in Catholicism by St Jacques. The epithet of Ogoun is *'Foutre tonnerre!'* (By thunder!) and he will demand a drink of rum at a Voodoo ceremony by shouting *'Grains moin frèt!'* (my testicles are cold). Charles Jean François claimed he was able to cure tuberculosis through the divine intervention of Ogoun Feraille – Lord of the Thunderbolt, also the preferred divinity of Jean-Jacques Dessalines.

We continued until we reached Palmiste, crouched in a valley of jungle. Here we asked directions for Lestin Yonard, the *bokor* of *bokors*, reckoned to be close to a hundred years of age. Seated on a rocking chair in the midst of his great sugar cane field, he was not happy to see us. Yonard would only confess to a belief in Guinée, the legendary African homeland where the *loas* hold permanent residence and to where the souls of the dead return. 'We are *neg Guinée*, the people of Africa,' he said defensively. 'The white man has no place here.'

The Haitian historian Roger Gaillard (a Marxist who became acquainted with André Breton) told me in Port-au-Prince one day: 'Life for the Haitian is only possible elsewhere, in another country. The upper classes obtain visas to take them to the United States, while the peasants believe they will return to the Valhalla of Guinée. Haiti as a nation does not exist. We are all of us in transit, without a home . . .'

After this tour of the Grande Cayemite we carried our dug-out across the beach at Anse-à-Macon and lowered it from our shoulders into the sea. The waters appeared calm enough, with waves like frilled scallops on the sand; but the sun was setting in a heavy bank of cloud over Jérémie and my guides knelt in prayer before clambering into the canoe. 'Bad wind over the islands,' Cerdieu remarked. 'Ask God, *le Bon Dieu*, for luck.'

Our dug-out rolled steadily, dipping now and then in a cloud of spindrift, as the guides negotiated the waves with skill. I took off my shoes and hung them round my neck by their laces; it would be easier, in the event of a capsize, to swim without their weight on the feet. Water kept splashing over the boat and it was a battle to bail out enough to keep us properly afloat. The joy of exploration soon vanished as the surf began to thunder and foam, making a see-saw of our canoe. Then my heart throbbed, fiercely, as Pricien and Cerdieu paddled to avoid a breaker. Three times the sea leapt over the canoe and flung bucketfuls of water on our heads. We were all of us soaked from the great whirls of spume and salt and my rucksack was a sopping bundle of cloth. Pricien seemed to find this amusing: '*Eh blanc, ça va?*'

It had been a knuckle-whitening voyage and a consolation when the sea lightened to a copper-cobalt blue, becoming less hummocky and lapping gently across streaks of yellow sandbank. These banks signalled the outer reaches of the archipelago of islets and soon enough a scattering of sandy knolls and mounds loomed to view in the distance like floating molehills. 'Which one do you want?' asked Cerdieu with a sidelong smile at Pricien.

It was now almost dark but I could vaguely descry a solitary clump of five or so palms. 'Let's make for those trees,' I suggested. The islet was called Moustique and about sixty people lived there – 'desperadoes', according to the guides. As we approached Moustique it seemed that all its inhabitants had gathered on the sands to witness the strange spectacle of a *blanc* being ferried towards them by canoe. I thought of Captain Cook on his last voyage to Hawaii, where he was killed in a hail of spears. 'Will they welcome us for the night?' I asked.

'No problem,' said the guides. 'You're the first foreigner that's ever been out here.'

This seemed a good enough reason to get rid of me but there was no turning back.

Trouser-legs rolled above the knees, we hauled our boat across the seashore at Moustique, an undertow sucking down wrack and shingle that scratched against our feet. The islanders came forward as a group and, keen to ingratiate myself, I greeted them with the absurdly formal words: '*Bonsoir, messieurs-dames.*' They watched as we unfurled a large palm-fibre pallet, well away from the surf, on which to sleep the night. Pricien and Cerdieu explained to the crowd that I was trying to research a book about Haiti and would they please leave us now, as we were all very tired. I felt dreadful – hair matted with salt, flesh cold and wrinkled from the water; but for the moment it was a relief to be left alone and I settled to writing my notes, cross-legged in the sand, with the light of an electric torch. After half an hour or so I shone the beam upwards and nearly leapt: the crowd had crept back in silence to gaze at me, the press of bodies so close I could feel their breath on my skin.

The intention, however, was friendly: they invited me to sample some taffia. Cerdieu, the more reserved of my guides, stayed behind trying to sleep while Pricien confessed a great enthusiasm for this raw rum.

The islet, perhaps one eighth of a mile square, was crowded with *caille-pailles,* one-room thatched huts built on sand floors. The doorways were hung with rows of drying fish and squid, giving a sweetish carrion smell. From inside the huts came a continuous clack of dominoes, and a faint susurrus of whispering broken by coughs. One of the islanders told us how he subsists entirely on fish; every day he hauls his catch by dug-out to Pestel, some two miles away, for sale in the market there. I asked him what sort of fish. There followed a long list of creatures unknown to me: Carangue, Cardinal, Bekine, Tazar, Peroquet, Soleil, Platelle, Pisquette . . . and the man offered to sell me a variety for $150. 'American dollars,' he specified. I declined the offer with the excuse that there was not enough room in my rucksack for quite so much food.

The rum shop – also of palm branches – was cluttered with countless bottles of taffia stoppered with miniature cob corns. In the pale liquid were marinating what appeared to be growths of pond weed. A man explained that this was *associ*, a herb which renders the alcohol nicely bitter. Each bottle of taffia cost three gourdes, about twenty British pence. I bought two of them and shared the liquor among several of the islanders. The rum tingled strongly in my fingertips and I gagged on the herb, acerbic as wormwood. Everyone laughed at my distaste and slapped me on the back.

I returned to our pallet feeling a little liverish and settled down to the discomfort of mosquitoes and a venomous little bug known in these parts as a *bigaille*. Presently an emaciated she-goat began to snuffle near by for scraps of food and a large ferret-like creature scrambled over a wattle-thatch roof. Rats, I guessed. At around ten o'clock I was woken by a rumble of drums accompanied by a rattling of pots and pans for rough music. Louder and louder came the drums, so they seemed to pound inside my head like the roaring which comes with fever.

I shook Pricien awake. 'What's going on?'

He yawned. And suddenly looked vacantly about him. 'Voodoo!' he said with a certain grimness. '*Service loa.*'

'Where?'

'Grand Gosier. Not far. Ten minutes by boat . . . Want to go there?'

'Yes, I do.'

There was not much light under the stars and I located our dug-out by torch. Then we pushed off for Grand Gosier, Big Throat, paddling in the direction of the muffled *boom . . . boom . . . tam*. In the distance I could see women disembark from boats wearing white dresses and kerchiefs, about to officiate at the ceremony. Pricien explained that they had come from other islands in the archipelago, attracted to Grand Gosier by the drumming which communicates throughout the night as a tele-graphic code. Depending on the breeze, this drumming would seem to sound from a great distance, like rolling, far-off thunder; at other times, close at hand with a sharp staccato message. The chanting of a monot-onous litany became louder as we approached, little oases of familiarity – '*libera nos a malo . . . exurge morti*' – mingled with hellfire shrieks and howls.

Stealthily, we beached our canoe on the sands and followed the drum-ming to the *tonnelle*, a great awning-like canopy of woven rattan which serves as the roof for an improvised Voodoo temple. The idea of intrud-ing my pale face into this gathering made me pause. 'Are you sure this'll be all right?' I asked Pricien.

'*Si le Bon Dieu veut,*' if God so wishes.

We insinuated ourselves into a crowd of spectators which had gathered at the outer edges of the temple. Any light from the moon was almost blocked, although a faint glow radiated over the beaten floor from an oil lamp nailed to the canopy. A few frightened children stared at me wide-eyed from behind the skirts of women. Otherwise no one cast me a glance: most people seemed to be stricken into a sort of ecstatic trance, oblivious of our presence.

Peering over a pair of shoulders I was confronted by a scene which filled me with some amazement. Twenty or so white-clad men and women staggered and reeled to the drumming as if drunk under the spirit possession, shoulders shaking. The *houngan* was probably the man wearing a red cassock with a large frilly white collar, his fingers and thumbs loaded with glittering rings and bangles. Growling strangely, face pearled with sweat, he sat astride a prostrate woman, working his arms up and down and screaming *'Out! Out! Out!'* – an exorcism perhaps. One celebrant stood still as foam collected on her lips, then threw back her head and began to gyrate her arms with rapid, scythe-like revolutions. Another man slithered along the ground as a serpent, muttering incomprehensible words apparently mingled with French and a little Spanish: *'Rounyou . . . vougnou . . . Sainte Croix de Jésus Christ . . . vougnou . . . diablo . . . aaaaiiii! . . .'* Whereupon he leapt to his feet, swayed on the spot, and writhed as though under the blows of an invisible whip. *'Bête méchante . . . muerte . . . Oh! Seigneur, mon Dieu . . .'*

I turned to Pricien. 'That man, his speech is completely unintelligible. What's the matter?'

My guide whispered: *'Il parle en langage,'* he's talking in tongues, or in the unknown language given by God – what Pentecostalists, Movers and Shakers call 'glossolalia'.

The priest in the red cassock began to shiver with spasmodic convulsions and pitched himself towards me as though projected by a spring; then he turned frantically round and round, stiffened and stood still with body bent forward, swayed and staggered. A woman caught him as he reeled off-balance and began to flounder about the floor doubled up, striking his forehead and twisting the arms. *'Li nans Guinée,'* Pricien continued in Creole – he's in Africa, meaning possessed.

Pricien then exclaimed: 'But I *know* that man! He's Pastor Wilfred Janvier, called by the people *Ti Jean*, Little John.'

'Pastor?'

'That's right. He belongs to the *Eglise de Dieu*, Church of God. A crazy man!'

'*What?* You mean this is a Protestant service?'

'It's Voodoo, but in the guise of Christianity,' Pricien corrected me.

I had heard how some Voodooists turn to Protestantism – *entrer dans le Protestant* – as protection from a hostile spirit. And the Church of God must appeal to these Haitians through its celebration of 'charismatic Christianity' – the movement of spiritual renewal that began in Kansas in 1901 with Pentecostalism and which claims inspiration from the descent of the Holy Spirit. The patterns of possession, ululalia, talking in tongues, holy-rolling and other 'anti-rational' practices of the modern Apostolic sectarians remain close to Voodoo (they were also close to John Wesley and to the wild militancy of General Booth's early Salvation Army); small psychological shift is required of a Haitian to make membership in such a church acceptable. One has only to think of the convulsionists and fanatical tumblers involved in Tennessee rattlesnake ceremonies, the way they shake and tremble before the Lord like the original Quakers.

'*Hallelujah!*', yelled Wilfred Janvier who had now apparently come out of his trance, sweating and jiggling his shoulder blades like an epileptic. The drumming struck a more urgent tempo as the celebrants fell rhythmically to the ground in a circle repeating 'H-a-l-l-e-l-u-j-a-h!' after their pastor. The drummers – *les tambouriers* – looked themselves entranced, bashing furiously on their rawhide membranes. Hands moved with such a virtuoso rapidity – the flat palm, the bunched hard tips of their fingers, the fisted knuckles – that it seemed to raise the divine ecstasy of these celebrants to a fever. Clothes were torn away unconsciously and two or three hot bodies collided with me, whirling away like dervishes. Pricien whispered that this was but a poor excuse for the pure Voodoo ritual where spirits are evoked through magical diagrams traced on the ground with corn and maize, the rites and libations conducted with solemn dignity.

Pastor Janvier was presiding over a Fundamentalist-Voodoo free-for-all, confounding Dahomey animism with the salvation-seeking of the evangelists. '*Hallelujah!*' He suddenly rapped his knuckles on a wooden table and silence fell in the temple. A young boy came forward to read from the Bible, in Creole. Pricien later informed me that the excerpt derived from St Paul's first epistle to the Corinthians, chapter 14: 'Follow after charity, and desire spiritual gifts, but rather that ye may prophesy. For he that speaketh in an unknown tongue speaketh not unto men, but unto God.' (It is curious to note that the clergy's handbook on exorcism, the *Rituale Romanum*, lists the uttering of such 'foreign' languages as one of the characteristics of bewitchment.)

The drumming began again and Little John the Pastor began to stagger, swoon and even somersault, shaking his frame from side to side amid whoops and cries of possession. *'Out! Out!'* My guide told me how the pastor had held a service on Grand Gosier every week for the past six months; by day he was a fisherman on Moustique.

'You mean he lives on our island? He's going to sleep there tonight with us?'

'I'm afraid so.'

'Ah.'

'In nomine Patris, et Filii, et Spiritus Sancti. Amen!' joked Pricien.

And so we paddled back to Moustique.

The slaves of colonial Saint Domingue were taken largely from western and central Africa: Dahomey, Guinea and the Congo. These three main areas included such tribes as the Aradas, Fons and Mines; the Nagos and Ibos; the Fangs and Monsombés. Each kingdom and tribe brought their particular traditions, language, gods, rituals, dances, the memory of their homelands and the names of their towns and rivers. (The word Voodoo itself is of Dahomean origin, meaning 'spirit' or 'deity'.) But within a week of debarkation at Saint Domingue, slaves were forced to embrace Christianity – a religious conversion which had been decreed by Louis XIV in his *Code Noir* of March 1685. Article Three states: 'We forbid all public practice of any religion except the Apostolic and Roman Catholic. We decree that all persons who act contrary to this prohibition shall be punished as rebels.' The article declares heretical the 'illicit and seditious conventicles' of Voodoo and warns that any master who permits his slaves to attend such assemblies will also be 'subject to punishment'.

It is obvious, however, that the forcible conversion of slaves did little to shake their belief in the animist divinities of Africa. As the colonial writer Father R. P. Labat notes in his huge book *Voyages aux Iles de l'Amérique* (1693–1705): 'The Negroes have no scruple in imitating the Philistines. They couple the Ark of the Covenant with Dagon, and secretly preserve all the superstitions of their ancient idolatrous cults with the ceremonies of the Christian religion. We may judge what sort of Christianity is the result . . .'

In colonial Saint Domingue – as in Haiti today – Voodoo was a means to escape the misery of poverty and oppression. The *Code Noir* itself authorized whipping of slaves, often with *lianes*, or reeds, supple and pliant like a whalebone. Mutilations were common; even the detonation of slaves with gunpowder ('to burn a little powder in the arse of a nigger' was a common expression among the plantocracy). This cruelty has not been forgotten: in the Musée du Panthéon National, a sleek underground structure built by Baby Doc across the road from the National Palace, the visitor is confronted with rusted iron manacles, chains, branding irons, muzzles, pokers and other implements (including a tin-plate mask designed to prevent slaves from eating sugar cane). 'For three centuries,' states a placard, 'our ancestors were subjected to the humiliation of being bought and sold at public markets, branded like beasts, and exposed to forced labour of an indescribable horror . . .'

Possession, the state of mind whereby an adept is said to be 'mounted' by a *loa*, was the most effectual antidote to that horror. The metaphor is drawn from a horse and its rider, and the actions and events during possession are the expression of the will of the rider, or spirit. (A Haitian proverb proclaims, 'Great gods cannot ride little horses.') Possession appears to be a psychological condition virtually indistinguishable from hysteria, with such clinical features as spasmodic convulsions, muscular contortions, fits of fainting and swooning where orgasms are not infrequent. It is peculiar to most religions practised in slavery – the cults of *santería* in Cuba and *cambois* in the French Antilles, the superstitions of the Deep South and the Mississippi Delta; but the most complete and extraordinary manifestation of Afro-American animism remains in Haiti, with Voodoo.

The great *Noiriste* Dr Jean Price Mars has described possession as 'a mystic state characterized by a delirium and splitting of the personality'. His son Dr Louis Mars, whom I later met in Port-au-Prince, broadly agreed. 'It is a species of psychoneurosis, perhaps the product of self-hypnotism or schizophrenia,' he said. Then he paused to consider the weight of this pronouncement: 'At least that's what I *think*.'

A frail and impeccably courteous man in his mid-eighties, Dr Louis Mars had studied in the Faculty of Medicine at the University of Haiti and received his psychiatric training in Paris and New York. Yet he was fundamentally nonplussed by possession, by what he called *'la crise de loa'*. He would only concede that it has been common to the Turkish sects of the Dervishes, the Indians of Mexico and their cult of the *mescal* hallucinogen, the Orientals and their system of Yoga concentration, the Dionysiac mysteries of ancient Greece – common to all these, and to Christianity during its periods of deepest mystical faith. 'Similar cases of entrancement and religious rapture,' said Dr Mars, 'have been recorded in the writings of St Angela of Foligno and the Carmelite nun, Mary Magdalen dei Pazzi, by St Teresa of Avila and by St John of the Cross.'

Dr Mars was briefly Haitian ambassador to Great Britain in the early days of Papa Doc, although like many *Noiristes* he was married to a mulatta so pale as to be almost white. 'Rhythm and dance,' Mrs Mars announced one night as we sipped papaya cocktails on the terrace of a most elegant home in the leafy suburbs of Pétionville, 'are almost an organic need for the blacks.'

Dr Mars bridled at this. 'Dark people, Madeleine,' he corrected her. '*Never* blacks.' Dr Mars went on in his morose cogitation of Voodoo: 'African mysticism is a most complicated thing, Mr Thomson. Many of those who are possessed would appear to suffer from auditive and visual hallucinations. I do not know. The French novelist Huysmans wrote that crowds are . . . "steam chambers of piety". And I believe one may talk about gatherings of Voodooists in much the same way. That is, by a process of hysteria and collective adoration of the divine, they invite the *loas* to come down from Olympus. Indeed the essential religious attitude of Voodoo is a recognition of the creaturely state – the *"Infinitum Excelsum Creatoris"* as proposed by St Thomas Aquinas. But all these inspired paroxysms, prophecies, trances and visions – they are most mysterious, no? . . .'

In his interesting study *The Crisis of Possession in Voodoo*, Dr Louis Mars records the case of a man on whom a testicular operation was being performed with insufficient anaesthetic. Suddenly, he broke into a Voodoo incantation and his expression of agonized pain subsided into one of absolute serenity, the operation following its course in complete calm. In the dark of the temple, celebrants lose themselves to another world where they are able to hold lighted candles under the chin, walk on broken glass and hold burning coals to their mouths. For just one night they are truly inspired – or perhaps 'enthused' (*OED*: in a state of rapturous or passionate eagerness).

When I awoke the next morning on Moustique, Pastor Wilfred Janvier emerged from his fisherman's hut with a faintly sheepish air. No longer the demented holy-roller of the night before, he politely suggested that I could do with a shave. As he sat me down with a broken mirror, razor and mug of salt sea water, women whom I had previously seen writhing wildly in the dust approached with smiles sweet as honey. I shall never forget their names: *Petit Oiseau, Petite Madame* and – she was quite a large lady – *Gros Morceau*. The white-gowned figures, the physical convulsions of last night – what had become of them? Then the Little Bird began to dance, very slowly, a cross between the samba and shimmy, the rhumba and cha-cha. Just as Oswald Durand had written:

> See her there, Francie-the-Mad,
>   entering the circle.
> She's possessed, she flies
>   – Gaze upon her face! . . .

X
Bolívar Was Here

> '"At three o'clock this afternoon I am leaving forever on the packet boat to Haiti," said Bolívar.'
>
> Gabriel García Márquez, *The General in his Labyrinth*

I was surprised to meet Simón Bolívar, the hero of South American independence, in Port-au-Prince one night. He was mounted on a black horse outside the Venezuelan embassy, illuminated by the sodium bars of a street lamp. His equestrian statue bore the words: 'If Men Are Bound by the Favours They Have Received, My Countrymen and I Shall Forever Love the Haitian People and the Worthy Rulers Who Make Them Happy. Simón Bolívar. 1783–1830'.

It is not widely known that Venezuela owes its independence to Haiti. On the first day of January 1816 Simón Bolívar stepped ashore at the south-western city of Les Cayes, where he raised an expedition to liberate Venezuela from the Spanish yoke. Robert Sutherland, an English entrepreneur stationed at Les Cayes, furnished Bolívar with a letter of introduction to the Haitian president, Alexandre Pétion, and on 2 January the two men met. Pétion agreed to finance the expedition on two conditions. First, that Bolívar undertake to abolish slavery in all the states he should liberate; second, that he recognize Haitian independence. This last was of crucial importance as Haiti was then insignificant in the swirl of world diplomacy, shunned by all Europe. It was not until 1862 that the United States acknowledged this country as the first independent Negro republic.

Simón Bolívar, *El Libertador*, consented to these conditions. And, while preparations for the expedition were under way, he wrote to Pétion:

I am overwhelmed with your favours. In everything you are magnanimous and kind. However, in my proclamation to the inhabitants of Venezuela and in the decrees I have to issue concerning the freedom of slaves, I do not know if I am allowed to express the feelings of my heart towards your Excellency and to leave to posterity an everlasting token of your philanthropy. I do not know, I say, if I may declare that you are the author of our liberty. I beg your Excellency to let me know his will on the matter.

While Pétion revered Bolívar, he was yet a man of great humility and refuted the designation 'author of Venezuelan independence'. Nevertheless, the expedition set sail from Les Cayes on 10 April 1816. With six schooners and one armed sloop, it comprised over three hundred Haitian volunteers and some thousand members of Venezuelan families driven into exile by the Spanish. All had been equipped by Pétion with rifles, powder, cartridges and provisions. Second-in-command was General Louis Brion, a mulatto from the island of Curaçao in the Dutch Antilles. He wore an English hussar jacket and scarlet pantaloons with a broad stripe of gold lace down each side, a field-marshal's hat topped by a large Prussian plume, and an enormous pair of dragoon boots complete with heavy gold spurs.

The tap-tap from Jérémie to Les Cayes was four hours late in departure. A rickety piece of junk, it was named *L'Espérance* and bore the hopeful legend: *'Souviens Que Tu Es Poussière'*, also to be found above the gates of the cemetery at Port-au-Prince. Haitians are generally a gracious people and one of the dubious pleasures of travel by tap-tap is the antique courtesy with which they salute one another as they clamber on board. Very soon there was standing room only, despite the sign which proclaimed in peculiar English: 'Passengers are not Permitted to Stand Forward While the Bus Is Either at a Standstill or Approaching in Motion.'

Riding tap-taps is a perilous business: accidents occur with horrific regularity owing to bald or flat tyres, and to the speed with which buses pull out in front of approaching traffic to avoid potholes. *'La Route Tue et Blesse'* is a common roadsign in Haiti, although no one pays it much attention. I felt unhappy about our driver: hunched over the open bonnet, he was pouring motor oil into the engine with a lighted cigarette glued to his lower lip, the Comme il Faut bobbing up and down as he engaged a passer-by in lively conversation.

'Allez, chauffeur!' An old woman grudgingly urged the driver to get a move on. Passengers continued to arrive – young girls shouldering sacks of charcoal, a man riding an ass who dismounted with a crate of Kola bottles. Then a beggar on crutches swung up to my window rattling an old Carnation milk tin against the side of the bus: *'Blanc, blanc. Ba'moin un gourde, blanc!'*

Presently the *Espérance* lurched into life, and a tape-recorded voice graced the passengers jammed in the back with a prayer designed expressly to guard against the danger of a road accident: *'Chers clients'*, it intoned. 'Let us pray to the *Bon Dieu* and to all the most merciful martyrs in heaven that we may be delivered safely unto our chosen destination. Amen.'

One more customer had yet to arrive. She waddled on board, a woman of substantial girth carrying two babies and an oil drum. In my experience the last person to mount a tap-tap is invariably very large, depriving the passengers of any remaining space. True to form, this bus would not leave until packed with more cargo than one might have thought possible. I surrendered my seat to the bulky newcomer and she eased herself on to the leopardskin upholstery with a *'Merci, chéri'*, later extracting a breast for the babies.

The *Espérance* creaked and jounced on the potholed road to Les Cayes. Young boys raced the tap-tap along the Grande Rue, offering us bananas. We soon left Jérémie to bucket along a coastal route, following a brilliant green line of palms that rimmed the shore. The bus was like a temple on wheels: a mass of religious trinketry – sacred hearts, rosaries – dangling from the rear-view mirror; the miniature gilded cage containing a toy nightingale which hung from the ceiling as a superstitious fetish; a plaster-cast Virgin affixed to the dashboard with one arm uplifted like a traffic signal to halt. Part of the windscreen had been shattered, I noticed, by bullets.

Passenger heads swayed in unison with the see-saw of the chassis. On we went, past the village of La Bastille with shacks festooned in bougainvillaea, uphill to Les Cayes which looks across the Caribbean Sea towards Colombia.

Situated on the south coast of the southern peninsula, Les Cayes is the third largest city in Haiti. It has a population of some thirty thousand, and its name is said to derive from the Spanish for 'coral'. This is a moot point, but according to the history books a ship cut adrift from Christopher Columbus's last great voyage of 1502 and foundered on the barrier reefs that lie a furlong out to sea from what is now Les Cayes: *'Los cayos!'* the corals, cried the captain.

Les Cayes has been famous since the days of Saint Domingue for its production of high-grade taffia. The British consul to Haiti in 1826, Charles Mackenzie, noted that enough of this rum was consumed by the cityfolk to 'rival the hard gin-drinking parts of London . . .' A further piece of information about the alcohol at Les Cayes was given to me by

Raymond Morpeau, secretary of the Haitian Société Bolívarienne. Namely, that the widely diffused slang expression 'OK' does not derive from the misspelled words 'Orl Korrect', but from the time Haitians stencilled the French words 'Aux Cayes' – meaning packaged at the Cayes – on wrapping round consignments of rum. In the early days when cargoes from all over the world arrived at New York, crates of merchandise were opened and examined as they came off ships. But freight-handlers would neglect to open packages marked 'Aux Cayes' in the knowledge that they contained the very finest rum. Thus the two French words became a general term of approval – pronounced and abbreviated in English as 'OK' . . .

A sudden explosion at the town of Beaumont and the *Espérance* groaned to a halt with a burst tyre. Then steam began to hiss from the bonnet of the uncapped radiator and we were advised to vacate our seats while the driver set about repairing the tap-tap. None of the passengers seemed the least put out by this incident; they took it as an opportunity to pee. Women began to squat on their hunkers in the undergrowth; men pissed willy-nilly against the hubcaps. We had broken down by the waters of the apparently icy cold Rivière Glace; the banks were shaded by masses of tufted bamboos which rose for hundreds of feet, tier upon tier above trees amid a myriad ferns. I watched a couple of turkeys furrowing the dust with their stiff tailfeathers. Then we were besieged by a crowd of women selling boiled eggs pickled in *sauce ti malice*, a piquant garnish made from chilli pepper and the peel of bitter orange.

I resented the colour of my skin as these women bustled about pressing their wares. *'Blanc! Blanc!'* They tugged at my shirt. 'Dollar! Dollar! For egg!' We were soon joined by three young girls each bearing a severed goat's head with eyes dead in their sockets like agate marbles. *'Americano! Americano!'* They waved the bloody produce before my face. 'Good to eat! Mmm!' one of the girls laughed, showing sharp little eye-teeth.

'Moin pas gin cuisine,' I protested, I don't have a kitchen.

No problem, she said: my mother can cook it for you.

All aboard the tap-tap, I reclaimed my seat and we continued on the upward climb through the Massif de la Hotte. Part of the journey took us through mountain forest with trees so close together that their interlacing branches formed a roof hanging with creepers. The Plaine des Cayes, by contrast, was flat as a postcard with paddyfields and wild ginger marshes.

Some weeks earlier I had spoken to Dr Louis Lamothe, the Bolivian consul in Haiti and author of *Alejandro Pétion Ayuda al Libertador Simón Bolívar*. A frail and bespectacled man with a degree in Spanish literature from the universities of both Santiago and Madrid, Dr Lamothe had told me how the friendship between Pétion and Bolívar was significant not only to the history of Haiti but also to the universal spirit of *'fraternidad humanas'*. Before Abraham Lincoln had raised his voice in the Anglo-Saxon world these two men on a small island in the Caribbean had, he said, 'proclaimed the application of the principles of liberty and equality enshrined in the Declaration of the Rights of Man at the time of the French Revolution'.

Dr Lamothe continued: 'Bolívar even sent Pétion his wonderful gold sword in gratitude to "the unsung author of our liberties". And this at a time when George Washington was perpetrating the most terrible cruelties against the slaves of America!'

It was a curious friendship: General Simón José Antonio de la Santísima Trinidad Bolívar y Palacios, descended from a wealthy Creole brought up in Hispaniola two centuries earlier (who asked permission of Philip II to import several tons of black slaves yearly to Venezuela); and Pétion, whose patronymic 'Little One' is said to derive from his days as a former slave. Venezuela has not forgotten its debt to Haiti. The capital city of Caracas where Bolívar was born is now graced by a statue of President Pétion, erected in 1916 on the centenary of the liberation of its slaves. Pétion never lived to witness the independence of Venezuela in 1830, but he would have certainly endorsed the *bolívar*, or the standard monetary unit of this country which he helped to liberate.

Dr Louis Lamothe had kindly provided me with the address of a man in Les Cayes who claimed to be a collateral descendant of Simón Bolívar.

Minutes before we reached Les Cayes there was another explosion, and the passengers broke into shrill yipes of laughter. This time the driver did not bother to change the flat tyre and we limped towards our destination on a ripped inner tube, rubber shredding against asphalt.

I got off by the entrance to Les Cayes which is dominated by a triumphal arch in honour of Pétion, daubed in red and blue after the colours of the Haitian flag. Coccyx bruised from the jolting of the bus, I trudged with my rucksack in search of a hotel. Les Cayes seemed to be a city of bicycles, hundreds of them weaving between the traffic, bells ringing. There are no hills in sight. I dodged the cycles to arrive at L'Auberge Bolívar, situated on the Rue Jean-Jacques Dessalines.

The hotel was cheap and rudimentary, my room pungent with the sharp ammonia smell of urine and noisy with Marley reggae piped from reception. I opened my rucksack to find that my plastic alarm clock had been crushed, the minute hand broken clean off. It must have been the fat woman who had used my bag for a cushion. Now I wished I had paid more heed to that notice in the tap-tap: *'Passagers, Surveillez Vos Effets!'*

The following morning I set out to explore Les Cayes and call on the descendant of Simón Bolívar, one Victor Bonostro.

It struck me as a sad city: ruined porticoes and collapsing Maugham verandahs, their paint faded to pastel as a ghostly reminder of prosperity. The streets appeared tolerably regular, though piled at their corners with mounds of rubbish, the gutters narrowed by filth. Rue Toussaint L'Ouverture passed before an ugly cathedral completed in 1908 with blocks of whitewashed cinder. According to a plaque, the stained-glass windows had been blown out during Hurricane Allen on 5 August 1980. They had not been replaced. The statue of Boisrond Tonnerre which stood near by on a plinth of pockmarked concrete had also suffered during the hurricane: one marble eye was missing; the other, which protruded like a ping-pong ball, had been restored with egg-yellow paint. This was the man who threatened to use the skin of a white man for parchment and his blood for ink when writing the declaration of Haitian independence. He was named Tonnerre – French for 'thunder' – because he was born at Les Cayes during an electric storm and this was quite in keeping with his character.

Rue Toussaint L'Ouverture eventually debouched into the dirty waters of the wharf. Here again I met Bolívar. Or, rather, a miserable memorial to *El Libertador* in the form of a concrete pyramid, most of it reclaimed by the sea. It was distempered to an algae-green and encrusted with barnacles. Black pigs snuffled about the detritus at my feet as I craned to decipher the worn inscription: *'Venezuela à Haïti. 28 Octobre 1953'*.

The memorial looked across the sea to Ile-à-Vache, vague and blurred in the distance like a faded watercolour. It was from this island that Captain Henry Morgan launched several raids against Colombia and the northern coast of Hispaniola. He came close, on one occasion, to the capital city of Santo Domingo which Sir Francis Drake had already sacked in 1586, when it was the seat of government for the Spanish colonies of Philip II. Doubloons, pistoles, pieces-of-eight; a fume of tobacco, the skull and cross-bones, smell of coarse snuff . . . Ile-à-Vache held promise of adventure.

I asked directions for Monsieur Bonostro's house. He was, apparently, something of an eccentric and most people dismissed him as pretty well non compos. He lived beneath the Ecole Commerce Victor Bonostro, a secretarial school which offered courses in typing. Every Sunday, Victor played clarinet and harmonium in the cathedral orchestra. He had even composed, they said, a piece of music entitled 'Bolívar and Bonostro, the Story of a Great Friendship'. He was seventy-six years old.

A young girl was sweeping the yard with a palm broom when I arrived. 'Victor's asleep,' she snapped. 'Walk in and wake him up.' He lay slouched in a chair before a television, the room gaudy with plastic roses, conch shells and a family photograph framed in curlicued gold with the inscription 'Mom's Pride and Joy'. A copy – most incongruous – of Molière's *Le Bourgeois Gentilhomme* lay open on the floor. I gave a loud cough. Victor jolted awake, darting his eyes sideways in quick appraisal of the intruder.

'Monsieur Bonostro, I'm sorry to disturb you. I was given your name by the Bolivian consul, Dr Lamothe, who said –'

'Sit down! Sit down!' The old mulatto belched into his hand and gave a great melon-slice of a grin. 'You've come to talk about my ancestor Simón Bolívar, n'est-ce pas?'

Victor Bonostro got up and shuffled over to a cabinet from which he removed a bottle of Barbancourt. 'This is the very best rum!' He poured me an extravagant measure. 'You must always look for the Blue Angel and Star on the label, proof that it's the genuine article. No contraband!'

Monsieur Bonostro gave a long and somewhat dubious interview, interrupted at half-hourly intervals by a plastic clock which chimed with an electronic rendering of *'Frère Jacques'*. He was well preserved for his years, the shock of white hair carefully brilliantined, an animal alertness to his pale blue eyes. He told a good story: 'My family originally came from Venezuela, where they carried the Spanish name Buenostro, later corrupted into the French Bonostro, n'est-ce pas? In 1813 they fled Venezuela for political reasons and eventually found asylum here in Les Cayes, after settling briefly in St Kitts and the Dominican Republic.'

Victor then explained how Simón Bolívar had lodged with the Buenostros in Les Cayes while preparing for his Venezuelan expedition. 'The house is still there, at 80 Rue Simón Bolívar, where I was born.'

'But how does that make you a descendant of Bolívar?'

Monsieur Bonostro appeared a little nettled by this question. 'That's simple.' He scratched his stubbled chin and leant towards me, lowering his voice. 'Between you and me, Bolívar was a bit of a Romeo. He was a terrible boozer too, but that's by the by. As I say, he liked to chase a bit of skirt – *il est allé pour les jupes!*' Victor told me how Bolívar had apparently fathered a baby boy by one of the Buenostro girls. 'And may I say how proud I am to be a descendant of Bolívar, *l'auteur de la liberté dans l'Amérique du Sud!* I feel as though I have more Venezuelan than Haitian blood in my veins.'

I asked Monsieur Bonostro if he had any proof of his ancestry. 'I used to. Unfortunately all the relevant documents were destroyed when my library was swept away in Hurricane Cleo on the twenty-fourth of August 1964. Or was it Hurricane Flora?' he blandly wondered.

This seemed to me typical of Haiti, where history has become so entangled with fiction that no one can really decipher the truth of anything. The notion that Simón Bolívar had brought a child into the Bonostro, or Buenostro, family has been preserved among the Cayennes as a fanciful tradition for generations. Eventually I felt the awful tiredness that comes with unexpected hospitality and took my leave of Señor Bonostro-Bolívar (as Victor occasionally signed himself).

Next day, I asked the owner of the Auberge Bolívar, Condé Marimon, whether he knew of anyone in Les Cayes who might further my researches into the Liberator. Monsieur Marimon was a strange man. He seemed to do nothing all day but mooch about the grounds of his hotel in a pair of Bermuda shorts, hawk spittle into the flower pots or shoot crows from the palm trees with an air rifle. The swimming pool was long since drained of water, dead leaves rustling in the deep end. Nevertheless, 'I know just the man for you,' he said. 'Professor Auguste Banatte. A ninety-year-old lawyer known locally as *le dernier philosophe.*'

Professor Banatte drew up three hours later in a battered Land-Rover. He was dressed with outmoded formality in an oversized pinstripe suit, a giant panama with the straw brim turned up in a jaunty fashion, and a frayed white shirt stained with what appeared to be tomato ketchup. I think he was the smallest man I had ever seen, with bird-like bones and a doll's face dark and wrinkled as a walnut.

'*Bonjour, monsieur.*' Auguste Banatte doffed his hat. 'I have heard all about you. And may I say how interested I am in you, for most young people these days have lost all memory of history.' He offered me a menthol Comme il Faut. 'But not you, I suspect.'

Curiously deferential, the professor led me to his Land-Rover with another doff of the panama. 'This is Jules.' He introduced me to the young boy behind the wheel. 'He is my nephew but today he acts as chauffeur on our historic tour of Les Cayes.'

As we bumped along I asked Professor Banatte about Victor Bonostro. Was he a hoax? 'In all likelihood, no. Unfortunately we have no means to establish the truth of his ancestry.' Professor Banatte took out another cigarette and occupied a moment in lighting it. 'Here in Les Cayes,' he continued, 'there is no written history, as the city archives were publicly burned on three occasions: 1800, 1805 and 1812.'

The professor was a quarry of encyclopaedic information and I wondered what he made of Anthony Trollope's comment on *El Libertador*: 'Bolívar had grand ideas of freedom, though doubtless he had grand ideas also of personal power and pre-eminence; as has been the case with most of those men who have moved or professed to move in the vanguard of liberty.'

'Trollope? I seem to remember reading *The Eustace Diamonds* one day, in French of course. But he was quite right, you know.' Auguste Banatte shot up in his seat as the Land-Rover negotiated a pothole. 'Bolívar was by no means perfect. For a start, he displayed signs of megalomania in his admiration for President Pétion's institution of life presidency.' (Bolívar even introduced this into the first constitution of Bolivia, making specific reference to the Haitian model.) 'Far worse, he depended on Haiti in order to win the war against the Spanish in Venezuela and then . . . betrayed us.'

The professor told how Bolívar had not only refused to recognize the independence of Haiti (on racialist grounds, he reckoned); he had also neglected to invite Haiti to the Congress of Panama which convened in 1825 to discuss the future of the five countries liberated by Bolívar: Colombia, Peru, Ecuador, Bolivia and Venezuela. 'And this despite the aid which we gave Bolívar in his hour of need: four thousand rifles with bayonets, five thousand pounds of gunpowder. The Cayennes have never forgiven Bolívar for his treachery.'

I wondered whether this explained the pitiful state of the monument in Les Cayes. 'No, no,' the professor laughed. 'That's only because of the madrepore coral, a sort of sea polyp which erodes absolutely everything round here.'

We arrived once more at the wharf. *'Arrêtez ici, garçon!'* Professor Banatte ordered Jules to switch off the ignition and explained how it was here, on the dusty Rue Cartagena, that the Spanish from Columbus's 1502 voyage placed the first stone of their new city. This part of Les Cayes was still named La Sabana, savannah, after the ship's crew who, impressed by the vegetable lushness of the coast, exclaimed *'Salva tierra de la sabana!'* – land saved from the desert! It was a miserable shanty town, its inhabitants wretchedly poor and glum with windfall sardines for food. 'Please excuse the water.' The professor apologized for the inconvenience of having to ford a small stream, tea-brown from drainage. 'What on earth has become of poor Haiti?' he complained, whacking a rusty tin can with his walking stick. 'We have been poisoned from the beginning by our terrible past.'

A scabby clapboard shack on Rue Simón Bolívar marked the spot where, according to folk history, the Buenostro family had fed and protected the architect of South American independence. 'The original house was blown into the sea during Hurricane Hazel on the twelfth of October 1954.' The professor shook his head. 'It was a night of apocalyptic storms. The roof of the Iron Market was wrenched clean away, the cathedral was full of people without homes.' Evidently, this second house had been punished by hurricanes subsequent to Hazel: the windows were supported from the sills by broomsticks; a couple of broken jalousies hung by their hinges.

In the front yard, under an almond tree, stood a gleaming tap-tap called *Mieux que Rien*, better than nothing. The owner, one Herman Lubin, announced: 'This is the house of Bolívar. Want to see inside?' Inside, a mule was lying loose stabled on some straw in a corner.

'Is that all?' I asked.

'Mais oui,' replied Herman, pulling strings of mango pulp from between his teeth. *'C'est deux dollars pour voir le mulet.'*

Professor Banatte was furious. 'Where's your shame!' he yelled at the startled tap-tap driver. 'We are here to follow in the footsteps of Bolívar, not pay homage to your mule.'

Back in the Land-Rover, the professor said we would now drive east in the direction of Cavaillon where stand the remains of L'Habitation Bonodo, the country house of General Jerome Maximilien Borgella. For most nights between 2 January and 10 April 1816 Simón Bolívar apparently slept at Bonodo, a guest of the mulatto general whom President Pétion had appointed Commandant of the *arrondissement* of Les Cayes.

'Bolívar only *ate* with the Buenostros,' specified Auguste Banatte. 'He never slept with them, whatever Victor might have told you.' As evidence, he referred me to the massive opus *Études sur l'histoire d'Haïti suivies de la vie du général J. M. Borgella* by one Beaubrun Ardouin. 'It was published in Paris from 1853 to 1860 but is now sadly out of print, like all the best books written by Haitian historians.'

This road was rugged and bad; it wound through attractive country-side with lianas like thick cables, bearded figs, fine wiry strands knotted in complimentary shades of green. Here and there one could see smoke curling upwards from charcoal pits, bluish in the conch-coloured dusk. Cavaillon was in ruins; no one was to be seen except a few soldiers, who stopped the Land-Rover to scrutinize my papers. Clearly illiterate, they feigned to read my passport, holding it upside down.

'*Arrêtez ici, Jules!*' But we could go no further, as our wheels were mired in mud. A bridle path planted with cabbage palms eventually led to a clearing in the middle of jungle on the outskirts of L'Habitation Bonodo. Near by the remnants of an eighteenth-century aqueduct lay concealed in the undergrowth; under its arches rusted several iron cauldrons – too heavy to move – employed by the colonial French for boiling syrup. 'How these ruins remind me of the chained ankles of my ancestors!' Professor Banatte exclaimed as Jules cleared a tangle of roots and creeper from a heavy slab of stone. An inscription began to emerge:

MARGUERITE NINON, CHEVALIER, DAME BORGELLA NÉE AU PETIT TROU DE NIPPES LE 31 JUILLET 1781 DÉCÉDÉE LE 13 MAI 1817

'Borgella's wife.' Professor Banatte removed his panama in gracious respect. 'A very beautiful woman, they say. Bolívar probably flirted with her.'

On we went, trousers stuck with thistle burrs from the vegetation along the banks of the Rivière Cavaillon. 'After you, please, sir. Let's go.' The professor spoke some English. Women riding sidesaddle to market passed by in the dust, their mules taking measured little steps, nodding their heads. Others went on foot, wearing colourful dresses with a reef taken in below the waist, raffia panniers balanced on their turbans. L'Habitation Bonodo was a splendid ruin, a heap of tumbled masonry scattered across a rice field which sloped seawards towards the Baie des Cayes. Tufts of broom and lance-tall grass sprouted from ornamental conduits and from the blue-tiled chute of a derelict chimney.

'Mustn't drink modder's ruin in the open like that, old man!' Professor Banatte exclaimed in English to a peasant swigging from a bottle of rum beneath a banana tree near by, and gestured his disapproval. The old man grunted, swayed back the blade of his machete and said, '*OK, m'sieur.*' The blade remained there, up in the air, for quite a while; I felt a little nervous. Then the peasant mumbled something in Creole about a buried treasure – *'une jarre'* – which he had spent the last twenty years trying to locate beneath the ruins of Bonodo. The professor explained how there is widespread belief in Haiti that the French buried much of their wealth before abandoning plantations to the insurgent slaves. Voodoo priests, he said, are sometimes employed to divine the whereabouts of this gold. Before General Borgella took up residency at Bonodo, the country house was owned by the Comte de Custines, a wealthy member of the plantocracy.

But it was sad to find a Haitian reduced to this state of inebriation – also quite unusual, as there is little alcoholism in Haiti. For the most part rum is consumed at Voodoo ceremonies, where it helps to induce possession. Talking to this Haitian, and to others before him, was to wonder whether life had changed very much since the days of slavery. 'I look for gold because my land will yield only a few ears of corn,' he said. 'Just a handful of maize.'

We drove back to Les Cayes in the mustering darkness, rain hammering tin nails on the roof of the Land-Rover.

The wretched memorial to Simón Bolívar was my point of departure for Ile-à-Vache. I set sail at three o'clock one Monday morning with a crowd of wharf stevedores and market women, the sails of our *shallop* stitched from old flour sacks and the prow cluttered with bailing tins. There was only dim starlight, the sky like black velvet picked with sequins. Though keeling a little to gunwale with the weight of merchandise – bags of flour, great Ali Baba jars of rice – the gentle pat and plash of water soon lulled the passengers to sleep. Slowly the waters slid by and I found a place amidships to rest my head.

The island was called by the Spanish the Isla de las Vacas and by the French the Ile des Vaches, after the preponderance there of beef cattle. Its aboriginal Arawak name, however, was Abaca, which anthropologists believe has little to do with cows. We find an early mention of this island in the writing of a buccaneer and navigator much admired by Samuel Taylor Coleridge – Captain William Dampier. From the first page of his mighty tome *A New Voyage Round the World*, published in 1697: 'We sailed with a prosperous gale without any impediment, or remarkable passage in our Voyage: unless that when we came in sight of the island of Hispaniola, and were coasting along on the South side of it by the Little Isle of Vacas, or Ash . . .'

It is curious how the Anglo-Saxons, more attentive to the sound than to the meaning, renamed it the Isle of Ash. One hundred and sixty-five years later, Abraham Lincoln referred to this island as 'Avache'. That was on 31 December 1862, when he signed a contract with a New Orleans adventurer and con-man, one Bernard Kock, to settle 5,000 emancipated American slaves on the island. This utopian scheme of Lincoln's was designed to atone for what he called the 'monstrous injustice of slavery'. Ile-à-Vache was to be the Freetown of the Caribbean, repatriated with slaves after the contemporary model of Liberia.

The programme was a disaster. Mr Kock had promised to feed his black men well, to erect comfortable houses, a church, a hospital, a school and to 'enforce wise and paternal regulations for the physical and moral good of my charges'. They would even receive a title to their gardens. But the result was rather less happy, despite a reduction in the original number of immigrants to 500.

The first official report on the Negro Deportation Plan came from James De Long, US consul at Les Cayes, who declared that, after one year, no houses had been erected except Kock's, that the settlers had nothing to eat but salt pork and coarse cornmeal. Forty had died of exposure while sick with smallpox. The second report from D. C. Donnohue, special US agent for the Secretary of the Interior, was more lamentable. When he reached Ile-à-Vache in July 1863 he found that a further forty-five of the freed men were dead, and an additional thirty-one of them gravely ill. Bernard Kock the 'nigger-breaker' had done nothing for his charges, only set them to work on twenty acres of cotton. He had provided six stocks, three dozen leg chains and five dozen handcuffs for the purpose. 'The singing of a man cast away upon a desolate island might be as appropriately considered as evidence of contentment and happiness, as the singing of a slave,' wrote the Negro abolitionist (and later consul general to Haiti) Frederick Douglass in his famous autobiography of 1845. 'The songs of the one and of the other are prompted by the same emotion.'

By 1864 the Haitian government ordered that Mr Kock and his black charges go home. Abraham Lincoln despaired: 'If any good reason exists why we should persevere longer in withholding our recognition of the independence and sovereignty of Haiti or Liberia, I am unable to discern it.' Several of Bernard Kock's slaves had fled into the hills of Ile-à-Vache and could not be found.

Dawn broke at around six o'clock. Clouts of pink sky and cloud lay mirrored in the sea as wavelets swilled across our bows to a gentle sculling of the oars. As we approached Ile-à-Vache there was a stink of fish gut; then a swarm of mosquitoes invaded the *shallop*, whining and drilling in our ears. I had already taken an additional dose of quinine, as there was a pandemic on Ile-à-Vache of malaria. Professor Banatte had told me how the terrain is swampy with salt water.

The anchor was fed carefully overside, some fifteen yards to shore of a town named Madame Bernard. We had to wade across water to reach land, skirts and trouser-legs hitched and rolled above the knee. Mud squelched underfoot: bits of coral pained my feet. The town lay in a wilderness of thorn acacias and devastated fields of millet. There were *marchandes* riding burro-back, children carrying on their heads red clay pitchers of rainwater. The Vachois – nine thousand of them on forty square miles of scurvy earth – subsist by exporting maize, potatoes, sugar cane and bananas to Les Cayes. Desperately poor, they are considered by the Cayennes to be a race of lunatics and absconders from justice, at the bottom of the social pile.

I was soon approached by the *chef de section*, an old Macoute called Antoine Jean-Baptiste. He dismounted from a horse and asked what business I had on his island.

'So you're American?'

'No, English.'

'What part of the United States is English?'

I noticed a revolver stuffed into the waistband of Jean-Baptiste's trousers. He was wearing a baseball cap stitched with the words: 'Showbiz Video Quizz Whizz'. A nasty sore had inflamed his left eyelid pink.

'England's near France. In Europe.'

At this he fairly laughed: 'Europe? So you come from the state of Europe in America?'

The Macoute would let me go only when I showed him my letter of introduction to Brother Jean Mauclair of the order of Les Petits Frères de Sainte Thérèse de l'Enfant Jésus. Brother Mauclair, a plump young priest with a smooth coffee face and effeminate manner, was well known on Ile-à-Vache. His mission at Madame Bernard was adjacent to the only Catholic church on the island, which stood in an old barracoon backyard littered with banana-trash and spent sugar cane. A yellowed map of Ile-à-Vache hung above the iron cot in my room at the mission. It showed towns which had been named, according to Brother Mauclair, after the French buccaneers who settled on this island at the time of Captain Morgan: Anse-à-Bernier, Boucan Charles, Pierre Le Nantais.

'Most Vachois believe Morgan buried treasure at Pointe Kock,' said the brother. 'His great galleon the *Oxford* sank near by.'

Pointe Kock? Was this the town where the human-flesh monger Bernard Kock had established his colony of American slaves? Sadly, Jean Mauclair had not heard of the Negro Deportation Plan. But he knew a good deal about Captain Morgan – boon-companion of King Charles II and Commander-in-Chief of the Royal Commission fighting England's first battles against Spain on American soil. Later, on my return to London, I was able to verify what Brother Mauclair had told me about this Welsh buccaneer and colonial governor.

In the early winter of 1669 Captain Morgan, armed with a privateering commission, determined to attack the fortified town of Cartagena in Colombia aboard the *Oxford*. This was the most powerful warship the English had then sent to the West Indies, of some three hundred tons and mounting thirty-six cannon. As Morgan set sail on the royal frigate from Ile-à-Vache, the chroniclers evoke a picture of rowdy hilarity – neither unique nor glamorous – as his crew 'drank many healths and discharged many guns, the common sign of mirth among seamen'. The noise of cannon-fire, the recoil of guns shaking the timbers, must have added to the gaiety, the singing and argument, as the buccaneers persisted in their drunken festivities. Finally the stores of gunpowder in the hold were exploded accidentally and the *Oxford* was rent apart, sinking within minutes. Three hundred and fifty-six English mariners perished. Saved by some freak of the explosion, Captain Morgan and the thirty men with whom he had been drinking in the officers' salon scrambled out of the smouldering wreckage and swam to shore.

No one spared a thought for the rest of the crew: for days their bodies floated to leeward of Ile-à-Vache and, according to the chronicles, foragers from Morgan's fleet rowed among them to salvage gold rings, as well as weapons and boots. The bloated flesh was left for sharks. This was not the only disaster which Captain Morgan encountered here. Returning in stormy weather from England to the West Indies in February 1675, his ship the *Jamaica Merchant* was driven ashore and wrecked on the rocks of Ile-à-Vache. 'We had all perished, had I not known where I was,' the buccaneer wrote home to London.

Brother Mauclair gave me the name of a *mambo*, or Voodoo priestess, who might be able to locate for me a quantity of Captain Morgan's treasure. 'She's illiterate and probably insane,' he told me. 'But she commands respect.'

Madame Lexima was thought to be one hundred and six years old and, as the mother of thirty-five children, something of a biological wonder. She lived by the sea at Pointe Kock in a small wattle-and-daub *caille mystères*, Voodoo temple, surrounded with pampas grass and poinsettia bushes whose flowers resembled wet red tissue paper. Dressed in a nylon jacket and blue silk scarf, the priestess sat on a wooden bench, spindly legs jack-knifed sideways. *'M'kontan oue wisit,'* I'm happy to see you here. Then she hissed, making a sound like insect wings rubbing together. The room was dark and heady with the stench of raw living. A single paraffin lamp illuminated a plastic doll's head, several empty bottles of rum (not, alas, of the Captain Morgan brand) and a wooden fetish representing Damballah Wedo, the supreme *loa* whose signature is similar to that of the Irish St Patrick – a serpent.

Madame Lexima threw back her head with a wolfish howl and spat into a bowl containing some sort of leaf-mulch. Was she possessed? I hoped so, as a *mambo* is able to prophesy only when in a state of mystic transport. I explained how I had come to seek her help in finding the buried treasure – the *jarre* – of Captain Morgan.

The priestess wiped her mouth with the back of her hand. 'Monsieur Morgan is more stubborn than millet under the mallet,' she proclaimed in Creole. 'But we shall try.' Whereupon the *mambo* produced a human skull yellow with age. This she put on the table between us, placed my right hand on the cranium, and hers on mine. In what was surely a skilful feat of legerdemain it moved across the wood, scudding to a corner of the table. This went on for quite a while but there was no psychic message from the Beyond, no communiqué dispatched from the Higher Life. It struck me as either a hoax or some insidious form of necromancy.

Fixing me with a glassy eye, Madame Lexima said: *'Bouch manjé tout manjé, min bouch pa palé tout pawòl!'* – a Haitian proverb which roughly translates as 'The mouth eats every food, but it can't speak all the words!' Or, put another way: there are some things which must always remain a secret.

'So you won't tell me where Captain Morgan buried his treasure?'

'No, *blanc*.'

'Why not?'

The priestess shrugged her shoulders. *'Se pa fot mwen,'* it's no fault of mine.

Madame Lexima would not allow me to leave until I had surrendered five dollars as a consultation fee. The homeward path to Brother Mauclair wound through sullen marsh-brown countryside; there was a tart odour of mango in the air and a sweetish scent of calabash that had spawned their thousand sticky seeds. Under a strong and unbroken sun, the earth was a milling of life and disease, swampy with the threat of malaria.

'When I first came to Ile-à-Vache the islanders despised me as a *blanc* who had no money,' said Sister Flora from Quebec. 'I managed to survive on a diet of maize but very nearly died from typhomalaria. And the Vachois wanted me to die, you know. They thought I was an evil white who had come to cast a spell.'

Then she said, 'Their racialism nearly turned me into a Negro-hater.'

Sister Flora (nicknamed by the islanders 'hell-on-wheels-Flora') had settled on Ile-à-Vache ten years ago to establish a hospital and small orphanage. 'This is where you come if you really want to test your missionary endeavour,' she told me. 'It's the most malarial area in the whole of Haiti, with about four epidemics of the disease each year.' A frail woman with large brown eyes and hair pulled back in a rubber band, Sister Flora explained how she has often to wear plastic sandals in church during the floods. 'There's no drainage on the island. Water simply festers in large pools, hatching mosquitoes which thrive under the shade of mango trees, out of the sun.'

Flora went on to say how the Vachois nearly lynched her when she suggested that they cut down their mangoes. 'Haitians aren't interested in the prevention of disease. They would rather have a new pair of trousers or some more food. They regard tuberculosis as simply another misfortune brought about by a malevolent spirit.' She explained how there is a sort of fatalistic resignation in the face of death on Ile-à-Vache, a collective belief that it takes only a throw of the dice to decide one's fate. 'There's nothing very much I can do about it, but my God I'm working as hard as I can.' Sister Flora touched the silver crucifix pinned to the linen of her starched white pinafore, and said: 'When a Vachoise reaches the age of thirty she's only the equivalent in physical strength of a sixty-year-old Canadian.'

One day on Ile-à-Vache I had passed a group of schoolchildren standing outside Brother Mauclair's mission. Clutching summing-slates and chanting by rote *'Deux fois deux font quatre, trois fois deux font six . . .'*, they suddenly rushed up to me and asked how old my parents were. 'Aren't they blind? Don't they walk around like this?' – and a little girl with hair like peppercorns demonstrated in hideous dumbshow how her mother could only walk with crutches.

Sister Flora led me on a tour of her hospital. It was a terminal hospice crowded with hookworm, malaria and malnutrition cases, some of them no more than two years of age. There were young boys sweating from the heat of tertian fever, out in the corridor under mosquito nets; and a teenage girl afflicted with AIDS, her forearm marked with the stigmata of needle-wounds. A child with hydrocephalus, her head swollen out of human semblance, interlaced her fingers in mine and began to cry.

'Polygamy,' said Sister Flora. 'That's the reason for this misery.'

Available accounts suggest that African patterns of plural marriage have existed in Haiti since the time of independence. Writing in 1830, Charles Mackenzie talks about a man 'not inaptly named Taureau' who, 'though his means were small, and his cottage still smaller . . . had a harem of no less than six wives'. Sir Spencer St John, British minister in Haiti some fifty years later, remarks that:

'In the interior, a well-to-do black lives openly with several wives, and I have seen the patriarch sitting at the door of the central house, with the huts all around in which his younger wives lived, as they could not be made to dwell under the same roof . . . The French priests attempted to alter this state of things, but they did not succeed, as the wives, surrounding the intruders, asked them what was to be their position if the husband selected one among them and abandoned the rest.'

Sister Flora considered polygamy an inevitable result of poverty. 'The more children, the more hands there are to carry pails of water from the village pump, to bring in the harvest of mangoes,' she said. 'Life is cheap in Haiti. What price the death of a child?'

Ile-à-Vache is the last land mass in the Caribbean Sea before you reach the continent of Latin America. It is six hundred and fifty miles by boat from Bolívar's Caracas. 'The Africans of Haiti possess a strength that is mightier than primeval fire,' the Liberator wrote on 20 April 1820 to General Francisco De Paula Santander, Vice-President of Cundinamarca in New Granada (now Colombia). 'And it is borne out by the maxims of politics and derived from the examples of history that any government which commits the folly of maintaining slavery will collapse.'

Haiti won its independence seventeen years before Venezuela, yet the folly of slavery remains. At the time of Dessalines the plantation system had collapsed as former slaves deserted the old land and disappeared into more remote territories – such as Ile-à-Vache – where they worked as sharecroppers or subsistence farmers. One result was that landowners began to lease smallholdings and returned to cities and towns – Port-au-Prince, Cap-Haïtien – where they furthered their careers as traders, officials, businessmen. Thus began a new tradition of absentee landlordism which still exists, with the emergence of a commercial and bureaucratic class that excluded the rural peasantry from power.

The Vachois may have lost all memory of slavery under France but a form of colonialism prevails among the urban mulattoes and among members of the black *classe intermédiaire* who marry with mulattoes. Their prosperity is largely founded on the degradation of those in the countryside.

The boat back to Les Cayes later that day was called *L'Amour du Travail* – love of work indeed.

XI

Yes, We Have No Parrots

'It seems that my father had large properties in Saint Domingue
. . . My mother, soon after my birth, accompanied my father
to the estate at Les Cayes, and she was one of the victims
during the ever-to-be-lamented period of the Negro insurrection.'

John James Audubon, *Journals*

Edward Lear had scant idea that there was a Haitian involvement with
the first book he published – *Illustrations of the Family of Psittacidae, or
Parrots*. His bird engravings were strongly influenced by those of the great
ornithologist and naturalist painter John James Audubon, who was born
in Haiti – and not, as many encyclopaedias still claim, in Louisiana.

Audubon himself neglects to mention in his *Journals* that he was
conceived at Les Cayes, the illegitimate child of a Creole from Saint
Domingue. 'I received light in the New World,' he says, but that is all.
He preferred to maintain the myth that he was descended from the son
of King Louis XVI of France. To this day, the people of Louisiana take
umbrage at those who insist their most famous artist was born in Haiti.
The Louisianais have even erected a memorial to Audubon on the banks
of the Mississippi, not far from New Orleans, which they demand for
his place of birth.

There are no memorials to Audubon in Haiti. But Edward Lear's early
mentor became national news in 1975 during the so-called 'Audubon
Stamp Scandal'. The authors of this infamy were Baby Doc's sister Nicole,
his ambassador to Spain, the director of Internal Revenue, the chief of
security at Port-au-Prince airport and the Haitian consul in Miami.
Together they conspired that delicate reproductions of bird watercolours
by Audubon should be printed as (fake) Haitian stamps in the Soviet Union
and later placed on world philatelist markets. They then bribed the State
Press director of Haiti to print a commemorative issue of the official
government broadsheet *Le Moniteur* announcing the Audubon stamps as
desirable rarities for those interested in both ornithology and philately.

The Philatelist Society of Switzerland indicated that they were satisfied with the apparently genuine edition of *Le Moniteur* and began to distribute copies of the paper to stamp-collectors throughout the world. Next, the conspirators persuaded Haitian postal officials to authenticate the Audubons with a first-day-of-issue postmark and the stamps were then sold to collectors via an entrepreneur in Miami. A small fortune accrued to the schemers until an enthusiastic Haitian philatelist (who happened to work at the Ministry of Commerce) declared the postage stamps outrageous fakes. In the first trial to be televised in Haiti, a gang of Duvalierist officials confessed their complicity in the forgeries and were subsequently imprisoned. Nicole Duvalier was judged exempt from any criminal charge and no doubt continued to reap money from the stamps which had gained additional value from the publicity surrounding the trial.

The man who the French anatomist Baron Cuvier claimed was the 'greatest naturalist-painter that ever lived' was born in the early hours of 25 April 1785 at Les Cayes. Audubon passed the first four years of his life on a plantation at the nearby coastal village of Gellée and I set out one morning to find the ruins. I was accompanied by a guide from L'Auberge Bolívar, one François Dimanche, who obliged me to hire expensive bicycles for the purpose. François claimed to know the precise location of the Audubon house; he led me across the marshy banks of the Rivière des Reaux, over rice fields and bogs which twittered with frock-tailed swallows, up escarpments that rattled with the noise of falling stones. For much of the time we had to carry our bicycles and I lost my temper when a young boy riding ass-back told me that Gellée was only five minutes away from the hotel on an asphalt road. 'Why this roundabout way to Audubon?' I shouted at François. 'Is it just to get more money out of me? I'm not a bloody tourist, you know.'

'OK,' and François pedalled ahead of me in hurt silence.

Gellée was a pleasant stretch of sand commanding a windward view of Ile-à-Vache. It was bordered by red-roofed adobe huts and rum shops noisy with the slap and clack of dominoes. Pelicans plunged into the sea to resurface with silver fish. Still smarting with annoyance at François, I asked some locals for directions to Audubon's house. No one had heard of the place and the answer was always the same: 'Everything old round here was *écrasé*, broken up, in hurricanes. Years ago. There's nothing left.'

I abandoned François to his bottle of rum (which he had bought with my money) and followed a man who really knew – at last! – where the

Audubon house was situated. For three hours we walked in what appeared to be circles, up and down sandbanks, until the guide announced: 'Nearly there. Ah! And here's the big plaque to – what's his name? – to Audubon . . . just here.'

'Where?'

'There! Why can't you see?'

The man pointed to a tattered billboard pasted with an advertisement for a cockfight. One of the gamecocks happened to bear the unlikely name 'Audubon'.

'See!' the man cried with a laugh. 'What did I tell you?'

We exchanged a long regard.

'Thank you,' I said. 'Thank you for your help.'

Back at the Auberge Bolívar I covered my head with eau-de-cologne and sat brooding in a foul temper beneath the fan blades.

The fate of Audubon's house was revealed to me some weeks later in Port-au-Prince by the president of the Haitian Red Cross, Dr William Fougère. 'It was destroyed in Hurricane Hazel,' he said. 'I am very sorry that you had to waste so much of your time in search of nothing.'

We sat in a study lined with row upon row of scientific journals bound in calf; a white hard-hat embossed with the words *'Croix Rouge Haitienne'* stood on top of an Edwardian roll-top desk. Dr Fougère was a nutritionist by profession, and had spent many years in Senegal conducting research into the causes of blindness. A cultured man in his middle fifties, he leafed through a copy of Audubon's *The Birds of America* and exclaimed, 'Such grace of design, such wonderful perspective and anatomical accuracy!' Then he echoed Cuvier's verdict on this monumental work. *'C'est le plus magnifique monument que l'homme ait élevé à la Nature.'*

Dr William Fougère was proud to be the great-great-grandson of John James Audubon's brother Belony Fougère, and he bridled when I mentioned the stamp scandal. 'It was typical of Duvalierism.' He shook his head. 'All that corruption, the abuse of power – typical!'

Dr Fougère had reason to complain: his father, Stéphane, nearly died in April 1963 when his house was destroyed by Papa Doc's militia. It was an accident, naturally: Stéphane Fougère just happened to live next door to Lieutenant François Benoit. Graham Greene described the horror in the *Sunday Telegraph*, 29 September 1963:

'A few minutes from the Hotel Oloffson one can see the blackened ruins of

Benoit's house. Benoit, one of Haiti's prize marksmen, was suspected of having been concerned in the attempted kidnapping of the President's children earlier this year. He took refuge in an Embassy and his house was set ablaze with petrol by the Tontons Macoute, who machine-gunned the flames . . .'

Stéphane Fougère managed to salvage from the charred mansion several papers which he had written on Audubon, and I was allowed to consult them in the hope of resolving the mystery of the artist's birth. To my knowledge, very little of the information which follows has appeared in any biography of John James Audubon.

The artist's unmarried mother, Mademoiselle Marie Rabin Fougère, was a Creole born of a wealthy French family from Bordeaux which had settled in Saint Domingue during the first years of the eighteenth century. (The meaning of the word 'Creole' is sometimes misunderstood: it should only be used of a person born in the West Indies of a race which is not indigenous to the islands: there may be white, mulatto or black Creoles – Mademoiselle Fougère was white.) The Fougères were in the business of slavery and even today there is an area in the north of Haiti named after the family. It was in this area, near the city of Cap-Haïtien, that Captain Jean Audubon fell in love with Mademoiselle Fougère.

Captain Audubon was then a retired officer of the French Royal Navy and had fought against the British in the Gulf of St Laurent, Canada, at the age of fourteen. In 1772 he determined to seek his fortune in Saint Domingue, where he trafficked in sugar, cotton, cocoa and indigo, having established plantations at both Les Cayes and Ile-à-Vache. Returning from Saint Domingue to France in the spring of 1779, his ship, the *Comte d' Artois*, was intercepted by a British man-o'-war. Captain Audubon was sent as prisoner to New York (at that time the possession of Admiral Howe) where he remained for over a year. The artist's father, then, was a gentleman entrepreneur or adventurer. And something of a philanderer, as he was already married to a certain Anne Moynet from Nantes when he first met Mademoiselle Fougère in 1783.

This affair incurred the wrath of the *famille Fougère*, who soon banished from Cap-Haïtien both the Mademoiselle, already pregnant, and her captain. On 19 April 1785 the lovers boarded a schooner for the southern coast of Saint Domingue. No sooner was the ship anchored at Les Cayes than Mademoiselle Fougère gave birth to the future artist, whom she named Jean-Jacques Fougère-Audubon. The captain and his mistress settled at Les Cayes as guests on the plantation of Monsieur Daniel Gellée, whose father was none other than the landscape painter Claude Lorraine (properly Claude Gellée). And here we find a curious digression in the papers salvaged from that terrible fire of April 1963: supposing Mademoiselle Fougère had in fact conceived Jean-Jacques by Monsieur Gellée (with whom she certainly conducted an affair), could it be that the genius of Claude Lorraine – 'le Raphael du Paysage' – passed to the grandchild who would one day become the greatest naturalist painter in the world? In which case, the boy's *de jure* father would have been Captain Audubon, and his *de facto de sanguinis* father Daniel Gellée.

This is far-fetched and remote; it is nevertheless certain that Mademoiselle Fougère was murdered in 1789 at the age of twenty-five during the slave revolt while Captain Audubon was away in Nantes. We do not know the manner of her death, but we can guess at its brutality from the contemporary accounts. Planters were hewed into pieces with cutlasses, eyes gouged out with knives, a carpenter was sawn in half, a man's severed head sewn into the belly of a pregnant woman with needle and twine. 'Human blood poured forth in torrents; the earth blackened with ashes, and the air tinted with pestilence,' writes the English eyewitness Bryan Edwards. 'Such are thy triumphs, philanthropy!'

Jean-Jacques and his younger brother Belony (without doubt the offspring of Captain Audubon and Mademoiselle Fougère) escaped to safety. Belony fled to Jérémie where he lived under his mother's name of Fougère, a distant ancestor of the current president of the Haitian Red Cross; and Jean-Jacques was removed by Captain Audubon from Les Cayes to France in the autumn of 1789, barely four years old, and now his legally adopted son. The young naturalist Jean-Jacques was baptized eleven years later at the Church of Saint-Emilien de Nantes under his father's name. And in 1803, at the age of eighteen, he went to live in America complete with a new English name: John James Audubon.

Audubon would have despaired at the state of the only Natural History Museum in Haiti, a taxidermist's nightmare located in the old Jesuit seminary at Port-au-Prince near the National Palace. Stuffed birds collected in the 1950s by a Swiss priest named Father Gasseur moulder behind cases of broken glass – here a wing eaten away by termites, there a piece of wire protruding from a breast without plumage. I tried to decipher the descriptions inked by hand on to yellowing luggage labels: Roseate Spoonbill (*Ajaja ajaja*), Caspian Tern (*Hydroprogne caspis*) . . .

'How much of this birdlife is left in Haiti?'

The curator answered silently with a gesture of one hand brought up to the level of the face, turning slowly at the wrist, which means 'Little or nothing'. Then he laughed: 'Only turkey-vultures and a few crows have survived the deforestation. And yes, we have no parrots.'

There was an overpowering stench of camphor, formaldehyde and decay.

'Wow! You're from England! Amazing!' The young Haitian spoke English with an American accent and wore a T-shirt with the words 'Surf Wave University'.

'So you know all the teams,' he presently remarked. 'Aston Villa, Luton, Arsenal, Nottingham Forest, *oui?*'

For some reason, the results of British football fixtures are printed every week in Haiti's conservative newspaper *Le Nouvelliste*. I had often found that the easiest way to convince people unable to believe that I came from an obscure country called England, and not America, was to say something like: 'Manchester City! Five-nil! 'Ere we go, 'ere we go . . .' Then the response: ''Ooligan! You are 'ooligan from the English country!' followed by the generous offer of a Comme il Faut or swig of rum. Twenty years ago in Haiti the mention of the word 'Liverpool' might have elicited the response: 'Oh, the Beatles!' Now it's 'Oh, John Barnes!' or, in the case of this particular Haitian:

'Chris Waddle! You know – he plays for Marseilles, used to be with Tottenham Hotspurs!'

'Um, yes. Chris . . .'

'So where are you headed for?'

We were sitting next to each other, Jacques Edma and I, in the most desirable seats of a tap-tap (those up front with the driver), about to leave Les Cayes for Anse d'Hainault on the southernmost tip of Haiti. I told him, 'Port Salut, I'm heading for Port Salut.'

'But that's where *I* live!' And Jacques insisted that I stay with his family there. It was my intention to reach the town of Les Anglais, roughly midway between Port Salut and Les Cayes, in time for Easter – for the simple reason that I was curious about its name: The English.

Our tap-tap, called 'Full Feeling', was some two hours late in departure. We were detained by a gaggle of market women who would not get off until they had persuaded all the passengers to buy a packet of *tablette noix*, a sort of nougat peculiar to Les Cayes. It is very saccharine, and will guarantee indigestion.

The road to Port Salut depressed me; it snaked through a desolate land-scape of mud-walled hamlets nestled in khaki grass, everything parched under a grudging sun. High clumps of dead sisal and thistle plants loomed at every twist in the road, coated with white dust. Not a tree or bird in sight, only fields of burned stubble. The chalky soil, harsh white in the limestone shining in the sun, is hostile to the cultivation even of wheat.

'Don't worry,' Jacques nudged me. 'You'll like Port Salut. It's paradise! Much nicer than Port-au-Prince, *la poubelle du pays*, the dustbin of the country.'

We arrived at Port Salut under a clear persimmon sky, which lent a supernatural glow to the fretwork mansards and verandahs of the tumble-down houses. In colonial times Port Salut was one of the three ports which linked Saint Domingue with Europe, the other two being Jacmel and Jérémie. Today the only legacy of France is in the names of two nearby sugar-cane plantations – Marcabée and Barbois, words which derive from the title of an eighteenth-century mayor of Port Salut, Marquis Barbé de Marbois. It is a wretched town, the smell of the place a potion of red clay and goat dung.

Jacques Edma's family lived in a shack plastered inside and out with lime over laths and thatched with straw. A couple of congo-bean shrubs grew in a handkerchief plot of land under a cane trellis; the bare front yard was fenced from a dirt road by a hedge of green succulent. Jacques's grandmother lay buried in this yard beneath the heavy slab of stone – painted a pale hospital green – which Haitians use as insurance against the resurrection of their dead. Outside the shack stood an advertisement: 'Pepsi, Rum, 7 Up, Rice, Fried Banana, Pork.' When not working as night porters in the local hospital, Monsieur and Madame Edma scrape a living by selling refreshments.

I was shown to my room by Jacques's father Vitalherne, a distinctly morose individual whose only words to me were, *'Il y a un pôt de nuit, si vous avez besoin.'* The chamber pot was a tin pail crawling with bugs which sat on a mat fashioned from banana branches, my bed. I unpacked to the yellow glow cast by a kerosene lamp, shadows flickering from its jagged flame against the wall and ceiling. Someone outside was singing a strange repetitive melody – I guessed it was Madame Edma, a tall and handsome woman dressed like a *mambo* with a straw hat worn over a white madras scarf. A knock at the door and Jacques came in with a bowl of oily *grillot* and a cassava pancake resembling chapati. 'Eat,' he said, and then left, closing the door.

I baulked at the sight of *grillot*, fried island pork: one morning at four in Port-au-Prince I had slipped out of the Hotel Oloffson to investigate a slum – La Saline – where I witnessed a slaughter of pigs. The makeshift abattoir stood over a network of streams, littered with a vulture's carnage of trotters and innards. Carcasses strung from low wooden gibbets were attacked by men with machetes, the awful noise of metal as it struck bone. There was a thick smell of a river at floodtide, of mud and blood; gobbets of offal lay in the sludge where they were devoured by dogs with fanged growls.

Live pigs were coshed squealing across the head with a length of lead piping, then upturned in the mud and covered in smouldering pieces of cardboard which would burn away the bristle and hair. A young boy afterwards inserted a metal tube under the pig's skin, and proceeded to blow until the hide could be swiftly removed from the carcass. (Meat spoils very quickly in Haiti: people are buried after a lapse of five hours maximum.) The butchers did not approve of my presence and asked me what I was doing at this ungodly hour, a *blanc* on his own in La Saline. Then came the insult *'vagabond!'* – a strong word of opprobrium in Haiti. I promptly left.

Since that time I had eaten mostly rice and fruit, and kept well away from the weevil-infested cuts of meat displayed in open markets. Unfortunately breakfast the next day at the Edmas' consisted of turtle flesh, goat and *diri et djondjon*, rice and black mushrooms – said to be the preferred food of Papa Doc.

Vitalherne Edma had been mistrustful of me; but as the day wore on he began to smile and even talk. He was curious to know whether I had been to Cuba. 'I spent five years there,' said Vitalherne. 'I cut cane. It was terrible labour, out there on the plantations where your back got all twisted up like a corkscrew. But life was too poor in Haiti. There was more wealth in Cuba, the folks lived at ease.' Then Vitalherne grinned to show a gold tooth. 'Cuban,' he said with some pride. 'Cuban tooth.'

'Why did you come back?'

Vitalherne explained that he had no sympathy with Castro. 'I got out on the last American plane to leave Cuba after Fidel came to power. It was the night of the twenty-eighth of September 1960, I was twenty years old. I remember how the plane – American Airlines – how it was full of Cubans trying to flee. There were people from Santo Domingo, from Puerto Rico too. We touched down at Kingston, in Jamaica, *oui*?' Vitalherne murmured with a smile. 'Then we flew to Port-au-Prince. I stayed there for two days, before catching the bus for Port Salut, where my mother lived. I've never been back to Port-au-Prince. In fact I've never left Port Salut, not since I came back from Cuba. Nor have I ever seen snow, not once, in all my life.'

Vitalherne was a *viejo* – the Spanish word which Haitians use to describe a migrant returned from Cuba. One thousand two hundred Haitians left their homes in 1913 to cut cane in Cuba under the auspices of the United Fruit Company of Boston (which succeeded in reducing Honduras to such a condition that it earned the original title of 'banana republic'). By 1920, the number of Haitian sugar workers in Cuba had reached some 36,000. This figure increased dramatically during the final years of the 1915–34 American occupation of Haiti when the Marines began to expel thousands of peasant farmers from their land, and employ them on construction sites.

The hero of Haiti's most celebrated novel, *Masters of the Dew*, by Jacques Roumain, was a *viejo*. Like Vitalherne, Manuel returns from Cuba with only a few pesos, but he brings to his compatriots a vision of a brighter future, persuading them that their poverty is not the result of divine retribution, but of their inability to organize as an efficient workforce. Manuel explains to his mother that the only hope lies in a monumental effort of collective labour ('co-operation is the friendship of the poor'), how this will bring an almost beatific sense of accomplishment:

There's heavenly business and there's earthly business. They're two different things, not the same. The sky's the pastureland of the angels. They're fortunate – they don't have to worry about eating and drinking. Of course, they have black angels to do the heavy work – like washing out the clouds or cleaning off the sun after a storm . . . but the earth is a battle day by day without truce, to clear the land, to plant, to weed and water it until the harvest comes. Then one morning you see your ripe fields spread out before you under the dew and you say – whoever you are – *'Me – I'm the Master of the dew!'* and your heart fills with pride.

Eventually, the villagers bring water to their fields made fallow from defor-estation, breaking the circle of famine through a *coumbite* or co-operative working bee where the men move forward across the land in a straight line, swinging their hoes in rhythm. This custom of fellowship and mutual aid probably derives from Dahomey, West Africa, and is still to be seen in the Haitian countryside. It is an extraordinary sight, as the men labour in concert to the beat of a drum or song chant and, in the words of Roumain, 'united as the fingers of the hand'.

The founder of the Haitian Communist Party as well as the Bureau of Ethnology, Jacques Roumain had studied anthropology at the Sorbonne and later became chargé d'affaires at the Haitian embassy in Mexico. When he published *Masters of the Dew* in 1944, he was hailed as the 'Zola of Haiti', and subsequently translated into a dozen languages. Edmund Wilson was too harsh when he wrote of this book that it was 'simply the inevitable Communist novel that is turned out in every country in compliance with the Kremlin's prescription'; but Roumain was certainly an idealist and perhaps naïve to hope that Communism might provide a solution to the chaos of Haiti's economy. The Americans, terrified by Castro, were of course fearful of the country's proximity to Cuba, and thus supported Papa Doc. 'The death or overthrow of François Duvalier would benefit the Communists,' proclaims a declassified CIA document from 1964. 'Extreme left-wing groups or individuals might under the circumstances emerge in a stronger and more dangerous position than they are today.'

Politics, however, is anathema to the majority of Haitian peasants. When I described the plot of Roumain's novel to Vitalherne, he shrugged his shoulders with the classic response: *'Moin pa fé politik,'* I'm not interested in politics. Tilling the fields from morning to evening, husking grains of millet, pounding manioc in a pestle, these Haitians have little time for affairs of state. Everything for them participates in the divinity: the sun, the moon, the stars, the slow changing of the seasons – all are bound in a natural magic. Roumain came closer to the truth about the Haitian peasantry when he wrote of their vision of heaven as the distant, half-remembered Africa from which their forebears had been uprooted:

> It's the long road to Guinea.
> No bright welcome will be made for you
> in the dark land of dark men:
> Under a smoky sky pierced by the cry of birds
> around the eye of the river
>   the eyelashes of the trees open on decaying light.
> There, there awaits you beside the water a quiet village,
> and the hut of your fathers, and the hard ancestral stone
>   where your head will rest at last.

Jacques Roumain died an alcoholic in 1944, aged thirty-seven.

On my last night in Port Salut I joined Jacques Edma and his drunken uncle, nicknamed 'Gros Lulu', for a game of dominoes under a shaded café hung with reed matting. *'Kouman ou ye, frère?'* how goes it, brother?; and *'Eh, amigo!'* The gamblers welcomed me with slaps on the back. Gros Lulu, dressed in a pink beret, sawn-off jeans, an eye-patch and some sort of sea-rover's medallion round his neck, managed to collapse the gaming table when he slapped a domino down with too much force, ripping the baize and scattering a stack of cards.

'Gros Lulu! You've been at the bottle again, *oui!*'

But all was forgiven in the spirituous approach to Easter, and soon the gambling swung into a *bamboche*, an improvised party with rum and tinny, tape-recorded samba or *méringue*. Vitalherne came to see what the noise was about, then began to shuffle to the music, sidling up to me with a question: *'M'sieur*, could you send me a Spanish grammar when you get back to England? I used to speak the language, in Cuba. A long time ago . . . now I've forgotten the verbs, OK, *compañero?'*

'Mais oui, compañero.'

We walked back to the shack in the rain; I did send him the dictionary.

It was still raining when I awoke the next day, feeling a little ill from the alcohol of the night before. I spent the grey and queasy morning trying to gather information about Les Anglais. Were there any buses there from Port Salut? How far away, how big was the town? But no one was able to give any description of the place – not even those who had been there. I decided to walk, followed by a small army of village *gamins* who straggled hopefully behind, asking for alms.

'Allez!' I shooed them away.

The road ran along lanes torn up by floods into deep holes and gullies; rain had churned the route to mud and I despaired of walking any further when a white UNESCO jeep approached, groaning behind me uphill. A *blanc* sat behind the wheel; I flagged him down and the vehicle slowed to a halt.

'To where you go?' The driver spoke with an unfamiliar accent, Middle European perhaps.

'Les Anglais. Any chance of a lift?'

'I go to Port-à-Piment, not far from the English.'

A stroke of luck. 'And in this heat!' he added. 'You'd die walking under the sun. Even the hens, they lay fried eggs in Haiti. So come with me.'

'Are there no buses to Les Anglais?'

'Buses – my God! Have you seen how wonderful the road is?' He laughed at his own understatement. 'It's a superhighway, let me tell you, a superhighway.'

'All right. Port-à-Piment.'

'My name's Milan.' The driver extended a hand. 'Milan Spiljak. I'm an engineer, from Yugoslavia. You know Sarajevo? That's where I live.'

Milan wore a UNESCO T-shirt ('Working to Keep the Dream Alive') and explained that he was involved in a project to build a road from Port-à-Piment to the mountain village of Rendel. 'But we get no thanks from the locals,' he complained. 'They only want our money. Dollars, dollars, always dollars, never mind that my national currency is the dinar!' Milan spat the words with some vitriol, tugging irritably at his visored cap; he was in his middle forties, pasty-faced with a curmudgeonly expression which seemed in keeping with the uncharitable remarks he made about Haiti: 'Dreadful country! Terrible food! Stupid people! Why you come here?'

At the town of Roche-à-Bateau we suddenly braked before a train of mules loaded with wood. The beasts reared in fright, one of them toppling a woman to the ground. Milan stepped on the accelerator. 'Here in Haiti you must forget about that Good Samaritan business' – a note of panic to his voice. 'Run somebody over, knock a person off his horse, and the villagers – they come at you with their machetes. It is not a joke.'

I turned round in my seat to see the mule charging after our jeep, scattering mangoes and grapefruit in the wake of its gallop. A couple of *marchandes* began to hurl stones at us; the projectiles fell several yards short of the jeep. Milan remained silent for the rest of our journey.

Port-à-Piment was made up of seventeen streets named after the Bible (Rue du Calvaire, Rue de la Passion, the Rues Saint Antoine and Saint Pierre). The gingerbread mansions were adorned with cuckoo-clock dormers and stately hinged doors, long since decayed but not without charm. There was the usual squalor: hogs haggling with roosters over mango rinds, shacks plastered in a thin layer of wicker with mud and crackled whitewash; but there was a brilliant, almost hallucinatory red to the hills around, which shone with the ruby-coloured fruit of capsicum chillis. Hence the curious name of the place: Pepper Port, Port-à-Piment.

Milan dropped me off by a pension unfortunately named the Hotel Sambo, at the intersection of Rue du Port and Rue Saint Augustin. 'Two dollars a night and the only auberge in town,' he said. It was Maundy

Thursday, three days before Easter. The owner of the Hotel Sambo, Madame Thoby, was a one-eyed woman whose face and hands were partially devoured by disease – two triangular cavities for a nose, tiny buds of flesh for fingers, skin like an elephant's hide. She wore a large gold bow in her tautly brushed hair, and a dress of pink Crimplene which she had put on that morning for Mass.

She took me to my room, lit by a flickering carbide lamp at the back of a yard full of wire chicken coops. 'OK, *blanc*?' She wanted to know what I thought of the lodgings. I told her they were fine, glancing round the shabby room with its enamel bowl and pitcher, the rope nailed to one wall for hanging clothes. Presently a young boy arrived to prepare a bath, pouring jugs of cold water into a zinc tub. '*Toilette, li fini*' – he held out a hand for a tip.

Behind the hotel, sunset was burning redly in a wilderness of trees. There was an orange glow of palm-branch fires where women were roasting pork in braziers. All I could hear was the cymbal-crash of waves along the beach, and the incessant concert of mosquitoes in my room. I went for a walk, past the cathedral of Notre-Dame de la Rosaire, and the cane-and-mud caserne where a soldier barred my way with a rifle, demanding to see my papers. I told him they were back at the hotel. '*Ça ne va pas de tout!*' He seemed pleased at my discomfort, nudging me in the chest with the butt of his gun. Threads of cotton protruded from his uniform where buttons should have been; a gaiter had slipped down over one ankle. I said, 'Just give me one minute and I'll fetch my passport. *Je reviens à l'instant.*'

'*Non! Venez!*' The guard shoved me through the entrance of the caserne. '*Venez avec moi, pour parler avec lieutenant!*' Inside the barracks, I was taken to an office where a fat man sat smoking a cheroot with his legs crossed nonchalantly on a desktop, a string vest exposed beneath his combat fatigues. Stacks of yellowing papers were piled on a filing cabinet, a half-empty bottle of rum and an ashtray containing cigarette ends by his side. Bolt-action rifles lay stashed around the office in wooden racks. '*Et alors?*' The lieutenant reached for his bottle and poured a drink, patting his big, taffia-tough stomach after permitting himself a burp. The guard mumbled some explanation in Creole to the effect that there was a stranger in town without any papers, without so much as a *laisser-passer*!

Lieutenant Saurel St Rameau stood up from behind the desk, a large pistol clapping his thigh. Hands clasped behind his back, he walked round me, appraising my face and clothes. *'Ecoutez, monsieur,'* he said evenly. 'There is a very serious state of insecurity in Haiti, after the departure of our president, *non*? So I must know who you are, what you are doing here, from where you come . . . *Je dois absolument savoir!'*

Once again I explained that my papers were back at the hotel. 'But that goes without saying. Of course you have papers!' Lieutenant St Rameau hesitated. Then after another pause: 'But how do I know they are genuine, that they belong to you, eh?'

This ridiculous interrogation continued until the lieutenant lost his calm and yelled at a guard to escort me to my hotel where I would collect passport and personal effects, and return to the caserne for further questioning.

Back at the barracks I was conducted to a small room, the walls flecked with red where insects had been squashed against the whitewash. An old Remington upright stood on a deal table, a sheet of paper already inserted into the carriage and letterheaded with the words *'Force d'Armée Haïti'*. The lieutenant had been replaced by his apparent senior, Monsieur Silaire Delafosse, the *Juge de Paix*, or Justice of the Peace, who seemed a little more mollient until he ordered a subaltern to search my body. This involved a patting and slapping of the hips and thighs, the laying of a hand under the testicles, and removal of my shoes. Then my particulars were taken down by a secretary behind the typewriter: age, nationality, profession, passport number . . .

'Je suis libre maintenant?' I knew that they had yet to search my ruck-sack, but tried to make light of the situation with another question: *'Il faut que je passe la nuit en prison?'*

Monsieur Delafosse was not amused. He grabbed my bag and tipped its contents on to the floor. Soldiers rifled through my effects without a gleam of friendliness or humour.

'And these?' The Justice of the Peace opened a packet of Arrêt.

'Those are tablets,' I tried to explain. 'For diarrhoea.'

'This?' He held up a paperback edition of the Metaphysical poets.

And so it went, question and answer, one object after another – tooth-brush, socks, an old German roadmap of Haiti, a thriller by Eric Ambler, a tin of detergent, a box of malaria pills, three sterilized hypodermic syringes in a first-aid kit (confiscated on the pretext that I might have been peddling in narcotics), plus a copy of the *South American Handbook* ('Haiti is especially interesting for the tourist who is avid for the out-of-the-way experience . . .').

Monsieur Delafosse let me go on payment of a fine for an *'attentat à l'ordre public'*, or breach of the peace.

Monsieur Silaire Delafosse struck me as a sort of Caribbean Judge Jeffreys, a man influenced in his dispensation of justice by pecuniary or political considerations. The legal system in Haiti is a disgrace: no prisoner has the right to be considered innocent until proven guilty and the law of bail is unknown. As the director of the Port-au-Prince Centre des Droits et Libertés Humaines, Jean-Jacques Honorat, later told me: 'Lawyers in Haiti are incapable of devising an equitable criminal or civil jurisprudence for the simple reason that they are corrupt. They can think of nothing but the meticulous tyrannies of the Roman and Napoleonic Codes.' He explained how a prisoner will give a sum of money to a guard; how the guard later negotiates some financial agreement with the judge; how the judge then grants unprovisional liberty to the accused. 'If you have no money, you may be confined in prison for years before being brought to trial. More likely, you will die of starvation or torture.'

Pinned to the wall of Monsieur Honorat's office was a quotation photocopied from *The Social Contract* by Rousseau: 'To renounce one's liberty is to renounce one's quality as a man, the rights of humanity and even its duties.'

'Rousseau should have come to Haiti,' said Jean-Jacques Honorat. 'Nowhere else in the West Indies will you find so flagrant an abuse of the rights of man. The barefaced perjury of the witnesses, the shameful perversions of the legal system . . . *Enfin, c'est une comédie!*' He went on to say how there is no such thing as an 'arrest' in Haiti. 'Arrest implies some form of legal arbitration. It would be more correct to say that people are . . . *abducted*. And the moment a man is abducted, he ceases to be a human being. Why? Because our legal system is homicidal, designed only to eliminate the individual.' According to Monsieur Honorat, there is no police registry in Haiti, let alone a prison registry. 'People are removed to jails which are accessible only to the military, where they vanish without trace, like the *desparecidos* of Argentina.'

In the Haitian countryside, a *juge de paix* will determine all contestations and trials. His function is similar to that performed by the old English country squire, who would sit as judge between neighbours who came to him with their disagreements. Rarely distinguished for either his moral discernment or ability to judge between right and wrong, the Justice of the Peace is 'invested with more local power', said Monsieur

Honorat, 'than the Queen of England'. (He will even order the execution of an enemy on the pretext of *'vagabondage'*.) Many of these paramilitary advocates are ignorant of the Penal Code, and are unable to comprehend those hundreds of Haitian laws founded on French precedents, as they speak no language other than Creole.

Criminal cases of the gravest sort are referred to Port-au-Prince by the Justice of the Peace. At the Palais de Justice I later witnessed the trial of three men from the Dominican Republic accused of armed robbery. Legal proceedings were a sorry farce; the principal judge, smoking cigarettes and insulting the inferior clerks, thundered at the assembled lawyers whom he tried without success to bring to order. Litigation was due to commence in the Chambre Correctionelle at ten in the morning but it was another four hours before the prisoners would arrive. The reason for their delay was attributed to the army vehicle which had blown a tyre while transporting the accused from the National Penitentiary a few minutes away. Argument broke out among the four substitute judges as to who should receive blame. One after the other they rose from their benches to read long extracts from the laws of the country enshrined in great dusty tomes which surrounded them almost as a barricade.

'Sir! Article forty-five of the *Code d'Instruction Criminelle*, dated the thirty-first of July 1835, states quite clearly that –'

'– This is absurd! Article nine of the Civil Code claims . . .'

And so on, each of these recitals heralded by the tinkling of a tiny sanctus bell and occasionally interrupted by gusts of wind from an open window which blew flurries of paper round the empty jury seats. Whether or not these readings had any bearing on the subject in hand seemed immaterial. They were mere formalities without purpose, part of a pageant. The principal judge banged his gavel against a volume of the Penal Code, sending dust from the cover. 'This is a farce and a masquerade! There is only one person who must take responsibility for the broken vehicle! The Minister of Transport!'

The 'farce' continued until the prisoners finally arrived in handcuffs. They had been made to walk the short distance under an escort of five police officers and ten soldiers.

Proceedings were about to begin when the principal judge asked, 'What has become of the other prisoners?' He removed his strange conical hat (fashioned from black crepe and what appeared to be tinfoil), and fumbled irritably with the ornamental frills of his cravat. 'According to my papers there should be three more Dominicans on trial today. Where are they?' Confused looks all round, then more argument. Someone in the public gallery threw a ball of paper at one of the lawyers.

At last we were able to begin and the accusations were read in florid French by a notary who fanned himself the while with a newspaper. Unfortunately the prisoners – a ragtaggle crew – were unable to understand a word since they spoke only Spanish. They cast one another expressions of blank incomprehension, shuffling their feet as the lawyers disputed some matter of protocol. The trial might have degenerated into a bun-fight had not the principal judge adjourned in camera to emerge some minutes later to suspend proceedings until an interpreter could be found.

After hours of frenzied altercation with lawyers quoting from several articles, it seemed, in one breath, the Dominicans were frog-marched back to the National Penitentiary in the furious two o'clock sun. They had been imprisoned for fourteen months awaiting trial and must have wondered if they would ever again see the light of day. 'The innocent might easily be convicted by the Haitian legal system, and the guilty escape,' Jean-Jacques Honorat had told me. But he was not entirely pessimistic about the possibility of penal reform: *'Tout tan tèt pa koupé, gin lespwa mete chapo,'* he added – a Haitian proverb which roughly translates as: 'For as long as your head is not cut off, there remains the hope that one day you will be able to wear a hat . . .'

That night, back at the hotel after my interrogation at the hands of the military, I intruded upon an argument which gave a rare insight into the heartland of Haitian culture and politics. Several people were seated round the kitchen table, drinking rum by the light of a candle. The *curé* of Notre-Dame de la Rosaire, Father François Thomas, was there; also the church organist, Cincinnatus Bibert, along with the owner of the hotel, Madame Thoby, and a military doctor, Gabriel L'Aventure, from the northern city of Cap-Haïtien. It seemed that Dr L'Aventure was the cause of the quarrel. 'You southerners make me sick!' (He was plainly drunk.) 'What have you ever done for Haiti? Nothing! Absolutely nothing! Parochial, that's what you are. It's a terrible sin, regionalism. Terrible! Me? I'm proud to be a Capois! We're better than the lot of you.'

'Oh come on, Gabriel!' The organist patted the doctor on the back. 'That's enough of your arrogance. Quite enough.'

'Ah shut up! *Taisez-vous, petit mec!'* Dr L'Aventure was obviously accustomed to barking orders, for he was attached to the notorious Dessalines

Barracks in Port-au-Prince. 'Complacent old fool! Just shut up! Pass me the bottle. I paid for it.'

Father Thomas yawned. 'I'm off to bed. I've had enough of this.'

'How dare you leave the room!' Gabriel reached across the table to grab the *curé* by his sleeve. 'I'm a doctor and I *know* that you are not in the least bit tired. Sit down! And that's an order!'

The doctor turned to me with what seemed a reproachful expression. 'And you! What do you think about these southern fools, eh?' He looked at me fixedly, like a man watching a film, and tried to draw me into his drunken argument. 'Surely you know how the north is more advanced culturally, how these southerners are completely without distinction and polish, eh?'

I told the doctor that I had not yet visited the north of Haiti. To which he replied, sharply: 'So what? That doesn't mean you are unable to take my point of view, as a cultivated European!'

The doctor's prejudice against the southern Haitian was apparently typical of the Capois. His lofty contempt may be explained by the fact that the south did not participate in the political violence during the early days of Haitian independence, isolated from the revolution by its geographical situation.

A southerner will often say of a northerner, *'Li Pagnol'* – he's Spanish – meaning a 'tough nut', 'fierce' or 'proud', presumably after the Spaniards who trafficked in slaves. The Department of the South, unlike that of the North, does not border on the Dominican Republic. It forms the lower jawbone of the giant crocodile's head of Haiti, where the influence is Gallic rather than Spanish. The Creole spoken by southerners is thus more influenced by classical French. *'Ça c'est pour moi'* becomes *'Sa se pou moin'*, but in the north, *'Sa se kinan-m.'*

Northerners are considered more industrious and economically advanced than their compatriots in the south, proud of their cultural and political pre-eminence. The intellectual movement of *Noirisme*, for example, never took a foothold in the south, traditional domain of mulattoes who had shunned the heritage of Africa. ('You! What the hell are you doing in this backwater?' Dr L'Aventure yelled at me. 'Why don't you just go to bed, like the rest of these southern cretins?') Perhaps this influence of France explains why the southerner is considered more cordial and more congenial than his northern counterpart, possessed of a happy-go-lucky exuberance and friendliness deficient in this foul-mouthed doctor from Cap-Haïtien.

Dr L'Aventure left the Hotel Sambo in high dudgeon, muttering to himself. After his departure Madame Thoby produced a supper of cartilaginous meat and cornmeal mush. 'Terrible food you get in the north,' she said. 'Absolutely terrible.'

I was now in some haste to get away from Port-à-Piment after my scrape with the military police. But curiosity still held me in Haiti; despite the pestering flies and my general fatigue from travel on alien ground, I wanted to continue. At this time memories of home were often recalled in my foreign thoughts. Much earlier, a friend had flown from London for a brief visit to Port-au-Prince; she had provided an interval of calm, kept me sane and dissuaded me from returning to England.

Aubelin Jolicœur had previously announced her arrival in the pages of *Le Nouvelliste*.

'Ah Laura – Laura, my dear!' The tittle-tattler came mincing up the steps of the Oloffson. 'So very pleased to meet you and how your beauty shines by candlelight! I see you as the Laura so beloved of Petrarch! Just as Dante was so enamoured of his Beatrice!' After this unusual overture, Jolicœur had arranged for his chauffeur to drive us round Port-au-Prince in the back of a Buick Sedan circa 1956. It was plushly upholstered in crimson velour; our gossip columnist sat in front reading an article about Victor Hugo.

'All right my darling?' he had asked Laura banteringly; and then: 'Are you in Haiti for Voodoo? Or for moonlit idylls beneath the palms?'

'I'm not quite sure.'

'Just make sure your friend Mr Thomson tells the truth about this beautiful country!' replied Jolicœur – with more emotion, I think, than he had intended to show.

I will, I thought, I certainly will.

Laura had left after three days and I was alone again.

XII

Easter at Les Anglais

'The lady behind the desk was adamant. There were no short-
term flights to the Caribbean. "There is, of course, Haiti,"
she added, dismissively, as if she were offering a package tour
to Beirut.'

David Blundy, *Daily Telegraph*, 16 September 1989

The only way to travel along this awful, rain-rutted road was to ride pillion
on a motorbike. A tap-tap would slither to a halt, wheels churning the
mud. The ancient BSA dispatch popped and spluttered with tiny explo-
sions of black smoke. Whenever we came to a particularly miry part of
the road I had to dismount and allow the driver to proceed. Then he
would yell as soon as he gained terra firma, the signal for me to run and
reclaim my seat.

Naked children emerged from huts made of packing cases and decayed
sign boards, leaping across our path with the familiar salutation: *'Blanc!
Bonjour blanc!'* It was a painful journey: often we had to stop and remove
the mud which clogged our wheels; twice we were thrown off balance,
pitched into the sludge.

The Petite Rivière des Anglais was blocked at its sandy-shoaled mouth
by an accumulation of mud, algae and water lilies. Upstream, the waters
were black and precipitous. I paid the motor-cyclist, removed my shoes
and began to wade across the river towards Les Anglais. Soon I noticed a
man gesticulating at me from the opposite bank, brandishing a machete.
He then splashed into the river holding a small rock in his other hand. I
stood still, horrified. A melon rind bobbed by on the skin of the current,
pursued by a rotten orange. Now the man was about ten yards from me;
he seemed beside himself with rage. 'You!' He raised the rock above his
head, screaming. 'You crazy or something walk around alone? Where you
go in Christ his name?' he asked in English.

'Les Anglais.' I struggled as the weight of my rucksack tilted me backwards.

'Who in Les Anglais? Who you seeing? I said, *who you* –' The man waded another step towards me, and widened the whites of his eyes. 'Who?'

'Monsieur Jean St Cyr.' It was the only name I knew. 'He's the Mayor,' I panicked, 'of Les Anglais.'

This seemed to appease. 'I see . . .' Then the man yelled in a military baritone, 'Son bitch Merican crazy man!'

'I'm English, not American . . . *Anglais.*'

He dropped his rock into the water. 'Excuse. I thought you Yankee.' Then his voice rose in pitch again. 'You lucky! Very lucky, my friend! If you tell me American I reduce your skull to matchwood. Then I decapitate you, here and now. And your head float off! Downstream! To sea!'

My command of Creole was not equal to this sort of situation and I asked in French why the man had taken me for an American. 'Because you look like Mormon! The colour of your skin, that short hair – just like Mormon. How I hate Mormons! Mafia! Macoutes! CIA, every one Mormon bad!' And with that the madman waded to shore in the direction of a *kalorin* or public wrestling match, where the object is to lay one's opponent flat on his back in the mud. We wished each other a happy Easter.

The muddy current broke on a crescent of sand and I went in search of the mayor.

The architecture of Les Anglais was similar to that of Port-à-Piment, but shabbier. Houses were small narrow clapboards peeling paint, their galvanized-iron roofs separated by drainage ditches choked with weeds and tin cans. Pools of stagnant water everywhere ran to broken culverts, also fouled with refuse. The town centre was a large paddock of beaten earth and thorned bramble, with the dilapidated aspect of a military encampment. A white neo-Gothic cathedral, ornamental as the Albert Memorial, happily relieved this desolation: its steeple, surmounted by a golden cross, was erected in 1907 by a French priest named François Hébelard of the Holy Order of Oblate Fathers. Around the corner, conspicuous by a fence snowy with honeysuckle, stood the mayor's house. A couple of *caranclous*, or turkey-vultures, roosted on the roof, silhouetted against the advancing dusk.

Jean St Cyr sat alone at his desk, tipped back in a chair with his legs crossed, holding a bottle of Kola on his knee. He was dressed casually in gabardine slacks and a blue sports shirt open to the waist. Another Macoute, I surmised. But no, this mayor was quite accommodating. *'Bienvenu!'* He offered me a beer and politely inquired after my business. 'Aha! A book about Haiti. Well then, I simply must tell you about Les Anglais,' and Monsieur St Cyr went on to explain how in the nineteenth century there used to be a sizeable English population from the old Crown Colonies of Barbados, Jamaica, St Lucia and St Vincent. Before that time, during the British occupation of southern Haiti which began in 1793, Les Anglais served as a port for the Royal Navy. Although not for very long. By the end of 1795 George III had apparently lost the initiative against the French in colonial Saint Domingue. The British were nevertheless terrified of the effect that an independent Haiti might have on nearby Jamaica, their own slave colony; and in February of the following year Whitehall sent the largest expedition – 27,000 men – ever to sail from the British Isles to the West Indies. The campaign proved a national disgrace: five million pounds were lost to the Treasury, along with the lives of thousands of men who might have been better deployed against the French in Europe.

Les Anglais functioned as a naval redoubt until June 1796, when Brigadier Thomas Maitland, British second-in-command at Saint Domingue, wrote home to his brother Lord Lauderdale: 'We have no business on this island where a Negro Free Government will arise out of the ashes of European despotism.' Maitland agreed to relinquish the south if Toussaint L'Ouverture would undertake not to interfere with the evacuation by sea of the remaining redcoats. The last British soldiers left Les Anglais in defeat at the beginning of October 1798, having recognized Toussaint as the legitimate ruler of Saint Domingue. It was the first time in history that a European army had surrendered to a black general. 'I found this colony dismembered, ruined, overrun by Spaniards, French and English, who fought over the pieces,' proclaimed a triumphant Toussaint. 'It is today purged of its enemies, quiet, pacified, and advances toward its complete restoration.' This was before the General was clapped in irons by Napoleon.

'I am very happy to have you here,' Monsieur St Cyr continued. 'Just one small problem' – his smile vanished – 'there is nowhere for you to stay.'

'No hotel?'

'No tourism, no hotel. Nothing.'

Jean St Cyr considered a moment. 'Unless we put you in the Hôtel de Ville.'

The Town Hall stood opposite a small beer and soda joint on Rue Colse (a corruption, apparently, of the English surname 'Coles'), surrounded by a fence of spider plants covered with prickles. It resembled more an African palaver-house than a municipal building, the windows caulked with newspaper and its tin roof nailed over guinea grass. St Cyr led the way with an acetylene lamp. 'Meet Oscar Chérubin.' The mayor introduced me to an old man slouched on a cane chair at the entrance. 'The caretaker. He's blind unfortunately but I was obliged to give him the job because he's my grandfather. Most nights Oscar sleeps here with his grandson Abnol. Poor Abnol, his parents died long ago.'

Oscar licked his dry, cracked lips and asked me for a cigarette. 'I am the guardian of the Hôtel,' he said impassively. 'I look after you.'

The mayor said, 'Don't mind Oscar. You'll be seeing quite a lot of him.' We proceeded through a partition of latticework reeds. 'Well, here's your room.' St Cyr placed the lamp on an old spruce table. A smell of mildew hit me forcibly. 'And there's your bed.' He pointed to a pallet of eucalyptus branches. 'I expect you'll be wanting something to eat before the Easter Vigil tonight. I'll send Abnol round with some food.'

The mayor extended a hand. 'See you at Midnight Mass then. Oh, and don't worry about the odd *chauve-souris*.' He held the lamp aloft and its rays fell on a fringe of loose fibres trailing from the palm-wood beams. A few hundred bats hung from these ceiling beams, tiny black bags like closed tulips. 'Funny!' Monsieur St Cyr exclaimed. 'Funny the way they hang head-down at rest!' Then he left me alone.

The acetylene lamp burned like some dim religious light; mindful of the bats, I lifted it by the wire handle and began to explore my room. A tattered line of red and blue bunting stretched from wall to wall. It was affixed at one end to a lurid study of Mary Magdalene and Jesus; and at the other, to a print of Jean-Jacques Dessalines dressed in a hussar jacket. A heap of untanned hides lay in a corner with an unusual assortment of junk including a gas cylinder, an old carburettor, a portable phonograph with a rusted crank, a soot-blackened saucepan and a broken perambulator.

At 9.30 p.m. from outside the Hôtel de Ville came the voice of a priest broadcasting the time for Easter Vigil – *la Veille Pascale* – through a megaphone. 'Father Jacques Saint of the Holy Order of Oblates summons all faithful to church at ten o'clock. Father Jacques . . .' The partition in my room was drawn aside and Abnol appeared with a tray supporting a blue coffee pot and two dishes under plastic fly covers. The food looked unappetizing: a stew of fish heads and rice swimming in oleo-margarine; half-cooked lumps of pork fat, soft and tallowy. Abnol could not have been more than six years old, his face smooth as terracotta. *'M'sieur, donnez-moi un cadeau.'* He made a gesture of eating. *'J'ai faim.'*

My stomach felt almost concave from hunger but I shared the supper with Abnol. Presently a beggar crawled through the partition, moving forward by lifting himself on his hands. *'Allez!'* Abnol yelled at this fearsome apparition. *'Allez! Vagabond!'* The beggar scuttled away sideways like a crab. In Haiti, you take what you can when you can. Abnol champed on his food.

A china-blue half-moon hung in the sky above the cathedral. Black-shawled women hurried to Mass in the mud, cursing the power cut. But there was light in the church and I could see that the celebrants were competitively dressed. Young girls wore rhinestone combs in their hair, mantillas of black lace; men arrived in straw hats, outsized suits and shiny cuff links. The fellow in front resembled the bridegroom on a Las Vegas wedding cake: large bow tie, frilly turquoise shirt. 'Misericordia!' He turned to me in the pews. 'A *blanc* in Les Anglais. Happy Easter, my friend.'

The windows of the cathedral were swathed in straw mats to shut out the heat; there was a scent of flowers heavy in the air like a funeral parlour. Candle stands were adorned with vine sprays and white heliotropes, the chancel with peacock-blue ribbons. In 1828 a British businessman, James Franklin, wrote that Haitians 'are not actuated by any religious feeling. Going to church is a mere matter of parade with them, and the female congregations which frequent the churches in Haiti appear better prepared for an opera . . .' There is little truth to this. While Haitians certainly dress in 'Sunday best', they are deeply religious, and most are nominally Catholic. In his proclamation of 10 October 1798 announcing the expulsion of the English, Toussaint L'Ouverture ordered thanks to the God of Hosts and recommended to his chief of corps that soldiers pray morning and evening, and faithfully attend Mass on Sundays. He reminded parents of their duty to teach the catechism to their children.

Dessalines himself sent a small number of black youths to Rome to be ordained by Pope Pius VII, so they might return and provide a black priesthood for the republic and bring Haiti into the theatre of European affairs. (As it happened, the Pope refused to consecrate these aspirants to holy orders, possibly through the intervention of Napoleon Bonaparte.) Yet the religion of the masses remains a gallimaufry of Voodoo and Catholicism where the *houngan* will recite the Roman liturgy – the Ave Maria, Pater Noster, Salve Regina and Creed – while invoking the spirits of ancestral

Africa. Voodoo makes frequent use of one particular sacrament of the Church – baptism. According to Father Roger Hallée, an American priest who works in the mountain village of Rendel some eight miles south of Les Anglais: 'If a child is not baptized, the *houngan* has no power of magic or medicine over him. A newborn unbaptized is merely a *choual*, a horse as they say in Creole, not a proper human being, just a half animal.'

Father Hallée had lived in Haiti for thirty years; he told me how scapulars, candles and even communion hosts are stolen from his church by Voodoo priests. 'They use these objects to counteract the force of an evil spell, or *wanga*,' he reasoned. 'And particularly so after someone dies before his time, when the first thing people ask themselves is: "Now who on earth were his enemies?" Because let me tell you this: in Haiti, there is never, ever such a thing as a natural death . . .'

The priest remembered a time five years ago when his parishioners found a list of people who had unexpectedly died – and of others who were about to die – on the person of a *bokor*. The sorcerer was brought before the police at Les Anglais for interrogation, where he confessed to dispatching his victims by mixing a noxious powder into their food. He managed, however, to bribe his way out of prison as the Justice of the Peace was complicit in the crimes. Two months later, a young farmer whose name had appeared on the list died all of a sudden while having a tooth extracted in the dentist's chair. 'I don't know whether this guy pegged out owing to an overdose of Novocaine or what,' said Father Hallée. 'But boy, when the dead farmer's family sent out a posse to capture the fugitive magician, all hell broke loose.'

The *bokor* was found cowering in fear at the nearby town of Dussable, protected by the Rendel chief of police. 'He was dragged out of hiding and summoned before a kangaroo court.' Father Hallée closed his eyes a moment, as though seeking strength. 'And then he was burned alive inside a rubber tyre.' The villagers had tape-recorded everything: a howling as the magician realized he was about to die, his final confession engulfed by flames. 'To this day I search for the man in possession of that terrible cassette.' The priest spoke in a small, dry voice. 'But I'll probably never find him,' he said with finality.

Some days after talking to Father Hallée I happened to be reading *The Beast of the Haitian Hills* by Philippe Thoby-Marcelin and Pierre Marcelin, Haitian brothers whom Edmund Wilson had commended to Vladimir Nabokov in 1948. The novel is a horrendous and witty grand-guignol tragi-comedy, anthropologically fascinating. It features a half-ferocious, night-prowling devil-dog beast with 'phosphorescent eyes', apparently in the service of Baron Samedi. It has been described as a cautionary tale addressed to those bourgeois Roman Catholic Haitians who choose to ignore the force of superstition, and appears to have frightened even one so stalwart as Sir John Betjeman. 'By the time the book was finished I almost believed in Voodoo myself,' he wrote in his review for the *Daily Telegraph*. The Westerner who comes to Haiti without knowledge of Voodoo is like a blind man walking on eggs and after three months in this country I had to readjust myself to an image of life more supernatural than supernormal.

Tam, tam, boom . . . Drumming had begun to sound for Mass, a steady rhythm from a battery of three *tambouriers* stationed before the altar. The drums were fashioned from hollow logs, tuned with pegs inserted in the sides and reinforced with twine wound round the stretched heads of cowhide or goatskin. These same drums are used in Voodoo ceremonies: the largest being the *manman*, the middle the *seconde* and the smallest the *bula*. Wearing a coat embroidered with gold silk, Father Jacques Saint of the Oblate Fathers commenced his reading from St Luke Chapter 24 ('And they found the stone rolled away from the sepulchre'). Then the church was put into darkness to symbolize the gloom of the tomb. A murky half-light like underexposed film, and an air of tense anticipation as several of the celebrants began to chant *'Lumière Jésus Christ! Lumière Jésus Christ!'* The Paschal liturgy and the Mass itself were all conducted in the dark until suddenly – to a great cheer – the lights came on and the congregation broke out in song: *'Alléluia! Le Christ est vivant!'*

When I returned that night to the Hôtel de Ville, Oscar Chérubin the caretaker was crouched in the doorway beneath an overhanging eave of cane, the white strip of an unlit cigarette hanging from his mouth. I struck a match for his Comme il Faut and inquired after the *chauve-souris*. Oscar gave a cold bray of laughter and swivelled his unseeing eyes. 'The bats,' I persisted. 'How are they?' But Oscar did not answer.

Back in my room I lit the acetylene lamp and there they were, countless bats reeling back and forth around the rafters. Instinctively, I ducked as they swooped close to my face and I hid under the bedclothes, though it was breathlessly hot. All night the flying mammals with their webs of leathery skin would emit a high-pitched squeaking, like the faint whirring blades of a helicopter. I had a dreadful night of it, all told.

* * *

The State Lottery Office – *Bureau de Borlette* – stood across the market square from the Hôtel de Ville. Every night a crowd of locals would bustle round the shack to place a cheap bet; as with many countries in what is now called the Third World, gambling is a way to tempt fate, and escape poverty. It is consequently the preferred pastime for most Haitians. *Borlette* was probably imported from Cuba by the *viejos*, Haitian migrants returned from cutting cane, who originally referred to the game in Spanish as '*la borlita*'. This is a supremely superstitious version of tombola and groups of excited gamblers will usually come equipped with copies of the *Tchala*. Mystically subtitled 'Premonitory Dreams and the Art of White Magic as told by the Spirits of Dygmatrimalion and Amaleck', the little booklet gives an individual lottery number to fit every conceivable dream, ranging from abattoir and apricot to machete, macaroni and revolver.

One night in Les Anglais I purchased a second-hand edition of the *Tchala* and took it back to the Town Hall. Turning the pages under the lamp, I was reminded of a leaflet which is readily available at newspaper kiosks in Naples, *La Smorfia*. This is a sort of gambling cabbala for addicts of lottery and contains such information as 'Dream of the Madonna: place a bet on 5', or 'Diego Maradona, 23'. The *Tchala* itself offered the following correspondence between numbers and dreams: Voodoo priest, 57; corpse, 60; electric plug, 53; diarrhoea, 47. I was particularly interested in: 'Bat: if hanging upside down from roof or branch, this signifies amorous upset. Place a bet on number 22.' The bats, needless to say, were out in force as I read the *Tchala* that night, but they never hit me, owing no doubt to their radar.

I got quite used to the bats; they enhanced an atmosphere which became ever more spooky as I studied the chapter addressed to gamblers 'who have no fear of the night'. Here I came across a prayer to be intoned at midnight during a full moon, guaranteed to bring propitious results. 'O great St Michael, Prince of the Celestial Armies, O great St Mark whose symbol is the Lion, O Archangel Gabriel exterminator of those unclean in mind and body, help me, guide me, care for my spirit in its sleep; commend me to Nabactamon, Legbat-Alemon, Jamabeth and Hectumen-Hali, that these most puissant Spirits of the Lottery may win me money.' Such a prolonged prayer – half Christian, half cabbalistic – would redound to the honour of Aleister Crowley, not to mention a Voodoo priest.

The mysticism, though, should not blind one to a sinister aspect of *borlette*; it is often controlled by Duvalierists. The next morning I heard through the *teledyòl* (grapevine) that the director of the National Lottery, a former lieutenant in the Haitian army by the name of Thony Pierre, had been reprimanded in court for rigging public lottery extractions. These he would attend in person armed with a Colt .45, accompanied by Tontons Macoute.

This connection between superstition and corruption inevitably involved Papa Doc. He even appointed a *bokor*, one Zacharie Delva, as his chief of Macoutes. Delva drove a large black limousine with a madly wailing siren; and in some areas of northern Haiti, peasants claim that human babies were sacrificed to his ceremonies.

'Here, this'll wake you up,' said Nino Cicinelli. 'It's what we call in Italy a *tirami su*, pick-me-up.' He poured some rum into the cup of coffee wedged between my knees. Then he switched on the ignition and we drove out of Les Anglais in the white light of dawn.

Nino worked as a mechanic for the same UNESCO project which involved Milan, who had earlier given me a lift to Port-à-Piment. I had to wait three days at Les Anglais for Nino the Italian to arrive: now that he had, my relief was great, as the only practicable way to reach the southern town of Tiburon fifteen miles away was by jeep. 'If it weren't for me, you'd have to spend the rest of your days in that filthy Hôtel de Ville,' Nino laughed as we groaned uphill through the village of Grosse Chaudière. '*Madonna mia!* What a fate! All those bats! Just being in the same room with bats can give you rabies!' Then he ground down through the gears as the jeep took a zigzagging descent amid clumps of spiny palmetto and up the other side along a flat and incredibly muddy shelf of land.

'How's the coffee?' He raised an eyebrow.

'Powerful. I feel pretty picked up.'

Nino removed his hands from the wheel a moment to check his appearance in the rear-view mirror, then swerved ('Phew! Close one, eh?') to avoid a man unyoking oxen in our way. 'Haitian rum!' he exclaimed. 'It's the best thing about this country. Otherwise, just Maggi Beef Noodle Soup or – *Spirito Santo!* – tinned American spaghetti. Can you imagine! My wife would have a fit.'

I warmed to Nino Cicinelli. He was a comic-strip caricature of the Southern Italian: short and dark, with slicked-back hair, flashing black eyes and a medallion of St Christopher round his neck. Born in the hills of Abruzzi near Rome, Nino had worked as a mechanic in all parts of French West Africa. 'But Haiti,' he spoke with a thick Roman accent, 'is a thousand times less developed than anywhere in Senegal, Gabon, or even the

Cameroon. At least you can buy Parmesan cheese in the supermarkets there. Here, never: only rice or burned bananas.'

For the rest of our journey we chatted in a desultory fashion about Marcello Mastroianni (whose rakish allure evidently appealed to Nino), the late Alberto Moravia and the Italian MP cum sex enthusiast Cicciolina (whom Nino had seen perform a striptease in Naples). We arrived at our destination in the drowsy heat of noon, the air dry and salty with a tang of sea. 'Say hello to Queen Elizabeth for me,' yelled Nino as he drove off in the direction of Source Chaude, a town miles away in the hinterland.

I was soon approached by the Tiburon *chef de section* who wore a white pith helmet, a nickel sheriff's badge and three grenades clipped to the webbing of his waistband. I produced my *laisser-passer* and explained to Gerard Alexis, this local chief of police, my intention to gather information on Tiburon for a book. A pig routed round our feet as the *chef* inspected my papers. Then he took my hand with unexpected friendliness and familiarity (though Haitian men often walk with fingers intermingled, I reminded myself), saying: 'Come, my friend.'

He led me to a chair under a bower of palm leaves. 'I'll fetch Gaspard the old schoolteacher.' The policeman released my hand. 'He'll be able to tell you everything you want to know about Tiburon.'

I sat there for some minutes, sipping from a bottle of warm soda, as people gathered. 'Where do you come from?' They stared at me as though I had descended on their village like an asteroid. 'What are you doing here?'

One old man asked if Miami was further from Haiti than England; an eight-year-old girl, fascinated by my cheap wristwatch with Roman numerals, wondered whether I spoke Latin. Presently the *chef de section* returned with Gaspard. Unfortunately, the schoolteacher was deaf; my questions had to be jotted down on the back of cigarette packets and it was approaching dusk, the sky stained to a sea-shell pink, by the time he had replied to all these written queries. Nevertheless, I learned the following:

The town was founded in 1737 by a group of Spanish who named it *Tiburón* – shark – after a rock near by which resembles the dorsal fin of that predatory fish. Of all the towns in southern Haiti, Tiburon is the one closest to Jamaica, which lies one hundred miles away across the Caribbean Sea. It was from Jamaica that the British arrived to occupy Tiburon on 3 February 1794 before they were expelled eight months later by the republican forces of Toussaint L'Ouverture. The victory is commemorated today by a Haitian fortress at Tiburon named Le Vainqueur, which is in ruins.

'What about Navassa?' An old man moved forward from the back of the crowd. 'Tell the *blanc* about Navassa!'

A murmur of assent, followed by a hubbub of people talking in low tones, and the chief of police got up to shout: 'No! We know nothing about this island.'

The old man persisted. 'Ah, nonsense, *mon cher!*' He wrote a question about Navassa on a flattened Comme il Faut wrapper. Gaspard read it, and proceeded to relate the history of the place which I was later able to substantiate from documents held at the Institut de St Louis de Gonzague, Port-au-Prince.

The island of Navassa lies about seventy-five miles east-north-east of Jamaica, and some thirty miles west of Cap Tiburon. Most Haitians have never heard of Navassa, this barren, waterless square mile of limestone thrust above the sea in the shape of a hummock. The Tiburonnais, though, often sail close to the island when fishing, and tell how the place is encircled with barbed wire. Many have seen helicopters land there during the night. There is no mention of Navassa on either my German roadmap of Haiti or on the ordnance survey of the country published for US pilots by the Defense Mapping Agency Aerospace Center, St Louis, Missouri. But then the Americans have reason to be secretive.

For centuries, the Haitian island of Navassa had remained uninhabited and apparently derelict, a home only for countless generations of sea birds. In September 1857, however, a Baltimore shipmaster named Peter Duncan took possession of Navassa under – of all things – the Guano Islands Act of 1856. This provided that 'whenever a citizen of the United States discovers a deposit of guano on any island . . . not within the lawful jurisdiction of any other Government, and not occupied by the citizens of any other Government, and takes peaceable possession thereof, and occupies the same, such island may be considered as appertaining to the U.S.' Mr Duncan discovered a million tons of bird shit on Navassa. This was a valuable amount in those days, for guano sold as fertilizer at $40 per ton. On 20 April 1858 a flotilla of Haitian gunships anchored off the island to protest.

The expedition was a failure; the Americans refused to leave. In November of that year, the Haitian commercial agent at Boston addressed a further protest to the US Secretary of State: Navassa, he stated, is a rightful dependency of the Negro Republic of Haiti. The agent was justified in his every objection to the American invasion, and turned to history as proof. Hispaniola, he said, was formally divided in 1697 by the Treaty of

Ryswick where Spain recognized French sovereignty over the newly named colony of Saint Domingue, which occupied the western third of the island and included the territory of Navassa. The guano island therefore became part of modern Haiti – formerly Saint Domingue – when Dessalines proclaimed independence from the French in 1804. The Secretary of State was not convinced of this argument and Navassa continued to reap dividends for the 'Yankee vagabond' Peter Duncan. In 1915 the Americans erected a lighthouse on the island; and according to the Tiburonnais, Navassa now functions as a radar base for the US Navy.

On my return to Port-au-Prince some weeks later, I went to the American embassy on Boulevard Harry Truman in the vain hope of gathering information about this mysterious island. Security was strict.

'Excuse me, sir. Is that a camera in your pocket?' The US Marine spoke to me from a tiny cubicle of bulletproof glass. All I could see of him was a pair of eyes, squinty slits beneath a peaked white cap. Above the cubicle hung a sign: AMERICA'S WARRIORS.

'No camera,' I declared.

'Please surrender your passport.'

I was then scanned in the usual fashion with a metal-detector by a man in military box-toed shoes who gave me a plastic identity tag for my lapel.

The then American ambassador to Haiti, Mr Alvin Adams, was in his middle forties, blond, and Ivy League in brown brogues, a blue-grey worsted suit and button-down shirt. A photograph of President Bush hung above his desk, garlanded with rosettes made from the Stars and Stripes.

'Why, hel-*lo*!' The ambassador rose to greet me. 'What can I do for you?'

'Hello. Well, it's a little delicate, but –'

'Ssssh!' Mr Adams put a finger to his lips. 'Did you say *delicate?*'

'Um?'

'OK, one moment.' The ambassador returned to his desk and pressed the intercom. 'Susan. Could you come up a moment?' He turned to me with a smile. 'She's my press officer, handles anything . . . delicate. Take a seat, won't you?'

We sat at either end of a sofa. Opposite, a large white baseball stood in a silver trophy on a filing cabinet. 'Smoke?' Mr Adams offered me a Comme il Faut. That was a good sign, an American diplomat who smoked Haitian cigarettes. I had even heard that he spoke fluent Creole. 'Sure I got the language.' The ambassador looked at me perplexedly. 'Can't get along without it.' This was in marked distinction to previous American ambassadors, most of whom were unable to master even French. Mr Adams explained how many Haitians now believe he was born as a feral child to a group of Creole-speaking missionaries in the mountains above Port-au-Prince. 'It's a Romulus and Remus sort of thing,' he laughed. 'You know, like the Tarzan myth.'

Susan Clyde arrived, an ample woman who grunted a brief greeting. 'I take it you're aware of the procedure of interview protocol.' She looked at me.

'I'm sorry?'

'Well, would you kindly turn off your tape-recorder?'

The press officer eased herself on to the sofa between myself and the ambassador, notebook in hand. I broached the awkward subject of the guano island.

'Navassa?' Mr Adams looked at Miss Clyde, Miss Clyde turned her gaze towards President Bush. There was a silence. 'Navassa.' The ambassador repeated the word as though it were unknown to him. 'Now that,' he said, 'is a question which I would rather you did not pose.' He straightened his tie. 'I myself of course have never been there.'

I related the story of how Navassa was appropriated by the Baltimore adventurer. 'I think,' Mr Adams answered placidly, 'that your version of history is, uh, correct.'

'So the island belongs to America?'

'As far as I know, it does not belong to . . . Haiti.'

'Is there still a good deal of bird dung on Navassa?'

'Oh I don't know about that.'

'Because the people of Tiburon claim the island is a radar base for –'

'That information is classified,' Miss Clyde interjected with absolute confidence.

Then I heard myself asking blankly whether the business of Navassa was not typical of US policy towards Haiti since 1804, which seems to have been controlled by a determination to deny the country any rightful degree of sovereignty or independence.

'Sovereignty or independence,' echoed Mr Adams with great seriousness. 'Well it's true. Up to a point. I mean, we *did* meddle in the affairs of Papa Doc. We even tried to get rid of him, in 1963, when he began to attack the Kennedy administration. But to say that Americans are in Haiti for strategic reasons – you know, Haiti seen through Cuban eyes – well, that's just crap. Things have changed. We're here to help establish a democracy, to ensure that the next president is not – repeat *not* – a chosen creature of the military.'

From what the ambassador was saying, it would seem that the success or failure of a Haitian government is still ultimately determined by diplomatic relations with the United States. But Mr Adams would not be pressed; he had an appointment elsewhere. As I left the embassy, he said: 'Haiti's one hell of a place. In many ways, it was the first Third World nation in the world. But how it will end, I don't know.'

'Well, that's the story of Navassa,' said Gaspard the deaf schoolteacher. The sky was illumined with a baleful red glow, darkening rapidly in the west. With help from the assembled Tiburonnais, I began to plan the next leg of my journey. They told me it was useless to return to Port-au-Prince via Les Anglais: the roads were flooded. It would be quicker to reach the capital by taking a boat to the south-western town of Les Irois, and proceed overland thence to Dame Marie where there was a possibility of a tap-tap to Jérémie. From Jérémie, another bus to Les Cayes; and then, if I could (these things always look so simple on a map), a second bus from Les Cayes in the direction of Port-au-Prince, passing the towns of Saint Louis du Sud, Aquin, Miragoâne, Petit Goâve and Léogâne.

Down by the shore, in the gathering night, one could see the single eye of a lighthouse winking in the distance from Navassa. 'Yankees,' the chief of police grinned as he led me seawards.

Shoes in hand, I clambered into the waiting boat and found a place by the prow. It was choked with old leaves and bits of cork. A sour musky smell came from the three oarsmen whose clothes were damp with sweat: they had been fishing since dawn for conches and their catch lay by the main mast, a pile of shells frilled with violet palates. *'Au revoir, blanc!'* The villagers waved as we rounded the breakwater and drifted out of sight.

Les Irois was located a little inland at the point of dead water created by the confluence of two small rivers. The village was named, they say, after Catholic Irish – *Irlandais* – who settled here after fleeing persecution at the hands of Oliver Cromwell. I could find no evidence of anything Hibernian in this foul-smelling place and began to inquire after transport. To my relief, an old produce truck was due to leave for Dame Marie in half an hour. I hopped on board and was immediately buttonholed by a young man who pointed with pride to the words across his T-shirt: 'Larry's Pool Hall and Pawn Shop'. Then he snorted in broken English, 'You! White man! Gonna buy me a visa?' and stared at me with sullen red-rimmed eyes. 'A visa to take me back to your country, eh?' I paid him no attention.

The man shouted, 'You! Rich boy! I'm talking to you!' He leant forward so that I could smell the alcohol on his breath. 'Felix, that's my name. Never forget. Repeat after me. F-E-L-I-X.' I mumbled the name and watched his Adam's apple rise and fall as he pressed his mouth to a bottle of rum. 'Good,' he belched. 'And you? What's your name?' – ignoring my irritation. 'What's that? I can't hear. Ian, you say. Ian . . . Jomsonne. Oh, I bet you're a *very* rich man.'

'No,' I said, resignedly.

'Ah, rubbish!' he went on, pleased. 'You *must* have money to travel around. Give me your name and address, Yan Yomsonne! Now!' His eyes seemed to search for a spot of guilt or uncertainty in me, on to which he could fasten like a lamprey. I began to feel a loathing for the man, for his cruel idiot smile and wheedling voice. He told me he came from a hamlet near Les Irois called Carcasse.

At last the truck clacked into life and off we lurched, a fine dust sifting through the floor. Felix would not leave me alone. 'Do you have a sister? Oh, I just know she's rich as hell.' He looked into my face and observed with satisfaction the symptoms of my discomfort. 'You know what, I'm going to marry your sister. Now what do you think about that, Yammy Yomsonne?'

To his and my surprise, I yelled: 'Shut up! Just . . . *shut up!*' My anger, I instantly saw, had its effect. From that moment, a sudden strangeness was set between me and this Haitian. He glared at me in silence until we reached Dame Marie where I caught the last tap-tap out of town.

XIII

Trollope and Turtle Soup

'She did not believe in God, but many gods: of food, light, of death, ruin. The *houngan* was in touch with these gods; he kept their secrets on his altar, could hear their voices in the rattle of a gourd, could dispense their power in a potion . . .'

Truman Capote, *House of Flowers*

I put in a handful of quarters; the jukebox clicked and whirred, then began to play a Cole Porter number: 'Do, do that Voodoo that you do so well . . .' No one else was here, the bar was deserted: Ricard, Metaxa, Strega, Custom House Distilled London Dry Gin, bottles covered in dust. A stuffed Siberian tiger, its pelt balding, snarled at me from the beams of the bare room. The walls were adorned with cracked elephant tusks, crossed polo sticks, yellowed menus from Maxim's in Paris.

Fifteen years ago when there was tourism, distinguished guests would sit here sipping gin slings – Helmut Berger, Baron Thyssen, Franco Rossellini and Twiggy to judge by the visitors' book. No longer. I was the sole customer at the Relais de l'Empereur, a large hotel in the town of Petit Goâve some forty miles west of Port-au-Prince. I arrived there after a gruelling journey from Les Cayes, bumping in a tap-tap over rough pastureland with stony heaths. It was the hot hour of day and I felt badly travel-stained, bitten by insects and thirsty for a frozen daiquiri. Sadly, the man at reception was a half-wit.

'Do you want a room with a fan?'

I said I did.

'We haven't any.'

'Then give me a room without a fan.'

The room, as it turned out, had a fan but it didn't work. A giant poster-canopied bed stood beneath the motionless blades, luxurious with linen sheets. The bath, even the bidet, was fitted with gold-plated taps; it was wonderfully indecent to find this ostentation in Haiti. I attacked the mini-bar and submerged myself in the bath, a welcome respite from the usual smell of peanuts and dung.

There was a small bookshelf with a collection of trashy paperbacks: *The Scorpion's Sting, The Lovely Wanton, The Season of the Machete* . . . Airport fiction: I assumed the books had been left by tourists bound from Miami. To my surprise, I found a copy of *Washington Square* by Henry James. Graham Greene suggested that the books to take on a journey are those which most closely contrast with the mood of the country you happen to read them in. He advised Anthony Trollope for Mexico ('a hating and hateful country'). I had made the mistake of taking Ronald Firbank to Haiti. His novels have too much an atmosphere of the hothouse to be read with proper enjoyment here. All that tropical sunlight, the Caribbean Sea, the blackamoors and blooming orchids: the writing skims across the page like a glittering dragonfly. But with Henry James, all fatigue was forgotten. For the first time in months I felt as though I had been returned to myself, happily repaired.

Misery treads fast on the heels of joy. When I came back to my room later that night I found that a good deal of money had been stolen from my wallet. I lodged a complaint with the owner, a man who seemed principally occupied in loafing with the dolly-birds of Petit Goâve. 'Naturally we shall do everything to alleviate the stress which has been caused to you,' he said, fibbing roundly (there was never any compensation). 'I need not tell you how profoundly I regret that this should have happened at the Relais de L'Empereur . . .'

So Henry James faded out and Haiti remained.

The Relais de l'Empereur is housed in the former residence of Faustin Soulouque, ruler of Haiti from 1847 to 1859, who is buried five minutes away beneath a hideous slab of concrete. Faustin constructed his home out of blocks of red stone imported from France as ship's ballast. It now resembles a storage depot.

Soulouque was a pompous emperor, an unsavoury hybrid of Idi Amin and Julius Caesar. Given to such imperial follies as the creation of a peerage with princes, counts, barons and numerous knights, he was lampooned by the French cartoonist Honoré Daumier as 'Monsieur Garibaldi-Robespierre-Napoléon Soulouque'. He ruled as a blatant despot and organized a force of secret police – the dreaded *zinglins* – which foreshadowed the Tontons Macoute. His court was preposterous, full of trumpery protocol; if Soulouque laughed, his chamberlain would pronounce, 'His Majesty is laughing. Gentlemen, you too are permitted to laugh.' Soulouque, an adept of African animism, was deeply superstitious and stories still circulate of how he was sworn in during a Voodoo ceremony with rum mixed in the blood of an ox sacrificed for the purpose; how a priest by accident presented the wafer to Soulouque at Mass the wrong side up, and was promptly executed on the grounds that he had cast a malignant spell.

The Dominicans called him a *'rey de farsa'*, a farcial king, and the *New York Herald* unkindly baptized him 'nigger Billy Bowlegs'. Victor Hugo, sickened by the regal pretensions of Napoleon III, regarded the French emperor and this Haitian autocrat as two of a kind:

> *Dieu dans sa sagesse a fait exprès cet homme*
> *Pour régner sur la France, ou bien sur Haïti.*

Soulouque is judged by modern historians, however, as a rather astute politician and his fears concerning an independent or hostile Dominican Republic were well founded. In his day, of course, Soulouque only encouraged the Western prejudice that slaves were quite incapable of civilized self-government. Anthony Trollope was explicitly pejorative. 'All the world knows that Soulouque is a black man. One blacker never endured the meridian heat of the sun,' he grumbled in his book *The West Indies and the Spanish Main*. 'He called together his army and put on the boots of Bombastes . . . and played, upon the whole, such a melodrama of autocratic tricks and fantasies as might have done honour to a white Nero.'

Eventually, Soulouque was overthrown in the usual fashion and exiled with his wife Princess Olive in January 1859. He was ferried to Jamaica on board a British steamer named the *Melbourne* at the precise moment Trollope was sailing towards Kingston from the southern coast of Cuba. This is a curious picture: Trollope, a great bumbling hulk of a man with pince-nez; and Soulouque, the dastardly dictator of Haiti, coal-hatch black but likewise stout and hale, chugging inexorably towards the author of *Barchester Towers*.

Arrived at Kingston, Faustin Soulouque put in at the Date-Tree Tavern where, according to Trollope, a group of furious Haitians whose relatives had perished at the hands of the tyrant's sword began to hold a 'dignity ball in token of their joy'. For three days they 'maintained their position in order that poor Soulouque might witness their rejoicing at his fall'. Trollope himself was resident directly opposite Soulouque, and says how grateful he is that the Emperor did not reserve a room in the same hotel. 'A few friends were to dine with me that day; and where would have been my turtle soup had Soulouque and his suite taken possession of the house?'

The Haitian authorities later allowed the deposed emperor to build a home in the town where he was born, Petit Goâve. The tawdry grandeur of this house which became a hotel might have appealed to Soulouque. Most of the furniture in the bar was reproduction Second Empire: candy-striped awnings tasselled like a circus horse, a chaise-longue upholstered in raw silk, gilded bronze columns. There were armchairs of buttoned red plush that looked as though they had been removed from some Bavarian schloss, high-back cane chairs, backgammon sets and even a live leopard named Sheba which padded about in the garden among the dislocated majolica tiles.

I ordered a whisky which was served in a chipped highball glass. Presently, a large Haitian walked into the bar wearing a sharp double-breasted suit. He told me he had travelled to Petit Goâve from his home in Los Angeles as the representative of a US computer company. 'Business here is wild.' He shook his head. 'We're back to the days of Al Capone and the Cosa Nostra, only it's the Mafia with a French touch – more sophisticated, underhand.'

The man described Petit Goâve as a town of smuggling and border-line enterprise, a vast clearing house for contraband. Go down to the wharf, he said: see for yourself, all those bags of Miami rice and stuff. 'It's bootleg, real bad booty, but the cops turn a blind eye.' He explained how there is no duty to pay on American rice, that it can undersell Haitian rice by more than half. Numerous other ports in Haiti also thrive on contraband – Saint Marc, Môle Saint Nicolas, Miragoâne and Gonaïves chief among them.

'Well, that's Haiti for you. You know about Felix Houphouët-Boigny?' The businessman looked at me with condescending curiosity.

I said I did not.

'Well, he's the President of the Côte d'Ivoire. Know what he said about Haiti?'

'No.'

'He said, *"Pauvre Haïti! Sí loin de Dieu et si près des Etats Unis."* That's what he said.'

'In which case, he was a plagiarist,' I countered.

'How so?' the Haitian demanded.

Pompously, I insisted that it was the nineteenth-century Mexican president Porfirio Díaz who had originally said, 'Poor Mexico! So far from God and so close to the United States.'

The man was visibly piqued at this and barked in his American accent: *'Garçon! Une autre crème de menthe!'*

Another powercut, and I decided to take a stroll along the wharf, perhaps to investigate the contraband. The broad midnight moon was shining clear and hundreds of bats dipped through the air under the one street-lamp outside the Caserne Soulouque, a dingy barracks more like a large horse stable. I passed a soldier, hand gripped tight on the hilt of his machete, and turned a corner at the Cathedral of St Pierre where a path took me through mud to the docks. Anchored some way to sea, and illuminated at the stern by a naphtha flare, was a small cargo ship named *Teddy Trader II.* Voices were borne to me on the breeze, English voices inflected with a Caribbean accent.

Round the ship bobbed six or so pirogues with lateen sails, bales of merchandise lowered into their hulls from pulleys hung with loops of rope. I walked further along the wharf and came to a crowd of Petitgoâviens arguing around boxes of produce ferried from *Teddy Trader II.* The labels read: 'Milcow – Fullcream Evaporated Milk Furnished by the People of the United States', 'Mr Ruby's Extra Fancy Long Grain Enriched Rice', 'Refined Miami Granulated Sugar' . . . An old woman sat on an upturned crate in the midst of this crowd, electronic calculator in hand. She caught sight of me and asked, 'Wat yu doam here now, mister?'

'Nothing, just out for a walk.'

'Is dat so?' She laughed. 'Me, I'm thinking you gwine report me to the police sho nuff.'

Her face, flame-lit, was kindly; she grinned like the Cheshire cat. 'Look, whitey,' she stood up, 'yuh want ah cigarette?' I accepted the offer and asked her, tentatively, about the cargo ship. 'Named it after my son,' she said with pride. 'God rest him in the grave.'

'So you own *Teddy Trader?'*

'Sho I do.'

The woman gave her name as Clarisse Shamoun. She had left Haiti, her native country, at the age of twelve to seek a fortune in Jamaica (hence the improbable accent), where she married a Lebanese. 'Can't justly say where he does be now,' said Madame Shamoun. 'He gone and left me, and it ain't seem right in the eyes of God to do such a thing.' In Kingston she established a shop called 'Hats for Happy Women' until it went bust thirty years ago. Then she went to Miami where she bought a cargo ship and began to export goods – rice, soap, lavatory paper, tomato paste, clothes, tinned sardines – to Haiti. *Teddy Trader* now leaves Florida for Petit Goâve once every fifteen days. Business is good and Madame Shamoun admires her crew. 'Most my boys come from Guyana, from Georgetown the capital. Or from Philippines.'

'Not from Haiti?'

'Oh no!' Madame Shamoun was adamant. They're too superstitious, she said, to qualify as professional seamen. 'Haitians frighten for God, but twice as scared of the devil!' And besides, she added, they might put 'bad stuff on *Teddy*'.

'Drugs?'

'Dat's what I say.'

This brought me to my delicate question: *is Teddy* a contraband ship?

'Whoever told you so told lies!' Madame Shamoun seemed to protest too much. Then she grinned again. 'Well, I ain't runnin' business here like a holy church.'

I asked if I could visit the ship with her.

'Oh why you ask?'

'Just . . . curiosity.'

'Hmmm. Well, I'm real busy tonight, and the hurrier I go, the behinder I get. But fair nuff, go down there and ask Ali for to take you over.'

She pointed to a dug-out beached in the surf beneath the wharf. 'Now gwan, gwan, be off with you!'

Ali was the chief mechanic for *Teddy*. He came from Georgetown. 'Touch the flesh, brother.' We shook hands. Waves broke like combers on the beach as we pushed out in our canoe. The tide was low, and there was a brilliant full moon. As we reached the ship, a companionway was lowered for us to scramble up the rungs. On board, I was led to the engine room where I was introduced to Lino the wireless operator, Terry the second engineer, and Ramon the cook. All were wall-eyed from alcohol. 'Is gin we drinkin', man.' They passed me a bottle of Bols. 'And tonight we been beautifying up the ship.' Ramon pointed to a picture of a naked woman decorated with Christmas-tree lights. I noticed a bottle of whisky – White Label – stuffed into a skipper's seaboot by the bunk. The boys were certainly merry, and some of them began to sing while gyrating to a lax samba.

Unfortunately the captain, Mr Macapagal from the Philippines, was sober and appeared reluctant to show me any cargo. All I ever saw, battened under a hatch of tarpaulin, was a gigantic pile of fabric – T-shirts, floral-print dresses, most of it already used. Haitians call this second-hand clothing *pépé* or sometimes *kenedi*, as large shipments came over from Miami in the days when Kennedy was in the White House. I had seen *pépé* for sale in every bidonville market – great bolts of multicoloured cloth, contraband in as much as it comes to Haiti without passing customs.

As I left *Teddy*, the ship lurched down to leeward. 'Wooah!' Ali steadied himself by gripping a table anchored to the deck. 'Careful how you go now, whitey!' he laughed. 'Specially with de women. One helluva ting does be happening here with AIDS.'

Heat and flies: heat and flies . . . The tap-tap to Léogâne lurched forward over potholes with a noise like startled poultry. Uphill through tracks of acacia shrub, and down again to the town of Fond des Nègres which was no more than a morass of mud. 'There is no de-luxe in Haiti.' A tooth-less man turned to me munching his cassava pancake. 'All of us is poor and miserable.' The rattletrap bus was named, with nice irony, *La Vie Est Drôle*. Life's a Laugh.

Black clouds overhead presaged rain. In this climate, you get wet twice: once from your own perspiration, and then from the rain. For most of my journey the heat had been stupefying: the sun in Haiti seems to kill every shadow, and they say anyone who has lived here for more than a month would probably need two blankets in hell.

Madame Beauharnais, mother-in-law of Josephine Bonaparte, kept a beautiful plantation in Léogâne which Dessalines destroyed, and I supposed the town was also in ruins, like the rest of Haiti. But it was my intention to stay the night at Léogâne with a Voodoo priest, Altesse Paul, whose name I had been given by the *houngan* Max Beauvoir. 'Altesse is the patriarch of Léogâne,' Beauvoir had told me. 'The Number One.'

Most unusually for Haiti, Max Beauvoir was a Voodoo priest with a middle-class background. The son of a physician, he left Haiti in his youth to study biochemical engineering in New York and at the Sorbonne in Paris. He speaks four languages fluently. Beauvoir became a *houngan* in 1974 when his grandfather asked him to do so from his deathbed, and is regarded by many as something of a mountebank. He was a proud and rather contradictious man (also extremely handsome) but I did admire his know-ledge of Voodoo. He had even been asked by a Tokyo academic about 'the correlation between Voodoo and Japanese history'.

When I met Max Beauvoir in his fashionable home just outside Port-au-Prince he was dressed like a yacht club habitué: white loafers with silver buckles, white cotton shirt, gold cigarette lighter. 'Voodoo is as old as humanity. It's a true religion, just as Mohammedanism, Buddhism or Christianity are true religions.' He conducted the interview from behind a desk with an IBM computer terminal, two telephones and an Anglepoise lamp. 'By which I mean, it's a set of beliefs and practices that deal with the spiritual forces of the universe, which keeps the individual in harmonious relation with these forces as they affect his life . . .'

Max Beauvoir asked whether I would like a 7 Up. He clapped his hands and a maid, Paulette, materialized on the instant bringing the drink. The study was adorned with pictures of gods, demons, metamorphoses, avatars; also with *vèvès* – elaborate designs of Dahomean origin usually traced on the ground of Voodoo temples in honour of various spirits. I noticed that the keys to Monsieur Beauvoir's Peugeot were placed next to an *açon*, a long-necked calabash enclosed in a loose cage of snake's vertebrae and coloured beads, used as a ceremonial rattle.

I asked Beauvoir whether he believed in God. 'As a Voodoo priest I place my faith in what we call the *Papa Bon Dieu*, which is not quite the same as your God.'

'In what way?'

Beauvoir explained, in his baritone voice: 'God for the Haitian is more like Fate or Destiny. He conjures no precise image, for he is too distant – *trop grand, trop lointain!* – to mean anything. Any natural disaster beyond the comprehension of ordinary folk, such as a hurricane or epidemic of disease, may be ascribed to the intervention of *Papa Bon Dieu*; but anything supernatural – a mysterious death, the appearance of a werewolf – will be directly accountable to the *loas*, or spirits.'

Monsieur Beauvoir reckons that Voodoo is so deeply engrained in Haiti that to hold elections here without acknowledging as much would be akin to 'conducting an election in Israel outside the spirit of Judaism'. His proud, high spirit would not allow that there are Catholic priests who wish to preserve the rites of African animism; Beauvoir is convinced of a conspiracy hatched by the Church to extirpate Voodoo. 'They think Haitians are simply whites with black skin and they want to ridicule our sacred images. Not that I am anti-religious myself' – he smiled tolerantly – 'although I do think that the Christians here in Haiti, particularly Americans, are cursed by a ferocious and destructive ignorance. Still, they are not beyond redemption. I believe they are capable of reform.'

This Olympian pronouncement was typical of Max Beauvoir and I left his house a little mystified by Voodoo; but at least I had a somewhat more precise idea of my ignorance than I did in the beginning.

I arrived at Léogâne under a low sky burdened with mizzly cold rain. Houses resembled small electric generators, tin-roofed, miserable in the leaden twilight. I had to ford a stream swollen by the spring cloudburst to reach Altesse Paul the *houngan*. Women stood thigh-deep in the waters washing clothes, their skirts tucked above their underwear. One of them yelled at me, '*Blanc!* Why don't you walk across like Jesus?' On the other side of the stream a small cinder path snaked through a thicket of baya-honda trees; a large carrion crow hopped ahead of me.

Soon I was lost for directions and inquired after Altesse at a run-down corner shop outside a Baptist church. The counter was piled with yams and cans of kerosene: the little old lady who stood behind them was barely visible. She seemed to flinch when I mentioned Altesse Paul. 'I don't want to get involved. People round here call him Doc, but he's a Voodoo man, makes me to feel the dead take possession of the whole of Léogâne.' She glanced at my Bible-black notebook. 'You a preacher?'

'Yes,' I lied.

'Then you know how the like of Altesse are an abomination unto the Lord. In God's good time the Voodoo men disappear.'

Such rousing words only strengthened my resolve to root out the *houngan*. However, the old woman did tell me where the spirit-raiser lived: walk straight down that road over there until you come to a tin shack with the sign *'Repassage des Cheveux'* (a beautician's where curly hair is ironed out flat), then turn left at a great thicket of rose-apple where a path takes you to Carrefour Meulier. 'And that's where the devil lives.' The woman spat the words.

'*Merci, madame.*'

'*OK, chéri. Bonne chance.*'

The path led through a dense canopy of forest full of whispering shadows, dwarf palms and frangipani, strange multiform trees with tentacular roots. Then I stumbled on a clearing of pounded earth scattered with white chicken feathers stuck together with dried blood, and I knew that I had arrived at Carrefour Meulier.

Altesse Paul lay groaning outside his *hounfour* – temple – on a straw pallet, too weak it seemed to chase away the hens pecking the ground around him. He was suffering, apparently, from *'faiblesse générale'*, whatever that meant. I handed the Voodoo priest my letter of introduction from Max Beauvoir and asked whether there was any chance tonight of a ceremony. 'Why do you want to know?' he snapped. I told him about the group of Protestant holy-rollers whose travesty of Voodoo I had witnessed on an island near Jérémie, that I was keen to see a true ceremony, the real thing.

The *houngan* fiddled with his necklace of vari-coloured teeth. 'I am flattered,' he said, propping his head on one elbow. 'Unfortunately, today is the first of May, Labour Day in Haiti, and Voodoo is not permitted on a public holiday.'

'What about tomorrow?'

There was a silence as Altesse stared at my shoes with a sort of fascinated admiration.

'I promise you a *service loa* for tomorrow night, but on one condition.'

'What?'

'That you give me your shoes.'

'But they're my only pair!'

'All right then, for forty dollars.'

'No!'

'*Trente,*' he said, opening his left hand rapidly three times in succession.

'No!'

Eventually, I was granted a ceremony for ten dollars. This demand for money did not surprise. A Voodoo priest is usually an astute businessman: faith, love of power and sheer cupidity are all entangled in his profession. As the people say, '*Houngan, c'est magasin. Gin un pile merchandise*' – he's like a shop, he has a lot of goods. Altesse Paul himself owned a small general store which sold rum, leaf tobacco, salt pork, dried codfish and unrefined red sugar. He combined in his person the functions of *curé*, mayor and bush doctor, a man both feared and respected by the villagers. The largest revenue for Altesse is derived from treatment of the sick, although to look at him one would not think so. He brought to mind a second-hand-car salesman: pencil moustache, pinchbeck jewellery, ignoble pot belly. Altesse snapped his fingers and one of his numerous cousins immediately came to dance attendance. 'Jacques!' The priest stood up bleary-eyed, scratching his crotch voluptuously. 'Fetch a bottle of rum for our guest.'

When the taffia arrived, the *houngan* rubbed a quantity of the stuff on both forearms. Then he spilt some more of the alcohol on the ground at the four cardinal points of the compass by way of a libation for the *loas*. 'Uncross your arms!' Altesse shouted at me. He explained that crossed arms would only impede the descent of the spirit tomorrow night. I apologized, and took a swig of the taffia which tasted of wood alcohol mixed with gunpowder. Immediately, I felt a dreadful burning in my temples. 'Don't worry,' the *houngan* assured me. 'It'll help you sleep and one must never forget either that alcohol is a food.'

I was to sleep the night in a granary of thatch and wattle built on stilts to protect the grain from weevils and assorted rodents big, apparently, as terriers. Behind this granary stood the *hounfour*, an open shed like a large garage painted with the advertisement: *'Altesse Paul: Mystique et Diabolique'*. Underneath these words was a crude representation of the Voodoo divinity Papa Legba, shown as a venerable old man in tattered trousers, terracotta pipe in his mouth and a large pouch of woven straw thrown over one shoulder. *'Legba-pied-cassé.'* Altesse pointed to the deity's broken foot swathed in bandages. Papa Legba is always the first to be invoked at a ceremony, as he is the protector of crossroads, journeys and beginnings. An ancient god, he was described by Sir Richard Burton in his gruesome book *Mission to the King of Dahomey* as 'a hideous spectacle with arms longer than a gorilla's, huge feet, and no legs to speak of. The mouth is a gash from ear to ear, and the eyes and teeth are of cowries, or painted ghastly white . . .' Evidently, Papa Legba underwent some form of metamorphosis in passage with the slaves from Dahomey to Haiti.

'Legba is the master of my White Magic temple,' Altesse Paul curtly announced. 'Baron Samedi is master of the Black Magic temple.'

I asked if I could see this second *hounfour*. The priest hesitated, then led me round the corner to a small door hung with four goat skulls and numerous tibias or shin bones bleached bicarbonate white by the sun. They made an attractive ossuary.

'C'est la chambre du Maître Terrible.' Altesse took one step back, paused, knocked five times on the door which he then opened and propelled me, forcibly, within. All was darkness until the priest shone an electric torch on to a scene of Dennis Wheatley imagining. The room was cluttered with miniature coffins to accommodate infants, decorated with sequins and bits of mirrored glass. On a raised pedestal stood a large white wooden cross surmounted by a battered high silk hat, an old pair of opera gloves pulled over either end of the crossbar. At the foot of this totem to Baron Samedi was a human skull wearing a wig of melted wax surrounded by tin bowls containing maize, gunpowder and withered chillies. In one corner

lay a collection of shackles and whips in memory of yesterday's slavery. There were also several *açons*, bottles of rum, a vigil lamp, and countless votive candles called *baleines*, or whales, after the blubber from which they used to be made. I noticed that a small crushed snake had been nailed to the lintel above the door, black with ants.

'I am able to resurrect people.' Altesse kept his eyes fixed gimlet-like on me.

'So you deal in zombis?'

The priest would not be drawn into any confession. All he said was, 'The affairs of the sheep are not for the nanny goat,' meaning I think that the affairs of black men are not for whites.

Back at the general store for more rum, and Altesse explained that there are two classes of ritual in Voodoo: Rada and Petro, never to be confused. The Rada Rite, named after the town of Allada which was conquered by the warlike Fons of Dahomey early in the eighteenth century, is the more gentle of the two. Here the *loas* are generally magnanimous, presided over by Erzulie Freda, the muse of beauty; they demand no more than chickens and white pigeons for sacrifice. The Petro Rite, by contrast, is *'plus raide'*, more rough. Its spirits are propitiated by a slaughter of hogs, goats, sheep, cows, dogs.

'And humans?'

'Only dead ones.' Altesse poured some taffia into a toothmug.

Petro, he went on, is the first step to the practice of Black Magic. The Olympiad of divinities involved in this rite is of awesome poignancy and hateful renown. It includes Erzulie z'yeux Rouges (or Marinette the Celestial Executioner), Baron Piquant, Congo Zandor and Papa Bakalou. These maleficent *loas* are worshipped for nefarious purposes.

'Which is what you do in that *hounfour* with the coffins?'

'Yes, but never on a public holiday.'

'Such as Christmas?'

'Easter, Christmas, National Tontons Macoute day on the twenty-ninth of July . . .'

According to Altesse, the drumming at a Rada Rite is ordered, rhythmically on the beat; at a Petro service, staccato, offbeat, sharp and unforgiving like the crack of a whip. I described to him a Voodoo ceremony which I had witnessed one night at Petit Goâve. Electric with nervous tension, very aggressive, it also involved a great deal of fire.

'Fire?' Altesse looked at me agog. 'Are you sure?'

'Absolutely.'

'Then it must have been a Petro Rite.' His expression changed to one of admiration bordering on beatitude. He said he had never heard of a *blanc* who had attended such a ceremony.

It was a disturbing spectacle, not one which I would care to see again. The priest, Norvilius Narcius, goaded his dancers with a whip and kept grunting unintelligible cries of *'Eh! Eh! Bomba! Heu! Heu!'* Many of the celebrants looked as though unhinged by a satanic seizure, stamping their feet to a wild rhumba. One woman may have been under the influence of Erzulie z'yeux Rouges, that dismal Hecate. Her skirt was rucked around the crotch and she bucked and writhed with tears streaming from tightly shut eyes. Oblivious of any pain, she held a fistful of burning whale-oil candles to her head, beneath her chin and under one armpit. There was a stench of scorched body hair. Then, with his cutlass, the *houngan* made a swift sign of the cross and sliced its blade clean through the neck of a goat.

The Petro Rite is believed to have originated at Petit Goâve around 1768, long before independence. Its name is probably a corruption of Don Pedro, a runaway mulatto slave from the Spanish half of Hispaniola who, according to the French colonial writer Moreau de Saint-Méry:

'abused the superstitious credulity of the blacks and gave them an idea of a dance, analogous to that of Voodoo, but where the movements are more hurried. To make it even more effective the slaves placed in the rum, which they drink while dancing, well crushed gun-powder. One has seen this dance, called Dance to Don Pedro, induce death . . .'

Yet after the slave died his followers raised him to the status of a *loa*, calling him Criminel-Pedro.

Petro is peculiar to Haiti. It reflects the rage and violence which threw off the shackles of slavery, and was often practised by the slaves before they engaged Napoleon. I hoped Altesse would not perform Petro for me tomorrow.

'No, no,' he said. 'We don't have enough goats.'

Outside the general store, darkness had fallen like the House of Usher.

Later that night in the granary a bowl of congo beans and roast goat was brought to me by a big-thighed, strong-buttocked woman wearing a bodice of roughly woven sisal fibre. I assumed that she was the *houngan*'s wife. For the sake of conversation, I asked her whether Altesse had made a good husband.

'But I'm not his wife,' smiling sweetly as she placed my food on a chair. 'I'm only *one* of his wives.' And with that she left, giving me a wink which I was unable to interpret.

The room stank like a rabbit hutch, and fetid vapours rose from the lavatory bowl. No sound, only a constant chorus outside of barking dogs. I decided to investigate and found stashed beneath my bed numerous cabbalistic or alchemical books. As I fanned through the pages of one, *La Science des Mages et ses Applications Théoriques et Pratiques*, a piece of paper fell to the floor. On it, written in a shaky hand, were words which had been taken from the Requiem Mass:

> *Dies irae, dies illa,*
> *Solvet saeclum in favilla . . .*

The words frightened like an unlucky number and I jammed a table against the door to shield me from any evil spirits abroad in the damp night wind. To judge by a strange story attached to the Voodoo version of *Macbeth* staged by Orson Welles at Harlem in 1935, the table would afford little protection.

This play, attended among others by Jean Cocteau, had been a great success and the spectacular use which Welles made of Haitian magic, colourful Caribbean costumes and even live goats ensured that it was the only black production in the history of American theatre which white people ever stood in queues to attend. The reviews, however, were indifferent, not least because Macduff wore a costume which lent him the outrageous appearance of Haile Selassie crossed with Toussaint L'Ouverture. One critic had been particularly uncharitable. The man who led the troupe of West African dancers in *Macbeth*, a genuine witch doctor by the name of Abdul who sported a pair of gold and diamond teeth, engaged Welles in the following conversation:

A: This critic, bad man?

W: Yes, he is a bad man.

A: You want me to make beri-beri on this bad man?

W: Yes, go right ahead and make all the beri-beri you want to.

A: We start drums now.

W: You go ahead and start the drums. Just be ready for the show tonight.

A: Drums begin now. Bad man dies twenty-three hours from now.

The critic died, as it happened, forty-eight hours later. Of pneumonia.

★ ★ ★

Next day, Altesse knocked on my door with the traditional morning greeting, *'Eh, la nuit?'* (And how was your night?), to which I gave the conven-
tional response, *'Pas plus mal, merci'* (No worse, thank you). I was in fact
shivering with a slight fever from grippe, for which the priest prescribed
a medicament concocted, he said, of garlic and castor oil. After my fears
of last night I decided to refuse this offer of help, and dissolved some
aspirin in gin which I had purchased at the Relais de l'Empereur.

The priest himself had made a remarkable recovery from his illness of
yesterday and moved about the temple with spacious, loping strides. As
evening approached, he donned a red shirt quilted together with a patchwork of cotton squares and appliquéd with small black crosses. This was
the uniform of a Voodoo priest and the mark of a *Gwos Neg*, Big Shot.
Thus attired, Altesse began to bark orders at members of his clan. Cousins
were chivvied, wives berated and I was careful not to cross my arms.

The ceremony that night was held to initiate a group of women into the
rank of *hounsi canzos*, or assistants to a Voodoo priest. For five days these
Rada neophytes had withdrawn from the world to devote themselves to
prayer and meditation. Forbidden to communicate with one another, they
had eaten only white food such as chicken and potatoes, mushrooms or
cornflour broth. The *hounsi* ceremony is one of the most elaborate which
an individual will undertake and I was privileged to be able to attend.
Inside the *hounfour*, Altesse greeted me with a firm handshake and a peculiar, triple pirouette-salute. 'Welcome,' he said. 'Thank you,' I replied,
returning his pirouette for the sake of symmetry.

The temple was already prepared for the initiation. At one end stood
the altar, a crude waist-high block of cement cluttered with offerings
consecrated to Erzulie Freda: bottles of Noilly Prat, Cassis, Martini, a
garland of flowers, a plastic necklace of multi-coloured beads, slices of
melon, sugar almonds, other bonbons, pistachios and several phials of
perfume. At the precise centre of the ceremonial enclosure was a large
pole called the *poteau-mitan*. This had been frescoed with the image of a
twisting snake, symbol of Damballah Wedo, harbinger of rain and patron
of rivers who speaks through the possessed in a barely intelligible hissing.
The *loas* are believed to descend the axis of this African maypole, and
platters of food – roasted corn soaked in syrup, cakes of maize – had been
left for their eventual propitiation.

Chairs were wedged against the walls of the temple and these were
now occupied by villagers who had arrived with bottles of rum, *baleines*

and Voodoo flags stitched with gilded spangles. One middle-aged woman of enormous bulk wore a black gauze gown with shiny buttons and a buccaneer's hat. Above these chairs hung coloured oleographs of Sts Isidore, Ulrique, Patrick and George. There was also a lurid chromolithograph of the Last Supper, pasted on the wall next to pages which had been torn from *Paris Match*. Everywhere, candles burned with an acrid odour, surrounded in the dark by little white coronas of heat, their wicks floating in coconut shells of oil.

The ceremony began with Altesse lifting a pitcher of water to the four quarters of the earth, then performing the *action de grâce* which consists of Catholic prayers intoned in a voice conversational in cadence, low with intimacy. It is the *houngan* alone who has power to summon the spirits into the dimension of the material world, whether as a physical presence or through possession. And it was Altesse who then began to invoke Papa Legba, accompanied by the officious rattle of his *açon*, a fetish adorned with a trellis of adder bones intertwined with glass pearls. The following is translated from a tape-recording made at the time:

> 'Mighty Legba, master of thresholds,
> Open the gates for us! Ago, ye!
> Legba, food and drink are provided;
> Family is gathered together with family;
> Oh Legba, open the gates for us,
> So that we may pass!'

This was answered in counterpoint by the *reine chantrelle*, or queen chorister, dressed in a blue silk robe:

> 'Papa Legba, limping along. Old bones, oh old bones,
> It is a long time since we have seen you, old bones!
> Legba who sits on the gate, give us the right to pass!'

Another pronouncement, this time in homage to Erzulie, and the drums began to beat a prolonged and perfectly syncopated introduction, monotonous as the slow tick of a metronome. (It is essential at this point that the *tambouriers* work in absolute concord: dancing will otherwise be thrown into confusion and the *loas* directly hampered in their epiphanic descent.) The chorus of drumming became more urgent, rising in volume, as thirteen women in white performed a ritual salutation before Altesse. This involved a full turn to the right, then to the left, then to the right again, each turn punctuated by a graceful curtsey, the whole concluded by kissing the ground three times on their knees. The female adepts then wheeled into line again, shuffling and singing with the cohesion of a *corps de ballet*.

The drums were still beating as Altesse concluded his invocation to Legba, waving in the air a large Damballah snake staff:

'Papa Legba, master of three crossroads!
Open the road for me! Ago, ye!
Do not let any evil spirits bar my path,
Let us in!'

Then the adepts began to revolve very slowly round the *poteau-mitan* arms akimbo, in a ritual dance to the long-lost gods of Dahomey, chanting this litany:

'Where does the sun rise?
It rises in the east.
Where does the sun set?
It sets in Guinée.'

Meanwhile a bottle of Barbancourt (three-star) was passed by relay from one villager to another, and finally to me. The rum was delicious but I was conscious of how peculiar my presence must have been in this temple amid fifty or so Haitians. They stared at me, not from any hostility (if I didn't drink, they laughed, I must be 'a woman'), but out of natural curiosity. Perhaps they found it perverse that a Westerner should be so interested in their own culture. I do not know; but the effect of Voodoo on a foreigner is certainly contagious. The drums, the candles, the chanting, dancing, alcohol and prayers – it all conspires to bring you, by degrees, to what Max Beauvoir had called a state of 'mystic exaltation'. As Aldous Huxley wrote in *The Devils of Loudun*: 'No man, however highly civilized, can listen for very long to African drumming . . . and retain intact his critical and self-conscious personality . . . If exposed long enough to the tom-toms and the singing, every one of our philosophers would end by capering and howling with the savages.'

Huxley might have been interested in the peculiar case of Maya Deren, a Russian-born American who travelled on a Guggenheim fellowship to Haiti in 1947, where she began to research her monumental thesis on Voodoo, *The Divine Horsemen*. Miss Deren was the James Frazer of Afro-American animist religions, a level-headed anthropologist who was nevertheless possessed – literally – by the spirit of Erzulie Freda. She lost consciousness for about four hours after having correctly performed an entire drum routine for a ceremony of which she had no previous knowledge.

This is not to give the impression that Voodoo, or at any rate the Rada ritual, is bacchanalian orgies and riotous assemblies, sanguinary in the extreme. Quite the contrary. In its purest form, one is impressed by the introverted sobriety of this religion, the meditative control with which the *houngan* will orchestrate the proceedings. I was astonished by the intricacy of the *vèvès* which Altesse began to trace with maize flour in front of the altar. Considerable skill is involved in the design of these cabbalistic motifs and the moment one of the adepts betrayed signs of possession – yabbering in a jumbled monologue, gyrating on one foot and then down on her hands and knees – Altesse pinched a small amount of flour between thumb and forefinger and, stooping low, let the maize sift to the ground in the form of his chosen *vèvè*. The speed of execution was absolutely prodigious. It took him about fifteen minutes to limn these elaborate scrolls and traceries in honour of Erzulie.

The stars clustered around this motif below are called *points d'arrestation*, stopping points. They afford the priest enough time between pinches of flour – sometimes of brick dust, powdered bark, ashes or even coffee grounds – to take a swig of rum or, in the case of Altesse, a puff of cigarette smoke.

'Jacques!' he said, tracing a *vèvè* to Agoué, 'a Comme il Faut!'

The cousin hurried across the temple to supply a cigarette. As he did so, Altesse belched and apologized – *'Pardon!'* – as if to placate the spirits.

A woman began to whirl round the *poteau-mitan*, gabbling and leering, rolling her hips and staring with gaping eyes. Although the trance was constantly suggested during this ceremony, it was never arrived at collectively. The rite was under control. Altesse shook his *açon* three times, making an impatient gesture with the burning end of his cigarette. Then the novices were borne into the temple like mummies wrapped in white sheets with only a hand protruding. They were carried on the backs of *hounsis* (a Dahomean word meaning 'spouse of the god') who had already been initiated, and these women now staggered through the crowd to deposit the bodies on the ground.

Then began a strange ritual in worship of Ayizan, the wife of Legba who is entrusted with exorcism of evil or impurity. The fronds of a giant palm branch, a tree sacred to Ayizan, were torn into strips so that they hung from a thin section of rib. Then the *hounsis* split each of these strips into even thinner shreds, so that the branch was like a huge plume of finest fringe. Bearing the branch in a processional that rotated to the right, to the left, and always revolving in a sensual movement of dance, the *hounsis* brushed it repetitively over the initiates who remained motionless beneath their sheets. Then a drum banged as its owner tested the membrane, and Altesse seized a squawking white rooster, waving it like a fan above the recumbent novices. The tempo of the drumming changed to an ominous roll as the priest began to intone:

> 'Damballah! Damballah! Blood will flow!
> The vein will open, blood will be drawn!'

When Altesse raised the chicken to his mouth, preparatory to crunching through its neck, I moved silently out of the temple, unable to withstand the dust, the cigar smoke, the smell of crowded, swaying bodies, and now this blood. Outside, the stored heat of the sun had dissipated to leave the air deliciously cool. The stars were brilliant overhead, burning blue round the platinum circle of the moon. 'I like the night and the sky better than the gods of men,' wrote Albert Camus after witnessing a Voodoo ceremony in Brazil.

One can sympathize with that verdict. However, the Haitian who sacrifices to the *loas*, who is possessed by them, who every week answers to the call of drums, is a Haitian ecstatically transformed, taken momentarily out of himself. Thus an ailing mother may become Loco Attison, god of medicine and wisdom; a down-trodden farmer might transform into Ogoun Feraille, vengeful Lord of the Thunderbolt; a young girl betrayed by her boyfriend, into Maman Brigitte, the fiery wife of Baron Samedi. In this sense, the world of Voodoo very precisely conforms to what Freud had to say about supernatural magic in *Totem and Taboo*: 'Spirits and demons are only projections of man's own emotional impulses . . . At the animistic stage men ascribe omnipotence to *themselves*.'

Voodoo then is an imaginary world of displaced desires, a fantastical theatre of the mind where – for just one night – you can trade your old clothes for a glittering costume worn by the divinities of ancestral Africa.

Nowhere in Haiti is this more apparent than at the Festival of Saut d'Eau which takes place every 16 July at a waterfall near Ville Bonheur (Happy Town), some forty miles north of the capital. The festival commemorates an apparition that occurred during the government of Faustin Soulouque of the Virgin Mary, who metamorphosed into a dove and flew into the whirling spray of the cascade, beating its wings to bless the waters. Soulouque interpreted this apparition as a sign from God that he should become emperor of Haiti and he even appointed members of his legislative cabinet – his ministers of finance, war, justice and foreign affairs – to verify the phenomenon. On 23 November 1849 Ville Bonheur was declared a place of national pilgrimage. Today it is the Lourdes of Haiti, as sacrosanct as the Basilica of Our Lady of Guadalupe in Mexico City.

One day I journeyed to Ville Bonheur by tap-tap. It was a wonderful morning, the sky overhead like a blue enamel bowl and the silence of the landscape broken only by a distant cawing of crows. When I arrived at Saut d'Eau, pilgrims stood sluicing themselves in the freezing waters of the fall, some of them naked. Others staggered about on dry land near by as if drunk, but in reality they were unhinged by the bountiful spirit of Erzulie Freda. Several acolytes had tied offerings of coloured cotton girdles round the branches of a sacred mapou, or pinned the bark with medals, ribbons, scapulars and lithographs of Catholic saints. I watched as a couple made a votive candle from half an orange with a penknife. They plugged it with cotton wool soaked in muskadel oil and then stuck the wool with a tiny wick, placing the orange in a hollow of the mapou where it flickered with a yellow flame.

Mapous are reverentially acknowledged to be inhabited by the *loas*, and they are tended by the Saudolese as hallowed property. In 1891 a

French priest, Father Lenouvel, cut down these mapous in an attempt to eradicate the demon Voodoo. He died in church the same day. Shortly after, driven by the missionary zeal of his predecessor, Father Cessens felled the remaining trees and suffered a paralytic stroke. He was buried a few months later at Ville Bonheur. These deaths were regarded by Haitians as retribution from both the Holy Madonna and the spirits of Voodoo, and they only confirmed the pilgrims in their belief that Saut d'Eau was a natural shrine whose waters would bring them out of misery into a state of mystic transport. Year after year they continued to arrive, by foot, truck, horseback and by chartered bus, almost as the Koran enjoins the faithful to visit Mecca.

Many of these pilgrims were dressed in penitential robes purchased from a *houngan*, and recited both rosaries and invocations to Damballah or Papa Legba. I was told that they will afterwards wear new clothes to begin a renewed life, taking the holy waters home in earthenware pitchers as gifts for those who are too old or ill to humble themselves before the falls of Saut d'Eau. 'Voodoo is the religion of the oppressed, of the poor. It is joyous, full of life,' the Episcopalian priest Roger Désir had told me in Port-au-Prince one night. 'Unfortunately, it has been completely Satanized.'

Roger Désir, a snowy-haired mulatto who had studied social science at Wayne University in Detroit, was unique for a Haitian Protestant in that he gave lectures in praise of what he called the 'rich vitality of Voodoo'; he had even translated the Bible into Creole. I asked him about the element of animal sacrifice in Voodoo: surely this verged on cruelty. 'Not at all!' the clergyman irritably declared. 'Unless of course you consider the Old Testament to be barbarous.' He referred me to the books of Leviticus, Numbers, Kings, Deuteronomy and Exodus. 'Just look at the liturgical regulations as prescribed by Yaweh for Moses and the people of Israel – slaughter your oxen, your sheep, the first-born of your sons, he told them. And let their fat burn in sweet odour to the Eternal, so that you may atone for the expiation of your souls at my altar! Or words to that effect.'

As we spoke, a Mitsubishi jeep drew up in the drive of Désir's house, opposite the Ministry of Information on Rue Delmas. 'Here they come!' The priest grinned in delight. 'The children of Mother Teresa!'

One by one they clambered out of their vehicle, Sisters of Charity wearing rubber flip-flops and white gowns trimmed with a blue border. The nuns giggled as Roger Désir embraced them with arms outstretched. Then he turned to me: 'How full of light these girls are! How happy, how *joyous*! They have the selflessness, that spirit of community which I fear Christianity has now lost. But not Voodoo, I hasten to add.' Désir spoke approvingly of the pilgrims at Saut d'Eau. 'You have seen for yourself how they care for the physically handicapped, how they give alms to the mendicants, distribute food to the needy, even to prostitutes.'

A headless rooster lay in the middle of the temple with its claws curled daintily in rigor mortis. The *vèvès* of last night had been trampled by the dancers into a mess like sawdust across a butcher's floor. A lone dog snuffled round the sacrifice; turkeys gobbled at husks of millet and two drums leant against the altar.

Altesse Paul emerged from his corner shop wearing a wide-brimmed smoke-tan cowboy hat. He held a damp towel to his face as though suffering from toothache.

'Yo!' But it was a half-hearted greeting.

'What's the matter?'

'Nothing,' he said. 'A minor alimentary disturbance.'

'Too much rum?'

'Too much rum,' he confirmed.

He handed me a Pepsi-Cola, hot from lying in the sun. I asked him how the ceremony went last night. 'Good,' he said. 'All the *hounsis* were initiated.'

'Well, goodbye, Altesse.'

But the *houngan* appeared reluctant to let me go. 'Life is full of mishaps,' he smiled, spreading out his hands with the palms upturned. 'With or without Voodoo.'

Then he said timidly, 'Or Christianity, which amounts to the same thing.'

I took my final leave, and set off in search of the tap-tap to Port-au-Prince, walking along a road thronged with pack animals, bootblacks, porters, beggars and ambulatory salesmen with sticks of ice cream, bottles of Kola and cuts of dubious meat. The sun meanwhile settled to its astonishing business of generating life in the midst of poverty.

XIV

Ways of Escape

'I have been present at Voodoo ceremonies in both Haiti and
Cuba: they much resembled each other, though perhaps the
Cuban ceremony was a bit Low Church, for I don't remem-
ber the priest in Cuba biting off the head of a live cock.'

Graham Greene in a letter to the *Tablet*, 8 February 1986

'*Hola, hombre!*'

It was Alfredo the Cuban, shooting craps across the kitchen table. The
gamblers shuffled their cards by the feeble glow of a candle-lantern, as
there was no electricity tonight in Port-au-Prince. Nor was there much
water. The lavatory upstairs made a frightful noise of choking and regur-
gitation.

'I dare say things are better in Havana.'

'*Si, verdad,*' Alfredo agreed. 'But Cuba no good, plenty bad people
there. Castro one big bastard, that not so, Johnny?'

It irritated me that Alfredo was unable to pronounce my first name.
He spoke a kind of terrible pimp's English.

'We see movie tonight, Johnny?' He tipped back his chair against the
wall and put on his hustling smile.

'No. It's too dangerous.'

Numerous reports had come through that day of further depredations
wrought on Port-au-Prince by marauding Macoutes: bombings, kidnap-
pings, rape, contamination of the water supply. The airport was closed.

'*Sangre de Cristo*, Johnny! You one big coward, talk like that. Plenty
good movies tonight, real good ones.' Alfredo read out loud from a newspaper. '*Karate Kick Boxer II, Vigilante Squad, Delta Force Commando, Dirty
Argus Does it Again —*'

We decided on a cinema off the Champ de Mars equipped with its
own generator. It was showing something called *Dead Bang* starring the
Miami beefcake Don Johnson.

The owner of our pension seemed reluctant to let us stray out of
doors. 'You'll get killed,' she said flatly.

Margot was the soul of affection. She bustled about in pinafore and madras scarf ironing shirts and fussing over guests with maternal solicitude. For three days she had nursed me during a bout of influenza, tendering a concoction of herbal tea hot with rum. The pension, situated in a suburb known as Canapé-Vert, was a ramshackle frame and old brick rooming house with a low crumbled balustrade, pink curtains and a tasselled red lamp in each room like a whorehouse. The walls were splashed with urine and there was very little to recommend the place save the presence of Margot.

I was interested, however, to discover that it stood near the hospital of Notre-Dame where Malcolm Lowry was obliged to recuperate one week in 1947 from delirium tremens. The author of *Under the Volcano* had reached Port-au-Prince by ship on New Year's Eve in time for Independence Day. He moved into the Oloffson with his beautiful Canadian wife Margerie Bonner, but began to drink unremittingly. According to a stringer for *Time-Life* magazine, he was seen to walk fully clothed into the hotel swimming pool still holding a glass of wine. Laconically, the journalist remarked of Lowry that 'he was conspicuously at odds with the message conveyed by his wife that he should not be encouraged or invited to drink anything'. The writer left Haiti on 12 February. 'Frankly I have no gift for writing,' he wrote from his hospital bed. 'I started by being a plagiarist . . . Now I am a drunkard again.'

Margot was meekly resigned. 'Go then, but at your own risk.'

'*Que mujer! Que mujer!*' The Cuban put his arm round her. 'Isn't she one wonderful woman, Johnny? Just like mother for me.'

The night air was dirty like a smoked ceiling, eerie with a barking of dogs and a distant chant of washerwomen. Shacks were lighted by tin lamps and resin torches. Port-au-Prince was benighted, its shops and streets abandoned as though under curfew.

A few men sat outside the cinema on dusty leather hassocks and packing crates, drinking rum in the light of a wavering Butagaz flame. A humpbacked beggar sidled up to us, hand outheld for alms. '*Viejo borracho!*' (Old drunkard) Alfredo gestured at him to go away. Inside, lightbulb filaments glimmered with a dim reddish orange and for the first ten minutes the film was projected upside down. This did not seem to matter as there was enough violence on screen to satisfy the audience. 'Mistair Don Johnson, he one good cop.' The Cuban grinned to show a set of large yellow teeth like a horse. 'Conducting like a crazy man and killing all *criminales*! Killing all *vagabundos*!'

Afterwards it thundered and rained; a savage scribble of lightning flashed across the night sky. For the moment there would be no gunfire from the Tontons Macoute; Haitians have a terror of wet weather. On our way back to Margot's, Alfredo confessed how the setting of the film – Boulder, Colorado – had reminded him of Russia. 'Nice and cool, lovely white ladies and plenty *plata*, much money!'

Alfredo had travelled to Moscow for the Olympic Games in the summer of 1980 and spoke fluent Russian from his days at school in Cuba. In 1976 he had been dragooned to fight alongside the Marxist troops in Angola, and still bore the scar of a bullet which had cut clean through the sinews of his right arm. It was Alfredo's dream to live in the United States, what he called 'Gringolandia'. He became a political recidivist and, on the run from the Cuban CDR (Committee for the Defence of the Revolution), he had tried to reach Miami. Instead he was washed up on the shores of Hispaniola.

Alfredo Negrin, aged thirty-eight and a former dental assistant in Havana, was considered a criminal. He belonged to a group of anti-Castro activists named Los Comandantes de la Noche, Commandants of the Night. Margot harboured him as a motherless child.

After the film, and throughout that night, the crackle of automatic fire could be heard at Margot's. It was impossible to tell from where it came, how close to the pension, because of the wind. One moment the shooting seemed to issue from somewhere beneath my window: sharp staccato bursts like metal struck against an anvil. Ten minutes later, there was only a distant sputter of Chinese crackers. The dictatorial president, Prosper Avril, had been ousted from Haiti three months ago, yet the Tontons Macoute goonshow was still very much on the road – with a ferocious struggle for power. It was curious, nevertheless, to note how perversely consoling this sound of gunfire became. The real terror lay in silence, when I began to wonder whether the shooting would start again. If so, when – and for how long?

'. . . We begin in January 1988.' Alfredo told me one night how he had fled from Cuba. 'I was in the western province of Pinar del Rio when I got the news that two of my colleagues had been arrested by the CDR. It was terrible, *muy triste*! They were flown by helicopter to a prison in the south where you just wait to die slowly. I saw no way out, Johnny! I considered myself dead . . .'

Alfredo went on, very solemn. 'I ran all night and day until I came once more to Havana. And from Havana I ran to Matanzas; and from Matanzas all the way to Guantánamo. From one end of Cuba to the other! A plenty bad journey, Johnny. No good. No *bueno*. I felt like a chicken without its head.'

Guantánamo is a depressing city of abandoned railway tracks, milling with soldiers, police and militiamen. It is about twenty miles north of the American naval base at the bottom of Guantánamo Bay, still the home of some 8,000 US personnel. Numerous Haitians work there at the missile plant.

'A friend in Guantánamo told me that he know of three Haitians who want to escape to Miami, by boat! So we set off one night, me and three Haitians in search of the United States. The boat have two motors and only one can of petrol. Five days we float at sea, Johnny! And we got lost! Ah, *muchas problemas*, terrible business. The coastline disappear completely! Only green sea and blue sky. And the waves, they get bigger and bigger, crashing like crazy over the boat. No water to drink, Johnny, so I sweat until there's no sweat left inside me. Then the sharks arrive to circle the boat. Snap, snap. They want to eat us up! And all this time we struggling with hunger and we seasick and I feel like, how you say, *nacido muerto*, like I was born dead . . .'

After four days and a night at sea they finally caught sight of lights flickering from a shore. *'Esto es Florida, hombres!'* exclaimed the captain. *'Estamos a Key West!'* It was, in fact, the Dominican Republic.

Alfredo said they were forced by storms to beach at a port named Pepillo Salcedo in the D.R. Whereupon the captain, a Cuban, determined to abandon his passengers, claiming that they had successfully reached the United States.

From Pepillo Salcedo, Alfredo and the three Haitians walked thirty miles to Dajabon where they stole across the frontier into the town of Ouanaminthe, Haiti. 'We very miserable, and it was real bad for me because I have no identification. No *papeles*! No *documentos*! No *pasaporte*!' From Ouanaminthe they trudged five days overland to Cap-Haïtien where a tap-tap took them to Port-au-Prince. Arrived at the capital, Alfredo slept for three nights with his companions in a park opposite the National Palace. 'Then one morning I wake up and find that the Haitians have left me. What am I going to do? I speak no Creole! I have no money!'

Fortunately, a market woman who had lived in Santiago de Cuba took pity on Alfredo. 'She give me banana fritters and she let me sleep on her porch until one night some men wearing uniforms came to take me away.' These were orderlies from the Haitian Red Cross and they drove Alfredo to their hospital near the main post office in Port-au-Prince. For three months the Cuban recuperated from dehydration.

Discharged from his ward, Alfredo idled through the days talking with Dominicans who would congregate around the statue of Simón Bolívar. They told him of an American cargo ship which was about to leave for Florida. 'So one night I swim across the filthy waters of the port with two Dominican men and we climb on to the ship . . .'

For three days they hid in the hull as stowaways, emerging at night to filch goods from the kitchen. 'I never see such lovely American food! All kinds of cookies and meat and jelly and bread, peanut butter! And bourbon too, *muy fuerte!*'

One night the ship's captain caught Alfredo and company foraging. 'He say nothing at all – *nada!* – but he must have betrayed us because soon after we get raided in our sleep by the Haitian Coast Guard. I remember that night: sixteenth November 1988, nearly one year after I flee from Cuba.'

The police set upon the stowaways with truncheons, beating Alfredo countless times across the skull and twice with a pistol over his left eye. '*Que barbaridad!* But they furious, Johnny. They hate me!' The Cuban explained that it was a question of colour. 'Because I'm black they think I'm Haitian, that I only pretending not to speak Creole. And so they shout at me in Spanish: "You wanna play games, little nigger? Very well, we soon teach you how to speak Creole." Then the sergeant start kicking into my stomach. He look crazy, Johnny, like his eyes rolled right back into his head! Kick, kick . . .'

Alfredo and the Dominicans were then bundled – hands and feet bound with electric flex – into the back of a jeep and transported to the National Penitentiary. 'From my understanding,' said the Cuban, 'even Alcatraz is better than this prison. Morning to night, *hombre*, all you hear is beating: beat, beat, beat with truncheons. For the first two weeks I feel unable to walk and I have to sleep next to shit and piss and brush my teeth in green water. You ask about our food? Always cob corn. And usually too much salt they put on the corn, so you can't eat it.'

Alfredo was eventually given a bed by a Colombian drug-dealer who massaged a cooling astringent of toothpaste on to his wounds, cauterizing the more severe cuts with lemon juice and the burning end of a cigarette. The Cuban was interned with numerous Tontons Macoute who had fallen foul of the deposed president, Prosper Avril. 'I remember one. We used to call him in Spanish *"Señor Rompe-Hueso"*, Mr Break-Bones. He a cruel bastard and one night he stab two Dominicans with the sharpened end of a spoon, then he bit off one of their ears for a joke you understand.' The officer in charge of the medical dispensary was apparently in a permanent state of intoxication from marijuana and rum. 'He wore black glasses to hide the eyes, all bloodshot from drink and drugs. And when I ask for aspirin, he yell: "*I* am the commander round here and it is *I* who give you five seconds to get out!" So that's a Haitian prison for you, Johnny.'

Alfredo Negrin remained for fifteen months without trial in the National Penitentiary of Port-au-Prince. He was eventually released through the intervention of the United Nations which now contributes towards the cost of his board and lodging. When I left Haiti, Alfredo was still attempting to contact his wife and daughter through Radio Martí (the Cuban-American radio station which broadcasts from Florida), to let them know that he was alive.

A week following our night at the cinema I was able to see the National Penitentiary for myself. But I was obliged beforehand to pay Alfredo a small fee for his help in securing the visit.

'*Bueno, gringo . . . La plata.*'

'Oh come on! I'm not a millionaire!'

'But Johnny! You my friend, *verdad*?'

Some time ago I had decided to move out of the Hotel Oloffson because it became too expensive and rum punches were no longer served with ice owing to power cuts and a broken refrigerator. Margot provided a dustier, noisier, more native brand of accommodation. The bathroom was littered with dead cockroaches and for some reason an old valise that I found behind my bed contained a stuffed mongoose. Food was good (strictly Creole), although the water was dirty and not to be consumed without sterilization tablets.

While I was content to remain at Margot's before journeying into the north of Haiti, the hurdy-gurdy clamour of Port-au-Prince had begun again to fray my nerves. Every night, in the bomb-torn darkness, came a terrible howling. Dogs, of course, small mangy, hurt-eyed creatures which ranged in packs. 'Don't worry. It's not your fault,' said the director of the Haitian-American Institute, Eleanor Snare. 'I've seen hardened travellers come to Haiti and flip out after twenty-four hours. We operate on Murphy's Law round here.'

The Haitian-American Institute at Port-au-Prince was primarily a language school and Eleanor had been connected with it for over twenty years. Yet she still retained the proprieties of her native New England. 'There are two things I never do: drink on my own at a bar, and smoke in the street.' In her youth she had known members of the Beat Generation such as Gregory Corso, Laurence Ferlinghetti, Gary Snyder, Kerouac and other writers who had wandered rootless from New York or California to San Francisco.

Eleanor was striking in appearance: quite tall with pale blue eyes and a moon-white complexion, her longish hair sun-bleached to a ghostly blonde. She resembled the American actress Elaine Stritch, her voice deep and gravelly from countless packets of Comme il Faut: dressed always in sandals with hand-made dresses of a billowing, tent-like design, Eleanor had two adopted Haitian children. Most people in Port-au-Prince had heard of her: 'Sure! I'm the fire hydrant that every dog in the neighbourhood knows.'

That was typical of her thorny wit. Eleanor maintained a certain distance however from the American colony in Haiti. 'I get a lot of invitations from my compatriots at the embassy to attend parties and I find these make very good bookmarks,' she smiled.

Eleanor was a woman of captivating charm, munificent in her hospitality: cigarettes and cups of coffee were dispensed with ungrudging generosity and I was grateful for the books she lent me on Haiti. The doors of her institute were usually open, even when bullets zinged round the Champ de Mars outside. Eleanor held the fort with implacable calm and was greatly admired by both students and employees; her sense of fair play, the impartial way in which she would redress a grievance, as well as her warmth and humour, inspired both loyalty and devotion. 'I'm here to stay,' she would remark with dogged fortitude. 'But after all these years in Haiti, I still feel as if I'm only a guest in a home. A *blanc* can never really get to know the Haitians. Not deep down, anyway.'

The years Eleanor had spent in Haiti gave her a privileged insight into the soul of this country. 'The Haitians are a very prideful people,' she had told me. 'And that pride can easily turn to arrogance. When it does, beware: it can often become an illogical arrogance, quite beyond reason.'

We were sitting that afternoon by the swimming pool at the Hotel Rancho in the mountain suburb of Pétionville. The Rancho was a lavish extravaganza of splashing fountains and Italianate marble floors much frequented in the 1950s by the New York crooner Harry Belafonte. It was a little shabby now, with the absence of any tourism. The buffet of Haitian food was carefully adapted to American tastes.

Eleanor stubbed out her cigarette and fished for another. 'They're often cruel, too, the Haitians – capable of enormous and perhaps unconscious cruelty.' She mentioned the ill-treatment of animals and children. 'But it can't be helped. Poverty does it. In Haiti, it's survival of the fittest.'

Eleanor had lent me a collection of popular Haitian folk tales entitled *Brother Bouki and Ti Malice*, much admired apparently by P. L. Travers, the author of *Mary Poppins*. I had been struck by the cruelty of Ti Malice, a cunning trickster in the mould of Renard or Brer Rabbit who removes the tongue of an enemy with a shard of broken glass, cuts off the tail and ears of a donkey, poisons a mango salad and eats his mother (seasoned with salt) because she costs too much to feed. Brother Bouki is presented as the comic foil for much of this horror. He is coarse, clumsy, thick-tongued, an easy mark for bullying from Ti Malice. Bouki is evidently the lesser mortal, and not a creature one should respect.

'Haitians admire Ti Malice,' said Eleanor, 'because he's the smart guy, the trump card. You and I might consider him sly and deceitful, treacherous and the rest of it, devoid indeed of any Western virtues of charity or compassion. For the Haitian, though, Ti Malice represents the very ideal of survival: shrewd, very adroit and so enduring that his stomach is always full of pig and rum. Bouki, by contrast, is just the poor old goat, a born loser.' Eleanor explained that country-folk in particular may emulate Ti Malice for the simple reason that no Haitian government has ever done anything to alleviate the misery of their lives.

She added: 'But the Haitians are also a gentle people, both lovable and loving. I have tried very hard to become their friend.' Clearly, Eleanor would not have remained in Haiti for so long had she not felt this degree of affection.

I offered to buy her a rum punch.

'No, no! This is the age of woman's liberation,' she amicably protested. 'I absolutely insist that I order the next round.'

The sun was about to disappear beyond the deckle-edged mountains, casting a reddish glow over the jutting palms and tin-roofed shanties. Soon all colour had vanished from Port-au-Prince and the leaves of the trees by the pool made a latticework of shadows against the sky.

'Well, here's to Haiti.' Eleanor clinked her glass against mine.

★　★　★

On the Boulevard Harry Truman, more or less at the end of the navigable road, stands a low white building with the sign 'National Research Institute'. Inside, Haitians sit on benches in the arsenic-coloured hall, awaiting the results of a blood test. Some look very ill; most, however, appear to be in perfect health, but the chances are nineteen in twenty that they too have AIDS. For seven years this institute has housed Cornell University's research project on the Acquired Immune Deficiency Syndrome in Haiti. A poster in the hall, showing a couple walking hand in hand away from a cemetery, cautions against polygamy and the one-night stand:

PA PRAN CHEMIN SIDA. YON SEL MADAM. YON SEL MARI.

Translated from the Creole: 'Don't take the road to AIDS. One wife only. One husband only.'

I asked Dr Jean William Pape, director of the research centre and something of a civic hero during this dreadful time of disease, whether there was any truth to the contention that AIDS originated in Haiti. 'None whatsoever. The ecology of Haiti closely resembles that of other Caribbean countries and there is no reason why a viral disease should localize itself to one island,' he replied. 'If AIDS were traditionally endemic in Haiti one would have expected it to occur with the same frequency in the neighbouring Dominican Republic, but it has not.'

Yet Haiti, to the detriment of both its national pride and tourist industry, is now irrevocably associated with AIDS. In the words of the American ambassador Mr Alvin Adams: 'I'm afraid it could become a question of: See Haiti and Die.'

This prejudice took hold in the popular imagination when the US Center for Disease Control in Atlanta defined Haitians in 1981 as a 'high-risk group'. Baby Doc immediately responded by closing clubs and bars in Port-au-Prince frequented by the homosexual community. But it was too late. In response to an editorial which appeared in the *New York Times* of 29 April 1990 ('Letting Haitians donate blood might expose at least 36 patients a year to the AIDS virus'), thousands of Haitian emigrants swarmed on to the streets of Long Island, the Bronx, Queens, New Jersey and Connecticut, in protest at what they considered to be a racialist affront.

'And it *was* a form of racialism,' said Dr Pape, himself a Haitian. 'To my mind, there can be no doubt that AIDS was imported to Haiti from abroad.'

He gave two reasons why the virus was probably introduced by tourists. 'First, outbreaks of the disease in this country were originally confined to males and not – as was the case with gonorrhoea for example – to members of both sexes.' (In 1989, the Research Institute found that seventy-five per cent of these men were bisexual, driven to prostitution through economic necessity.) 'And second, the disease was peculiar only to urban areas of Haiti, largely to the red-light district of the capital visited by foreign homosexuals.'

An article which appeared in the *British Medical Journal*, dated 4 August 1984, confirms Dr Pape in his belief. It began:

AIDS was probably introduced to Haiti by vacationing American homosexuals for whom the island was a fashionable resort in the late 1970s. It is easy to see how in a poor country a young man, not necessarily homosexual, might become intimately involved with an affluent group of foreigners.

It concluded: 'AIDS in the United States would seem to antedate that in Haiti.'

According to Dr Pape, the virus has now entered the sanctuary of the Haitian countryside. 'It is almost impossible to locate and quarantine the victims because there are no beds specially for AIDS patients anywhere in Haiti. People usually go back to their families to die,' he said.

The extent of the disease in Haiti is not known; it is certainly pandemic and there is even a theory that Voodoo had fostered its voraciousness. 'People used to think that there might be some obscure connection between AIDS and the consumption of sacrificial animal blood,' said Dr Pape. 'This is most unlikely. And we must also dispel the myth that Voodoo incorporates any widespread cult of scarification with rusted knives or needles, such as one may find with certain tribes in Africa.' The problem, said Dr Pape, lies in remedies prescribed for AIDS by *houngans*, many of which involve the use of old hypodermic needles. 'Most of these Voodoo priests are charlatans. They come to me every day at the Research Institute with assurances that they have successfully cured a patient of chronic diarrhoea, and therefore of AIDS supposedly, since the former is usually a symptom of the disease.'

The Voodoo priest Max Beauvoir claims to have healed no fewer than six people of *diare masisi*, faggot's diarrhoea, as AIDS is commonly and cruelly known in Haiti. 'A further six are doing very well,' he smiled suavely. Dr Jean Pape gave me the names of two more *houngans* in the business of miracle remedies: Daniel C. Claude and Matthieu Antoine. I decided to seek them out.

* * *

An eccentric form of transport at Port-au-Prince comes in the form of a cheap taxi or jitney called a *publique*. It is usually identifiable by a letter 'P' prefixing the licence number or by a red kerchief tied to the rear-view mirror. The driver will stop wherever he chooses and pick up whomever or however many passengers he so desires. *Publiques* are not to be recommended for the fastidious tourist; they go like the wind, careering over pavements or the wrong way up one-way streets, and you will often have to share your seat with a live pig or brace of roosters. Once I endured an entire journey with a very large market woman sprawled across my lap. '*Ça va, chéri?*' She wanted to know whether I was comfortable.

But the *publique* is certainly cheap as you share the cost of the journey with other passengers so I flagged one down outside the Research Institute to take me directly to Daniel C. Claude.

'Enoch!'

'*Ah mon cher Thomson!*' Enoch thumped the steering wheel with the flat of his hand. 'I thought you'd gone back to England!'

It was my old friend. I hadn't seen Enoch in months, not since I'd set out with him to investigate a community of Polish black mountain people.

Fortunately, the *publique* was empty and Enoch agreed to take me to Pétionville where the Voodoo priest lived. He untied the red cloth from his mirror. 'We won't be needing this any more,' he grinned. 'It'll be quicker without it.'

We drove along the Avenue John Brown, pitching and rocking over potholes until we came to a billboard by the roadside. 'AIDS Is *Not* an Incurable Disease,' it proclaimed. 'Fever, Bronchitis, Intestinal Upsets, Maladies of the Skin, Mental Palsy, Folly of the Brain . . . After 22 Days You Will Be Cured.' Several of the rs and ss were printed backwards.

'This must be where the *houngan* lives. Come on.'

'No, no. I'll stay in my car.'

'Why?'

'I'm a Baptist, *mon cher*, Voodoo makes me feel . . . uneasy.'

An arrow pointed down a ravine to an adobe hut surrounded by a cactus fence. I could see a few goats wandering in and out of a yard, bleating at a couple of rutting dogs. Clinging to vines and roots I clambered down over stones slippery with excreta. Then I stumbled upon a notice – '*Daniel C. Claude. Sauveur du Monde*' – affixed to a corrugated aluminium door. I rapped against the metal. It was a day of pestilential heat. The door was opened by a middle-aged man removing wax from his ears with a toothpick.

'Are you the Saviour of the World?'

'I am Daniel, a man greatly beloved.'

'The Saviour?'

'Yes.'

'Could I have a few words?'

'You may enter.'

The *houngan* wore a bracelet of beer-bottle caps, and the nail of a little finger – knife-sharp and shiny as a Chinese man's – was lacquered with red varnish.

He led me to a room about six by ten feet, cluttered with discarded soft-drink cans, an empty refrigerator and an old television. Daniel scratched his left armpit with monkey-like solemnity, then lay down on a sackcloth bed.

'I have cured a total of one thousand five hundred and seven people of AIDS,' he said with a serene stare. 'They paid me seven dollars American each.'

'Show me the people you have saved,' I asked, startled by this information.

'I do not have the time.'

The Saviour seemed to ponder awhile. Then, with a fine assumption of affability, he said: 'Since you are a dear friend I will show you one of my patients.'

Daniel clapped his hands. There was silence until a voice at my side whispered *'Bonjour.'* I turned round to behold a skeletal young man frail as a fishbone. The Saviour explained how this fellow's wife had died of AIDS, how he had proved to be HIV positive, how he was now free of the virus.

'Allez! Marche! Vite!' The Voodoo priest gestured at the poor man to go away. I felt sick.

'Would you like,' Daniel queried blandly, 'to see how I cured him?' He reached under the bed and pulled out a five-gallon white plastic bucket. There was a stomach-grabbing stench of vegetable decay as he prised off the lid. A mass of decomposing leaf-mulch floated in the bucket.

The Saviour told me that he injects this horrible unguent into his patients. He does not bother to sterilize the needles, and there is no electricity with which to run the refrigerator.

'Where did you get the recipe for that . . . liquid from?'

'*C'est un don de Dieu,*' pursued the Saviour of the World. 'A gift from God. The cure came to me in a night vision.'

He got up and walked towards a cupboard from which he removed a dog-eared copy of the Bible. 'Turn to the Book of Daniel.' He handed me the volume. The relevant pages were spattered with candlewax and scribbled over in ball-point with the following words: '*Daniel la Délivrance . . . Daniel le Miracle . . . Daniel l'ange de Dieu*'.

Clearly the Saviour of the World saw himself as the biblical Daniel reincarnated, or perhaps as Belshazzar, master of magicians and ruler of Babylon. Daniel C. Claude retrieved the Bible and began to read out loud:

'. . . Daniel was preferred above the presidents and princes, because an excellent spirit was in him; and the king thought to set him over the whole realm . . .'

The Saviour closed the book. 'Did you listen to those mighty words?'

'Look, I really must go.'

'Not unless you give me five dollars.'

'For what?'

'For your consultation.'

I left Daniel to his foul den and scrambled frantically up the slope towards Enoch. 'May your crops fail!' I heard the Saviour wailing behind me with a low, dog-like grief.

We drove off in a warm, fine spring drizzle, taking the road to Kenscoff where the second *houngan* mentioned by Dr Pape – Matthieu Antoine – was reputed to live.

The morning mists had rolled away from the mountains. It was a beautiful day. We wheezed uphill through thickets of crimson *flamboyant* trees and tall poinsettia plants heavy with bright blooms, to an Alpine height of six thousand feet where mangoes, avocados and even raspberries grow. *Marchandes*, an endless line of strong, graceful women, swayed past with headbaskets of fruit. They were on their way to the Iron Market in Port-au-Prince some ten miles away. The return journey would also be made on foot.

'I'm glad that God did not make me a woman, *mon cher*. Far better to drive a taxi,' Enoch remarked.

We bumped across the pebbles of a dry river bed, through a pine forest which concealed the ruins of two magnificent fortifications built by Dessalines – Fort Jacques and Fort Alexandre – then along a flint-studded red clay road which took us to Monsieur Antoine. He was a great gnarled hulk of a *houngan* wearing a pair of fire-engine-red socks, shiny-seated nylon trousers and a black plastic bomber jacket repaired with strips of insulating tape. His baseball cap was embroidered with the peculiar legend 'I Love Top Vice Turbo Digital'.

Enoch remained in his *publique*, well away from the house. He need not have been so wary of Matthieu Antoine for he was an unexpectedly amiable soul. Appallingly, both his daughter and son-in-law had died of AIDS.

'There was nothing I could do about their deaths,' he said with an awful resignation. 'It was God, *Papa Bon Dieu*, who ordered that they should die.'

I asked Matthieu if he could provide any effectual antidote against AIDS. Yes, he said, a mixture of *pois congo* (beans which are also used to cure smallpox, impotence and jaundice), *acajou* (a herb otherwise used to prevent dysentery) and a fern called *mouri levé*. He mashes these ingredients into a magical restorative with a pestle and mortar, then administers the potion with a syringe. The Voodoo divinity who presides over this prescription is Ti Jean Petro, characterized as having no feet yet extremely agile in climbing trees.

'Does it work?'

'Yes,' replied Matthieu. '*De haut en bas*, from head to foot.'

Then he swallowed a spectacular measure of rum.

The pity of AIDS in Haiti is that even the middle classes, as a last resort, will seek treatment for the virus from a Voodoo priest. As Dr Pape had said: 'The people have to be educated. It is so hard for the mass of the population to understand that, first, you can be infected but apparently in very good health; and second, that the virus may kill as much as ten years after it has entered the host . . .'

I woke up in a blue, almost dawn light. There had been more gunfire at Margot's that night but no one mentioned it at breakfast. Her guests had become blasé.

Alfredo was looking very spruce, this being the morning of our visit to the National Penitentiary. Margot had ironed a clean white shirt for him and he smelt of sickly after-shave or lilac condiment oil. 'What for you ah wear dirty jeans, Johnny? They no *policia* in the prison. They *diablos*. Murderers. Is good you look more clean and fresh, like you ah going to a party. Then we have better chance of making the police talk nice to us. OK?'

I changed into a more respectable pair of trousers.

'*Vamos!*' Alfredo led the way. I was a little nervous, as our plan was to report at the police headquarters as human rights activists affiliated with a spurious organization called 'The United Front of Freedom for Prisoners'. Alfredo had forged UFFP credentials in order to visit the prison, and was evidently accustomed to this sort of cloak-and-dagger subterfuge. 'For why you worried, Johnny? The military take one look at these *documentos* and we get inside jail. I promise.'

I was uncertain about the moral implications of this visit and felt some guilt at my dissembled persona. What was I trying to do? What was I looking for? I was not in Haiti with a mission on behalf of Amnesty International, say, or of PEN. Neither was I simply interfering with the plight of unfortunates to file a sensational report. But one cannot remain blind to the arbitrary illegality of the judicial system in this country, to the blatant financial corruption of the armed forces, the fact that Haiti (at least when I was there) had been a military despotism in the hands of a single man. My own detention in the barracks at Port-à-Piment still rankled and now I was to see the very worst of the military. Pompously, I wanted to bring their injustice to the attention of other people.

The yellow and maroon building bore the words *Quartier Générale du Dept. Militaire de la Police de Port-au-Prince*. A military policeman, the brass-work of his uniform badly tarnished, barred our entrance with an Uzi machine gun. I noticed that both his trigger finger and right thumb were missing . . . probably can't shoot straight. Aloud I said: 'We are trying to find the office of Colonel Gabriel Bellegarde.' Then I took out my passport and held it up. The guard effected a salute and stepped aside.

So far so good. Upstairs in the army headquarters numerous officials bustled about their tiresome duties. One man was in the process of collapsing a gatling on a desktop; others ambled around clutching manila envelopes, banging rubber stamps on bits of paper. Alfredo caught sight of a fat khaki-clad man smoking cigarettes.

'Fucking Macoute!' the Cuban hissed. 'Plenty bad bastard. In prison we call him Commando Stingray.'

Alfredo explained that this was the thug who had dealt him all those blows on the night of his arrest. 'I kill him, Johnny.' He slammed his hard fist into a cupped hand.

We had to wait three hours until the Colonel summoned us into his office. He was a man who fancied he could speak English.

'Are you extraneous or are you of this place?' he asked me.

'I am extraneous and my colleague Alfredo here is also extraneous. I come from England and –'

'No, Johnny,' Alfredo nudged me, whispering in my ear, 'is better you say American.'

'I am American and my colleague here is also –' I quickly returned – 'from the USA. In fact he lives in Miami.' My heart thumped wildly in fear.

'This is odd,' the colonel mused, greatly interested. 'Because first you say . . . English? And then American. Now what need for you to make disguise?' He began to speak some Spanish. 'What are you from? *Inglés? Español? Americano? Alemán? Russo?*'

'We are American, Colonel. There can be no doubt that we are –'

'All right.' He rose from behind a large mahogany desk, patting the leather of his Sam Browne. 'Now may I see your papers?'

We produced our counterfeit UFFP documents and the Colonel carefully noted the details. 'You have no passport?' he asked the Cuban.

'No mistair. I har no papers. I leave them in Miami.'

'I see.' The colonel paused briefly in his reflections. Then he informed me summarily: 'Your passport, monsieur, is strange. British? What is this?'

'British,' Alfredo swiftly interposed, 'is one of the fifty federal states of America. It is near Miami.'

The Colonel looked dazedly round the room. 'British.' He repeated this peculiar word. 'British . . . You know, I never heard the place mention!' He laughed. And we laughed too, from nerves.

'But I think it best,' the colonel motioned his cigar towards a typewriter, 'that you compose me a formal letter explaining precisely why you so wish to visit our National Penitentiary, giving more details of –'

'The problem is that I'm leaving Haiti next week,' I fibbed. 'And with all respect . . .'

The colonel picked up a telephone and dialled direct to the National Penitentiary where he spoke to a certain Major Clerjeune, otherwise entitled 'Chef du Service d'Investigation et Anti-Gang'.

'Will you require a chauffeur?' the Colonel asked politely. 'No? Well, I wish you a happy flight back to British.'

We all shook hands.

The penitentiary, situated at the intersection of Rue de Champ de Mars and Rue du Centre, was a low building crumbling to decay and painted a patchy leprous yellow. The walls were damp from a deep sour heat, the windows made of rusted iron bars. Outside, a crowd of Haitians had assembled with parcels of food for relatives or boyfriends; a woman with an infant told us how her brother had been shot dead that morning – one bullet to the head, another in the back – for attempting to escape.

'Violent deaths are natural deaths here,' wrote Graham Greene in *The Comedians*.

We held up our credentials to a man on the other side of a judas-hole. There was a rattle of chains and a banging of bolts as the door swung open. My attention was immediately caught by a couple of soldiers urinating nonchalantly over the forecourt flagstones. Others sat on the ground playing cards, backs propped against rifles. The place had more the appearance of a lunatic asylum than a prison. Inmates wandered round in pyjamas with shaved heads (where clearly they had been beaten by guards). One large man sat sphinx-like on a limestone block, knitting with a ball of wool. '*Ou la soule, avant!*' a guard howled at him in Creole. (You there, alone, step forward!) The prisoner gave no reply.

Major Clerjeune was so impressed by our UFFP cards that he allowed us to inspect the penitentiary unaccompanied; he did not recognize Alfredo as a former inmate because the Cuban had lowered his voice and donned a pair of sunglasses. The prisoners, though, began to shout '*Cubano Alfredo!*' patting him on the back, and '*Hola, extranjero!*'

I had never seen such a collection of beaten physiognomies: scarred, gnarled and bruised, a man with a broken nose and a large torn ear; another with the bloodshot eyes of a mandrill, his mouth hanging open to expose a set of iodine-brown teeth. I recognized two of the Dominicans – Julio and Narcisso – whose trial I had attended not so long ago at the Palais de Justice. They looked at me briefly, averting their eyes.

Prisoners jostled round, picking at my clothes. A man with a patriarchal air came forward to greet me. He had the face of an Iroquois who might have stepped from the pages of Fenimore Cooper – brown and weather-burned, with long straggly locks of ink-black hair.

'*Gracias por su visita, amigo.*'

'*De nada,*' I replied.

This, as I later found, was the Colombian drug-dealer who originally provided Alfredo with a bed. He had arrived at Cap-Haïtien by boat in August 1983, carrying twenty-five kilos of cocaine and ten bags of marijuana weighing fifteen pounds apiece. Seven years he had languished in this prison without trial. As we walked across a makeshift football pitch the word got round that I was affiliated to a human rights delegation (Alfredo had long since dropped his pretence). The Colombian, a self-appointed spokesman for the other prisoners, said: *'Aqui esta moriendo la gente por falta de alimentos y medicina!'*

'What's he saying, Alfredo?'

'He say that people are dying here from shortage of food and medicine. Is true, Johnny. All they have to eat each day is piece of cobcorn and a cassava pancake. I *know!*'

'Sí, sí,' said the Colombian. *'No hay remedio.'* There's nothing to be done.

We came to the principal jail, a room the size of a small barn suffused with a dim underwater light. There was a dreadful stench like old eggs, no doubt from the open culverts which served as lavatories. Six hundred inmates sleep on palm-fibre pallets, shoulder to shoulder, with only tallow candles for light at night. It had the air of a makeshift hospital on a battle-field, the floor strewn with straw and empty sardine tins. A one-eyed man holding a blue transistor radio to his ear hobbled up to me; the hair was matted with blood and he bore a nasty bruise to his face. 'We die . . . *comme les chiens,'* was all he could bring himself to say before collapsing again on his pallet. Another Dominican prisoner was drunk, with a blistering flow of invective to command.

'Callate!' Alfredo stiff-armed the man into a corner and told him to shut up. 'This Johnny is good man. *Muy simpático!* He wanna help. And he no speak the Español. He American.'

'But he's not' – the Dominican made this important point – 'going to help us, is he?'

I remained silent, wishing now that I had never come to this place.

'Of course he is,' Alfredo quietly exclaimed, 'and one day you'll thank him.'

Prisoners began furtively to hand me their pleas for help, scribbled on the back of flattened silver paper from cigarette packets, then folded into neat little squares and slipped into my pocket. These notes were illegal (and could lead to serious trouble if the wardens discovered them on my person); I read them once I had returned to Margot's later that day, and they gave clear evidence of corruption within the prison. Many were written in good French.

From Délega Limorin. *'Mon bien cher ami,'* it began. 'I was arrested on 30 December 1979 after a woman wrongly accused me of stealing $200.

I have been condemned to eight years in prison; the guards have agreed to set me free if I give them $400 but I do not have a cent to my name. *Faites une chose pour moi. Merci.*'

Ulrick Georges, who had remained at the National Penitentiary for eight years pending trial – guilty of petty theft:

I have a family of seven in Jacmel and none of my children knows whether I am alive. At Tribunal five years ago the shopkeeper from whom I stole some bananas implored the judge to set me free but they took me back to prison all the same. I would be grateful if you could cast an eye over my case and please do something for my children *parce qui'ils souffrent beaucoup de mon absence.*

I had been given about thirty of these pathetic notes; a particularly alarming one came from Serrier Franty who had killed a man in the northern city of Port-de-Paix, chopped him up and left the dismembered parts of his body at the doorstep of the victim's wife. 'Fifteen years in jail without trial,' it read, 'and if I ever get out I'll take a machete to the President of Haiti.'

I followed Alfredo to the most feared part of the National Penitentiary – the *cachot*, or solitary confinement cell. There was a press of faces here at a small grated door, staring at me. From the glow of my lighter, it seemed scarcely large enough to accommodate a small horse. The prisoners began to spit, rattling the bars of their cell. Alfredo, fortunately, was equal to the occasion and managed to placate them with a promise that they would see the light of day through the philanthropic intervention of the UFFP.

That was enough for me. I had committed an offence against these prisoners and felt shame as an impostor, trespassing on their lives.

'You OK, Johnny?' Alfredo asked as we regained the Rue du Centre. 'No.'

'Ah, well. Just make sure you tell the truth of what you see in prison.' To which, more or less humorously, he added: 'There are times when even you gringos speak the truth.'

The National Palace showed glaring white against the cobalt of a cloudless sky. Other buildings, decrepit in the broiling heat, bore the varnish of red dust which covers all things in Haiti like a disease.

In March 1985 Amnesty International published a report on the mass jailings, torture and general abuse of prisoners in this country under Duvalierism. Ernst Benjamin, a member of the Christian Democrat Party, gave this account of his treatment by the Tontons Macoute in the Dessalines Barracks:

A torturer called G hit me eight times on my right ear with the palm of his hand and four times on my left ear. Blood was running from my ears when the Colonel ordered him to use a stick. I was then beaten with this stick by a second lieutenant. On the orders of the Colonel, G hit me continuously while I was standing up. He stopped when I was about to soil my trousers. I was let out of the torture room for a moment in order to tie the bottoms of my trousers with string so that the Colonel's interrogation and torture room would not get dirty . . .

That night of 16 October (1984) I felt I was dying. I spent two months and four days in prison, being interrogated under torture six times. I was beaten, given electric shocks, and made to stand to attention for prolonged periods. This last torture would make anyone confess like an automaton.

René Théodore, General Secretary of the Haitian Communist Party (PUCH), later elaborated: 'This is a land of sentimental nostalgia, of political necrophilia.' Nothing had changed, he said, since the days of Papa Doc when membership of the Haitian Communist Party was declared illegal. 'It still means certain death, even for those who are merely friends of members. Justice? Nonsense. No Haitian has ever been put on trial. He is either murdered in prison or shot dead on the streets.' Monsieur Théodore himself never leaves the PUCH headquarters at 82 Champ de Mars without a bodyguard.

As I left his office at two o'clock that afternoon there was an explosion from the direction of the police headquarters followed by a burst of machine-gun fire. 'Another coup d'état perhaps?' Réné Théodore glanced very calmly at his wristwatch. 'I should say it's about time.'

XV

A Paintbox Possessed

'. . . those poor bastards in Haiti, the artists, who got too
much, too soon, from Selden Rodman and the other folk-
doters on the subject of primitive genius, so they're all down
there at this moment carving African masks out of mahogany
– what I mean is, they never *had* an African mask in Haiti
before Selden Rodman got there.'

Tom Wolfe,
The Kandy-Kolored Tangerine-Flake Streamline Baby

The Episcopal Cathedral of the Holy Trinity, two blocks north of the
National Palace in Port-au-Prince, is a dreary Gothic affair, the cemetery full of broken bone-white slabs. Tombs are overhung with dropping
maidenhair and ivy but their surroundings are scarcely romantic, still less
reposeful.

But the barn-like interior was ablaze with fantastical murals, both apse
and transepts an efflorescence of Haitian colours which had never existed
in nature: pink spears of sugar cane, Nile-green animals, market women
painted russet, maroon and slate grey, banana trees of stormy purple, everything aglow like coloured silks. I was astonished by the aboriginal purity
of the designs: primitive, their exotic imaginary landscapes reminiscent of
Le Douanier Rousseau. Many of these murals were executed with the
geometric precision of maize-flour *vèvès*. They reminded me too of religious oleographs from Europe or of socialist-realist oils from Latin America,
as though Marc Chagall had been crossed with Diego Rivera.

Haitian art is inseparable from Voodoo. The American poet and art
historian Selden Rodman, who both inaugurated and directed the painting of this cathedral in 1949, later told me: 'Should Voodoo ever vanish,
the miraculous art of Haiti may vanish with it, quick as you can say
Rumpelstiltskin.'

Mr Rodman was born in 1909, but looked sprightly in an orange
T-shirt, tennis shoes and a green eyeshade. His home near Pétionville was
adorned with paintings by the Haitian artists Ramphis and Stivenson

Magloire, and by their mother Louisiane Saint-Fleurant. They were exqui-site: large canvases with snake-like divinities stippled in brilliant dot patterns rather like the pinpoint style in abstract paintings, glimmering gold as the tesserae in Byzantine mosaics. 'There are no schools of Haitian art,' said Mr Rodman. 'Everyone is an original.'

Selden Rodman should know. He had been associated with the art of this island since 1948 when he published his book *Renaissance in Haiti*, the first ever on the subject and much admired by Patrick Leigh Fermor. In the early days of the Second World War Mr Rodman's verse play about Toussaint L'Ouverture, *The Revolutionists,* was produced at Port-au-Prince; it won considerable acclaim and the author was subsequently decorated with the Haitian Legion of Honour.

The art of this country, like Voodoo, represents a triumph of the imaginary world over the real and many of these cathedral murals had been influenced by the *mythos* of Black Magic. In one, a man runs to a Voodoo ceremony clutching a sacrificial rooster; another shows a hog slaughtered in the rites. It lies upside down on a bed of plantain leaves surrounded by adepts in the throes of possession. One man was evidently a zombi, a victim of premature interment at the hands of a *bokor* and later revivified as a cataleptic. Prominent above the altar beneath a host of trumpeting angels was a large all-seeing eye of Masonic design, suspended in the ether like a psychedelic polyp.

In 1949 the Anglican Bishop of Haiti, an American named Alfred Voegeli, agreed to commission these murals on the grounds that it 'pays to be crazy at times'; but there was nevertheless some consternation at the juxtaposition of Christian symbolism with that of Voodoo. *The Marriage Feast at Cana*, painted on the south transept wall by Wilson Bigaud, clutters the scene of Christ's first miracle with drums, horns, conches and clay jars called *govis* which are believed to contain the spir-its of the dead. It is pure syncretism, the union or reconciliation of diverse religious beliefs. In the case of Bigaud, there may also have been a conflict of belief. The artist was barely twenty-two years old when he first began to paint, hailed by Selden Rodman as the 'Brueghel of Haiti'; but he suffered a nervous breakdown almost as soon as he took a brush to his important mural, *The Last Judgement*. This painting – unfinished – portrayed demons so terrifying that Bigaud became himself the victim of his own imagination. The *loas*, he said, had taken revenge and been transformed into the leather-winged devils of Christian iconography. He entered a mental hospital and subsequently ran away to the United States.

Other, less dramatic, problems presented themselves in the creation of these magnificent murals. Mr Rodman relates how the artist Philomé Obin agonized over the propriety of depicting Christ in *The Last Supper* as a black Haitian. He compromised by painting the Saviour as a mulatto with distinctly Caucasian features surrounded by disciples both Negro and white. Every morning before he began to paint, Obin would kneel in prayer and intone from a Protestant hymnal:

> *'Mon Sauveur mourrit sur la Croix*
> *Grâce à l'Agneau de Dieu'*

There is something here of the medieval artist or craftsman who would paint the interior of a church with a sense of proud participation in the work of God. One thinks of how Giotto decorated the walls of the Arena chapel in Padua under the guiding numen of the Blessed Virgin, of how both he and Cimabue painted frescoes in the name of St Francis of Assisi. The great Haitian artist André Pierre will claim divine tutelage not only from the Catholic saints but also from the *loas*. He is unable to paint until their inspiration is upon him, or perhaps once he has consumed a quart of rum.

André Pierre lives just outside Port-au-Prince in Croix-des-Missions, a village dotted with humble mud-baked dwellings. Numerous churches – Eglise Baptiste de Calvaire, Eglise Methodiste Libre, Eglise de Nazaren – give promise of evangelical salvation but André Pierre is a Voodoo priest and his thoughts wander less to heaven than to the earth. 'Everything comes from the soil, from *la terre*.' He tilted out a jigger of the rum which I had proffered as a gift, and placed the bottle next to a canvas daubed with the trellised heart of Erzulie Freda. 'Everything! Even man, the holy saints and the Pope in Rome, all created with the dust of this earth! But the first magic of the world was made by God, who lives in the sky.' This, indeed, is the credo of most Haitian peasants; to believe in the spirits is to believe in the earth. God is altogether too remote for everyday worship.

Pierre returned to his chair beneath the greenish penumbra of a fig tree and considered a moment. He wore a grubby white shirt and a pair of spectacles Sellotaped at the bridge. One brown eye was clouded by cataract. Pierre picked up a brush of chicken feathers. 'Without the inspiration of the earth,' he announced, 'I am unable to paint with the hand of God.' Then he began to dab a smidgeon of gouache – Prussian blue

– on to a wonderful painting of Loco Attison, the Voodoo divinity of medicine and knowledge, disguised as St Joseph. The colours here were rich and lustrous: trees, flowers, blades of grass, greenswards, a clearing in a forest, all glowing violet and brilliant orange. 'Ah the beauty of holiness!' André Pierre swallowed another swig of rum and his voice took on a strange vibrancy of emotion . . . 'The beauty of holiness.'

André Malraux, the French novelist, connoisseur of Haitian art and former Minister for Cultural Affairs under de Gaulle, praised André Pierre as *'le plus grand naïf vivant'*. But Pierre has rarely cared for such encomia. Sixty-seven years he has lived in this same tumble-down shack at Croix-des-Missions without a telephone. His origins are a little uncertain, although they evidently are humble. 'In the early days I was a *cultivateur*,' said André Pierre with a faintly alarming giggle. 'A fieldhand.' Other Haitian painters have been cobblers, bakers, tailors, fishermen; Louisiane Saint-Fleurant was a cook until it was discovered that she could paint. Today she lives in a small shop of her own in a ravine above Pétionville market, a timid old lady with hair that stands in unkempt little clumps, stiff with dust and gypsum.

I asked André Pierre why he chose to paint. 'It was decreed by the spirit of God.' A mischievous glint came to the old man's eye. Was he married? *'Oui, un peu.'* The artist cackled. *'J'ai plusieurs femmes.'* Had he become a Voodoo divinity himself, entered the pantheon of animist deities? 'Yes, I think so. Possibly!' Pierre led me into a dingy room pungent with the smell of paint and rum. He lit a coconut-oil lamp and a soft glow fell upon five or six paintings. 'Baron Samedi,' said Pierre, pointing with a brush to a mustachioed figure standing at a crossroads in the midst of jungle. His skull-and-crossbones tricorne, tipped at a rakish angle, and black undertaker's coat were stitched with sequins like a pearly king's. Smoke from Pierre's lamp fumed blackly up the wall and the Baron glared at me with graveyard eyes.

'Is he dangerous, the Baron?'

'He is powerful,' André Pierre corrected me. *'Très, très puissant*, with the right to decide who should live or die!'

'Tell me, is Voodoo ever evil?'

'No! It is only men who make zombis; men like Papa Doc, as crooked as the devil's toes!' Pierre added in Creole: *'Wanga, moun qui fait sa*, it is mortals alone who create black magic.'

Another painting showed Damballah Wedo, whose counterpart in the Catholic calendar is St Patrick. Twin serpents curled round his shepherd's staff and a double rainbow of rich luminosity arched across the fore-ground. I noticed how Damballah's feet were fused into the earth like the roots of a tree, as if the deity had been spirited from the pages of Ovid's *Metamorphoses*.

'And this,' said André Pierre, 'is Queen Elizabeth.'

'Of Great Britain?' I queried.

'Yes, I think so.'

The artist explained how the painting had been commissioned by a man in London who specified that the sovereign be transformed into a *loa*. There she sat, Queen Elizabeth II, ensconced on a golden throne surrounded by animals like prehistoric cave figures, and by a rich prolif-eration of leaves and hibiscus and convolvulus. Her Majesty's face had darkened to a shade of chocolate.

The miracle in these paintings was that nothing had been slyly trans-posed from Western art or literature. You might detect the influence here and there of a carnival backdrop or cinema poster, a commercial hoard-ing or indeed an advertisement which André Pierre may have seen in one of the shops at Croix-des-Missions (Dynasty Dry Cleaning, Chez Dodo); ultimately, though, Pierre was inspired and guided in his art only by the divinities of Dahomey, by the spiritual history of Haiti.

Common to most Haitian *naïfs*, Pierre will refuse to paint the misery of life in a slum or bidonville. His themes are legendary, religious or hermetic, drawn from memory or simply pure invention, as in the manner of another Haitian artist, Préfète Duffaut. Philippe Auguste adorned his canvases with giant fruits and flowers, Gauguin bathing beauties, carnival masks and mermaid-tailed divinities. But Duffaut was the master of pure decoration. His paradisal landscapes are built from strange capes and impossible peninsulas, overhung with cloudless skies of inky blueness. Philomé Obin occasionally referred to the schoolbook history of Haiti, depicting the arrest of Toussaint L'Ouverture or the assassination of Dessalines; but even these paintings resemble surrealist distortions of eighteenth-century prints with their French viceroys in fantastical strands of brocade or frog embroidery, the exaggerated plumes of peacock feathers.

Rarely is there any hint of contemporary affairs or politics in the art of Haiti, although it is true that the young and gifted Haitian painter Edouard Duval-Càrrié once executed a portrait of Baby Doc which showed the dictator in a lace wedding dress and holding a suicidal revolver to his head. 'It could have got me into trouble,' Edouard had told me in

Paris where he now works above the Musée des Arts Africans et Océaniens. 'I prefer to live in France.'

As I left André Pierre to the bottle of rum, he began to sing, rocking to and fro on his rattan chair beneath the fig tree. I misquote from memory:

> 'Here I am Damballah Wedo
> Holding a thunderstone in one hand
> I am the water's beating heart
> I slither on my back
> With my seven serpents
> I am the rainbow . . .'

Artists in Haiti will usually find sponsorship with an individual benefactor, often someone who owns a gallery. One of the largest galleries in Port-au-Prince is run by Issa El Saïëh, a Haitian-Syrian who has provided indefatigable support for André Pierre. Issa (as everyone calls him) is an astute businessman with considerable experience in real estate and his gallery behind the Hotel Oloffson on the Rue Chile is also his home, a sturdy construction with tall shutter doors, pine floors and a spacious balcony screened with sweet-smelling honeysuckle.

'I remember I sold a Philippe Auguste to Graham Greene for a really crazy sum, something like fifty dollars American!' Issa poured himself another cup of Turkish coffee and looked at me shrewdly. 'Know what that painting would fetch today? Five thousand dollars minimum. Not that I'm always hot-footing after money, you understand. But just what in the name of creation was I doing selling a picture so *cheap*?'

Issa was born in Haiti to Palestinians from Bethlehem but had spent his youth in the United States. 'We're direct descendants of the Crusaders,' he told me. 'All the women in my family had a holy cross tattooed on their wrists.' Issa's great-uncle Solomon owned a shop in Port-au-Prince selling pots and pans and his grandfather Moussa Talamas was one of the brokers who arranged the sale of the Iron Market to Haiti from America.

'But my father thought Haitians were just a buncha mean no-count folk and he didn't want me to grow up here in Port-au-Prince,' said Issa, patting another yawn. 'So at the age of five he packed my bags for New York and that was that.' In America, Issa learned how to play basketball and became a bandleader. 'That's me there.' He pointed to an old black-and-white photograph of himself with Charlie Parker. 'Used to perform on clarinet and sax with Charlie in the Café Society Club NY. Those were the days! We'd raise holy hell at that venue . . .'

I asked Issa why he came back to Port-au-Prince. 'Oh, for a whole headful of reasons,' he said. 'For one thing, I wanted to make some money. Besides, this is where I was born!' Issa went on to open the first department store in Haiti and in 1957, the year Doctor Duvalier took power, he decided to establish a gallery. Six years later Graham Greene arrived in Port-au-Prince and they became friends. 'Every day he'd sit here in this very room talking to me about Haiti, gathering information for *The Comedians.*' Issa remembered those days with affection. 'He was a great guy, Greene. Had to drive him to a brothel once, strictly for the purposes of research you understand. He was a boozer, too, though I never saw him drunk. But was he *religious*! I mean really Jesus-bitten. Sonofagun used to keep a great crucifix by his bed – room number eleven that was, in the Oloffson. To frighten away the zombis I guess. But he was funny, you know. He made me laugh.'

Issa is a spirited raconteur and, by his own account, a man who has performed 'a lot of cloak-and-dagger stuff' in the days when he was a secret anti-Duvalierist. Once he flew from the United States with a plan to overthrow Papa Doc concealed in the sole of his shoe. 'I had to smuggle the thing into the kitchen of the El Rancho Hotel under cover of dark. Macoutes were on to me as fast as lightning.'

Issa appears, thinly veiled, as the Syrian storekeeper Hamit in *The Comedians*. 'And when Greene found out that I'd been arrested by Papa Doc, he killed me off in the book,' said Issa. 'Poor Hamit, found dead in an open sewer on the edge of Port-au-Prince. Greene obviously thought that anyone who went to jail in those days would never come out alive.' Issa puckered his eyes. 'I'm sure Greene would think I was *still* dead,' he said ruefully.

The Galerie Issa was a confusion of iron sculptures fashioned from flattened petrol drums, mahogany plates, bowls and masks, small cedar boxes decorated by hand with vivid jungle scenes, a few items in sisal or straw and hundreds of paintings pushed willy-nilly into racks or suspended from the ceiling by hooks like coat hangers. Many were of excellent quality, in particular those by Gérard Valcin and André Normil. Issa is almost avuncular in the care and attention which he lavishes on these and other artists, ensuring that they are adequately fed and paid. Hard-nosed merchant but also provider, Issa commands great respect and is furthermore impatient of those who wax lyrical about the art he sells.

'I run a business,' he told me with natural modesty, 'and not a salon.'

When André Breton travelled to Port-au-Prince in the winter of 1945, accompanied by the great Cuban artist Wifredo Lam, he purchased a number of Haitian pictures. 'These should revolutionize French painting,' he is reported to have said; 'it needs a revolution.' Breton arrived a year after the celebrated renaissance of Haitian art inaugurated by one De Witt Peters, an American watercolourist who moved to Haiti on a wartime assignment to teach English. Legend tells that the American stumbled on a bar in Mont Rouis with this sign over the doorway: *'Ici La Renaissance'*. Hector Hyppolite, a Voodoo priest apprenticed to the trade of cobbler, had decorated the tavern with frescoes of birds, fruit, flowers; and Mr Peters was so impressed by these that he embarked on an enthusiastic quest to disinter more examples of primitive art in Haiti.

In 1944, having established Hyppolite as the Henri Rousseau of Haitian artists, De Witt Peters and Selden Rodman opened the Centre d'Art in Port-au-Prince. This became a place of instruction for all Haitian artists, a sort of Caribbean Ecole de Paris. The Renaissance had begun; Voodoo art became the fashion.

But Issa El Saiëh doubts whether there was ever a reawakening in the first place. 'There has been painting here for as long as memory,' he said. 'Goes right back to the days of slavery.'

This opinion was endorsed by a character I met some months later on my return to London, Sheldon Williams. 'It was no revelation, the Centre d'Art, no damned miracle on the road to Damascus! De Witt Peters just happened to be in the right place at the right time!' Mr Williams spoke at his home in Stoke Newington, adorned with gold rococo chairs upholstered in purple plush and only one or two objects from Haiti, among them a hollow half-gourd painted by André Pierre and a metal sculpture in the form of a devil by Seresier Louisjuste.

Sheldon Williams, born in County Cork, is the foremost expert in Great Britain on Haitian art; his book *Voodoo and the Art of Haiti* was the result of several trips in search of paintings for dealers in Switzerland, France and England. Mr Williams, himself no mean painter of abstracts, has also known Wifredo Lam and other surrealists interested in Voodoo.

'Now where the hell was I?' he asked in a curious transatlantic drawl reminiscent of Christopher Isherwood. 'Oh yes! Well, Haitian art began *long* before the days of Hector Hyppolite and company. Since time immemorial the Voodoo priest has sought to express the inexpressible through *vèvès* and whatnot, cabbalistic symbols and designs on the odd temple wall. With De Witt Peters, this suddenly developed into Art with a capital A! And it became big business, with an awful lot of cultural perfidy and money-fodder pictures floating about for the American market, I might add!'

It was eleven o'clock on a frosty winter morning and logs glowed orange in the grate of an open fire. Mr Williams, swathed in a silk dressing gown and smoking explosive cheroots specially imported from the Cameroon, rose from his chair, remarking: 'Care for anything to eat or drink?' He returned ten minutes later with a bottle of retsina and a plate of broken digestive biscuits. 'I'm afraid it's all I've got. My wife's in New Zealand you see.'

Mr Williams described himself quaintly as a *'flâneur'* and 'caddis fly', a moth-like insect whose pond larvae build houses from bits of twig or shell. He possessed a marvellous set of gold teeth, and numerous rings of esoteric design glittered on his fingers. Of elfin build and height, his appearance was all the more striking for a great mop of unruly white hair. 'My relation to Haitian art is exactly like that of the caddis.' He flicked the butt of his Cameroonian cheroot on to the hearth and lit another. 'I latch on to everything, collecting in a haphazard way.'

What was it about Haitian paintings that gave Mr Williams such pleasure? 'I was impressed by the honest clarity of the artists, by their unconscious wisdom,' he said. 'People like Hyppolite seemed to be working in a state of childlike wonder, as if they had been touched by God. I mean they had this . . . charisma. Look at André Pierre! He's what I'd call the official portrait painter of the *loas*. Absolutely top notch. You know, I could swear on my own heartbeat that I saw the same sort of thing happening with the Expressionists when I visited Germany as a young boy. Distortion, jarring colours, breaking with the shackles of proportion!'

Sheldon Williams has travelled widely: he fought in the Spanish Civil War; his ship was sunk by Messerschmitts in the Arctic Sea and he was shot at twice in Port-au-Prince outside the National Palace. 'It was Papa Doc's fault, probably. One was always meeting him in those days. Frightful creature. Just sat there like a sack of coal.'

Mr Williams first visited Haiti when he was sixteen. He explained how he saw an advertisement in *The Times* one day offering a job on a sugar plantation in the Dominican Republic. 'I jumped at the opportunity. In fact I stole my father's stamp collection, flogged it for ninety-six quid and used the money to pay for my passage all the way to Haiti.'

Haitian art proved a revelation. 'I was staggered by what I saw,' he went on. 'Unfortunately, being young, poor and stupid, I never spent my precious dollars on any paintings, which would have only cost me the equivalent of a few English shillings.'

I asked Sheldon Williams why Haiti alone among black countries should have produced such splendid art. 'Damn good question and it all comes back to our old friend Voodoo,' he replied. Mr Williams believes that the early expulsion of the French by the black slaves of Saint Domingue enabled this religion to thrive on the island as nowhere else in the Caribbean or the South American mainland. 'What you get in Haiti is this incredibly rich mixture of dance and symbol and song, with the culture of France grafted on to that of the hundreds of tribes transplanted from Africa. The result of this great cultural salad, this whole *maelstrom* of currents and influences, is that some eight hundred very good artists are working in Haiti today.'

Sheldon Williams drained another glass of resinated white wine and walked me to his front door. 'Voodoo's the ticket, my boy!' he said jovially. 'But watch out for zombis. Their curse is like poison. Ha ha!'

I caught the number 73 bus back home from Stoke Newington.

The rain had begun; it fell perpendicular and steady, drumming into a heavy downpour. A great wind swept across the roof of the Hotel Oloffson, dislodging tiles. 'Don't worry,' said Dr Carlos Jara, placing his glass on a table with a beach umbrella in the middle. 'I've lived in Haiti long enough to know that it'll be over in a minute.' Dr Jara is a wealthy psychiatrist who fled his native Chile during the early days of the Pinochet regime. With Latin blue-black hair and sad brown eyes, he was dressed in a crisp pair of white linen trousers and a short-sleeved shirt, silver pen clipped to the breast pocket.

I had arranged with Dr Jara to visit a community of peasant artisans living fifteen miles above Port-au-Prince in the hamlet of Soisson-la-Montagne. The community was founded in 1974 by two Haitian intellectuals, Tiga Garoute and Maude Robert, who had provided the peasants with brushes and pots of paint in the hope that they would produce primitive art inspired, haphazard, by the spirits of Voodoo. The five Haitian artists originally associated with this project – Levoy Exil, Prosper Pierre-Louis, Denis Smith, Dieuseul Paul and Louisiane Saint-Fleurant herself – are still working at Soisson-la-Montagne; I was interested to see how they had fared since André Malraux visited in late 1975.

Malraux was so impressed by Saint-Soleil, as the community was then known, that he lavished over twenty pages on its artists in his monumental study of religious iconography, *L'Intemporel*. Malraux appears in particular to have been struck by the painted cemetery at Soisson-la-Montagne which he likened to a nomadic or Merovingian graveyard daubed with the nightmarish masks and skeletons of James Ensor, the decadent Belgian artist. In almost hallucinatory prose, Malraux goes on to describe how the tombstones had been decorated with a 'furious freedom, but not infantile'; how 'Africa has found its genius for colour in poor Haiti, and in her alone . . .' He hails the artists as 'sacred' and mentions their names in the same chapter which he devotes to Rouault, Uccello, Raphael and Van Gogh.

Perhaps Malraux, ill and already approaching death by the time he arrived in Haiti, had been a little affected by the apocalyptic reception he received at Soisson-la-Montagne. Apparently, an artist had stepped in front of the venerable Frenchman brandishing a pitchfork and yelled: '*André! Je suis le Fils du Soleil! Nous avons décidé de tuer la Bête!*' Malraux, by his own admission, was nonplussed by this salutation. He called it a 'Babylonian harangue'.

The breeze in the aftermath of the rain was warm and clammy, like the breath of a panting dog. A lop-eared mutt in fact shook itself on the verandah of the Oloffson, spattering a guest with mud.

We set off in Dr Jara's red four-wheel-drive jeep, passing a group of men by the roadside in their ragged underdrawers. On we drove, climbing upwards through gigantic clumps of hills damp and glistening in the filtered green light. I was fortunate to have Dr Jara as guide and cicerone, for he owns one of the largest collections of Haitian art in the world, well over five thousand paintings.

Someone had cleared a narrow but practicable path to the cemetery at Soisson-la-Montagne. A large black cross to Baron Samedi stood at the entrance, pieces of burned banana placed at its foot on a platter next to clumps of red and purple rags. 'Offerings for the God of Death,' said Dr Jara as he knelt to place his own offering – a silver coin – by the unholy rood.

Little remained of the tombstone paintings so admired by Malraux; their paint, faded to an insipid green or pink, had been washed away by the rain. Soisson-la-Montagne appeared to be deserted, a morning multitude of cock-crows the only sound. In the distance I could see smoke rising from charcoal pits like Red Indian signals; and beyond, the pastel-blue horizon of the sea. Following in the footsteps of Malraux had brought me a peaceful patch of countryside, but nothing else.

We drove a mile or so from the cemetery to a concrete studio perched on the side of a hill where I met Prosper Pierre-Louis, Denis Smith and Dieuseul Paul. Prosper, a former hairdresser and the son of a Voodoo priest, achieved some notoriety in 1984 when his painting of Damballah Wedo appeared on the cover of the Port-au-Prince telephone directory, and his clothes suggested that he was not a poor man. He wore a *Playboy* T-shirt, a metal pendant the size of a Brazil nut, bell-bottom trousers and a spivvish fedora with a golden chain-belt like Jimi Hendrix.

Sheldon Williams would later express a fear that Haitian art might suffer from contact with the West. 'Money from dealers in the United States has already corrupted quite a few artists,' came the verdict. 'Suffice it to look at poor old J. B. Chéry. He was a fine artist until he discovered he could earn a fortune by painting small children with gigantic melons on their heads and twee stuff like that, turning out rubbishy art for a fast buck.'

The paintings at Soisson-la-Montagne confirmed, I think, the truth in this. They seemed to have been hurried out of the studio for the international market like so many copybook prints off a conveyor belt. Most of them leant towards an extreme and rather facile abstraction, lazy dots and squiggles, with the work of one artist almost indistinguishable from that of another. It was not always so. André Malraux had written that these artists would paint *'pour une fonction magique'* – that they were moved by the animist divinities, capable all the same of producing work which compared with Matisse. To judge by an extraordinary painting by Prosper Pierre-Louis which appears in *L'Intemporel*, this was certainly true. No longer: what I saw was copperplate reproduction.

Dieuseul Paul, a one-time farmer now dressed in a 'Surf Wave and Ski Company' sweatshirt, spoke in mystical terms about Malraux. 'When I first set eyes on him it was as though I had already seen him before. He had great presence, and a spirit of fire . . . Poor André! He wrote the last page of our community. I think he must be in heaven now.' In 1977, the artists of Soisson-la-Montagne organized a pilgrimage to Paris where they left flowers at the grave of Malraux.

'They *are* good artists, you know, really,' said Dr Carlos Jara as we drove back to Port-au-Prince. To my mind they had surrendered, if understandably, the brush and easel for a roll of banknotes.

XVI

A Brush with Zombis

'It is not so much undue haste as inexcusable carelessness that
must be blamed for the premature burying of persons who
are not already dead.'

From 'Burying Cholera Patients Alive', *Lancet*,
23 August 1884

The backyard was a menagerie of cooped doves and rabbits, with a pile
of broom-sweepings by the outdoor lavatory. From the kitchen came a
soft smell of a hen boiling in a pot; Madame Marie Nuñez had decapitated the creature that morning with a sharp machete. No restaurant in
Haiti has a very distinguished menu but at least the food here was fresh.
Large lobster were hauled from the Bay of Saint Marc and served soon
after with a pitcher of reasonable wine. The ice was of dubious provenance,
however, and on two occasions I found a bluebottle trapped like an insect
in amber.

Madame Nuñez was the patron of the Hotel Carré d'As in the old
coffee port of Saint Marc, some sixty miles north of the capital. The
hotel, a handsome clapboard with wooden arcades, stood opposite a Shell
petrol station on the Rue Christophe. Tap-taps would refuel there before
grinding northwards to Cap-Haïtien. My bed was very dusty, the mattress
moulded by earlier tenants; and it was difficult to sleep with the electric
dynamo of the hotel droning all night over the thin wail of mosquito
wings. For three mornings now I had been woken by an impassioned
harangue from Madame Nuñez as she scolded her sons for speaking Creole
at table:

'*Français! Ici vous parlez français!*'

To which the children would chant in derisive Creole: '*Palé fransé pa
di lespri pou sa!*' – just because you speak French doesn't mean you've got
a good mind.

Marie Nuñez was a large mulatta whose straw hats for church were
adorned with clusters of celluloid fruit. She was pleased with her corn-
flower eyes and pale skin the colour of rum. 'I'm so sorry about the

outdoor lavatory,' she had apologized. 'They all lack a satisfactory convenience, these magnificent old buildings.' Her father Antonio Nuñez, a Spaniard who married a black Haitian, had built the hotel. 'It's haunted,' said Madame Nuñez. 'But then, *vous savez*, this whole island is haunted . . .'

It was Lafortune Félix who told me where to find the zombi. 'At the Baptist mission in Passe Reine,' he said. 'Be careful. He's a body without a soul, *un corps cadavre* . . .'

Monsieur Félix is an artist of great originality and variety; none of his paintings is the same, although they have a single theme. Voodoo for Félix is always a force for fear and trepidation. His landscapes are claustrophobic with lowering skies black as pitch; zombis glare at you with a saturnine eye. *Ibo mange chien, Offrande par Maître Lucifer, Cérémonie Sacrifice Simbie Wandezo* . . . these titles are typical of his paintings. But the gloom is transfigured, quite magically, by a riot of dream-like foliage brilliant in colour like the surrealist designs of Odilon Redon: stalks of chartreuse green, saffron yellow, leaves the colour of ultramarine, cerulean blue and burnished gold.

I first saw these paintings at an exhibition – Les Visions Magiques de Lafortune Félix – organized by Dr and Mme Carlos Jara at the Museum of Haitian Art in Port-au-Prince. The opening night was a rather soigné affair, with the beau monde of Haiti dressed in tropical white. Monsieur Félix, though, was absent. According to Dr Jara, the artist had suffered a turbulent dream of living inhumation in which he struggled to free himself from the confines of a coffin.

Lafortune Félix was an elusive character; no one in Saint Marc seemed to know of his whereabouts. Perhaps they were confused by the several different names which he had used since 1958. I eventually located the road – more a goat track – down which the artist lived and asked directions of a man walking towards me.

He was about sixty, crabbed in expression, with two gold teeth, a sparse moustache and oblique little eyes. His breath was tainted faintly with rum. Apropos it seemed of nothing, he snapped: 'Who told you how to get here?'

All I could say, stupidly, was: 'Nobody. I mean I walked. Why do –'

'I am the man you are looking for,' and he flashed me a furious glance.

I mentioned to Lafortune Félix the name of Carlos Jara; Jara owns four hundred paintings by this artist, and acts as his agent.

'Eh bien mon ami,' Monsieur Félix grinned. *'Venez avec moi.'*

His house, a sturdy construction with concrete floors, overlooked a jungle-like profusion of tropical fernery and a luminescent variety of shrub. Evidently the artist had made more money since 1933, when he was born in a humble shack at the nearby village of Pont Sondé. Feeble electricity in the studio trembled and wavered; there was an odour somewhere of resin burning in a censer. Paint pots, palettes, tubes of gouache, all provided by Dr Jara and neatly arranged beneath an easel. Lafortune Félix removed several paintings from a pine chest. One, entitled *Le Grand Magicien de l'Afrique Guinée*, was inspired by the fearsome Petro divinity, Bossu of the Three Horns, a red-eyed hunchback.

'The bad, the evil *loas* have adopted me,' said Monsieur Félix. 'I have more nightmares than dreams. Sometimes the spirits come to me in my sleep and tell me which colour paint I must use.'

He described one such delirium. 'The spirits asked me last night how to paint a milk coconut and I replied, "You must mix the following colours: yellow, citron and apricot. Then you will have your coconut" . . .'

Lafortune Félix continued in a voice without expression:

'Then the gods, several of them, they came forward to congratulate me: *"Ah, monsieur! Vous êtes artiste,"* and shook my hand.'

The artist produced a painting of a zombi. It showed an automaton creature howling beneath a moon, a moon like a slice of snow. 'The *corps cadavres* work in fields by night,' Lafortune Félix whispered the words. 'They have soulless eyes and crouch in their sleep like brutes.'

'Where can I find one?' I inquired.

The village of Passe Reine stands seventy miles north of Saint Marc in a valley dotted with banana trees and fat-trunked ficus. The zombi, a gentleman by the name of Clairvius Narcisse, was harboured at the Baptist mission here by two Americans, Paul and Patsy Bailey. It was a blustery day; the wind was near to being a gale and mangoes fell with a thud into the open compound of the mission.

'This here wind's no humorous matter,' Pastor Bailey smoothed his tousled hair as he came to greet me. 'Thought it had got quieted down this morning but, Lord's sake, you coulda fooled me. Just a while back I had a young boy shinny up that mango yonder, fetch some fruit. Next thing he's blown clean out the branches. Seems he broke a bone or two . . .'

The pastor was a stocky man: thickset limbs, a lantern jaw: but jovial in manner, with a beaming smile.

'So what brings you here?'

There was some hesitation; I did not want to broach the subject of the living dead for fear of giving offence with undue haste.

Pastor Bailey repeated his question. 'Tell me straight, what brings you here? A man don't have no secrets from God, leastways if he's a Christian he don't.'

I explained that I was gathering material for a book on Haiti, and left it at that.

'Well, don't fret yourself overly,' he smiled. 'Just you come inside and meet the wife.'

Patsy Bailey sat on a rocking chair in a small room lined with copies of the Bible; a bunch of unripe bananas hung by a hook from the ceiling and, propped above the refrigerator, a block of mahogany carved with the word: JESUS. Mrs Bailey looked very pale, with fine ginger hair fluffed into a childish aureole around an oval, apple-like face. She was strangely beautiful but in the frail way of a pressed flower; her eyes were a faded periwinkle-blue.

Paul introduced me. 'Mighty pleased,' she got up totteringly from the rocker, 'to meet you,' extending a tiny hand. 'And I just want you to know, Ian, that you're welcome here most any afternoon. I hope you feel at ease with us here in this house of the Lord.'

It seemed strange that the Baileys, having settled in Haiti for almost forty years, had never been to a Voodoo ceremony. 'Now listen here and don't mistake me,' Pastor Bailey drawled. 'I don't mind if Haitians use drums and things like that at a military parade, or special state functions. But Lord, don't let's have any trouble from them *Voodoo* drums! Leastways not while I'm around.'

'Paul's right. We don't never allow drums in church.'

'Why not?' I asked.

'It don't make any difference for why not!' replied Mrs Bailey. 'I know good and well that Jesus'll never redeem folk that play drums in church. Why, it makes my flesh crawl just to think about how –'

Pastor Bailey interrupted ' – to think about how there's this darn business with Voodoo of burying folk in a premature fashion, I mean before they're certified *daid*!'

The Baptists looked at me.

'Dead?' I faltered, alarmed but definitely interested. 'You mean –'

'I mean just what I say: *daid*.' The pastor turned to his wife. 'And Patsy, the way I look at it, you can't get any more bestial' – he pronounced it *beestial* – 'than burying folk alive. It's just way outa line, that kind of behaviour.'

Patsy described how a zombi, Fancina Illeus, had wandered into the mission one day in 1979. 'She was, oh, all fragile like with her head bent low, you see. And she couldn't bear to see no sight of the sun, after being underground in the dark like that. Her hands were crossed over her chest, just like the way they bury folk hereabouts, and she slept at night with her feet crossed at the ankles too. Oh, such a real sweet person she was, so I called her Ti Femme, Little Woman, and we gave her a home. Land's sake I just wanted to . . . *lasso* her soul for the Lord! Well, it seemed a harmless thing to do.'

Pastor Bailey added gruffly, 'We were pretty shook up when Ti Femme arrived. Seems she'd been through most everything possible in the way of a nightmare. Beaten, chained to a bed, roped to a tree. I don't wonder she couldn't make head nor tails of her situation . . .'

I asked if I could talk to Ti Femme.

'Oh no, she's *daid*,' said Patsy. 'Died a year back.'

'That's right,' the pastor remarked. 'And the dead are dead and can stay that way.'

There was a silence.

'Mind you,' Paul cleared his throat, 'we *do* have another zombi here, feller name of Clairvius, Clairvius Narcisse. Lord, he was in a bad way when we took him in, pantslegs all torn up, great scar down his face where the coffin nail went through. Seems he was put underground by a *bokor*, one Joseph Jean. Nobody knows what happened to *him*. Police located not hide nor hair of the evil man.'

'Could I talk to Monsieur Narcisse?'

'Why sure you can! He's a mighty good boy, a real Uncle Remus and sweet as pie!' the Pastor beamed.

'But can he speak?'

'Sure can. He don't really know how to read and write, mind. But he'll talk. He's lively, talky as a jaybird!'

Pastor Bailey led me across the windswept compound to a hut where the zombi lived. 'He was buried alive some thirty years ago,' the Baptist said. 'Tombstone's still there, not far away in Pont Sondé. Lord, it's enough to shame the dead . . .'

Apparently, the inscription reads: *'Ici Repose Clairvius N'*.

In the West we have the quick and the dead; in Haiti, they have the quick, the dead and a third category – the zombi. Neither a ghost nor a man who, like Lazarus has been raised from the dead, a zombi is one that was taken for dead after the ministrations of a witch doctor, then buried alive and resuscitated shortly afterwards. They have attendant brain damage due to anoxia, or oxygen deprivation, that results from severely diminished respiration. The victim survives as a virtual vegetable – no longer able to distinguish between hallucination and reality, an automaton without character or will, blindly obedient to the dictates of a *bokor*.

The middle classes of Haiti will dismiss any talk of zombis as mere *folklorisme*; but there is no doubt that premature sepulture exists in this country. It is the subject indeed of *Hadriana in all my Dreams*, a wonderful novel by the Haitian writer René Depestre which in 1988 won the French Prix Renaudot. Set in Jacmel during carnival, it tells the story of a beautiful woman from France, Hadriana Siloé, who falls dead in church the moment she pronounces the words 'I do' before her bridegroom. Hadriana is buried and later revivified by a *bokor* with the aid of a magical powder. Forty years on she appears in Utah, of all places, as the reincarnation of Simbie-la-Source, the Voodoo divinity of rain. The plot may appear, with its peculiar resonance of the marvellous, to be implausible. Depestre, though, is certainly familiar with the practice of Voodoo and for him, as for most of his compatriots, the zombi is simply a part of what he calls the *'surréalisme quotidien'* of Haiti, a peculiar fact of everyday life. Perhaps it is no coincidence that this novel is dedicated to the memory of André Breton; it is a work of grand and consuming poetry.

In the popular belief, then, zombis are literally members of the living dead – corpses which have been removed from the grave and endowed by sorcery with a mechanical semblance of life. A *bokor* will insist that the poison he secretly administers to a victim in the form of a powder has the power to kill outright; that the victim is then exhumed and later reanimated as a walking corpse – *un corps cadavre* – by means of a magical antidote. This is nonsense. People are in fact buried alive, as the powder induces in the victim a state of catalepsy or apparent death such as Juliet was to experience from the phial of distilled liquor offered her by Friar Laurence:

> '. . . no pulse
> Shall keep his native progress, but surcease:
> No warmth, no breath, shall testify thou livest . . .'

The antidote itself is probably no more than a potion designed to prevent the victim from ultimately succumbing to the poisonous effect of the original powder; and not, contrary to what a *bokor* may believe, to revive him from the dead.

The pharmacology of zombi powder is not precisely known, in spite of diligent ethnobotanical research conducted into its chemical composition. It is believed, however, that a nerve agent – tetrodotoxin (TTX) – produced by the puffer fish may be one of the ingredients which brings about a state of catalepsy in the victim. TTX is one of the most potent neurotoxins known: it was used by Ian Fleming in an unsuccessful attempt to kill 007 in *From Russia With Love*, and is to be found in blowfish, globefish, balloonfish, swellfish, toadfish and porcupine fish of the suborder Gymnodontes. Scientists have also found traces of tetrodotoxin in certain frogs (genus *Atelopus*) from Costa Rica, the Pacific goby (*Gobius criniger*), the Australian octopus (*Hapalochlaena maculosa*) whose bite may be fatal to man, and in the Californian newt (genus *Taricha*).

Poisoning by TTX produces symptoms similar to those suffered by victims of myasthenia gravis (muscular atrophy that results from an antibody which blocks the action of motor nerve impulses), and zombi powder. Namely: an initial prickling sensation in the face and limbs which may progress to ataxia (inability to co-ordinate the actions of muscles involved in movement), double vision, respiratory distress, profuse sweating and hypothermia. If death occurs it usually does so within twenty-four hours owing to respiratory paralysis. Most patients remain conscious until shortly before they die; but there are numerous cases, particularly in Japan, where a victim of puffer-fish poisoning has been pronounced dead and subsequently recovered in the morgue or on the way to the crematorium.

The term 'zombi' was probably imported to Haiti by Portuguese slave traders from Africa, where in the language of the Bonda tribe we find the word 'zumbi'. But the practice of restoring vitality to a seeming corpse was also widespread in Jamaica. Matthew Gregory Lewis, author of that chain-rattling masterpiece of romantic medievalism *The Castle Spectre*, records in his Jamaican diaries a peculiar ceremony conducted on that island by a witch doctor. The following appears under the entry for 25 February 1817:

At the end of two or three hours he returns with a large bundle of herbs, from some of which he squeezes the juice into the mouth of the dead person; with others he anoints his eyes and stains the tips of his fingers; accompanying the ceremony with a great variety of grotesque actions, and chanting all the while something between a song and a howl, while the assistants, hand-in-hand, dance slowly round them in a circle, stamping the ground loudly with their feet to keep time with his chant. A considerable time elapses before the desired effect is produced, but at length the corpse gradually recovers animation and rises from the ground perfectly recovered.

Mr Lewis comments further on the *bokor*, or Obi man:

After this proof of his power, those who wish to be revenged upon their enemies apply to the sorcerer for some of the same powder which produced apparent death upon their companion; and, as they never employ the means used for his recovery, of course the powder once administered never fails to be lastingly fatal . . .

It is usually as a result of some act of vengeance or form of justice that a Haitian will be transformed into a zombi. Guilt or innocence is determined in such cases by a tribunal of community elders affiliated to one of the numerous secret societies which still exist in Haiti as political adjuncts of Voodoo. Broadly, these are pseudo-Masonic associations for mutual aid. Members are protected against individuals who may try to rob them of their land, or in some way outrage the honour of their families. In the southern town of Port-à-Piment I had spoken to a schoolteacher, Saurel Descombes, whose younger brother had reportedly been consigned alive to the tomb by members of a secret society from Trou Bonbon, a village near Jérémie, all because he had transgressed over some marital matter.

The society bore the nightmarish title of Bizango and the teacher told me that there are numerous other such confraternities in Haiti: Mackanda, Vlinbindingue, Zobop, Mazanza, Congo, Sindindin, Shanpwel, La Société Grand Drap and the Cochon Sans Poil (hairless pig). According to Saurel Descombes, these societies demand the sacrifice at their ceremonies of a *cabrit sans cornes*.

'A hornless goat?' I had asked the teacher to elaborate.

'Yes,' he pulled a face. 'A human being.'

It should be stressed here that zombification is strictly the concern of *magie noire* or black magic; it has little to do with the generally peaceable creed of Voodoo.

★ ★ ★

Clairvius Narcisse sat outside his hut on a rattan chair, an old man with extinguished, glassy eyes. His blank expression was, Pastor Bailey told me, typical of the *corps cadavre*; the Tontons Macoute themselves took to wearing sunglasses in order to make peasants think they were zombis. A bottle of taffia, stoppered with a baby cobcorn, stood by the old man's feet.

'I died in 1962.' Clairvius took a long swig of the rum, running a finger along the railway-track scar on his right cheek. 'When they buried me I could hear everything that was happening, but I couldn't move, speak or do anything.'

Monsieur Narcisse had related this story many times before and spoke in broken deadpan sentences. 'The funeral was on Thursday and I was dug up on Saturday,' he recalled. 'My mouth felt full of earth.'

Clairvius might have hailed from the pages of a story by Edgar Allan Poe. The old man described the fumes of the damp soil underground, the heavy oppression of the lungs, his thoughts of the air and grass above. 'The earth opened at night and I sat up,' he claimed. 'Then men from the society hit me like this – ha! ha! ha! – three times across the face.'

Pastor Bailey interrupted. 'That's right! The witch doctor and his men came down and slapped the poor man bowlegged.'

'Why?'

He explained that this was to kill the *gros-bon-ange*, or soul, of the victim. 'Took away ever' bit of his good big angel they did. It's the first step toward zombification.'

Clairvius smiled thinly. 'Then they made me smell something. Some powder. I was taken back to the house of the *bokor* and he healed the wound on my face.'

The potency of the original poison (for 'powder' we should presumably read 'antidote') must have been such that it effected the total cessation of all apparent functions of vitality in Clairvius Narcisse. Taken sick with shortness of breath and high blood pressure, he was admitted to the Albert Schweitzer Hospital some fifteen miles east of Pont Sondé in the ragged town of Deschapelles. According to records there, he died on 2 May 1962 at 1.15 p.m. of 'malignant hypertension and uraemia'. But his decease was only seeming. As Poe wrote of the cataleptic in *Premature Burial*: 'Sometimes the patient lies, for a day only, or even a shorter period, in a species of exaggerated lethargy. He is senseless and externally motionless; but the pulsation of the heart is still faintly perceptible . . .'

★　★　★

It is curious that Narcisse was declared dead in a hospital where the physicians are trained largely in the United States, Canada, France, Belgium, Italy and Switzerland. The hospital had been founded in 1956 in tribute to Albert Schweitzer who established an infirmary in French Equatorial Africa to combat leprosy. Sadly I was unable to talk to the director of the Schweitzer Hospital, Dr William Larimer Mellon, as he died shortly before my arrival in Haiti.

A smell of carbolic and antiseptic swabs permeated the wards; infants lay in metal cots equipped with oxygen cylinders or nutrient tubes, suffering from miliary tuberculosis and kwashiorkor protein deficiency. They looked like tiny old people, their skin shrivelled and stomachs distended. Adults languished under mosquito nets, many of them victim to malnutrition complications as well as to pneumonia, meningitis, sepsis malaria, typhoid, internal parasites. Their sores had been stained purple with antiseptic gentian, a plant which is scarcely used in medicine today.

Yet the Schweitzer is one of the best hospitals in Haiti; it is equipped with one hundred and sixteen in-patient beds, and a further forty beds for overnight observation. There is a good pharmacy and dispensary, a vaccination clinic, diagnostic laboratories for bacteriology and haematology; isolation, paediatric and terminal wards.

'So how could the doctors have blundered in their diagnosis of Narcisse?'

'I don't quite understand your question.' Mrs Gwen Mellon was on the defensive. 'All I hope,' she gazed into the distance at the Cahos mountain range and the plateaux rippled with maize fields. 'I just hope you write in your book that we are here to save lives and fight disease.'

We spoke in her garden under the dappled shade of a huge banyan planted by Mrs Mellon's late husband. There were several Cayenne cherry trees which had grown from seeds sent by Dr Albert Schweitzer from his hospital in Lambarene. Gwen Mellon, a native of New Jersey, was a handsome woman, tall and fine-boned, distinctly patrician in manner; but she would not be drawn on the subject of Clairvius Narcisse.

'Well, you know, it goes without saying that witch doctors mistreat patients, but so do all doctors, sometimes.' She looked at me. 'But *bokors* are the best psychiatrists in Haiti, believe me. Many of their . . . remedies are extremely efficacious. After all, medicine began by trial and error. Witch doctors understand the magic in plants and herbs much better than we do.'

When I left the hospital I walked to the market at Deschapelles. It was full of women in old calico smocks, haggling and clucking over merchandise that must have escaped from a supplies warehouse at the Schweitzer: Nestlé cream, Fab detergent, even Lea and Perrin sauce. A young boy approached waving a packet of pills. 'Give me five cents!' He stared at me with the dead eyes of malnutrition. 'Give me . . .' I looked at the packet: the pills contained powerful antibiotics – tetracycline, ampicillin, streptomycin. (This last can damage the kidneys and interfere with hearing in older people.)

'Where did you get these from?'

'*Bokor!*' the boy grinned. 'For *pici-pici*, for injection!'

Revived or galvanized into movement within three days of his entombment, Narcisse was set to work as a zombi in a field, weeding and planting. He worked ferociously and tirelessly for his master, a pitiful drudge without consciousness of his surroundings. This may explain why zombification is the most terrible of curses: it represents a return to the slavery that Toussaint L'Ouverture had abolished. Narcisse said he was sold – '*vendu*' – as a zombi by his two brothers. Apparently, there had been argument over the lease of a piece of family land. Handsome profit is to be made from this trade in slavery. In the hills above Jacmel I had spoken to a *bokor* named Balthazar Alexon who was reputed to harbour several zombis – four men and four women – in a sort of cowshed. 'Can I talk to them?' I had asked.

'No,' came the reply. 'They are still working, guarding my fruit trees and gardens, not ready to be seen.'

I offered the witch doctor a packet of Comme il Faut. 'Cigarettes will not do,' he had said. 'If you want to see my zombis you will have to give me thirty thousand American dollars.' As I left, the *bokor* cracked a giant whip close to my feet. 'I am known all over the world!' he shouted. 'In Martinique, in New York . . .'

At first, Clairvius Narcisse said he lived in a large hangar with two hundred and fifty other zombis, nine of whom were women. They were set heavy dull tasks, and beaten like dumb beasts if they slackened. After two years one of the *corps cadavres*, in a rare fit of rage, killed a witch doctor with a blow to his neck from a hoe. Whereupon the *bokor's* widow fed the slaves on food mixed with salt, which apparently returned them to an awareness of their humanity, and so they escaped. Salt, according to the Haitian superstition, provides the only panacea for living death and a zombi's diet is kept scrupulously free of any saline preservative. Narcisse said he roamed the hills of Haiti for sixteen years, finally returning to his family in early 1980 when he became something of a national celebrity. Haitian journalists sought him for interviews; psychiatrists examined him for brain damage.

After an hour of talking to me, Clairvius's face was a study in chagrin, hanging jaw and vacant gaze.

'I do hope he hasn't lapsed into permanent insensibility.'

'No, no. He acts like that ever' day,' returned Pastor Bailey. 'You know how it is, the nerves get a little . . . unstrung.'

As I left the Baptist mission, Patsy gave me a huge burlap sack full of mangoes. 'Well so long, Ian.' She said goodbye in the dimming light.

On board the tap-tap for Saint Marc I was pestered for alms by numerous market women. *'Blanc, blanc!'* They pawed at my shirt. 'Give me one dollar! Give me money!'

My nerves also felt a little unstrung and, churlishly, I played a cruel trick. 'Here, have as many of these as you like.' I opened the sack of mangoes and let the women fall upon my booty. Then, at an opportune moment, I said: 'They were given to me by a zombi.' In horror the *marchandes* dropped their mangoes like so many hot potatoes. They did not bother me again.

The Hotel Carré d'As was tranquil that night: a whirr somewhere of a Singer sewing machine, doves cooing in the eaves, the usual chatter of domesticated guinea fowl and maidservants singing to the rhythm of their dry reed brooms. There is a witch doctor near by – Marcel Pierre – who trafficks in the living dead. He is mentioned in a book about Haitian zombis entitled *The Serpent and the Rainbow*. The author of this study, Wade Davis of the Botanical Museum at Harvard University, is convinced that tetrodotoxin constitutes one of the ingredients of zombi power. Marcel Pierre had provided him with a sample of poison which was later submitted for laboratory analysis; it contained pulverized broiled pufferfish.

'Don't be back too late,' chirped Madame Nuñez as I left the hotel in search of Marcel Pierre.

Marcel Pierre was evidently renowned in Saint Marc. He ran a nightclub called the Eagle Bar from which he rarely emerged during the day. The club was situated some distance from my hotel in a dusty part of town known as Portail des Guêpes, Wasps' Gate. A yellow electric bulb dangled over the entrance; the club was a cinder-block dive and, stepping through the bead curtains, I was approached by a svelte young girl wearing a bra and pants.

'*Bonsoir, chéri.*' She raised an eyebrow. '*Vous cherchez l'amour?*'

There was a reek of cheap whorehouse perfume; the brothel was hot and fuggy. One could have cultivated orchids.

'No,' I said. 'I'm looking for Marcel Pierre.'

The hooker, a Dominican I guessed, dismissed me in a shrugging, cynical manner, '*Ay, madre mía!*' and sauntered off in search of the patron.

I took a seat beneath a large hand-painted sign: '*Pas de Crédit*'.

Marcel Pierre emerged some ten minutes later. He was a tall muscular chap, sporting a pair of wraparound sunglasses like Ray Charles. '*Bienvenu, blanc.*' He shook my hand in a vice-like grip. One of his feet, unbuckled in a black plastic sandal, was horribly swollen. The faintest soupçon of a moustache graced an upper lip beaded with sweat.

'I would like to talk with you if possible about zombis.'

Marcel Pierre removed his glasses, glanced at me with the quick black eyes of a lizard. He wore a dirty blue golf cap back-to-front, stitched with the words 'Rich Stars'.

'You will have to pay.'

'How much?'

'One thousand dollars.'

We negotiated a slightly more reasonable fee and Marcel Pierre led me into an antechamber behind the Eagle Bar, where he eased a padlock from the door. Then he lit a candle and showed me to a chair. The flame illuminated a plastic doll with a silver key around its neck ('*une garde loup-garou*' said Pierre – a protective charm against werewolves), a small cupboard revealing a lurid chromolithograph of St Jacques (identified in Voodoo with Ogoun Feraille the divinity of war), several coils of snakeskin which hung from the ceiling on lengths of twine, a variety of dirty detergent bottles, a large whip and a rusty insecticide aerosol. The floor I noticed was puddled with rum and castor oil, and trampled with a jetsam of charred sticks or palm branches.

Marcel Pierre removed an old sheet from the table in front of us. Beneath it rested two human skulls caked in scales of graveyard mud and three thigh bones. Both craniums, the witch doctor said, had been 'grated', the parings then calcined over a fire and ground into a powder with a pestle and mortar. 'But they're no good now for zombi poison.' He shook his head with theatrical disapproval. 'Far too old.' How did Pierre obtain these bones? They were purchased, he replied, from a '*fossoyeur*', gravedigger, in the cemetery at Saint Marc.

'Disgusting,' I said. 'Go on.'

'They cost me sixty dollars. Quite a good price.'

I put it to Marcel Pierre that Article 249 of the Haitian Penal Code would declare him a criminal. Translated, this reads: 'It shall be counted as attempted murder to employ substances which, without causing death, produce a lethargic state more or less prolonged . . . If following this lethargic state the person is buried it shall be qualified as murder and will be punished by death.'

Pierre sucked on his Comme il Faut, exhaled. 'There are two kinds of dead,' he said. 'Dead of the *bokor* and dead of God. The dead of the *bokor* are capable of resuscitation, but the dead of God cannot be resuscitated.'

'So the dead of the witch doctor are more fortunate?'

'Naturally.'

Our conversation died abruptly; one cannot argue with this kind of logic.

Marcel Pierre then produced two desiccated black toads stoppered in jam jars like specimens from the Natural History Museum. One, he said, was called *crapaud bouga*; the other, *crapaud de mer*. Their backs were pitted with wart-like bullae said to be venomous. Dried in the sun, these toads are then roasted over a fire and ground into a noxious talcum. Toads and human bones: René Depestre mentions these in *Hadriana in all my Dreams* as components of the catalepsy powder, as does Wade Davis in another of his studies, *Passage of Darkness: The Ethnobiology of the Haitian Zombi*.

My next exhibit was a dried spherical fish with a distended gullet sac, bristling with small spines. *'Poisson-globe.'* Pierre cast me a critical glance. Then, snapping a spine, he merely observed: 'It'll kill you.'

According to Wade Davis, this is a species of puffer fish known in Haiti as the *fou-fou* (Latin tag: *Diodon hystrix*) and its toxin, TTX, inhibits the conduction of nerve impulses. 'I am dying to eat puffer fish, but I don't want to die' is a popular proverb in Japan where the piquant culinary dish of *fugu* fish (literally seahog) is a common cause of puffer poisoning. An article which appeared in the *Lancet* (2 June 1984) under the arresting title 'Puffers, Gourmands, and Zombification', explains that while the Japanese appreciate the obvious risk in eating this epicure's delight (it is a gastronomic form of Russian roulette), they nevertheless enjoy the exhilarating physiological after-effects of warmth, flushing of the skin, mild paraesthesiae (tingling) of tongue or lips, an overwhelming euphoria. The article also mentions that *fugu* testes are prescribed in Japan as a powerful aphrodisiac when swallowed with a measure of *sake*.

Cooking does not eliminate the TTX in puffer fish as some organs (gonads, liver, skin) are extremely toxic. The author of this article relates how a fourteen-year-old boy was admitted to hospital in New South Wales after ingestion of a puffer; he was suffering from acute apnoea (a dramatic pause in breathing which is sometimes characteristic of deep sleep in the elderly), and a marked dilation of the pupils. 'The resuscitation team expected anoxic brain damage, but the boy recovered and described vividly his helpless state of paralysis, which the physicians regarded as coma but in which he could hear their conversation.'

Captain Cook himself almost died from tetrodotoxin. In his book *Second Voyage of Discovery Towards the South Pole and Round the World* the English navigator relates for the year 1774 how he ate the liver and roe of a puffer fish for supper near the Polynesian Islands. At about three o'clock the following morning he was seized by a terrible numbness of the limbs. 'I had almost lost the sense of feeling,' he wrote. 'Nor could I distinguish between light and heavy bodies . . . a quart pot full of water and a feather being the same in my hand.' When a group of islanders saw the type of fish eaten, they made signs to Cook, by rubbing their stomachs and closing their eyes, that it was poisonous and caused drowsiness or death. Cook was revived with an emetic, but a pig on board ship which snuffled the remaining entrails was less fortunate and expired.

To the ingredients of puffer fish, calcined human remains and pulverized black toads must be added those of a small white tree frog (*Osteopilus dominicencis*), polychaete worms with numerous bristles on their footstumps which inflict a mild paralysis, the skin of an extremely toxic New World toad known in Latin as the *Bufo marinus*, sundry millipedes, tarantulas and lizards. All these, once ground together into a powder, are reportedly capable of producing the phenomenon of living death.

It would seem that this unsavoury medicament is absorbed cutaneously, through the skin. 'I sprinkle the powder over the entrance to my victim's house.' Marcel Pierre looked unconcernedly at the puffer fish.

The corpse, so called, is then buried. 'You have to be on good terms with a grave-digger,' he added dryly. 'I always go to the cemetery with a *badjikan*, assistant to a witch doctor, for help and protection.'

A zombi, all told, is a human body deprived of its conscious powers of cerebration. This is a fate worse than death yet Clairvius Narcisse, in terms quite literally 'ecstatic' (*OED*: subject to trance, catalepsy, rapturous emotion), had described how in the Albert Schweitzer Hospital he lay on his apparent deathbed to watch his body float upwards into another realm where he felt very content and absolutely without fear. The advanced symptoms of known tetrodotoxin poisoning in fact merge very closely with what Western physicians term the autoscopic near-death experience (NDE). Autoscopy has been registered in medical literature as happening to those who emerge from anaesthesia as well as to others who have been revived after a temporary suspension of their cardiovascular activity.

People like Narcisse who have been at the frontier of death speak of an ineffable dimension where all intuitive sense of time is lost, and where the act of dying is acknowledged as something calm and even beautiful. Here we might recall the peculiar case of the great atheist philosopher A. J. Ayer who described in a letter to the *Spectator* (30 July 1988) how he had suffered a 'somewhat agonizing but very astonishing experience' in hospital when his brain had continued to function during the four minutes of a heart arrest. The description which the late Sir Alfred gave of his almost mystic enrapture bears an uncanny resemblance to the (garbled) accounts of near death as given by zombis. This is not to say that the author of *Language, Truth and Logic* had met with a peculiarly Haitian or indeed very religious experience ('One might well fall back on the Christian doctrine of the resurrection of the body,' the logical positivist begrudged). But Professor Ayer, like Clairvius Narcisse, had experienced a profound separation between his material body and some airy aspect of himself that hovered above the flesh. Then, apparently, he had been returned to his corporeal being and all was normal.

Haitians will resort to any number of ruses to circumvent the possible resurrection of a body. The corpse may be killed again, in the course of sepulchral obsequies, with a knife or stake through the heart as in the Dracula legend; care is taken too that no parts belonging to the dead matter – hair, fingernails – should remain above ground, for fear that they might otherwise be turned to magic or malevolent use. In short, all measures are taken to ensure that a body submit absolutely to corporeal dissolution and not to the 'Tragicall abomination', as Sir Thomas Browne wrote in *Urne-Buriall*, of being 'knav'd out of our graves . . . to delight and sport our Enemies'.

This horror of premature inhumation is not confined to Haiti; it swept across Victorian Europe, when people took the most extraordinary precautions to guarantee that they were buried in the 'final insensibility of death', as R. L. Stevenson put it. Fyodor Dostoevsky urged that his burial be delayed five days lest his decease be a condition of catalepsy or 'catatonic schizophrenia'. Bishop Berkeley ordered that one or more of his veins should be opened, so that his blood drain away in definitive confirmation that he was no longer a living mortal. In modern times, Leopold Bloom from Joyce's *Ulysses* wonders whether a friend had really died, and suggests: 'They ought to have some law to pierce the heart to make sure, or an electric clock or a telephone in the coffin and some kind of canvas airhole. Flag of distress . . .'

I asked Marcel Pierre how many people he had retrieved from the subterranean world of the seeming dead. 'I can't remember,' he said flatly. 'Hundreds. I've lost count.'

Might I see some examples of his magnificent work?

The witch doctor paused, then: 'Impossible. My zombis work far away – *une belle distance* – in the countryside. I took the spirit from their bodies and then sold them at a good price.'

The candle began to flicker and soon the room was in darkness. Pierre lit another stub of wax. There was a knock on the door and a young girl entered, looking very ill and frail. Her name, she said, was Jocelyn Willis. *'Moi, je suis une petite feuille.'* Jocelyn gazed with admiration at Marcel Pierre.

A 'small leaf' is the term for one who has sought treatment from a witch doctor or *houngan*. 'Jocelyn,' Pierre suddenly interposed. 'Roll up your sleeve!' The girl did as she was told. Her forearm bore a pattern of elaborate cicatrices made by scarifying the body. 'It's a protection,' Pierre explained. *'Une protection contre les mauvaises esprits.'*

'How did you do it?' I asked the *bokor*.

'With a Gillette.' He used the proprietary term. 'A razor blade.'

What was the matter with Jocelyn Willis?

'Malaria,' said Pierre. He then produced a number of tiny envelopes containing powder made, he assured me, of aloe plant (*Aloe vera*), which produces a nauseous bitter purgative, and spiky candelabra cactus (*Amyris maritima*) known locally as Shrove Tuesday ashes.

'I treat malaria with this powder,' Pierre continued, crushing some buds of cactus into the palm of his hand. 'Here,' he offered. 'Smell this.'

I did; it brought tears to my eyes and a sensation of burning in the nose.

Marcel Pierre laughed, a deep booming laugh midway between a cackle and a visceral gurgle. The cactus, he told me, was also used to resurrect a zombi from the grave.

'Oh good!' I replied in an attempt to be jocular. 'So now I'm a white man returned to life, a *zombi blanc.*'

'*Oui, oui!*' Pierre crowed and chortled with laughter at my apparent funny-man act. '*Zombi blanc!*' clutching his stomach. '*Zombi blanc . . .!*'

Jocelyn quietly left the room, kissing Marcel on the forehead. The witch doctor regained his composure, wiping away a tear with the back of his hand.

He went on, becalmed. 'It takes about thirty minutes to revive the *faux cadavre*, false corpse, from the tomb by means of a zombi antidote. Then you slap the resurrected body across the face' (this was just as Narcisse had told me) 'three times.'

I asked Pierre to elaborate on other components of the antidote (also administered as a powder). His ingredients tallied exactly with those mentioned by Wade Davis. There were several species of recognized hallucinogens, in particular *Datura Metel* and *Datura Stramonium* – both known in the picturesque native tongue as '*kokonm-zombi*', zombi's cucumber. This herbaceous plant is a strong narcotic and contains alkaloids which, ingested, may result in amnesia. Peruvian Indians use it as a stuporific intoxicant and the Hausa people of Nigeria impregnate their ritual beverages with the sap of its trumpet-shaped flowers. (A variety of datura grows in Great Britain on dunghills and in waste places.) Among the other components of this antidote are: bois caca (*Capparis jamaicensis*) which is a universal tisane sometimes used to protect newborn children; and the bark of *cadavre gaté*, a tree endowed in Voodoo with various healing properties.

Marcel Pierre gave a litany of other plants, leaves, venomous animal entrails, cordials and infusions. Too many; he began to sound like one of the witches in *Macbeth*:

> 'Fillet of a fenny snake,
> In the cauldron boil and bake;
> Eye of newt and toe of frog,
> Wool of bat, and tongue of dog . . .'

There was no mention, I am happy to report, of 'baboon's blood' or 'nose of Turk'.

I was about to leave when I noticed in the guttering light of the candle a tattered blood-red jerkin. It was suspended from a coat hanger above the human skulls. Marcel Pierre remarked my curiosity. 'I wear that every sixth of January.' He glared at me with a critical eye. 'It's to celebrate Ogoun Feraille.'

Feraille is one of the Petro divinities worshipped by adepts of the Bizango Society. I asked Pierre if he was a member.

He stood up. There was a long silence.

'Indeed I am. We meet every Wednesday in Saint Marc, and no,' he said, answering another question, 'you cannot attend. It is very dangerous. You have to be an initiate. There are passwords.'

'Such as?'

The witch doctor would not be caught off guard.

And what sort of protection would initiation afford me?

'Everything, *mon cher blanc*! You can leave at midnight for Cap-Haïtien and fear nothing . . . You can meet a band of horned devils carrying torches in their hands, but they will step aside to let you through.'

When I told Marcel Pierre that I would very much like to attend a Bizango ceremony, he suddenly wheeled round and shrieked at me. *'Ça pique les esprits!'* – it stirs up the spirits, *'qui se fâchent!'* – who get angry. Then, in Creole: *'Yo ap manjé ou!'* – they'll eat you up.

And with a twinkle in the eye, he whispered: 'I shall see to it that they eat you up.'

Marcel Pierre appeared to consider this threat quite seriously. So I took my leave, walking home in the soft night breeze. The Hotel Carré d'As was in darkness; Madame Nuñez and her brood were sound asleep. There was only the raw electric glare of a single bulb above the porch. I climbed the precipitous flight of stairs silently. When I reached my bedroom I lit a mosquito coil and listened to the rain puttering gently against the window. It was Monday, two days before the next Bizango ceremony. Saint Marc in the rain smelt curiously of flowers.

XVII

Initiation Rites

'The Voodoo priest, perhaps recognizing a kindred spirit, has
promised to initiate me by fire . . . do you think that is a
really good idea?'

Malcolm Lowry in a letter (Haiti, February 1947)
to his editor Albert Erskine

Saint Marc, dilapidated and decaying, must once have been quite beautiful. A building like a doll's house fashioned from wooden lace stood
opposite my hotel, its ruined clapboard façade overgrown with rose vine.
A 1931 fire-engine manufactured by Chevrolet, complete with pump and
coiled hose, rusted outside the Town Hall, a remnant of colonization
under the United States. And at the further end of the street under the
Venus Bar (five cents for a shot of whisky) mouldered a magnificent
mansion in the Southern vernacular style with Confederate Doric arches,
pillars and a balcony of curlicued iron.

There was, nevertheless, an air of mildew. The flea-pit cinema had
been pasted with tattered advertisements for such films as *Siegfried the
Invincible* and *Cauchemar de Vietnam*; an abandoned plantation near by bore
the mahogany hub of a sugar mill manufactured by John Gordon &
Company, London.

Saint Marc was occupied by the British between 1793 and 1798 and
they built two strongholds – the forts Churchill and Brisbane – which
overlook the town from an eminence of rock above the poster-blue sea.
A glance at the *Haitian Journal of Lieutenant Howard, York Hussars* will
confirm the futility of this occupation. No sooner had the British arrived
at Saint Marc than they were devastated by yellow fever and pernicious
malaria. 'Broiling on a gridiron must be fool's play to the heat in this
town,' Thomas Howard coolly observed; and one can imagine how disease
spread among these hussars who wore uniforms of tight breeches, Hessian
boots, fur-trimmed dolmans and forage caps with tassels and heavy green
piping. Lieutenant Howard relates how he drank himself into oblivion
with bottles of claret and madeira, crying: 'Oh, man, why wast thou

Born thus to perish distant from thy Native Land without a Friend to close thine eyes?'

In 1802, having expelled the British, Dessalines reduced Saint Marc to rubble so it could not be reclaimed by the invading armies of Napoleon. The town was later restored to comparative grandeur and its cathedral, surrounded by greenish shrub bush, is now a striking building in the Tropical Gothic style. Nailed to the white stone walls is a curious plaque:

IT WAS FROM HERE THAT A GROUP OF NATIONAL VOLUN-
TEERS LEFT IN 1779 TO BATTLE FOR THE INDEPENDENCE
OF THE UNITED STATES OF AMERICA. THEIR BLOOD WAS
SHED WITH GENEROSITY AT SAVANNAH AND YORKTOWN.

Many clandestine shipments of arms and ammunition were sent by the French from Saint Domingue to aid the insurgent colonists in America. In 1779 Admiral Charles-Hector d'Estaing sailed from Saint Marc to command the siege of Savannah in which six hundred mulatto and black troops fought courageously against the British. Among these Haitian volunteers was an eleven-year-old boy named Henri Christophe, then a slave-orderly to a French officer but later crowned king of Haiti. (As monarch he built a residence outside Saint Marc which is still dignified with the title of palace; it is now a converted *scierie* – saw-mill – long since abandoned, crawling with mongrel whelps and rats.) In 1781 a further fleet of Haitians left Saint Marc to defeat Lord Cornwallis at Lynnhaven Bay in Florida; by preventing his army from escaping across the sea they helped bring about the decisive surrender of Great Britain at Yorktown.

The Yankees did not forget the support which King Louis XVI had offered the Colonies during the American War of Independence; hundreds of French later left Haiti during the slave revolt to seek political asylum in the United States. They came flooding into Boston, Philadelphia, Baltimore, Charleston and New Orleans, bringing wild tales of burning, terrorism, rapine and death. In 1787 Jean Berard and his family fled their plantation near Saint Marc, arriving at New York two years before the triumphal inauguration of Washington as President of America. The family was accompanied by their Haitian slave Pierre Toussaint (no relative of Toussaint L'Ouverture) who at the time of writing is a candidate to become the first black American saint. Monsignor Robert O'Connell, Vice-Postulator of the Pierre Toussaint Guild in New York, tells me: 'Rome has accepted the process of canonization. The least we can hope for now is that Toussaint will be beatified and made venerable.'

I first read about Pierre Toussaint in a lurid history entitled *Black Pearl: the Hairdresser from Haiti* (1956). The authors, Mr and Mrs Arthur Sheehan, describe how Toussaint lived to be the most celebrated hairdresser in old New York, arranging immense architectural bouffants of powder and pomatum on the heads of fashionable ladies about town; he was also a philanthropist, devoting his income to works of charity along the Battery and the Bowery. In collaboration with the world's first religious community specifically for black women – the Oblate Sisters of Providence – he opened a refuge and school in New York for outcast children.

Toussaint's death in 1853 at the age of eighty-seven was mourned throughout New York. One newspaper began its obituary: 'Pierre was respected and beloved by widely different classes of the city . . . He possessed a sense of the appropriate, a self-respect, and a uniformity of demeanour which amounted to genius.' The freed slave was buried at Old St Patrick's cemetery in south Manhattan, where thirty thousand of New York's early Catholics are laid to rest. On 15 December 1990 the London *Independent* announced that Toussaint's skeleton had been exhumed. 'He may become a saint of the Catholic Church,' it confirmed.

A dragonfly hung like a humming-bird in suspension, its wings stirring the sand on an English cannon, then it flitted to a clump of broom and dithered awhile before flying over the precipice. The sky up here is a rarefied pure blue; there is no human sound amid the ruins of Fort Churchill, only a gobbling somewhere of turkey-cocks. Nor is there much vegetation – cotton dust balls, globes of thistledown, desiccated weed.

The fort commands a superlative view of Saint Marc. Way below, the Gulf of La Gonâve – a limpid world of sand shoals and shallow bays. To the south, the promontory of Anse Pirogue, a yellow grain silo, the knitting-needle spire of a cathedral; to the north, an isthmus called Pointe Table au Diable, the disreputable Eagle Bar, tap-taps hurtling along the pitted blacktop roadway to Cap-Haïtien (grandiosely called Route Nationale Numéro Un), a scattering of metal-roofed shacks known collectively as Cité Miami, and the brownish ribbon of the Rivière des Guêpes.

General George Churchill had installed a total of ten cannon here ('heavy guns that would greatly annoy an enemy', according to Lieutenant Howard); but today they are in an inexplicable state of confusion, as though hurled about by a poltergeist.

'What happened?' I asked my guide Aliès Pimba, a frail bat-boned man who worked as a notary in the Town Hall at Saint Marc.

'Loups-garous.' His eyes gleamed with excitement.

Werewolves? Now it seemed there was no limit to the freakish rami-fications of Voodoo. I was incredulous of this superstitious jabberwocky, and not a little impatient. Aliès, though, had become a friend. I did not want to hurt any feelings.

He directed me to the north side of the fort where, heaped round a litter of squashed cigarette ends, there was a number of offerings to the animist divinities – iron nails, guttered stubs of candles, small rocks and stones tied with braided string.

'Bizango.' Aliès looked at me guardedly.

'Are you a member?'

There was silence.

'Many people are members.'

Now I saw my chance: one can only attend a Bizango ceremony if invited to do so by an associate, and I felt sufficiently confident of my relationship with Aliès to broach the subject.

Aliès was prepared to offer an invitation, but said he would first have to gain permission from his superior, a certain Monsieur Mortelle, Emperor of the secret society. Any intruder is otherwise regarded as a stranger, a spy, an alien – and 'punished accordingly'.

'Eaten for supper?' I ventured.

'They say we eat people,' Aliès did not laugh, 'and we do, but only in the sense that we can take their breath of life.'

'You mean turn them into zombis?'

He answered with an evasion: 'A *blanc* should not dabble in such matters.'

For the educated classes of Haiti, Bizango and other secret societies are mystico-criminal cabals whose members stalk the streets at night in practice of black magic or an extreme form of Petro worship (*'Petro sauvage'*). Associates are bound by an oath of allegiance to the *'djab'*, or devil; and they venerate such feared Petro divinities as Erzulie Cœur Noir, Baron Cimetière, Maman Brigitte, Prince Zandor and a she-devil whose symbol is the screech owl – Marinette Bois-Sèche. We find in Bizango almost every leering apparition of the sabbaths which once crowded the dossiers of ecclesiastical tribunals in the days of witch-hunting and the Inquisition, cannibalism among them. An article which appeared in *The Times* (14 December 1908) stated that '. . . the question of whether human flesh is eaten in connection with the Voodoo ceremonies is a perplexing one, which it is impossible to answer with any degree of confidence'.

Yet within the space of one year, 1888–9, two books had appeared in Britain which claimed that cannibalism was rife in Haiti. These were *Hayti: or the Black Republic* by a former diplomat in that country, Sir Spencer St John, and *The English in the West Indies* by the historian James Anthony Froude.

St John (who maintained that he had the 'testimony of ocular witnesses') wrote how the neck and shoulders of a human being had appeared one day in the market at Port-au-Prince, how he found two men devouring a corpse in the Jacmel penitentiary, how human flesh was sold as pork at Saint Marc. There is no end in this book to racialist tales about 'the fetish worship of Negroes from Africa' and the worst concerns a French priest who attends a Bizango ceremony to find the boiled skull of a child in the middle of a temple whose walls had been pasted with pages from the *Illustrated London News*. James Anthony Froude, a friend of Carlyle, is generous enough to concede that these stories of human heads and limbs may be the product of 'anti-Negro prejudice'. In Jacmel, however, he likens his hotelier to '. . . some ogress of the *Arabian Nights* capable of devouring, if she found them palatable, any number of salt babies'.

Almost a century before Sir Spencer St John gave his infamous account of a cannibalistic 'Congo Bean Stew', Lieutenant Howard had noted in his journal that 'Man-eating is a thing not at all uncommon among the Caribee Negroes . . .' Aliès Pimba's description of Bizango tallied quite closely with the fieldwork conducted since the late 1970s into this secret society by a young Haitian anthropologist, Michel Laguerre.

'Bizango is not a criminal society,' Aliès lowered his voice to little more than a whisper, 'it is a judicial body that gives protection against exploitation by outsiders. A member feels assured that no one will try and rob him and, if wrongfully arrested by the police, he can count on the Bizango leaders to use their contacts to set him free.'

Similarly, a Sicilian might seek to defend the Mafia as a benevolent freemasonry or Honoured Confraternity where family and group loyalties take precedence over civic pride or the state. In Haiti, as in Sicily, notions of public service and social conscience have never properly existed; in the absence of government, of the law, Bizango has founded its own law, primitive though it may be. Again like the Mafia, secret societies in Haiti form a dense capillary network of cabals, cliques and camarillas bound to each other through a system of patronage and cliental contacts. Members know that they must aid each other, side with their friends, and with the friends of their friends, to fight against the capricious actions of an outsider.

Bizango is apparently structured to form a pyramid. From pinnacle to base, members carry the following titles: Emperor, Honorary President, First Queen, Second and Third Queen, Directing Queen, Flying Queen (or Werewolf), Flag Queen, Society Mother, General, Prince, Prime Minister, Auditor, Lawyer, Secretary, Treasurer, Brigadier-General, Supervisor, Intendant, Prefect of Discipline, Major, Executioner, Assistant Executioner, Hunter, Guard, Sentinel-Scout, Soldier. The Emperor is a prototype Capo Mafia or great overseer, a man to whom peasants turn in times of need. He must ensure that his members do not talk (Aliès Pimba was prepared to reveal the purpose of Bizango, but not its secret language, strict rules or names of individual associates); and there is swift reprisal for an adept who breaks the silence, who betrays what a Sicilian might call the code of *omertà*.

Michel Laguerre has written in his recent thesis, *Voodoo and Politics in Haiti* (1989), that the word Bizango may be traced to one of the tribes imported to Haiti from the Bissagot Islands, an archipelago located off the coast of Kakonda between Sierra Leone and Cape Verde. It would seem that tribesmen from Bissagot participated in the formation of maroon communities – groups of fugitive slaves who escaped to live as outlaws in the woods or mountains, where they practised a form of guerrilla warfare against the plantocracy. Laguerre argues that the mentality of maroon fraternities has continued to exist in contemporary Haiti through the formation of secret societies. Members of Bizango no longer fight, of course, against the supremacy of *blancs*, but 'they still stand strong to keep safe the boundaries of power in their local communities'. Just as maroons understood that secrecy would facilitate the raids they conducted on plantations (passwords were required for communication between accomplice slaves), so affiliates of Bizango deploy pseudo-Masonic codes or handshakes to strengthen a spirit of solidarity in their community, and to differentiate friends from spies.

Aliès Pimba told me that there was a total of ten secret societies in Saint Marc; that they convened every Wednesday at midnight for a ceremony or séance. Today was Wednesday so it was now or never.

'How old are you?' Aliès asked with a crooked smile.

'Why do you want to know?'

'Because you can only attend a séance,' he added in explanation, 'if you are over twenty-five.'

* * *

Later that afternoon Aliès Pimba came to the Hotel Carré d'As with news that Monsieur Mortelle (apparently an old friend and domino crony) had agreed to my participation in Bizango.

Aliès appeared a little vexed when I asked him how this had come about. 'No questions!' His voice was tight with emotion. 'Come with me.'

We arrived at a corner shop on Rue Dauphine where I was instructed to buy a packet of tallow candles and three bottles of rum. 'Gifts for the Emperor,' said Aliès. 'Now go home and sleep.' The shop, I noticed, bore a lurid image of St Michael, bane of demons.

We left the Carré d'As at half past eleven; not one star showed in the curtain of cloud, it was a night without light. Aliès carried a lamp fashioned from a condensed-milk can.

'Pick up some of these,' he advised, bending to gather a handful of stones. 'There are bad dogs round here.'

Presently we gained the Avenue Privert where a pack of tawny pariahs came out of the shadows by the Mormon church, snapping and barking at our approach. Aliès flung a missile in their midst and it struck with a dullish thud.

'Dogs should be considered a natural hazard,' he said stiffly. 'Like werewolves.'

The road took us into a clearing of forest.

'How far now to Monsieur Mortelle?'

'His people are coming,' Aliès replied with apparent irrelevance, and then: 'Stand still!'

There was a smell in the air of rubber smouldering and I could hear a low chanting of voices which grew louder as a group of men and women, twelve or so, materialized from deep within the forest. They moved at the pace of a funeral cortège, bearing torches made of palm branches that burned with a fierce flame. These were the diabolical noctambulists of Bizango and they wore black trousers or skirts with a large black cross stitched to their red shirts.

'Order and respect for the night!' Aliès said in a loud firm voice.

A man bearing a banner of black and red (the colours, incidentally, of the Haitian flag under Papa Doc) came forward and repeated: 'Order and respect for the night!'

There followed a complicated procedure of handshakes and *mots de passage*, passwords.

'Who are you?'

'*Bêtes Sereines*. Animals of the Evening Dew,' Aliès answered.

'Who is your God?'

'Baron Cimetière.'

'Where are you coming from?'

'I come from the fist.'

'Where are you going?'

'I am going to the fingers.'

One may laugh in retrospect; at the time I was frankly terrified. Any intruder encountered after midnight by a secret society runs the risk, they say, of being 'eaten'. The man who stood in face of Aliès was muscular as a dockworker, with cold beady eyes. He was not effusive in his greeting:

'Who is the *blanc* by your side?' He looked at me with stern disapproval.

'He comes by invitation.'

'Of the Emperor?'

'Of the same.'

The hostility relaxed somewhat, then more passwords:

'What is your goal?'

Aliès said: 'To live as sweet as honey, bitter as gall – *douce kou miel, anmé kou fiel*.'

'When they admitted you, who was there?'

'Good people.'

'Who were they?'

He answered with a list of names, among them a local magistrate and a former member of the Tontons Macoute.

There was a muffled rumble of drums as we approached the séance. The cortège preceded us into the temple while a man on guard outside cracked a whip, or *fwet kash*, to block our entrance. He was a Sentinel-Scout and mechanically intoned:

'Those who belong

Come in!

Those who don't belong

Go away!'

Aliès Pimba asked to speak with Monsieur Mortelle the Emperor. This man emerged five minutes later, tall and stooped with a thin columnar neck and yellowish eyes behind spectacles.

'Greetings!' It was a cordial enough welcome, as he took my packet of candles and the three bottles of Barbancourt. 'We have been expecting you.'

Aliès exchanged a few cryptic words with the Emperor who considered awhile, then:

'You may enter,' he said in a tone of confident authority.

The room was much like any other Voodoo temple, painted with the garish pinks and blues of souvenir ashtrays; in one corner a smoking oil lamp cast a soft glow over a plastic figurine of Christ in the Agony of the Garden. Etched on to the wall above this religious gewgaw were three initials: J.S.H.

'*Jésus Sauveur de l'Homme*,' the Emperor explained as he led me by the hand to one of the rude chairs arranged round the temple.

Then he politely asked if I would care for a drink.

'Rum?'

'Yes please.'

'Ice?'

'No ice, thank you.'

I wondered what next – potato crisps, canapés? But I was grateful for the alcohol; it would calm my nerves.

The twelve members of the Bizango cortège had taken positions at the farther end of the temple, where they stared at me from beneath a gigantic painting of the *djab* with horns and bifurcated tongue like a gargoyle in the gutter of a medieval church. The white plaster ceiling was daubed with a red heart impaled by a dagger, symbol of Erzulie Dantor, the Black Virgin.

Monsieur Mortelle returned with a bottle and glass.

'Drink as much as you like,' he said, his voice cool and remote as Mephistopheles. 'Remember that you are a guest in our home.'

I had no clear idea what to expect and I was astonished that the Emperor should have allowed me to use my tape-recorder. The proceedings, however, amounted to little: for the first two hours Monsieur Mortelle presided over a ceremony of the sort which was now quite familiar to me. There were numerous prayers in the name of Catholic saints:

'Ste Philomène, ouvrez la porte,
Ouvrez la porte du paradis . . .'

. . . as he traced cabbalistic signs in front of the altar with maize flour. Bottles of rum were passed by relay from one celebrant to another, myself included; soon I felt quite tipsy.

At two in the morning precisely, Monsieur Mortelle struck the altar with the flat of a ceremonial sword, shouting:

'*Aye aye zobop!*

Aye ya aye zobop!'

Silence fell in the temple as a man stood up to blow three prolonged and very mournful notes through the lip of a *lambi*, conch shell. This was followed by a song of warning, which I translate from Creole:

> 'Baron la Croix! Marinette!
> People and friends of Bizango,
> Be wary of what you say.
> What we see today,
> We won't reveal.
> If we do,
> We'll eat our tongues.'

Then the Sentinel-Scout cracked his whip and ordered: '*Wete po, mete po!*' – remove skin, put skin! This was a metaphor for the adornment of ritual society dress – bright green shifts trimmed with red and black ribbon, shako-shaped hats in the same colours, the garb of Bizango.

I swiftly flipped the cassette in my recorder as the Emperor marched across the temple towards me and sat by my side. 'You have two choices,' pouring himself another glass of rum. 'Either you leave now or I initiate you into Bizango.'

Aliès Pimba joined the conversation. 'Excuse me, Grand Master of the Night, if I interrupt.' Turning to me with a scared glance: 'You heard what he said: and your decision?'

The devil take the hindmost. 'Initiation,' I risked.

'Very good,' Monsieur Mortelle replied, 'but you will have to pay for your hat.'

'How much?'

'Ten dollars. Do you have it?'

The hat reminded me of the sort I had worn at school as a Sea Scout – lozenge-shaped, only black and red instead of blue and white. The Emperor eased it over my head and then proceeded to the altar where he was met by two men – the *Lansé* (Major) and *Chasseur* (Hunter) – who performed a strange ritual with swords and flags that must surely have derived from a Masonic lodge, the Philadelphia Circle, established at Le Cap in 1740. This body was devoted in principle to the ideals of Voltaire and even maintained contact with that most illustrious Freemason,

Benjamin Franklin; in practice, however, members were among the outstanding defenders of slavery until the Circle was eventually commandeered by the revolutionary slaves.

By the 1840s every small town in Haiti had its Masonic lodge: La Vraie Gloire, Vallée de Josaphat, Zélateurs de la Verité, La Respectable Loge des Coeurs Réunis . . . Most ministers in Emperor Soulouque's government were Freemasons and there is certainly some connection in Haiti – albeit obscure – between Masons, Voodoo and secret societies (or *sectes rouges*) such as Bizango. Indeed Voodoo priests will often adopt the star of Solomon as a private motto.

One day in Port-au-Prince I had interviewed the Very Venerable M. Jean Gousse, First Deputy Master of Le Grand Orient d'Haiti. He was a great enthusiast of arcana, conversant with the Mystical Legates of Camelot, the Hermetic Order of the Golden Dawn and also with the Duke of Kent (himself a Grand Master); but he would not be pressed on the subject of Bizango.

'No, no,' he touched his pendant silver triangle. 'It's too much of a mystery.'

Then he had handed me his visiting card written in English. It was embossed with a weird riddle-me-ree: 'What is a Mason? A Mason is a Man and a Brother whose trust is in God. He meets you on the Level and acts upon the Square. Truth is his Compass and he is ever Plumb. He has a Grip on all that is Rite . . .'

Swords were returned to their scabbards – a rasp of metal against metal – as the Emperor, Major and Hunter wheeled about to salute the *djab*. Monsieur Mortelle took me to a small room adjacent to the temple where a guttering candle revealed the tools of a grave-digger propped against a table: spade, pick and hoe, also the symbols of Baron Samedi who occasionally assumes such names as Trois-Pelles, Trois-Piquois, Trois-Houes. A number of rusted cutlasses were stuck into the earthen floor, beneath what looked like a photograph of ice-hockey champions. But it was difficult to tell: the chamber was in dingy chiaroscuro. The Emperor motioned me to a chair while the Secretary noted my particulars: date of birth, nationality, et cetera.

Monsieur Mortelle then snuffed out the candle, leaning close to me in the dark. 'Now listen to what I have to say . . .' And so began a sermon to stress the importance of secrecy to the survival of Bizango, and to impress upon me the seriousness of the step which I was about to take. It was delivered in French, so that I could understand. 'After you have become a member of our society, certain spirits will guide you for the rest of your life. Do you follow?'

'Yes. I follow.'

'And these spirits will offer protection, so that you will be free to walk in the night no matter when and where you so desire. You need fear nothing, no one will harm you. Do I make myself clear?' I nodded. 'Good. Now listen carefully. In a short while I shall leave you. Ten minutes later the Executioner will come to fetch you with a *corde* (hangman's noose) and a *poignard* (dagger). Again you have nothing to fear.'

My expression must have revealed the anxiety I felt, for Monsieur Mortelle clapped a consoling hand on my shoulder. *'Du courage, mon vieux!'*

Then, out of the blue, he asked: *'Vous voulez une gazeuse?'*

It was like the offer of a cigarette before a firing squad.

'Coca-Cola?' he specified.

The drink arrived, lukewarm and saccharine to the taste. Then the Emperor left me.

For reasons of professional secrecy I shall not reveal every detail of my initiation. It would amount to a betrayal of trust, as very soon I would take an oath inviting extreme penalties if ever I disclosed the secrets of Bizango. And I am fearful (despite my rational self) of malevolent repercussion; I thought of the famous curse of the boy Pharaoh, King Tutankhamen, where fourteen people connected with the opening of his tomb died in violent or mysterious circumstances over as many years (one from an infected mosquito bite in Egypt; another killed in a car crash near Columbus, Texas). Still, as Voltaire said: 'The superstitious man is dominated by the fanatic, and becomes one . . . Do not be so idiotic as to believe that your garden will be damaged by hail if you fail to dance the Pyrrhic of the Cordaxian.' However, I must confess that I had never been as frightened in Haiti, either before or after, than I was on that night: it felt that the end was now at hand and I would be fortunate to return to England.

From outside my chamber I could hear a regular, insistent rhythm of drumming, broken by wilder surges and mingled with invocations to Beelzebub or the Lord of Flies from the Old Testament, to Lucifer, St Radegund and (I think) Astoreth, the ancient Semitic goddess of sexual passion. At this point I only hoped that my tape-recorder was still operating outside – that nobody had put a hex on the thing so as to jam the spools. Fragments of other prayers reached me, most of them apparently nonsensical:

> *'Marie vien Jésus moi*
> *Grâce ô Grâce*
> *Déshabille Déshabille*
> *Grâce Marie Grâce'*

I glanced at the illuminated dial of my watch; the Executioner was a little late in arriving.

The chamber door flew open and a blaze of light hurt my eyes. The awful man stood before me – rope in one hand, dagger in the other, wearing a conical hood with slits for eyes like a member of the Ku-Klux-Klan.

It was useless to protest; the noose was looped around my neck (careful of my new hat!) and I was led out of the Chambre Symbolique into the temple.

There I was obliged to kneel before a small coffin painted the familiar black and red with a decorative inlay of filigree round the edge of the lid. This coffin – known as the *madoulé* – is a central icon of Bizango and it usually contains the society funds. For my initiation, though, it had been planted all round with tiny *baleines* that flickered like so many candles on a birthday cake. Still wearing the noose, I was instructed by the Emperor to hold a lighted black tallow and a book of Catholic prayers called the *Ange Conducteur* (published, I noticed, in Marseilles). Presently the lid of the *madoulé* was removed to reveal a human skull which was placed by my side next to the Executioner's dagger.

'Repeat after me –' Monsieur Mortelle stood with his sword unsheathed, the drummers hammering wildly at their maps of skin – *'je jure et promets –'*

'I swear and promise –'

'In the name of Baron la Croix and all the devils –'

'In the name of . . .'

'Never to reveal the secrets of Bizango. And if I do, may a terrible fate befall me.'

Then I was asked to stand up as the Secretary read from a scroll:

'Saint Marc, twenty-second May nineteen ninety. By all the power of the *Vénérable Maître* Jehovah and by the high ordinance of the Diabolic, *Suprème Auteur de l'Univers*, we hereby declare that Monsieur Yam Jonsomme, citizen of British, will now be initiated into Bizango.'

Two Queens stepped forward and removed from their prayer satchels a plastic detergent bottle. These contained a fine white powder which was puffed from the nozzles until I was enveloped in a cloud of talcum. 'Breathe deep of the powder,' the Emperor advised. I hesitated, suspicious of its chemical composition. 'No, no. *Deep!*' I obeyed and immediately felt nauseous, also elated, almost transported. Then the other members of Bizango inhaled from this cloud and fell about sneezing, some of them gasping. The scene was like an advertisement for a successful joke-shop gimmick but the Emperor was serious: 'From this moment,' he said in a tone that could not be denied, 'you will be immune to any powder put in your path by an enemy.'

His eyes shifted nervously. 'And now, monsieur, we shall initiate you into the three degrees of Bizango.' These all revolved around the *madoulé*; during the night, secret societies place one of these coffins at a *carrefour*, crossroad, to prevent any intruder from stealing on a ceremony uninvited. The coffin is usually guarded by the Sentinel-Scout and it may appear in any one of the following ways: first, unadorned; second, with a candle stuck to the lid; third, with the candle plus a bottle of rum. There is a sequence, accordingly, of three quite different ritual gestures which a stranger must perform before he or she is allowed to pass the coffin and proceed to the séance as a recognized member of a secret society. It would be otiose to relate every one of these complicated gestures. I will only mention that they involved swinging the right leg, then the left, over one end of the *madoulé*; a series of rapid genuflections; running round the coffin to shout 'Ha! Ha! Ha!' three times; pouring rum on to the ground in the outline of an inverted cross; and spraying the alcohol from one's mouth over the left shoulder.

I was unable initially to master the mathematical precision of these movements but Monsieur Mortelle was patient with my clumsiness. He even congratulated me on my apparent progress: *'Félicitations, mon cher blanc! Vous êtes très intelligent.'*

This was followed by initiation into a series of secret handshakes, what the Emperor termed *'l'attouchement'* (his index finger pushed against the upper palm of my right hand, pressing the finger on my skin so that I became aware of a sign); and this in turn by a series of passwords of which I give two examples:

'Who is your mother?'

'She is the *veuve* (widow).'

'Who is your father?'

'I have no such person.'

And the second:

'What are you during the night?'

'I am a *Bête Sereine*.'

'From whence your particular *feuille* (leaf)?'

'From the *mombin bâtard*.'

As I already knew, this last is the name of a common tree in Haiti whose leaves are used to drive away evil spirits and *loups-garous*.

My initiation closed with a ceremony which I recognized from Voodoo as being the *Brûler Zin*, whereby an adept is rendered invulnerable to fire. Iron filings were sifted into a porcelain alembic and set ablaze with the aid of a demijohn of rum. My hands were held by Monsieur Mortelle over the flame for roughly thirty seconds and I felt no pain.

'*Messieurs et dames de la Société, bonne nuit!*' he proclaimed to spontaneous applause.

And then, '*Unissons-nous les frères maçonniques!*' to further, more vigorous, applause – stamping of feet, whistling, cheering and hosannas (also for me) of congratulations.

We left the séance, Aliès Pimba and I, at around four in the morning. The ringed moon illuminated half the sky and Avenue Privert was deserted. There was a faint smell on the air of night-flowering plants, of garden lilacs mingled with a stench of mud and shrimp that drifted from the sea.

I was no longer afraid of the lingering dogs and felt, somehow, immune from danger. Then again, I was a bit drunk on the ceremonial rum: liquor lends a deceiving courage.

'If you ever have any trouble with Bizango,' Aliès said ambiguously, 'come to me.'

'Trouble?'

'I mean trouble from enemies, from the bad spirits. Last night Baron Samedi appeared to me in my sleep. He had red eyes and –'

'Christ, Aliès!' I thought it wise to change the conversation. 'Stop going on about it.'

A strong breeze rustled the trees as we approached the Town Hall; above the Venus Bar a half-strength lamp fizzed and crackled from a faulty connection.

I was still confused as to why I should have been welcomed to the inner sanctum of Bizango. While I knew that a neophyte must attend meetings for an entire year before he or she may be accepted as an eligible

member (oaths and ordeals are revealed step by gradual step), I had nevertheless been pitched into a world that remains barred to most Haitians.
Aliès, for his part, had perceptibly changed in his attitude towards me.
He appeared more friendly, less suspicious, now that I was an initiate. It
was as though I had been admitted to a special intimacy.

'You can't go back to the Carré d'As,' Aliès laughed. 'Not at this hour.
Madame Nuñez would have a fit.' He kindly offered a bed for the night
in the Town Hall.

When we reached this building I saw that a piece of paper had been
nailed to the main portal; it bore the image of a coffin, crudely sketched
in pencil, with the words: *'MON FRÈRE, ÊTES-VOUS COMPAG-
NON?'* The note had evidently been put there purposely – whether out
of devilry or Masonic solidarity, Aliès would not say. But he began a fit
of shuddering that clucked his teeth together.

'What's the matter?'

'Nothing.' He fumbled with the padlock and inched the portal open.

I struck a match against the darkness inside. It flared briefly and burned
my thumb. There was a glint of moonlight from one window, enough
light to guide one's step.

Aliès moved across the floor to what looked like a desk, from which
he removed a candle-lantern. 'This,' he said, lighting the wick, 'should
help you see.'

A plastic sofa showed in the tottering light of the wick. 'If you don't
mind,' Aliès began to spread a sheet across the cushions, 'this is where
you'll sleep.'

Then he led me to the portal. 'See those?' He pointed to three sizeable stones resting on the floor. 'I want you to push them against the
door after I've gone.'

'Why?'

'For protection,' he said.

A long silence followed his words.

'Monsieur?'

'What?'

'Monsieur, you know how I work like a mule in the Town Hall. The
government hasn't paid me in months. Could you I wonder give me a
small . . . *douceur*?'

I told him that I had spent most of my money on the hat.

'Well, give me whatever you have.'

It amounted to about fifty English pence.

'*Merci bien.*' He shook my hand in the way Monsieur Mortelle had demonstrated. '*Merci, mon frère.*'

I rolled the stones against the door as Aliès padlocked it from the other side. Then I returned to my sofa, lantern in hand, and prepared for sleep. Despite my night of Bizango I soon lay quite becalmed, warmly fuddled. Within a few minutes I felt the encroachment of drowsiness.

It did not last very long.

'That you, Aliès?'

I thought I could hear a slow beat of footsteps, as of one probing his way along a passage in the dark.

'Aliès?'

Then came the regular sound, it seemed, of someone splitting wood with a hatchet.

I groped for my candle-lantern, lit it, and took myself in the direction of the noise. Thud, thud, thud – it grew louder as I approached a door which opened on to a steep flight of stairs. I began to ascend, feeling before me every inch, testing the steps to ensure that they were solid underfoot.

I paused at the stairhead by a second door surmounted by a fanlight of broken glass, and gently eased it open. A great room lay before me on to which the moon, nearly full, shone brightly through a single open window. Its casement banged on hinges against the wall, blown by the sea-breeze to and fro. Thud, thud . . . I was relieved that this was no human sound, and with a calmer heart my wits returned.

I looked around. The room resembled a school assembly hall, but with a musty smell of disuse; floorboards exposed disconnected rusty pipes; countless bats swooped in and out of an old skylight like pigeons from a dovecote. Holding up the lantern I trod gingerly over the wooden boards towards the window. It gave on to a labyrinth of sailing ships anchored in the cove of the public market. I could see a group of men unloading crates of merchandise from a hull – contraband no doubt. Turning to my left I came to a wall adorned with prints freckled brown with age. They represented scenes from the dead grandeur of colonial France – plantation homes that would be set to the torch by slaves; an overseer in a riding suit of white drill, brass spurs on a pair of laced leather boots; the component parts of an antiquarian telescope eyeglass – an illustration perhaps from Diderot's *Encyclopédie*.

Beneath these prints were busts of Jean-Jacques Dessalines, Toussaint L'Ouverture and President Alexandre Pétion balanced on fluted wooden pillars. The great men glared at me from beneath tricorne hats, toy marbles cemented into their eye-sockets. Dessalines wore a blue uniform coat sprayed with brass buttons (the colours crudely daubed) with heavy gold chevrons on the shoulders.

I bolted the casement window, my curiosity satisfied, and made to walk across the room towards the staircase. I was about to descend when there was a faint sound of calling. A rapid glance at the casement: it was securely latched. I listened for a moment and thought I heard someone murmur 'Jan' or 'Yam' . . .

Panic took hold of me again and the boozy sense of well-being evaporated. I hurried downstairs.

Alone in the dark I felt illicit as a burglar, sweating in the motionless air. Did the voice belong to Aliès? If so, I was unable to fathom from what direction it came. In the low keening of the night wind, he could move unheard. Perhaps he had come back for more money. I shut my eyes – it helped to keep away the fear – and listened unwillingly for footsteps. But they never came and there was a sort of armistice of the nerves until all of a sudden the building echoed with a monotonous undertone of talk, a concert of stage-whispers and jumbled conversation. Then it was quickly quiet again, and only silence.

I wondered later whether these voices were not the figment of an auditory hallucination caused by the ceremonial powder I had inhaled: at the time, though, the witchery felt real enough (or else it had the palpable distinctness of a nightmare) and for two hours I sat rigid on the sofa smoking Comme il Faut until there was a blueness in the sky of dawn. Then I clambered out of a basement window for breakfast at the Hotel Carré d'As, my appetite roused by the rum.

It was a revivifying meal of mango and cornflakes; the sequence of the night's events seemed remoter than a dream. I paid the bill and walked along the Rue de l'Eglise in search of transport out of town.

Soon I noticed an old Plymouth lurching towards me burdened with passengers. I flagged the truck to a halt and managed to communicate with the driver in sign language and pig-Creole that my destination was Gonaïves forty miles north of Saint Marc. The driver said he was bound for Souvenance from where it would be another eight miles on foot. I hopped on board.

We bumped along through fields of tall cane, the rough surface rattling the vehicle so ruthlessly it threatened to break the axle. Passengers were accustomed to this discomfort; one woman stood stalwart with a sun-baked calabash balanced on her head as though it had been welded to the scalp; as protection against the dust, others wore polythene shower-caps which inflated in the breeze to resemble exotic jellyfish. Now and again we passed a desolate cluster of shops and churches with American names – The New Easy Pentecostal Tabernacle (Wash Your Spirit!); Early Bird Exterminating Company (RIP Mr Pest!) – which became less frequent as we drove into the Artibonite Valley.

Here the landscape broadened into fallow slopes camouflaged with thick grass and blooming millet, paddy-fields emerald green and level as a billiard table. The 36,000 hectares of irrigated land in the Artibonite rank as the most fertile in all Haiti; they are cultivated as far as the eye can see with the completeness of a garden and produce sufficient vari-eties of rice – marianiti, fortuna, cristal, montedivi – to feed the entire country.

A footpath from Souvenance took me across several streams which forked as babbling effluents from the Petite Rivière de l'Artibonite. There were wild orchids and fire-tipped *flamboyants*, yellow sulphur flowers and interesting rope trees. Amid the matted vegetation I espied a kingfisher – plumbago blue – and the odd stork that flapped upwards to glide away into a speckling of cloud. Never had I seen so many huts belonging to Voodoo priests. They were indicated by thin poles of bamboo tied at one end with a red or blue kerchief and they quivered in the breeze like dry-fly rods. The principal temple here has 'Souvenance Mystique' painted in large letters over the entrance, with a Masonic five-pointed star and a pair of mathematical dividers underneath.

Try as I might, Bizango would not leave. My mind was still clotted and shaken by the events of last night. Approaching Gonaïves some hours later, however, the experience began to fade slowly into the mind as a delirium born in sleep; and the ritual hat, folded at the bottom of my rucksack, lay as a remembrance of things too strange for comprehension. I had come through, that much was certain; but at what cost, I preferred not to consider.

XVIII

From Dessalines to Duvalier

'I easily survived three extended trips to Haiti during the reign
of Papa Doc, but when Baby Jean-Claude picked up his crown
my feeling was that the end was at hand. Blessed are the poor,
says the Book, but it could hardly have been commending
this kind of poverty.'

Norman Lewis, *To Run Across the Sea*

The sexton cracked his knuckles, stretched and yawned. 'Claire Heureuse?'
pondering awhile. 'I think she's over there, by that old fellow.'

He pointed beyond some broken cherubs to the bust of a bald man
that resembled a lycée professor.

'Thank you.'

It is fitting that Claire Heureuse – Happy Claire – should be buried
in the enormous grey cemetery of Gonaïves: it was in this city that her
husband, Jean-Jacques Dessalines, declared Haitian independence. Little is
known of the woman. Thomas Madiou's monumental seven-volume
Histoire d'Haïti (1848) reveals only that she had married in the town of
Léogâne (Toussaint L'Ouverture was best man); that she was a gentle soul
who 'glowed with majesty' dressed in a blue satin gown stitched with
gold and silver bees. This paucity of information may have some connection with the animosity that Madiou, a mulatto, bore Dessalines, the black
emperor. Apropos of his gruesome assassination in 1806, the historian
grudgingly observed: 'Let us remember how the Romans grew to detest
Romulus because he became a tyrant; they only promoted him to a place
among the gods because he was the founder of Rome.'

A small elderly woman in black stood with bowed head over the tomb.
I approached with slowing steps, not wishing to disturb. The inscription
proclaimed:

*ICI REPOSE MADAME JEAN-JACQUES DESSALINES. PASSANT,
SI TU DESIRES SAVOIR CE QUE FUT CETTE FEMME, CON-
SULTE LES PREMIERES PAGES DE NOTRE HISTOIRE.*

No date of birth or death – although we know from Madiou that Claire's mother, Marie Elizabeth, died somewhere in the Artibonite Valley at the age of fifty-six: 2 November 1805.

Following the proclamation of independence on 1 January 1804, Dessalines ordered a capital city to be constructed twenty miles south of Gonaïves at L'Habitation Marchand; it was to be named Dessalinesville (in the same way that Papa Doc would build a town called Duvalierville), protected by eight forts with the bizarre names of Décidé, Doco, Culbuté, Innocent, Ecrasé, Source, Débuté and Fin du Monde.

Dessalines, as this city is known today, seems a ghost of its former self. It has the dreamy, suspended atmosphere of Sunday afternoon; a solitary beggar moves up and down the streets, plate in hand like a verger. It was once a *'jolie petite ville'* with horse-racing from nine in the morning until two in the afternoon. Twenty thousand people lived here and they would greet their emperor with 'Hail Duclos!', the name he carried, as a former slave, or with the more respectful title 'Papa Jacques'.

It is a mystery why Jean-Jacques Dessalines should have moved the capital of Haiti from Port-au-Prince to a place inland, thus isolating his subjects from contact with the world outside. He would have been quite unaware of plans to overthrow him, many of which were percolating in the maritime cities of Les Cayes and Cap-Haïtien. The Emperor continued to live in despotic solitude, and famously advised his courtiers to: *'Plumez la poule; mais prenez garde qu'elle ne crie'.* This dictum – pluck the chicken but make sure it does not squawk – roughly intends: reap your fortune to the detriment of the state, but avoid a public outcry. It was much practised by Jean-Claude Duvalier.

Dessalines was toppled from power in a manner which was to prove a model for several subsequent rulers: stoned and torn to pieces by rebel officers in Port-au-Prince, his headless corpse displayed in Place du Gouvernement. Henri Christophe, the future king of Haiti, immediately wrote to Claire Heureuse, fearful for her safety at Dessalinesville. His letter (21 October 1806) is the last record we have of any correspondence with *Sa Majesté l'Impératrice* and it accused the assassins of dividing Haiti at a time when 'we should be thinking of nothing but completing our defences and preparing to meet the enemy. Very guilty men have played a part in this business.'

For 'enemy' one should of course read 'France'.

Gonaïves – *la Cité de l'Indépendance* – is the fourth largest conurbation in

Haiti and is known to foreign correspondents as 'the ugliest place in the Antilles'. The wildly modernist cathedral at Place d'Armes is in the shape of a triangle (or perhaps a bishop's mitre), the white masonry chipped and stained yellow. A monument to Dessalines stands in front, very futuristic in the form of a ship's prow with the Emperor at the helm brandishing a Haitian flag. The nearby Place Bouteille is named after its concrete wine bottle (the size of a small grain silo) erected as memorial to Boisrond Tonnerre, secretary to Dessalines and by all accounts a heavy drinker. Curiously there is no statue of Jean-Baptiste Dessables, a black inhabitant of Gonaïves who in 1779 became the founding father of Chicago. Dessables is, however, commemorated on the Statue of Liberty.

Street names in Gonaïves are grandiose – Rue de la Révolution, de l'Egalité, des Sans Culottes, de la Patrie – but the city is really a wilderness of dust, of dust and loose sand charged with saline particles so that the slightest breeze will aggravate the eyes and lungs. Sixty thousand people live in Gonaïves and it is famous, they say, for two products: malaria and matchsticks. A single factory – *Les Allumettes Haïtiennes S.A.* – employs perhaps thirty people to manufacture matches from planks of New Orleans aspen and Colombian poplar. The building was closed when I arrived, with only a lingering smell of phosphorus. 'I don't know what to do,' bemoaned Jean-Charles Fred, Chief of Production. 'For thirteen years we had a monopoly on Haitian matches.' He explained that the factory had been made redundant by Swedish and Czechoslovakian matches dumped as contraband in Gonaïves.

'They come off Haitian ships returning from Miami,' added Monsieur Fred.

'Will the factory ever open again?'

'I doubt it,' he said with deep gloom. 'The harbour police are involved.'

The largest shanty in Gonaïves, Raboteau, is a collection of mud and palm-leaf hovels scattered among dusty paths where plots of land are staked with sugar-cane stalks. On 27 November 1985 the slum-dwellers rose in protest against the government of Baby Doc; they were joined by students from the school of the Immaculate Conception, four of whom were killed by army bullets and fourteen more seriously wounded. This bloody repression will not be forgotten; it led directly to the fall of Jean-Claude a few months later. Berthony Cambronne, a pupil at the school, has written numerous poems in memory of his dead colleagues. They lean heavily on Lamartine, Alfred de Vigny and Verlaine, writers still studied by Haitian schoolchildren.

'And this,' Berthony produced a sheaf of crumpled typescripts from his satchel, 'is a poem I wrote after reading Victor Hugo's *Sara la Baigneuse*.'

'It's a pretty turn in the earlier manner of the Parnassian poets,' interjected Yvens Michel, also a burgeoning poet.

I liked Yvens and his friend Berthony. They had kindly found a hotel for me in Gonaïves, one of three. The Auberge Topaze – high prices, thin walls – stood opposite the Tropic Full Force Night Club and the yellow-brick Caserne Toussaint L'Ouverture. Soldiers would emerge at ten every morning from these barracks to raise the Haitian flag and the military band was conducted by a man with cavalier disregard for tune or time. This grated on the ears but a worse irritation was that the door to my bedroom could only be opened with a kitchen knife obtained at reception (there was no key). Compensation for this inconvenience came in bottles of excellent Nine Star beer, usually served at state banquets in Peking but sold in my hotel as contraband.

Not so far from the Topaze, at the intersection of Rue Geffrard and Rue du Quai, stands a memorial to Admiral Hammerton Killick, an exuberantly moustachioed adventure seaman from Scotland who became the occasion for a dramatic episode in Haitian history. This is not widely known, but until the First World War Germany imported a significant percentage of Haiti's coffee harvest and there were frequent visits by German gunboats to these waters where they competed with the United States for strategic control of the Caribbean basin. Conflict over territorial rights culminated in September 1902 when a German steamer carrying arms for President Nord Alexis of Haiti was captured in Gonaïves by Admiral Killick, himself a supporter of the presidential aspirant Antenor Firmin, and likewise pro-American. The German government sent a gunboat, the *Panther*, in reprisal. Although it is not clear why Killick should have pledged loyalty to either party, nevertheless he decided to blow up both himself and the *Crête-à-Pierrot*, his own ship, rather than surrender.

Evidently, the London *Times* considered this a significant international incident: the newspaper's correspondent in Berlin was allowed an entire page (9 September) in which to describe it. 'The explosion in the after powder chamber made it impossible for the *Panther* to take the vessel in tow, as further conflagrations might occur. Since the guns mounted forward were still serviceable, the German commandant, Herr Eckermann, further exploded both the boiler and powder chamber with shell-fire. When this took place the *Crête-à-Pierrot* (built at Hull in 1895) broke in two and sank. Admiral Killick was on board . . .'

The sinking of this ship ensured victory for Nord Alexis but Hammerton Killick has nevertheless earned a place among Haiti's most revered national heroes; his gallant gesture was immortalized in a play, simply entitled *Crête-à-Pierrot*, by the Haitian writer Charles Moravia.

Early one afternoon I left the Auberge Topaze to meet Berthony at his family house on Rue Lamartinière, a low-gabled wooden shack with a large front room that opened on to the street. We had arranged to visit the hamlet of Ennery where Toussaint L'Ouverture kept a residence at the time of his seizure by the French.

Berthony asked me first to join him in a cup of coffee. We sat on upturned wooden crates while a big white-haired woman at the other end of the room chewed noisily on a chicken bone.

'That's Grandmother,' said Berthony. 'Don't mind her.'

My coffee arrived, bitter and grainy.

Then the young poet asked absent-mindedly: 'Have you ever been to the Tuileries Palace?'

The question appeared quite surreal in this shabby room.

'I think it was destroyed by fire, long ago. Why do you want to know?'

Berthony explained. 'Toussaint's teenage sons, Placide and Isaac, were summoned to the Palace – by Napoleon – a couple of weeks before they left France to meet their father at Ennery. That's what we learned at school.'

Thomas Madiou relates how Placide and Isaac L'Ouverture were removed from their school in Paris, the Collège de la Marche, to arrive at the Tuileries some time in October 1801. In the presence of their tutor, Abbé Coison, the boys were lavished with gifts of military costumes and gleaming suits of armour; high officials then entertained them to a sumptuous banquet. The flattery was politic: Bonaparte was poised to carry war against Saint Domingue, to reinstate slavery on the island and destroy Toussaint L'Ouverture. He assured Isaac and Placide that the French government had none but peaceful intentions, that the expedition was designed merely to strengthen Saint Domingue against its enemies.

The trickery was carried further when Napoleon persuaded the boys that they should depart for Saint Domingue with the French fleet, and inform their father in advance that the expedition was of friendly intent. The brothers set sail in December 1801 from the harbour of Brest; they were accompanied on board the frigate *Syrène* by the Abbé Coisnon; and on the flagship *Océan* was Napoleon's brother-in-law

General Leclerc, now appointed First Magistrate of Saint Domingue.

Neither Leclerc nor Coisnon had any scruples of conscience; arrived at Saint Domingue, the priest was dispatched by Leclerc to Ennery, with Placide and Isaac as unwitting decoys in the ensuing war planned by France. Coisnon took with him a long letter addressed to Toussaint L'Ouverture from Bonaparte, a masterpiece of duplicity which guaranteed both liberty to the black slaves and vague threats to their leader should he refuse to assist Leclerc in government of the island.

To Citizen Toussaint, General-in-Chief of the Army of Saint Domingue

. . . We have pleasure in hoping that you will be the first to pay homage to the nation which counts you in the number of her most illustrious citizens, both for the services which you have rendered, and for the talents and force of character with which nature has endowed you. Conduct contrary to this would be irreconcilable with the idea which we have formed of you and would dig before your feet a precipice which, in causing your own ruin, might contribute to the ruin of those brave negroes whose courage we love, and whose rebellion we should be sorry to find ourselves compelled to punish . . .

Paris, 27 Brumaire Year 10 (18 November 1801)

The First Consul, (Signed), BONAPARTE.

The Reverend John Beard describes in his *Life of Toussaint L'Ouverture* (1853, the first such biography in Britain) how Placide and Isaac were greeted along the road to Ennery by crowds of freed slaves happy to see the General's children back from Paris. The news that they had come to convey tidings of goodwill and friendly assurances to Toussaint was gladly received, although the crowds must have wondered at Coisnon, who maintained a cautious distance from the celebrations.

As they approached Ennery on the evening of 9 February, the brothers left behind them 'all horrible images of civil war – old men, women, children, flying from fire and sword' and soon came 'into view of peaceful scenes, the work of their father's genius – cultivated fields, abundant crops, happy families'. Toussaint was away, but early the next day 'the sound of a trumpet and the rattling of horses' feet announced his arrival', writes the Reverend Beard.

Within a matter of days the elaborate deception of Napoleon was exposed and Coisnon himself executed by Dessalines. With his last strength the priest scratched this quatrain on to the wall of his prison:

> O cold and damp abode of crime and punishment
> Where crime's disciples languish with the innocent!
> What dread, what suffering you hold in store,
> Yet cannot daunt the man whose heart is pure.

The stone which bears this sorry inscription is now to be found in the National Museum at Port-au-Prince.

It was almost sundown by the time we caught our tap-tap to Ennery. Yvens Michel was also with us. Inspired perhaps by the crimson cirrus clouds above, he began to recite several of his own poems.

> *'Oh! Princesse de mes tendres rêves!*
> *Même dans mes songes érotiques*
> *Je t'imagine en robe d'Eve . . .'*

I listened to him with amusement and some perturbation, as the recital drew looks of hostility from passengers on the bus, one of whom yelled reproachfully 'L.B.H.!' – an acronym for *'l'argent blanc pour Haïtien'*; it meant that Yvens and Berthony had decided to command a fee as guides. This was true, but they were of poor families; in their shoes I would have done the same.

Our bus, *Le Vent du Christ*, negotiated the dangerous turns and ravines in a reckless way, bucketing past the villages of Les Poteaux, La Coupe and Passe Reine. Then the road dipped like a roller-coaster over low, scrubby hills and after five miles we came to Ennery.

This is an old market town with an abandoned TELECO (Haitian Telecommunications) office and a breeze-block jail. Dog ordure was everywhere in the streets and a soldier lay slouched outside the prison. There is a broken obelisk in the middle of a sugar estate with the words: *'Ici a Habité Toussaint L'Ouverture'*. Only traces of his residence remain, a couple of walls in a state of ruin.

'Are you disappointed?' Berthony asked.

'Disappointed?' His question did not rate a reply. The tropics are merciless to ruins; everything is allowed to die or decay in the onslaught of heat and rain, the creepers and insects: dwellings that are abandoned for a single year have the appearance of centuries of dereliction. The history of Haiti had fired my imagination, but there was little on which it would thrive.

We understand from the history books that Placide and Isaac threw themselves into Toussaint's arms while tears streamed down the cheeks of the august old soldier. At the opportune moment, Coisnon stepped forward with a solemn reminder of duty to France ('Is this the faithful servant of the Republic whom I see?') and produced Napoleon's letter from which the state seal was suspended by a silk cord.

Toussaint looked at just half of this compound of cajolery and menace, delivered some three months after its date. To the priest he made a dignified response: 'You, Maître Coisnon, whom I consider as the preceptor of my sons, and the envoy of France, must confess that the words and letter of the First Consul are altogether in opposition to the conduct of General Leclerc; those announce peace – he makes war on me.'

Conversation was prolonged far into the night, and Toussaint could not contain his indignation as he realized that his sons were being offered him as the price of his surrender. He told the priest that while he owed his fellow citizens the sacrifice of his life, he would send the boys back lest Leclerc should think they were bound to their father by coercion or undue influence. On the night of 11 February 1802 Toussaint dispatched Isaac and Placide to Leclerc with a letter proposing a suspension of hostilities. Two days later the young men returned with a message from Leclerc. It promised that if Toussaint came alone to negotiate, all would be well. Otherwise, a proclamation would declare him an enemy of the French nation.

The allure of this ultimatum was not enough, the threat impotent. Toussaint resolved to employ all his energies for the maintenance of the liberties he had achieved. His sons, with their obvious love of France, implored him to yield; but Toussaint remained inflexible. 'My children, make your choice: France or Saint Domingue; whatever it is, I shall always love you.' Isaac declared for France; Placide threw himself on his father and weeping said: 'I fear the future, I fear slavery; I am ready to fight against it; I renounce France.'

Toussaint L'Ouverture immediately invested Placide with the command of a battalion of his guard; Madame L'Ouverture persuaded Isaac to change his mind and the son agreed to stay, a reluctant enemy of Napoleon.

This scene (reproduced in countless Haitian paintings) was reported to Leclerc, who now wrote to Napoleon: 'Toussaint is the most false and deceitful man in the world.'

L'Ouverture meanwhile addressed his troops: 'You are going to fight against men who have neither faith, law nor religion. They promise you liberty, they intend your servitude . . . The mother-country, misled by the Consul, is no longer anything to you but a stepmother . . .'

A decisive victory was struck for the black troops on 4 March 1802 when they held against Leclerc at the fortress of Crête-à-Pierrot near the town of Petite Rivière de l'Artibonite. Toussaint entrusted Dessalines with the defence; he stood on the ramparts naked to the waist in dirty boots and a hat pierced by a bullet. 'We are going to be attacked,' he yelled while holding a lighted torch above a keg of powder. 'If the French put their feet in here, I shall blow up everything.' One thousand eight hundred Frenchmen perished in the siege.

On 7 June 1802, Toussaint L'Ouverture was arrested and sent as prisoner to France; his wife, sons, niece and aide-de-camp were also taken. Soldiers rifled his house, stole money and jewels, burned the family papers. 'The wide earth will take cognisance of what thou didst attempt and achieve,' the Reverend Beard addresses Toussaint L'Ouverture, 'and pronounce thee a benefactor, not of thy colour, but of thy kind.'

The task of establishing the first black republic in the modern world now fell to Dessalines alone.

On the night of my visit to Ennery, a group of artists and intellectuals called Zanfan Tradisyon Ayisyen (Children of the Haitian Tradition) was due to convene on a banana plantation near Gonaïves. ZANTRAY had been established in May 1986 to preserve and protect Voodoo during the riots that followed the overthrow of Baby Doc – to counter what the *houngan* Max Beauvoir had called 'the imbecile unholiness of destroying the ancestral religion of Dahomey'. When I asked Berthony and Yvens if they would accompany me to the meeting, the young poets chimed in chorus: 'Certainly not! ZANTRAY is evil!'

They claimed that the president of this group, a Voodoo priest named Hérard Simon, was for many years chief of the Tontons Macoute in Gonaïves and also a man who 'serves with both hands', meaning in thrall to good and bad.

However, Yvens arranged for a taxi to take me there. It was actually a moped with the word 'Taxi' painted over the mudguard, and the driver, known locally as Marc Charlatan, wore a pair of aviation goggles and a plastic hard-hat, numerous pinchbeck trinkets and a goatee beard. As we drove to the plantation in the starred and palmy night, myself on the pillion seat, Marc kept shouting: 'Do you need a car radio? Half price?'

'No thanks.'

'How about an electric portable fan?'

'A what?' I could scarcely hear him, above the labouring phut-phut of the engine.

'A fan or maybe some light bulbs?'

'Not for me.'

'Do you know Hérard Simon?'

I said I did not.

'He's a good friend. Last week I sold him a washing machine.'

A path took us through forest with a great nocturnal concert of crickets and croaking frogs, and finally to the plantation where a Voodoo ceremony was about to commence in honour of Macaya, a mythical slave. There was an air of festivity with groups of market women selling boiled fish and plantain, bottles of rum discoloured with grenadilla to a syrupy red. The branches of a breadfruit tree were strung with bunting and a smell of fritters hung heavy in the night.

'That's Hérard Simon,' Marc Charlatan pointed to a bald fat man whose eyes bulged like a Pekinese dog's. He was seated in conference with other members of ZANTRAY, the table draped with the flag of Benin (formerly Dahomey) which is a red star against a green background. A white cross stood in front, the sleeves of an ancient naval tunic fitted over the horizontal arms: I recognized this mould-spotted tailcoat with gold epaulettes as the symbol of Agoué, the divinity of water. Simon and his confederates soon began to chant a hymn in praise of the god, punctuating each verse with *'Abobo!'* – Voodoo for 'Amen'. Then they each scooped a handful of earth which they blessed with their lips.

I introduced myself to Hérard Simon and he mumbled a brief greeting. His voice was gruff and husky, edged with a tone of menace. He asked throatily, 'Are you another *blanc* in search of the sensational?'

'No,' I said with feeble defiance. 'Not the sensational. Just . . .'

He looked at me with a trace of humour. 'Well, what then?'

One sensed that Simon was a man accustomed to giving orders. He had great presence, a bulky importance – despite the badly eroded teeth – with arms as thick as pit-beams and a very ample paunch. He clicked open the fasteners of his plastic attaché case and removed a packet of cigarettes. 'Here, have one of these.' He offered me a menthol Comme il Faut. 'They don't rasp the throat so much.' Then he lit one for himself and blew out the smoke.

He added: 'Whenever people wish to destroy Voodoo they level the accusation that it is purely evil, with every sin in the calendar. Well, you know the French proverb: *Quand on veut noyer son chien on l'accuse de la rage* – when you want to drown your dog you accuse it of having rabies . . .'

Hérard Simon was a cultured man and had recently travelled to Ouidah at the invitation of the last king of Dahomey, Agoli-Agbo, to attend tribal ceremonies that marked the centenary of the death of this monarch's father Roi Glélé. 'Everyone in Haiti is a Voodooist including the Bishop of Port-au-Prince,' Simon pursued. 'The upper classes practise the religion in secret, *en tapis noir* – under cover of dark.'

He went on to say that even a mulatto family whose children have received their education in Paris may be subservient to the animist divinities. 'Voodoo will be brought into their household by a black cook or maid. It's inevitable.'

I said, 'To the Western mind this may sound rather sinister.'

Monsieur Simon gave a curious bubble of a laugh. 'Sinister? Nonsense, *mon ami*. Voodoo is very close to Catholicism. Just as Erzulie Freda was once a good woman who existed in Dahomey, so Saint Louis was once a good king who existed in medieval France. The two religions canonize alike.'

I asked Simon about ZANTRAY.

'It's a *mise en garde*, a protection, against unholy priests,' he said. 'Against any Christians who might seek to eradicate Voodoo.' Then, abruptly: 'I am summoned by Macaya and it is time for me to go,' rising from the table and rubbing his hands together. 'André!' he yelled at a man near by. 'Bring me another bottle of rum!'

Yvens and Berthony were good Catholics, and critical of Dessalines for his practice of Voodoo. The Emperor's allegiance to this religion is well known: he worshipped numerous Petro divinities of fire and gunpowder – Ogoun Feraille, Brise Pimba, Marinette Bois-Sèche; and the troops were so superstitiously affected by his utterances that they believed death in battle would bring a glorious afterlife in the heaven of Guinée. Soon after his assassination Dessalines entered the Voodoo pantheon as a *loa*; adepts now chant his name at ceremonies in a sort of abracadabresque mantra:

> Better to die, oh Dessalines, than run away,
> Dessalines, oh Dessalines the powerful,
> Long live liberty!

I was not surprised, therefore, to find that the fortress of Crête-à-Pierrot

is now a place of worship. In the centre stands a large cross to Baron
Samedi painted with the simple legend: *'J. J. Dessalines. Bataille. Le 4 Mars'*.

Curiously, the first official persecution of Voodoo was when Jean-
Jacques Dessalines led a battalion from his 8th Regiment to a ceremony
near Port-au-Prince and murdered fifty of the celebrants.

Politics, rather than religion, was at the root of this massacre in 1801;
Dessalines was so much in awe of Voodoo that *mambos* (priestesses) taught
him how to divine the intentions of a man by the humidity or dryness
of the tobacco inside his snuffbox.

The most horrific repression of Voodoo came after Baby Doc fled the
country on 7 February 1986. According to Max Beauvoir, over one thousand Voodoo priests and priestesses were slaughtered by 'Christian bigots',
both Catholic and Protestant, in the course of anti-Duvalierist reprisals.
Beauvoir, whose house was attacked and his brother-in-law shot, has
subsequently logged the names of these victims on to his computer and
written a book about the massacres entitled *Voodoo and Persecution*. 'It is
not yet published because I fear for my life,' he told me. 'Unfortunately
we do not have the sort of police protection in Haiti that is offered
Salman Rushdie in your country. My IBM is nevertheless an important
weapon against the Christians. I can analyse their tactics.'

Beauvoir said that men and women were hunted down by mobs and
killed with stones and machetes; some were branded as *loups garous* and
disembowelled, others were mutilated, burned and tortured. He was
convinced that Father Jean Bertrand Aristide, the radical Catholic priest
who later became President of Haiti, orchestrated many of the killings.
'Aristide even published an illustrated leaflet which encouraged people to
rip babies from the bellies of pregnant mothers.'

This is an exaggeration; the leaflet, *One Hundred Biblical Verses for De-
Duvalierisation*, does indeed contain an illustration of a pregnant woman,
but there is no direct encouragement to eviscerate her unborn. The picture
is captioned with a line from the Book of Psalms: 'The wicked are
estranged from the womb; they go astray as soon as they are born, speaking lies' – words which elicit from Beauvoir the Pavlovian response:
'Aristide is a murderer.'

The incidents are terrifying, however, and they certainly occurred.
Madame Pierrot, one of the wealthiest *mambos* in Haiti with additional
homes in Miami and Paris, was fortunate to escape. On 26 February 1986
her huge four-storey house on Rue Fouchard, not far from the cemetery in Port-au-Prince, was gutted: a rout of frenzied neighbours stole

nineteen television sets, decapitated and set fire to her ten dogs, ripped out electric plugs (to sell on the streets), and ran off with five thousand dollars. 'They were jealous of my wealth,' said Madame Pierrot. 'It had nothing to do with religion or politics.' Thirty of the crowd were shot dead by police.

Two months later the London *Daily Mail* reported: 'Radio Lumière, a network run by a Baptist group, appears to have started the killings with a call to uproot the sorcerers.' One can believe it: many Protestant priests in Haiti have denounced Voodoo as 'Satanic' and called on *houngans* to renounce their faith. Near Léogâne, in a mountain village called La Colline, is a large community of evangelists who belong to something called the Christianville Foundation Inc. As one might expect, this is an American concern (based in Florida with outlets in Mechanicsville, West Virginia, and in Knoxville, Tennessee); there is a large church that resembles a McDonald's hamburger emporium and a Vacation Bible School for six hundred local children. In the words of the Christianville Newsletter, infants are taught to 'play kickball, participate in summer camps, sing songs for Mother's Day and replace Voodoo with the Gospels of Our Lord Jesus Christ'. This is the usual stuff of missionary endeavour – to help, to edify, to set divine examples. Max Beauvoir, though, maintains that the Americans were complicit in the killings. The director of Christianville, Wayne Herget, was wary of me.

'You're a journalist aren't you?'

'I'm actually researching a travel book,' I said in extenuation.

'Sorry, but I can't help. I don't mean to be evasive. I just don't know anything.'

As Wayne showed me to the door I asked him to explain the purpose of Christianville.

'To bring Christ's love to Haiti,' he said mechanically, 'and to perpetuate the effective ongoing of our ministry.'

'I dare say Voodoo must sometimes get in the way.'

'Let's just say that we eliminate all the . . . dubious variables.'

For churchmen of an evangelical calling, the fight against Voodoo in 1986 was a war unto death, with the God-fearing Children of Light pitched against a benighted horde of infidels. For others, perhaps Father Aristide among them, the killings served a political purpose: to eradicate Duvalierism. We know that François Duvalier was interested in Voodoo as an amateur ethnologist. During the presidential campaign of 1957 he told reporters: 'Every country has its own folklore. It's part of the patrimony. It is so in

England, in Japan, and Central Europe. Grieg took his musical themes from Norwegian folk culture. Similarly we should exploit the richness of Voodoo folklore for our national literature.'

No sooner elected as president, however, than Papa Doc began to enlist Voodoo priests as spies and informants on the peasants. *Houngans* from the most isolated areas of Haiti were summoned to the National Palace and required to report on members of their congregations; it was thus possible for Papa Doc to reach the masses outside Port-au-Prince and submit them to his control.

The network of espionage was rendered more efficient when numerous *houngans* were recruited into the Tontons Macoute. It became quite common to see a priest presiding over a ceremony with a revolver clapped to his thigh, the Duvalierist flag displayed above the sacrificial altar. In the village of Digue near Les Anglais I had spoken to a Voodoo priest who served as a Macoute in the governments of both Papa and Baby Doc. Guillaume Seide was an old man now, a little short of breath, but nevertheless happy to show me his threadbare uniform – red kerchief, denim fatigues – and a silver medal awarded him in November 1984 by Jean-Claude Duvalier for years of faithful service. This last resembled a triangular sheriff's badge, stamped with the words: '*Agent de Police Rurale Numéro 20617*'.

A Voodoo priest like Guillaume Seide would have joined the Tontons Macoute in order to become a prominent figure of authority in the community, to maintain control over his own domain, to ensure a monthly salary from the government, and also because, no doubt, he had no alternative. In a poor country like Haiti, these motives must be accounted as only too human; it was unfortunate for some of these *houngans* that they rose to political pre-eminence under the Duvaliers, otherwise they might have survived the massacres.

No Haitian president prior to Doctor Duvalier took such pains to dominate the religion of Voodoo (secret societies such as Bizango were heavily infiltrated by the Tontons Macoute and Madame Pierrot herself was patronized by both Baby Doc and his brutish chief of police Roger Lafontant); but it was not only Voodoo that Papa Doc chose to contaminate with his baleful brand of politics. His influence extended to the Catholic Church, to education, the army, newspapers, and to the cinema. Once crowds had been incited by Catholic priests or pastors of the Protestant faith to exorcize the demon of Duvalierism, *houngans* became an easy prey; they were blamed or punished for the sins of others, sacrificed as scapegoats. Worse, how many of these Voodoo priests were ever Macoutes?

The morning after my meeting with Hérard Simon I awoke at the Auberge Topaze in sheets of coarse cotton softened after countless washings: the taps gave only a trickle of lukewarm water and the communal lavatory was choked as usual. Into the fifth day at Gonaïves and I had really had enough: even the bottles of Peking beer began to cloy.

Early in the day before the sun rose too high in the sky I said farewell to Yvens and Berthony, catching a bus westward to Port-de-Paix. From there I would eventually take a boat to Ile de la Tortue. My visit was inspired by an old book entitled *Turtle Island – Goodbye*. The author of this autobiography, Father Roger Riou, describes how he set sail from Le Havre in 1938 with a 'wish to be among the wretched of the earth' and eventually found them on Ile de la Tortue. This island was 'considered the refuse heap of Haiti' – inhabited by lunatics, syphilitics, lepers and the tubercular whose 'faces were eaten away with the horrible sores of yaws'. Father Riou had intended to remain there for only six months. He stayed for twenty-two years: 'I did not think it possible that one could descend much lower into the hell of human suffering.'

The French priest began to treat the islanders with the few medicaments his suitcase contained. ('My first operation was to yank a molar with my sewing machine screwdriver, for lack of forceps.') When these ran out Father Riou gave injections of sterile water, to maintain morale and show that someone cared. He taught his parishioners how to read and write, and cultivate the land. Conditions were appalling; rats swarmed everywhere ('when I fell asleep, they'd bite my toes'), children were riddled with worms and chiggers, adults with gonorrhoea. There was an epidemic of tetanus caused by midwives who cut the umbilical cord with a machete. Gradually help arrived from abroad. The wretched dispensary became a small but efficient hospital; four chapels and a school were built, some of the worst endemic diseases were eradicated and the crops at last began to flourish.

In March 1968, however, Father Riou was deported by Papa Doc after he had publicly denounced the Tontons Macoute. He was never allowed to resume his work on Turtle Island.

The winter before my departure to Haiti I went to Paris in search of this unusual priest; he had grown in my imagination as a composite of Graham Greene's mysterious Mr Querry from *A Burnt Out Case* (who worked among lepers in the Belgian Congo) and Mr Kurtz, the up-river ivory agent in Conrad's *Heart of Darkness*. Riou was at any rate larger than life; in his autobiography we see him riding horseback into the Haitian interior as a bush curé in pith helmet and black soutane, living with the charms and spells of Voodoo. I had been given his last known address but I suspected that the man might now be dead, for he was born in 1909.

There was a presbytery on Rue de la Tombe-Issoire owned by the Catholic Order of Montfort, to which Riou had belonged. Inquiries there revealed that the priest was still resident near the Belgian frontier in a small village called Rogny, not far from the cathedral city of Laon. It was New Year's Day when I met Father Riou, the great flat meadows of Rogny covered in snow.

'How about a glass of Calvados?' The priest was in a celebratory mood. 'It was Maigret's favourite tipple, much better than Haitian rum.'

Riou was a large man, well preserved for his age, with spiky grey hair and the rubicund complexion of those accustomed to drink. Champing vigorously on the butt of a cigar, he bore a marked resemblance to Anthony Quinn (coincidentally, Quinn was to play Riou in the film *Adieu la Tortue*, but it was never made); and he possessed a salty sense of humour, a rough wit, that must have served him well in the slums of Le Havre where he grew up. During the First World War, when Riou was eight, he stole from army stores and sold his loot on the black market. From petty thief he graduated, like Jean Genet, to amateur pimp and was sent at the age of nineteen to reform school where he decided on the improbable vocation of priest. He was never a very pious clergyman: 'Several times in Haiti I caught scabies and the itching became unbearable,' Father Riou remembered. 'And I had to laugh when I found myself taking advantage of a *Dominus vobiscum* and turned towards the congregation to scratch my backside against the altar cloth.'

Lunch was prepared by Roger Riou's housekeeper and general amanuensis Madame Antoinette, twenty years his junior and previously married to a former French ambassador to Haiti. She kept a beady eye on the Father's consumption of alcohol – 'Roger! I think you've already had enough' – and removed a bottle of Burgundy out of reach. When she left the room the priest gave me a conspiratorial wink. 'Quick! Pass me the wine!' He swiftly poured himself another glass.

'Before I went to Haiti I never believed in the devil. Now I do. Voodoo is diabolical and never let anyone tell you otherwise.' Riou considered a moment, then with a groan: 'Once I found a nest of snakes hidden in three ceremonial drums; they had been fattened on consecrated eucharistic offerings.'

I asked Father Riou if he had ever been to a Voodoo ceremony. 'It would be like going to a whorehouse!' he exclaimed with sudden school-boy coarseness. 'Of course not. Besides, all you'll ever see is Voodoo faked for a white audience, with great bleeding Christs and over-deco-rated Virgins. Not the real thing. No *blanc* is allowed to know the true mystery of Voodoo and everything in Haiti that remains inexplicable to whites may be ascribed to this simple fact.'

Roger Riou then led me to a glass-fronted bookcase lined with the works of Victor Hugo, and various relics from Ile de la Tortue – Arawak Indian arrowheads chipped from obsidian, granite knives and hatchets, an axe-head of rose-coloured flint. 'I gave away most of my archaeological finds to the Museum of Mankind in Paris,' Riou said. 'But this' – he unlocked a cabinet with a key – 'is my prize possession.' It was a medal of white enamel in the form of the Maltese cross, suspended from a pink silk ribbon. 'Papa Doc decorated me with the silly thing,' the priest shrugged. 'It's the Haitian Ordre Honneur et Mérite.'

'I thought you were thrown out of Haiti.'

'Oh but I *was*. In the early days, though, Papa Doc was quite prepared to tolerate me. Not that I ever liked the man. He was *rusé* – crafty – like a fox.'

I asked Father Riou how he had eventually come to grief with the dictator.

'It happened one day in Port-de-Paix, when I noticed a store selling medicine that I alone received in Red Cross parcels. I knew it had been stolen by the Tontons Macoute at customs. So I denounced the militia as dishonest. This was an extraditable offence of course and some months later at Turtle Island, during Lent, a band of Macoutes flung themselves on me brandishing clubs. "Kill Father Riou!" they yelled. Then I was arrested in my white soutane, the one I usually wore for Mass, and shipped to Port-au-Prince. A Bible was my only possession. I read it on the plane to Rome, because my heart was broken.'

Father Riou returned to Turtle Island on four brief occasions after his deportation in 1968, the last in 1972 when the Roger Riou Foundation was established as a charity with volunteers in Canada, France and Belgium. This foundation still exists on Ile de la Tortue and Riou provided me with a letter of introduction to the priest who now lives there, Gaston Aragon.

'What will I make of Turtle Island?'

'It's very cut-off. Newspapers come by boat and they always arrive late. I only learned of Hemingway's death eight months after it happened. It's a beautiful island (watch out for the barracudas) but you mustn't stand idle for a second. If you do, you'll drown in despair and drink.'

I left Rogny village with a complimentary bottle of Calvados.

The bus from Gonaïves to Port-de-Paix was upholstered in woven straw and oilcloth. Everything – including the motor – was held together with baling wire. For three hours we jounced through a glaring wasteland of dusty cane fields and candelabra-cactus. Raptors circled overhead in the porcelain blue as the sun rose behind a hill to burn away the mist. The landscape was barren with the colours of white pipeclay and red oxide.

We broke down at the town of Gros-Morne, then at La Boutique, and a third time at Chansolme. Father Roger Riou had told me: 'Life in Haiti hesitates on the verge between tragedy and comedy. Remember that, and you'll retain your sanity.'

Ile de la Tortue was clearly visible from the pier at Port-de-Paix, a level tongue of rock some thirty miles in length, separated from the mainland by the Canal du Vent and named by the Spanish after a great sea turtle: *tortuga de mar*. Father Riou was convinced that the bustling activity of Port-de-Paix, the boisterous yelling in its corridor streets, derived from the time when La Tortue was home to so many buccaneers. One or two of the sloops which ferry cargo across the canal fly the skull and two crossed thigh bones. I could foresee adventure, despite the insufferable heat in Port-de-Paix.

XIX

The Pirates and the Priest

'The greatest stronghold of the buccaneers was Ile de la Tortue,
a small island lying off the west coast of Hispaniola. Here in
their most piping days flourished a buccaneer republic where
the seamen made their own laws. And what a curious mixture
they were, those irreligious scoundrels, the gracious or grace-
less, childishly evil, first Brethren of Turtle Island . . .'

From *'The Pirates' Who's Who* by Philip Gosse,
London, 1924

The smell of Port-de-Paix, compact of jasmine and drainage, was reminiscent of Tangier. Not only the fragrance, but the beetling activity in
its taverns and warehouses, in the smoky huddle of huts along the water-
front. Dusty, green-jalousied dispensaries offered medicines of dubious
efficacy; and tired little shops in the open-air market displayed American
goods – Hamburger Helper Sauce Mix, New Freedom Panty Tampons –
behind windows opaque with grime.

Portpaiciens are renowned for their flair in commerce and a joke hereabouts is that Port-de-Paix is the capital of Miami. The pier is thus
thronged with seamen bound to and from Florida on ships stowed with
contraband – whisky, rice, perhaps narcotics. These vessels, wave-worn
and fretted by surf, are powered by a wood-fed boiler and they resemble
miniature Mississippi paddle-steamers with a wheel on each side. Those
that survive the storms arrive at Miami in under three days. For the
Portpaiciens, then, the capital of Haiti might as well be Erewhon. Many
of the *armateurs* – shipowners – are ignorant of where Port-au-Prince is
even situated: the United States is closer to home by far and it is said
that the inhabitants of nearby Ile de la Tortue subsist largely on food
smuggled from Florida.

Father Roger Riou had lent me a book by one of the most illustrious
of corsairs from Turtle Island, a certain Louis-Adhemar-Timothée Le
Golif, also known as Captain Borgnefesse (one-buttock) from the enemy

cannon-ball which had blown away part of his posterior. His journals give a racy chronicle of life on the island from 1630 until the Treaty of Ryswick in 1697 – the Homeric age of fugitive adventurers such as Henry Morgan who sailed to Ile de la Tortue at the age of twenty-four having escaped forced labour in Barbados. Arrived at Turtle Island, Morgan was dragooned into a group of desperado sea-dogs named the Brethren of the Coast. Their members swore an oath of initiation upon cutlass, crucifix, and a human skull set in the centre of a torn black bunting.

These Brethren were a strange assembly of Catholics hunted down in Cromwellian England, Huguenots persecuted in France, political dissenters and soldiers of fortune from all nations (Brandenburgers, Hollanders, Irishmen). They lived without women, often in couples, and neither acknowledged nor owned individual property. Huts were built of brushwood thatched with leaves or oxen hides dried in the sun; they slept rough on the ground in hog-skin boots and pantaloons of coarse linen steeped in the blood of slaughtered animals. Captain Borgnefesse relates how he hunted wild boar on Ile de la Tortue with the most hirsute, filthy and foul-smelling men he had ever approached. 'And when I say *approached*, I am not speaking figuratively. I had to submit to the practices of those men who had no women . . .'

According to that amusing record of villainy *The Pirates' Who's Who*, Brethren learned from the few surviving Arawak Indians on Turtle Island how to cure beef on a sort of turnspit or barbecue which they called a *'boucan'*, hence the French word *'boucanier'* and the English 'buccaneer'. It is curious that the British should have adopted this term from their French comrades, while the latter soon took the title of *'flibustier'*, which is the Anglo-Saxon word 'free-booter' (or perhaps 'flyboot') pronounced in the Gallic manner. At any rate, it was from the pirate commonwealth of Turtle Island that these Brethren launched their most spectacular offensive operations against the Spanish, sacking the ports of Maracaibo, Santa Marta, Porto Bello and Veracruz.

Before I set sail for Ile de la Tortue, I determined to locate a *houngan* so ancient that he could apparently remember meeting Lloyd George and Clemenceau at the League of Nations.

Eliezer Legba Cadet lived in a small village north of Port-de-Paix called Château Dessalines. I had to ford the brown waters of a great confluence – the Trois-Rivières – in order to reach this Voodoo priest. The sight of a *blanc* wading with shoes in hand over mud and shingle drew howls of laughter from women who sat on the banks washing clothes.

'You are white, we black,' they joshed. 'Give to us ten dollars.'

'No money' – I returned the pleasantry. 'Ask the Tontons Macoute for cash.'

I had learned that comedy is the best antidote to begging in Haiti and the women soon left me alone, slapping their thighs and shrieking.

On the opposite side of the Trois-Rivières the waters broke over a beach curved like the quarter-moon of a fingernail. Here a dusty path led uphill through a banana plantation. There was a tropic afternoon scent of vanilla and mango, the sky hot and blue, a rasp of cicadas from the ceiba trees. I asked for directions at a makeshift refreshment stall and the owner, swigging from a bottle of Mateus Rosé, said with pride:

'Papa Cadet is the patriarch of Port-de-Paix. Not a leaf can move upon a tree without the permission of this great and very good man. Did you know that he was born in 1898?' He pointed in the middle distance to a large building made from a patchwork of palmfrond and corrugated siding. 'That's where he lives.'

I paid the man for a gaseous fruit drink and continued on my way.

Eliezer Legba Cadet was seated naked to the waist in a wheelchair. He wore a grubby T-shirt repaired with cobbler's hemp that bore the prohibition: 'No Skate-Boarding'. Sightless, the old man turned in my direction and felt for me with a hand outstretched.

'Aha!' He ran the tips of his fingers gently over my face. 'I can tell that you are good of heart, my friend. You radiate a pinkish light that bespeaks an excellent psychic aura . . .'

I did not know what to say: 'Thank you' seemed inappropriate, although a friend in Port-au-Prince had forewarned that this Voodoo priest was 'un homme mystique'. He had corresponded in his day with Pope John XXIII, President Kennedy and the Dalai Lama of Tibet.

'Are you the sort that reaches out for the ancient understanding?' the houngan pursued with a puzzled frown. 'I think you must be,' he suddenly beamed, 'for in my blindness I see an image of the great Stonehenge!'

In good French, with a certain roughness to the syntax, Monsieur Cadet explained that he had travelled to Britain in the spring of April 1919 on behalf of Marcus Mosiah Garvey, the Jamaican black national-ist leader. In London he interviewed soldiers from Africa and America ('and as many coloured folk from the Orient') on the subject of black emancipation.

The son of a prosperous dyewood merchant from Port-de-Paix, Eliezer Legba Cadet had graduated in 1916 from the esteemed Haitian college of St Louis de Gonzague and later supported himself as an auto-mechanic in Paris where he met the wealthy socialite Nancy Cunard, champion of black civil liberties, and patron too of James Joyce. At the age of forty-five Monsieur Cadet established a successful fruit cannery in Haiti, but he had been animated all his life by the teachings of Garvey.

'It was Marcus alone who ensured that the plight of Africans, and of people of African descent, should become a part of the political conscious-ness of the world,' said Monsieur Cadet. 'He appointed me High Commissioner of his Universal Negro Improvement Association and made it my job to lay the grievances of our brethren and race before the demo-cratic peoples of Europe at the Paris Peace Conference; I remember sitting opposite Mr Woodrow Wilson, a nice man but he spoke no French.'

The Voodoo priest raised an outspanned hand and began to recite a stanza – in English – from the UNIA Convention Hymn:

> 'Our fathers bore the stinging lash
> Of centuries of slavery's crime;
> But we are here without abash,
> For we shall win in God's good time . . .'

Monsieur Cadet sat silent awhile in dejected meditation, then went on: 'The League of Nations was a disaster for the UNIA. Mr Wilson was really the sole omnipotent of the conference and he had no interest in the blacks, even though thousands of us had fought alongside the Allied powers . . . Marcus Garvey and I were left without a voice.'

Eliezer Cadet added, testily: 'So I left the conference under the pretext of going outside to take some air. And that was when I met Lloyd George. Well, he was polite enough you know (and even offered me a cigar) but I did not trust him, for he was the principal representative of the British Empire and perhaps a little prejudiced against the coloured peoples of this world . . .' Monsieur Cadet broke into a smile, flashing one gold tooth in an impish way. 'But the cigar was good.'

After Paris, Eliezer Cadet worked on Garvey's Harlem newspaper *Negro World* and for the Black Star Line, a steamship company that intended to link black communities in the USA with those in the Caribbean.

'But I soon became disillusioned. Garvey was wrongly convicted of fraud and sent to prison; the cause of Negro emancipation crumbled in face of the white man and I suffered a *crise de foi* – a crisis of faith – that was so strong, it obliged me to convert from Catholicism to Voodoo. And let me tell you this: not even your *Encyclopaedia Britannica*, nor the Larousse Dictionary, could show the knowledge that has been given me by the *loas*. I am suffused with their light, my friend, with their holy love!'

At this point a bread-fruit tumbled heavily to earth outside, as though shaken by the force of Monsieur Cadet's pronouncement. The old man laughed richly, adding: *'C'est le Bon Dieu qui m'avait donné la voix; mais c'est Voodoo qui m'avait donné la lumière!'*

When I told Eliezer Cadet that I soon intended to explore Ile de la Tortue, he frowned: 'You will be in bad hands there, and the hands are those of Father Gaston Aragon. He is what we call in Creole a *bouch kabrit*, a goat's mouth – one who brings bad luck. Why? Because he's an ecclesiastical dictator and bears the proselytizing cross like a bludgeon, submitting the poor Tortugans to the worst of a white man's Christianity. I would go further: Father Aragon represents everything that Marcus Garvey had taught me to fight against: he's as life-murdering as the Spanish in El Dorado . . .'

Eyes unfocused with mute fury, the Voodoo priest gave a bold blank stare. I was taken aback by the vehemence of his denunciation, quite unexpected from a man previously so gentle in manner; naturally, I now felt some anxiety at meeting Father Aragon. 'He is secretly affianced, in my view, to the Devil,' Monsieur Cadet added with sudden ferocity. Then he abruptly changed course: 'But fear not; good will triumph!'

The light was failing as I left this remarkable old man and in the darkling countryside clouds were heavy with coming rain. Papa Cadet had impressed me with the strength of his convictions, his sense of humour. And he plainly sought enlightenment into the nature of this world, for the walls of his room had been pasted with astral charts, zodiac cycles and predictive calculations after Nostradamus – the stuff of mediums and moonshine, and maybe of lost souls.

The clouds broke with a torrential downpour and it was good to arrive once more at the Hotel Bienvenu in the centre of Port-de-Paix, where there was tax-free Captain Morgan rum.

It had rained all night and next day I stepped gingerly along the mud-churned streets, passing the cathedral on Rue Estimé where all the civil and ecclesiastical authorities, the congregations and schools of Port-de-Paix had gathered to celebrate a Te Deum in honour of National Flag Day: 18 May. Then down to the pier, which was milling as usual with a species of businesswoman known locally as *madame sara* from a migratory bird of the same name that attacks supplies of food, millet in particular. These women are as much a part of this filibustering city, the aggressive carpetbaggery of the place, as the *armateurs*; they travel great distances, selling direct to export houses in Miami, San Juan, Puerto Rico and Santo Domingo. Many of them possess a relative or second home in Florida's Palm Beach and one can see them, night and day, standing hands on hips in front of their shops in Port-de-Paix, resplendent in straw hats trimmed with crinoline flowers. They display their wares with pride – bolts of Siamese cloth, trousers, blouses, dresses, cakes of soap, articles of hardware or haberdashery.

The sloop to Turtle Island was of rough-hewn planking with sails sewn from random swatches of fabric; the number of passengers plus oxen, pigs, goats and sacks of grain was such that she rode very low in the water. Some of the women had stripped to pants and brassieres made of stoutish cloth, concealing their dresses in plastic bags to ensure that they would reach the island with dry clothes. Water lapped placidly against the sides of the boat as she swung broadside across a deep basin called the Careenage where corsairs were reputed to haul their ships; then we were running with a gentle breeze over the dirty, bronze-sequined sea towards Ile de la Tortue. But there were ominous flurries of rain overhead and the Canal du Vent is a very treacherous stretch of water. 'It can play some mean tricks,' Father Riou had told me. 'After drifting in a flat calm, your boat may rise to the tops of dizzying waves that send human and animal cargo reeling in every direction . . .'

Soon enough high seas came to buffet our sloop, her bow lifting clear out of the water and then crashing down as we were thrown into a steep roll, heaving the stomach. Rounded loaves of cassava bread, piled fore and aft to keep dry, were swept overboard where they swiftly disintegrated; then the rudder was loosened and carried away in the glassy green waves. Women began to holler in panic while men fell over each other, scrambling from one side to the other in a valiant attempt to restore the boat's trim. Most passengers, including myself, inevitably vomited into chamber pots or mess tins kept aboard for the purpose, the stinking contents thrown over either gunwale.

The skipper managed to keep on course while the deckhand steered with an oar over the stern. After three hours or so we had almost reached Turtle Island, abreast of the jetty at Pointe des Oiseaux, when we were forced to cross diagonally against a strong headwind, tacking back towards

Port-de-Paix five or six times. Passengers had to duck their heads as the boom of the mainsail was swung this way and that, at the will of the gusts. It was thus thirty miles, instead of the usual fifteen, that we had travelled before arriving at safe anchorage. There was a great quantity of sea sloshing about the plankings, afloat with tiny dead fish.

Even in the wrangle of disembarking, Ile de la Tortue appeared a magical island: the sea by Pointe des Oiseaux was a beautiful limpid blue, ebbing over a pink brain-like configuration of coral. As I walked uphill to the village of Palmiste where Father Aragon lived, the path snaked through a vast tangle of tropic vegetation and fluttering birdlife that cannot have changed since the days of Jean Esquemeling. He was a Fleming who arrived at Turtle Island in 1666 to work as a barber surgeon for the French West Indies Company. In his famous book *The Buccaneers of America*, he wrote: 'Huge flocks of wild Pigeons resort to this island of Tortuga, and about the sea-shores great multitudes of Crabs are everywhere to be found. These are good to feed servants and slaves, who find them very pleasing to the palate, yet withal very hurtful to the sight.' Esquemeling identified two varieties of palm – *palma espinosa* (prickle palm) and *palma vinosa* (wine palm); a species of hairy spider 'as big as an ordinary egg with four black teeth like those of a rabbit'; and great thickets of candlewood. Much of this creeping wildlife has been laid to waste since the days of Henry Morgan and Captain Borgnefesse, but Roger Riou had spoken of a *'fécondité admirable'* and the toll of woodcutting is not as grievous here as elsewhere in Haiti.

At the village of Tandron I caught one of the few tap-taps on this island (its population of twenty-five thousand mostly travel by donkey); fancifully named *La Belle Tortugaise*, the bus carried several planks of wood which protruded dangerously from its sides. The driver was so intrigued by the sight of me – 'Where do you come from? Do you have many wives?' – that he neglected to keep his eye on the road. It was not long before there was an almighty thwack as the planks knocked an old man into a thicket of gorse where he lay groaning. This was not an auspicious arrival (never mind the heroic crossing by boat) and very soon an angry crowd had gathered to threaten the driver and myself with rocks. I was terrified: stories abound in Haiti of locals wreaking vengeance – usually with a dozen gashes about the body from a machete – on those who have caused an accident. We managed to placate the villagers with an offer of money and by suggesting we take the victim (his nose was streaming blood) to hospital.

'You all right, uncle?'

But the wounded man did not reply to the driver's question; he just badgered me for more money.

The hospital, a modest collection of breeze-block wards three miles away in Palmiste, had been built by Father Riou himself and electricity was still powered by small 300-watt motors which he had received from the United States as Korean War surplus. A plaque outside an embryonic ophthalmology department proclaimed: '*1958: François Duvalier, Président de la République, P. R. Roger Riou*'. I felt a million miles from that snow-grey afternoon at Rogny and life on Ile de la Tortue had surely improved since Riou had described it: the only evidence of misery in the hospital was a child who lay suffering from tetanus, several hens tied to the foot of her bed. We referred the old man to out-patients and I proceeded to the presbytery where I found Father Gaston Aragon seated at table for lunch.

This middle-aged priest from Alsace bore an uncanny resemblance to the suet-faced chief of police, Hank Quinlan, as played by Orson Welles in *Touch of Evil*: bulging thyroidal eyes, grim-jawed, his nylon shirt damp under the armpits. 'I said pork, not chicken!' The priest shoved his plate towards a woman who looked quite terrified. There was a great quantity of food on the table: wedges of cheese, plates of jerked beef, a bottle of Chartreuse, two pots of Dijon mustard, all of it stashed like booty in front of Aragon.

'Yes?' He looked at me without interest. 'What can I do for you?'

I said I had come with a letter from Roger Riou requesting permission for me to sleep at the presbytery.

Aragon stuffed the envelope into his breast pocket, and waved me to a place opposite two Haitian priests who sat in silence awaiting their share of food. The padre then indulged in a second helping of soup which he drank from the edge of his plate like an Edwardian trencherman. 'What religion are you? I hope you're not a wretched Baptist,' he fiercely inquired. 'Baptism is a dreadful babel of a religion, same as Voodoo. We're trying to polish off the whole crowd of them.'

There was no doubt who held the whiphand here: Eliezer Cadet had called Father Aragon '*le roi blanc de la Tortue*'. In his short story 'An Outpost of Progress', Conrad described two Belgian empire-builders who were helpless away from their fellows, living in the middle of Africa 'like blind men in a large room, aware only of what came into contact with them, but unable to see the general aspect of things'. They might have been Father Aragon, big fish in a small bowl. Now the Alsatian scoffed his mess of potage with such ravenous abandon that the loose flesh on his face shook a little. 'I teach a life on this island which is in keeping with the evangelic principles: poverty, chastity, obedience,' he said crossly. 'If you want to stay here you will have to respect what I say.'

Aragon threw me a triangle of La Vache qui Rit. 'Eat as much as you like,' he generously offered. The Haitians smiled at me; they were evidently accustomed to the ill-mannered bluntness of their Father Superior. Aragon interposed in a tone of impatience: 'Where's my pork?'

Then he spoke into his plate: 'Servilus! Show the Englishman to his quarters.'

The Haitian priest got up and did as he was told.

My room was low and dark, obscurely animal in smell, with a whiff of naphthalene. There was a cheap reproduction of the *Laughing Cavalier* on one wall, a discoloured South Seas Gauguin on another. The sink had lost its enamel and the washstand glass was smeared with toothpaste. I removed my salt-encrusted clothes and lay beneath the closed canopy of the mosquito net, feeling depressed. I had arrived with such an exalted expectation of Ile de la Tortue. From my reading at least, it seemed a Stevensonian island of uninhabited sandy coves and grottoes, with squids entangled in bridal-veil transparencies, and the barracuda which is 'more pertinacious in its attacks than the shark, taking a very handsome nip out of a gentleman's carcass', according to a nineteenth-century guide to the Caribbean.

I dozed, woke, dozed, unable to sleep. Roger Riou's map in hand, I took a path outside the presbytery that ran seaward from the administrative centre of Palmiste with its hospital, caserne, Tribunal de Paix and Hôtel de Ville. It led to Basse-Terre where Riou had spoken of some pirate cannon. They were still there, mouldering in the ruins of two fortifications perched a mile apart on top of a reddish cliff.

According to Riou's diligent notes, one fort had been built by the first elected warden of the Brethren, a Frenchman named Le Vasseur who traded in plunder or stolen goods with the West Indies Company of Louis XIV; the other by the great Bertrand d'Ogeron, Knight of the Holy Sepulchre. He was sent to colonize for France by Louis, who had realized that these buccaneers (whether English, French or Dutch) would prove a valuable card for his hand in the dangerous game played by European kings in the Caribbean. The Brethren defied d'Ogeron, and he menaced them with a 'shipload of chains from France'. But this was an idle threat, for the governor had brought with him instead one hundred and fifty young women from the brothels and 'closed houses' of French ports – volunteers for matrimony and the first housework on Turtle Island. When this cargo was offered for sale, the buccaneers bid 'every doubloon and piece-of-eight in their purses'. D'Ogeron consequently ruled Ile de la Tortue for twelve happy years until his death in 1676.

The Cuban writer Alejo Carpentier relates in *The Kingdom of this World*, his dazzling novel of Haiti in the time of Toussaint L'Ouverture, that Pauline Bonaparte would repair to the tranquillity of Basse-Terre to read the memoirs of Jean Esquemeling. One might allow for a little exaggeration here (Napoleon's favourite sister was not a literary woman), but it is nevertheless certain that Pauline had journeyed to Saint Domingue with her husband, General Leclerc, in 1802.

From the available biographies of Pauline, we understand that she moaned pitifully at having to leave the excitement of Paris and 'live in exile among serpents and savages'. During this crisis, the celebrated Duchess d'Abrantès (later Madame Junot) paid the young woman a visit and tactfully suggested that '. . . the snakes would do her no harm, if there were any in the Antilles; that the savages were equally innocuous; that it was not there that people were roasted on spits, and I concluded my speech by telling her that she would look very pretty, dressed *à la Creole*'. Becalmed, Madame la Générale began to pack her hampers with silk turbans, Mauritian kerchiefs, whalebone basques and billowing muslin skirts – a trousseau that was certainly worthy of Pauline, who had proclaimed: 'I am the first lady of the land and I reign like Josephine.'

Napoleon had good reason to remove his wayward sister from France, albeit for a brief season. Pauline had indulged in certain indiscretions ('I am on excellent terms with my brother: I have slept with him twice') which occasioned a good deal of gossip. The more garrulous of chroniclers reveal that she had conceived a violent passion for the famous tragedian Pierre Lafont, who in May 1799 scored an unqualified success at the Comédie Française with his role as Achilles. Bonaparte, for his part, 'perceived no more certain remedy than to place a distance of fifteen hundred leagues between this beauty and her lover'. (Although he was outraged by the delay of twenty-three days that passed before the squadron could weigh anchor for Saint Domingue – owing to the number of courtiers, musicians and buffoons that Pauline insisted she take on board.)

If the First Consul was relieved to be rid of Pauline, he was more than happy to distance himself from his brother-in-law General Leclerc, a diminutive fair-haired man whom soldiers nicknamed 'the blond Napoleon' after his evident desire to ape the Emperor. The obscure birth of Leclerc in the provincial town of Pontoise disquieted the pride of Bonaparte (persons of 'low condition' arrived every day in Paris to claim a blood kinship with the Consul's sister), and we may imagine that Napoleon was not especially distressed when news eventually reached him that Leclerc had died in Saint Domingue of yellow fever.

At Saint Domingue the rapid spread of disease soon obliged Pauline and her husband to seek sanctuary on Ile de la Tortue where for several months they lodged on the plantation of Raymond Labatut, a slave-driver from Gascony. The setting was salubrious – a temperate breeze, orange blossoms, the gentle swell and whisper of the sea – and it was not long before Turtle Island became a vast infirmary for French troops wounded in the war against Toussaint L'Ouverture. Pauline, however, blithely abandoned herself to the captivating reveries of love (for she had a beautiful physique, the face of 'an idealized puffin', and a habit of promiscuity), lounging beneath a bower of frangipani and oleanders where 'certain gentlemen of colour were not permitted to sigh in vain'.

Father Riou had marked on his map a location called Château Pauline, five miles west of Basse-Terre in the hamlet of Pagne. I was curious to visit. 'This is where Madame la Générale indulged her most extravagant follies. A slave rubbed her with almond cream, then he fanned her with palmfronds and stroked her feet with peacock feathers . . .' the priest had told me.

All that remained of Pauline's house were four low brick walls in a waste of parched earth and cactus, thornscrub and neem.

The château, so called, was a disappointment after Habitation Leclerc in Port-au-Prince, an opulent hotel built on the former estate of Pauline Bonaparte. In the days when there was tourism, a replica of Canova's notorious nude statue of Pauline (*Venus Victrix – Victorious Venus*) would welcome guests in the reception hall. Sadly, it was stolen by the Tontons Macoute when they commandeered the Habitation after Baby Doc had fled the country, and the hotel is now boarded up; but one can still see the ivy-covered satyrs and the magnificent stables which Pauline had built for herself, a woman whom the poet Lamartine likened to a Grecian Aphrodite with the rays of the setting sun playing over her marble bust.

When a young American named Mary Hassal (her sister was married to a French officer) called on Pauline at Turtle Island, she found the woman lying on a chaise-longue in a room darkened by venetian blinds. 'She is small, fair,' the American wrote:

with blue eyes and flaxen hair. Her face is expressive of sweetness but without spirit. She has a voluptuous mouth and is rendered more interesting by an air of languor which spreads itself over her whole frame. She hates reading, and though passionately fond of music plays no instrument . . . She can do nothing but dance.

The dancing came to an end one afternoon when General Leclerc returned to Ile de la Tortue a very sick man, his body shaken by ominous chills and his eyes jaundiced. On 5 May 1802, Leclerc wrote to Napoleon: 'Do not think of establishing slavery here for some time. Yellow fever, what they call the Siamese disease, is making such frightful progress that I cannot think where it will end. For the last two weeks I have been losing from 30 to 50 men a day . . .'

Pauline had the doors of her house scored with aromatic plants and tobacco strippings; she consulted a Voodoo doctor whose peculiar remedies – fumigation with indigo, driving nails to form a cross in the trunk of a lemon tree – 'stirred up in her the lees of old Corsican blood, which was more akin to the living cosmogony of the Negro than to the lies of the Directory', according to Alejo Carpentier. General Leclerc insisted that Pauline return to France, but she refused to go unless he gave her one hundred thousand francs.

'My sister Murat has a carriage of her own [she complained]. She writes to me about it herself, to infuriate me, chattering about fêtes and balls and everything that Bonaparte is doing for her. That's why I must have the money, so I may own a more beautiful carriage than she has, and so that she can see me finely dressed at the Tuileries . . .'

Charles Victor Emanuel Leclerc died at Ile de la Tortue on 2 November 1802, not yet thirty years of age. The following day an untimely letter arrived from Napoleon: 'Pauline ought not to fear death, since she would die gloriously in dying with the army and in being of service to you, her husband.' Pauline returned with her husband's body to France, apparently heartbroken. Dressed in black, she cut off all her hair to lay beside him in the cedar coffin. 'Pauline knows, of course,' commented Bonaparte, 'that cropping her hair will make it grow twice as luxuriantly.'

The First Consul deposited Leclerc's body amid much pomp in the Panthéon and Pauline meanwhile settled to win herself another husband.

She found him in Prince Camillo Borghese, one of the wealthiest men in Europe, in whose Florentine palace she died at the age of forty-five.

'THE LORD IS GOOD,' hollered the white man from behind his lectern. And these words were shouted back, in joyful unison, by his congregation. 'Ay-men,' somebody chimed. And then, louder still: 'I said ay-*men!*' The faithful broke into a romping, foot-stomping spiritual loud enough to loosen the galvanized roofing from the building.

The Baptist church at Pagne, run by a young American pastor named Randy Moore, stood in the hard noon glare like a piece of giant white marzipan. Clearly there was some rivalry with Catholics for the salvation of Haitian souls as the walls had been daubed with slogans denouncing Father Aragon as *'un prêtre sauvage'* and even, in Creole, as *'masisi'*, homosexual. No one had bothered to scrub away these insults; to judge by the gleam of paint, they had probably been renewed. The reading inside, interrupted by much brotherly shaking of hands, was from the Book of Ezekiel; and thought for the day: 'Catholics and Voodoo priests are wrong to employ the Virgin as an intermediary between man and God. It is only Christ who maketh intercession.'

Musical accompaniment was provided by a laid-back fellow in sunglasses with rings on his fingers the size of Klondike nuggets. His electric guitar was plugged into an amplifier next to Pastor Moore, who now began a heated homily in praise of the Protestant faith:

'Brothers and sisters!' shaking a tambourine with golden jingles, 'know that we are against the magic charms used by Voodooists and Catholic priests to ensnare the people like so many helpless birds. And I say to you: do not be yoked together with unbelievers. For what do righteousness and wickedness have in common?'

'Praise God! *All the way!*' interjected Randy's friend Bob, a fellow-Baptist from Virginia. Having pronounced this apostrophe, Bob resumed his seat to yell again: 'Voodoo is of the Devil!' adding rather unnecessarily, I thought: 'It is a . . . Haitian religion!'

'You betcha, Bob!' Pastor Moore clapped his hands. 'And thank you for your contribution there.' Turning once more to the congregation: 'So let me say it again: sorcerers, idolaters, the sexually immoral . . .'

I wondered how much of this sermon the assembled Haitians were able to comprehend, for Bob and Randy spoke in English only. Then Bob stood up again and addressed the celebrants through a microphone: 'Well, I've only been on Turtle for a week now, but it's been like a real, uh, *experience* you know. Sure I miss the Baptist cook-outs, the family suppers and volleyball tournaments back home at Virginia, but gee, I just . . . *know* the Lord is with you all and I sure hope He'll, uh, be with you always. It's real great to be here, that's all.'

Rapturous applause from the Haitians as Pastor Moore (whom I had already met) summoned me from the back of the church where I thought I would not be noticed. 'Ian, how about a few words to accompany Bob's? Whaddeya say?'

'No really, I –'

'Come on!' Randy said in a tone of reproach. 'Why doantcha?'

Reluctantly, I mounted to the podium where a sea of black faces stared at me in mute incomprehension. An old fear of Sunday school returned as I approached the microphone, days when I was pressed as a child to read from the scriptures in a clear, strong voice. But this was worse, for I felt myself complicit in the white man's business of proselytizing, preaching to the natives like Father Aragon. The pews were filled with large ladies in even larger lurid hats; one old man in a battered fedora gave a toothless grin of encouragement as I cleared my throat.

'*Chat pran lang moin.*'

I had no sooner spoken than the congregation fell about laughing. '*Blanc capab palé Creole!*' they yelled in delight.

'What did you say?' asked Bob in a voice I could hardly catch, drowned in the uproar.

'I said the cat had got my tongue.'

'That so?' He looked at me askance. 'On accounta the coloured folk you mean?'

'Of course not!' I was irritated by his racialist antipathy.

After the service, Randy was apologetic: 'We meant no harm, asking you to speak like that. So how about if we make it up to you with a bite to eat? We serve the best French fries in Hay-di, no kidding.'

So it was chips and barbecue sauce at the Baptist mission. Lunch began relaxedly enough, although conversation seemed to unfold like the questions and answers in a phrase book:

'Will you have another plate of fries?'

'Thank you, I have had two plates already.'

Of a sudden, Bob began to wilt from heat. He was in any case a pallid young man, and overweight; now his face looked as though it had been dusted with chalk and, lifting his awkward weight from the chair, he groaned: 'Man, I feel kinda funny.'

Then the poor man ran from the kitchen with a hand over his mouth. 'Will he be all right?' I asked Randy.

'It's the tropics.' He grinned unhappily. 'Takes a while to get used to the sun – course, that's not counting the dirty water and Haitian food.'

'How long have you been on Ile de la Tortue?'

'Best part of ten months now, but I intend to stay for fifteen years. It won't be easy: as a messenger of the Gospel I get to feel awful lonely on Turtle, what with the battle against Voodoo and those . . . watch-callem –'

'*Houngans?*'

'Yeah, buncha knuckleheads! They give me a whole lot of mission-ary stress, you know. So it'll be good to head back to Virginia once in a while, say hello to Mom and Pop. Care for some banana Kool-Aid?'

Randy poured himself another beaker. 'When I first came to Turtle I got the shock of my life. There I am, minding my business, when news came through on the radio that an American real-estate company was planning to purchase the island and turn it into a giant vacation resort! I mean what's the *idea*? I'm newly arrived at Turtle, and the islanders act like they wanna lynch me . . .'

According to a May 1989 edition of the weekly newspaper *Haïti Progrès*, the plan to purchase Ile de la Tortue was proposed by an American company called Lenz International Incorporated, specialists in tourism for Disney World. Prosper Avril, then the tyrannical President of Haiti, secretly agreed to lease the island for a hundred and ninety-eight years, over which time she would evolve as a kind of sovereign nation, the inhabitants deported and only able to return if they possessed an appropriate pass-port. Destined to become *'un paradis pour touristes millionnaires'*, La Tortue would boast an international airport, eight thousand hotel beds, ten golf courses, and two thousand de-luxe holiday homes. All this, at a cost to Lenz International of $13,535 billion.

It was not the only time that a Haitian ruler had sought to profit by the sale of national territory. Avril was preceded in 1883 by President Louis Salomon, who had likewise proposed the cession of La Tortue to America. As the buccaneers were first to realize, this island is of strate-gic importance in the Caribbean – equidistant from Cuba and the Dominican Republic, a convenient route of access to Mexico and, from the day it began operations in 1914, to the Panama Canal. In 1981,' fear of Fidel Castro persuaded the United States to bargain with Baby Doc for the purchase of Môle St Nicolas, a city discovered by Christopher Columbus on the north-western coast of Haiti some sixty miles from the eastern tip of Cuba. It was reported at the time that the first American bid of $500 million for the Môle had been rejected by Duvalier; the second, it was said, had raised the sum to $780 million. By 1985, talks were still in progress: they collapsed a year later when Baby was deposed. With hindsight, it seems quite possible that the proposed sale of Ile de la Tortue had less to do with Lenz International (or Disney World) than with the US military base at Guantánamo in Cuba, possession of which theoretically expires at the end of this century: America has long favoured an alternative base, and what better than an island which strategically guards the Windward Passage to the Caribbean?

'Anyway, now that Turtle's *not* for sale, I know what I've got to do,' Randy continued, brightening. 'Eradicate Voodoo and fight the Catholics.'

Talking to Randy, it became clear that he was impregnably armoured, by his good intentions, against argument: Catholicism and Voodoo alike were inadmissible, and there could be no further quarrel. I looked at his pinched white face with its aggressive little chin, the curly black hair shaped like a tonsure round a patch of baldness and the drab brown eyes behind wire-frame spectacles. He resembled a civil servant down on his luck; but innocent and naïve, blinded by the infallible rightness of his calling.

Randy went on, his voice low and monotonous: 'It's been ten years now that Aragon's had complete control of Turtle, and he's a real tough titty: "Do like me, and you'll do right, otherwise get out". Well, we Baptists will have the laugh on him yet – Jesus Christ ordains as much.'

'How?'

'It's more than a conflict of personalities.' Randy ignored my question. 'There's the clothing too. As fundamentalists, we just don't go in for the Catholic type of gear. I mean, a man can wear a cassock and go to hell the same way still and you better believe it.'

'So you think there's such a place as hell?'

'Sure! We're in it now, here in Hay-di.'

I'd had enough; dusk was gathering, the sky a yellowish pink like brickdust.

'Thanks for the French fries.'

'You're welcome.'

We shook hands perfunctorily.

★ ★ ★

When I returned to the presbytery, Father Aragon was glooming around in his dressing gown. I tried my best to be polite, but:

'Where the hell have you been?' He turned on me with the speed of a biting dog.

'For a walk.'

Perhaps the priest had been at prayer: there was an odour of burning tallow, stearin and wax.

'Is there any supper left?'

'You're too late,' Aragon answered huffily.

'Then I may as well go to bed.'

'No, oh, no!' He advanced towards me, a breeze through the open window belling the cotton of his gown. 'You can always have something to eat in my room . . .' and he made as if to take my arm.

It seemed wise to settle this matter expeditiously: I could smell the alcohol on Aragon's breath.

'I'm not hungry.'

'Leave me if you must,' he said in a terrible voice.

Walking away I turned at the door to see the priest pass a heavy hand across his face.

Back in my room that night, under the mosquito net, came the steady zing of an insect near my ear. It did not bother; I was confused by Father Aragon's behaviour. He was by all accounts a man who took pleasure in the adversity of others; he seemed cruel, arrogant and self-satisfied, yet he had shown himself vulnerable as though it was the warmth of companionship he most desired. Perhaps he had tried to find a substitute for this in God, but it was not a God one could easily recognize – merciless, without compassion. 'Anyone who is not a Catholic will be sent to a Christless grave. They are less than dust,' I had heard him say one day.

I lit an oil lamp, adjusting the wick. Moths fluttered round the flame; there was no sound, only a dog howling at the moon and then, as usual, the clatter of Father Aragon as he made for the urinoir next door, emptying his bladder with the door left open.

The following day, however, something happened to convince me that there was in fact some splinter of malice in the heart of Father Aragon. It had long been my intention to visit Pointe Ouest, a hamlet on the westernmost tip of Ile de la Tortue twenty-odd miles from the presbytery at Palmiste. It was from here that Henry Morgan had attacked the

Spanish fortification at Saint Jago, now in the Dominican Republic. This was the young Welshman's blooding in adventure and it was my romantic belief that a trek to Pointe Ouest across the unfrequented uplands of Ile de la Tortue would show the spirit of an explorer. I explained this to Aragon.

'You may be right,' he said, picking his teeth. 'It's very . . . isolated down there, *terrain inconnu*. I can give you a lift as far as La Vallée. From there it's ten or so miles to Pointe Ouest.' He promised to collect me at Pointe Ouest some time in mid-afternoon.

What the priest did not say was that there is no traffic or transport beyond La Vallée. It was hot as an oven that morning, and the sun blazed back like metal.

Groups of unshod urchins pestered for money as our truck got lumberingly under way; Aragon accelerated through these children – 'Geev-me-ten-cents-Meester' – like a man possessed, only braking when we came to a rope stretched taut across the road, attached at one end to an ox.

'How they stink, those animals.' Aragon sniffed from a Benzedrex inhaler as a farmer goaded the offending beast from out of our way. 'How Haiti stinks.' These were his only words for the entire journey.

At La Vallée I helped Aragon unload his truck of supplies for the Catholic dispensary: two hurricane lamps, a box of hypodermic syringes, several cans of Shell Company gasoline.

'I'm sure you'll enjoy the walk,' Aragon smiled. 'Lovely landscape . . .' Then he added: 'If you see any Voodoo priests, tell them to watch out.'

'Oh!' I said, not at all consoled.

'At Pointe Ouest, then,' and Father Aragon drove back to Palmiste.

The landscape was of diminishing fertility – tufts of rank or stubbly shrub, salt flats studded with the shrivelled flowers of peanut plants. Several miles from the dispensary I found a small lake of brackish water, the Lac de La Vallée, bordered by shacks which had sprung up like weeds. In contrast to the east of Ile de la Tortue, there were few trees: only cacti, a couple of dismal willows, pieces of driftwood white and huge as the lashed bones of a dinosaur. I was reminded of paintings by Sidney Nolan. Then, on the further side of the water, a flurry of colour like pink alabaster. It was a flock of flamingos, giant birds raising their wings from the brine of the lake, bills angled down in search of food. The image struck me with the force almost of an epiphany – here, amid this desolation, the *phoenicopterus ruber*, roseate flamingo. It lifted the heart.

I continued westward, blithely ignorant of the fate in store.

Towards noon the sun became high and painfully fierce, hanging vertical in the sky. Still, it seemed there was enough water in my rucksack to slake any thirst. A red dust road took me across land with not a soul in sight: the countryside was entirely depopulated so that, in a modest way, I began to feel the romance of solitude. Soon I came to a vast plain of sand and flints, dipping after four miles into a steep ravine that was difficult to negotiate, owing to a loose course of scree, and to clumps of palmetto whose spines would pierce my feet, even through rubber-soled plimsolls. Irrationally, I began to curse the French priest: why hadn't he told me about these plants?

A further four miles over sharp and burning ground, and Pointe Ouest showed on the horizon; I could smell a salt dampness of the sea.

The villagers at Pointe Ouest paid no attention to my coming. There were only a few straw huts – *cailles-pailles* – built close to the tide and turning shingle; most of the inhabitants were busy trawling for fish, casting nets from boats that rocked like toys on the broad, furrowed waves. The wind came directly off the Atlantic; it was damp with a soft, seafret rain, cool against sunburned skin.

A gnarled and twisted blackness of larval rocks, very brittle underfoot stretched towards a solitary lighthouse. I wondered what sort of upheavals had formed this igneous matter: it contained fan-shaped fossils, bedded crustaceans, tracks and burrows of prehistoric organisms. By the lighthouse I sat on a sandhill grown over with a sort of marram grass, and decided to swim. I wished later that I had not; twice I accidentally gulped a quantity of sea water that would bring an awful thirst; then my trousers were drenched by a rogue wave, so that wearing them caused a fierce salt-rash. But I had no intention of walking home in underwear: Haitians have a nice facility in sexual innuendo and one could imagine their taunts: '*Eh blanc! Blanc nudiste, baisez-moi, OK!*'

It was now early afternoon; twenty miles to Palmiste, and still no sign of Father Aragon. He was supposed to have met me here at Pointe Ouest a good two hours ago. I eventually gave up on him: walking without halt I should be able to reach the presbytery before the abrupt equatorial nightfall. Very soon I was limping from blisters: fragments of larval rock had insinuated like iron filings and, with the palmetto spines, made it almost unbearable to walk. The canvas of my cheap plimsolls chafed against skin unprotected by socks. First I tried to cushion the shoes with leaves of paper torn from my notebook, but perspiration made a mush of them like papier-mâché. Then it was barefoot for a while, yet the heat made me hop like a man on burning coals. It was now so insupportably hot that breathing seared the lungs; when the water ran out after two hours, I played at catching salt-drops of sweat in my mouth. Surely Father Aragon, I wanted to yell, surely he would come lurching towards me in that truck of his.

There were no trees with promise of shade, no pool of water among rocks, and in the heat I began to trudge at a mechanical pace: must conserve energy.

About five miles more and my eyelids had turned granular from particles of blown dust and sand; I made a turban of my shirt but it did not lessen the roaring in my head, nor the heat. Then, way ahead in the level sunset, I could see the sparkle of Lac de la Vallée. I began to run, hobble rather, so great was the relief. After ten minutes it emerged that this was no lake: only a vast wall of rock that glittered with mica crystals.

Night was blinking with fireflies when I finally reached La Vallée. The dispensary had closed, the flamingos had gone, and the only available water was served in dirty gourds by a market woman. I was past caring about hepatitis and drank the stuff.

'Another.' I held out the empty gourd.

'Mes-z-amis!' exclaimed the young woman. 'What's the matter with you?'

'I don't know. Another. Please.'

A baby girl cried in her arms.

'She's very beautiful, your daughter.'

'Merci, chéri,' replied the woman with a touch of coquetry.

'Another, please,' changing the subject.

The water chilled me, and I swayed with a sort of nausea.

'More?'

'No. How much is that?' I pointed to a large melon.

'Two gourdes.'

'I want it.'

The marchande split the fruit with a machete and I devoured the pithy flesh like an animal, pips and all, as she stared at me in meditative silence.

'Are you a priest?'

'No I am not.'

I asked her if she had seen any sign today of Father Aragon.

'Gwos neg blanc?' she replied. 'You mean the fat white man?'

'Yes, him.'

The woman shook her head. Aragon had not been seen since early that morning. I thanked her for this information and went away in a rage: it now seemed certain that the priest had abandoned me, for whatever motive.

Seven o'clock, said the bright minute-hand of my watch: in my condition, I would be lucky to reach the presbytery on foot before the first light of dawn. I began to bargain with local *armateurs* for their price by motorboat to the seashore hamlet nearest Palmiste: La Cayonne. Sixty dollars, they said: nothing less. Petrol costs money, you know. It was another hour before I found a man who would agree to a third of this fee. Then I found out why: he had no outboard, only sails.

The tide was at high slack and a teenage boy, the skipper's son, stripped to his underclothes to dive into the sea close to shore, emerging seconds later with small rocks for ballast. These were heaved over the gunwale and rolled into the bilges of the hold. Soon the boat tended to the winds, and her canvas lay quietly back, throwing a pleasant shade. 'There's the breeze,' said the boy, drawing up the anchor on a rope. 'Only three hours to La Cayonne. No problem.'

This was not to be, for the winds dwindled to a mere cat's paw of breath; rising and falling over the smooth swell, we seemed barely to inch along the southern coast of Ile de la Tortue and the only sound, now that the sails had been hauled home, was a regular grind of oars in the rowlocks. First I tried to sleep resting my chin on drawn-up knees, then huddled against my rucksack in the prow; but the slow, monotonous swishing of the waves kept me awake. There was nothing to do now but watch the vanishing trails of foam on the water, white with phosphorescence under the sickle-shaped moon.

It was three in the morning when we arrived at La Cayonne: seven hours to cross seven leagues of sea. Under my feet the jetty sounded like a drum in the overpowering silence of the night and I was frightened of what lay ahead. There would certainly be dogs, and the wrath of Father Aragon, so I loaded my pockets with stones for protection. The path uphill to Palmiste was difficult to locate as my torch gave only a feeble beam. Stumbling footsore over rocks I lost my bearings on a goat track that disappeared as a dead-end into the maw of the dark. I stood still; there it was again, a low murmuring of voices broken by sudden lamentations, shrieks and ululations. Approaching the source of this sound I could see candles burning yellow in an air thick with incense.

It was a *veillée*, a funeral watch, such as I had already witnessed in the

Haitian countryside. The moment a person dies he is laid on a deathbed strewn with roses or tuberoses, the jaw taped shut, both nose and ears plugged with cotton. Mourners will buy enormous quantities of food and the best wine when attending a feast for the dead, or *manger loas*. Often it is an occasion for mirthful riot and eating; but the wake tonight seemed subdued and, fearful of my reception as a foreigner, I had no desire to intrude. It was evident that the corpse had been dressed in his best clothes and seated in a chair under a palm tree, a cigarette placed in the mouth.

Quickly turning, I laboured on uphill. Then a young man came after me brandishing a heavy walking stick.

'What are you doing on your own?' He spread wide his arms in disbelief. 'At this hour?'

I must have looked aggrieved, for the man then asked: 'Are you lost?'

'I don't know. Is this the way to Palmiste?'

'Palmiste?' He exclaimed. 'Of course not! I'll show you the way. Wait there.'

The man vanished for a moment, returning with a metal trident used by villagers to impale squid or fish, and as protection against wild dogs.

'For your security, *blanc*.' He handed me the weapon.

'No thanks.' I asked to borrow his stick instead as my knees were beginning to lock.

Up, wearily up, myself lagging behind . . .

The feeblest suggestion of daylight had begun to show in the sky when we reached Palmiste. Brushwood fires had been lit in the fields by farmers ready for another day's work and there was a scent in the air of dew and lemon balm. A thin drizzle came slanting, strange and beautiful, across the pale light as we approached the presbytery; but Father Aragon was nowhere to be found. With malicious delight I stole a bottle of beer from his refrigerator and carried it to my room where, utterly wearied, I listened to the rain as it rang down on the roof-sheets.

I never saw Gaston Aragon again. His maid told me he had left for Port-de-Paix that morning two hours after I returned from Pointe Ouest. The following night, however, I returned to the presbytery to see the end of a cigar glowing in the dark of his office. When I mentioned this to the maid she told me that I must have been dreaming. 'But you are young yet,' she added with unconscious sadness, 'and let Father Aragon be a lesson to you of how none of us is ever perfect.'

★ ★ ★

On 7 December 1492, Christopher Columbus entered a harbour which he named Valparaiso, now Port-de-Paix. Only two days before, he had sailed within first sight of Haiti – a land that Ferdinand and Isabella would christen Hispaniola, Little Spain. In his monumental biography, *The Life and Voyages of Christopher Columbus*, Washington Irving describes Haiti as 'one of the most beautiful islands in the world, and doomed to be one of the most unfortunate'. This was well said: Columbus had discovered an earthly paradise in unknown seas, with fertile forests and running water, yet within fifty years some half a million of the Taino-Arawak Indians had perished in the Spanish gold mines and pre-Columbian culture had all but vanished from the island.

This annihilation was brought to the attention of colonial Spain by Father Bartolmé de Las Casas, that famous missionary philanthropist, in his *Brevisima Relación de la Destrucción de las Indias Occidentales*. The book (much admired by Sir Walter Raleigh) is a strong denunciation of brutality towards the Indians and tells how the Spanish 'made a law among themselves, that for one Christian whom the natives killed, the Christians should kill a hundred natives'. Las Casas was not exaggerating. 'Our men made bets as to who would slit an Indian in two, or cut off his head at one blow; or they opened up his bowels. They tore the babes from their mothers' breast by their feet, and dashed their heads against the rocks . . .'

Father Las Casas was so vigorous in his condemnation of Indian slavery ('the system is impossible and intolerable') that by the year 1542 he had achieved its abolition. His measure was too late to prevent the destruction of the Taino-Arawaks and instead brought about the dawn of African slavery in the New World. As an alternative to the cruelty of submitting the indigenous peoples of the Caribbean to heavy labour (for which they were constitutionally unsuited), Las Casas suggested the importation of black men from the Spanish colonies. Thus the first shipment of slaves to Haiti and the beginning of all subsequent sorrows in the Caribbean. To this odd twist of philanthropy we owe, up and down the Americas, endless things: 'the mythological dimensions of Abraham Lincoln; the five hundred thousand dead of the Civil War; and the entrance of the verb *to lynch* into the thirteenth edition of the dictionary of the Spanish Academy . . .', according to Jorge Luis Borges.

There is no practicable route from Port-de-Paix to my final destination, Cap-Haïtien: only garbage-laden gullies where vehicles scatter clots of mud, rutty ox-cart tracks. Far better to return to Gonaïves and proceed along a glorified cinder track beaten hard into the level smoothness of asphalt. I had sailed across the Canal du Vent with the intention of travelling directly to Cap-Haïtien, but there was nevertheless a detour I wanted to make: seventy miles along the road from Gonaïves and you arrive at the town of Limbé. This is the home of Dr William Hodges, a Baptist missionary and archaeologist who has devoted almost thirty years of his life in search of Navidad.

Navidad was the first edifice built by Europeans in the Western Hemisphere. It was constructed out of timber salvaged from Columbus's flagship the *Santa Maria*, which sank in a bay off Cap-Haïtien at around midnight on 24 December 1492. Columbus interpreted this wreck as providential intervention: it had been decreed by God that the ship should run aground in order that a settlement be established near by. So, with help from Taino Indians ('timid beyond cure', wrote Columbus), the Spanish dismantled the wreck and brought it piecemeal to shore. Then they built a primitive fortress with a moat and tower which they designated Navidad in memory of their having survived the shipwreck on Nativity, Christmas Day. The Indian *cacique* or chief, Guacanagarí, lavished on Columbus various gifts of gold masks and a 'statue of pure gold as large as the Admiral himself' (in the words of one eyewitness). On 4 January 1493, the Admiral then set sail for Castile with news of treasure, leaving behind a garrison of thirty-nine men which included a physician, caulker, cooper, tailor and gunner.

When Columbus returned eleven months later on his second voyage he found that Navidad had been burned and his men killed by Indians, presumably as a reprisal against brutalities inflicted on them. These Spanish were the first casualties ever in the long series of colonial wars to be waged in the New World; we know from Las Casas that Guacanagarí himself was forced to flee 'from the massacres and cruelty of the Christians' and 'died a wanderer in the mountains, ruined and deprived of his state'. Yet, if one is to believe the chroniclers, Columbus felt no sorrow, gave no word in elegy for his own two score dead, only 'much grief at the sight of the ruins of the houses and the fort'. The absence of any mineral treasures traded with the Indians was a disaster; Columbus had hoped that Navidad would gather so much gold that it would help Ferdinand and Isabella in their ambition to conquer the Holy Land. 'If ever I forget the thought of thee, O Jerusalem,' he proclaimed, 'let my tongue cleave to the roof of my mouth.' Driven by his thirst for seaborne glory the Admiral moved up the coast of Hispaniola and established a new settlement at La

Isabella, due east of the present-day Dominican city of Monte Cristi. Navidad was soon covered with the wild luxuriance of tropical vegetation and slowly receded into legend.

Dr William Hodges is last in line of several who have attempted to locate the site of Navidad, among them the French historian Moreau de Saint-Méry and Washington Irving. Saint-Méry believed the settlement was situated in the north at Habitation Montholon where he identified some skeletal remains as those of Columbus's men, killed and buried by the Indians. Irving himself was convinced that Navidad lay a short distance inland from the nearby village of Petite Anse, two miles south-west of what is now the airport at Cap-Haïtien. Both men, it seems, were wrong. Irving had been misled in his geography by an American tradesman with whom he corresponded in Cap-Haïtien ('very obliging and interesting letters', but sadly inaccurate) and Saint-Méry was in reality looking at the cemetery of Puerto Reale, a city founded in 1504 as a point of debarkation for Indian and African slaves, rediscovered in 1974 by Dr Hodges himself.

Navidad remained a closed book until *National Geographic* reported in November 1987 that Dr Hodges had unearthed the remains of a large Indian town at the site of En Bas Saline, Habitation Minioc, in a remote corner of the Département du Nord. It was claimed that this might be the long-lost settlement of the *cacique* Guacanagarí, where Columbus very clearly states that he built Navidad in the last week of 1492 and the first week of 1493. Excavations carried out under the auspices of the University of Florida brought to light several shards of pottery, the posts and balks of Indian dwellings and those of a European well. There was a mass of scalloped nails, pieces of broken iron kettles, and a variety of Spanish artefacts: brass scabbard ornaments, copper jingles, a home-made pommel for a sword handle, the trigger-guard of a blunderbuss, a large number of lead musket balls. Also, the bones of animals probably transported from Seville, including the jaw of a pig. One has no reason to doubt the integrity of Dr Hodges: he has been rigorous in the location of all Indian sites in northern Haiti, the examination of geological changes in relation to coast and river positions as they appeared in the fifteenth century, the consultation of French and Spanish colonial documents, even the enlistment of Haitian farmers as guides.

Limbé was a small, attractive town where washing hung out of windows as it does in Naples; the flower-bowered houses were built with steeply canted roofs, and there was everywhere a thumping of pestles husking the evening rice. I was a little nervous of meeting Dr William Hodges; he had the reputation of a cold and rather formal civility ('He may or may not be pleased to see you,' a friend had told me), and a watchful alertness. He was regarded by Haitians as a strange magic-man, drilling holes in the ground in search of gold: either mad or dangerously inspired. Dr Hodges has no telephone and I had come without a letter of introduction.

He was not pleased to see me.

'I think you could have chosen a more propitious time to call upon me,' he remarked with calm irritation. 'I am currently at supper with my family.' The old-fashioned propriety of his diction, the leisurely composure with which he surveyed my face and clothes, brought to mind a school headmaster.

I told him my business, that I was researching a book on Haiti, and was curious about the history of Navidad.

There was a short silence; then Dr Hodges said, quietly: 'I take it that you are also aware of the fact that you have come to Haiti at the worst possible moment? Haitians are doing their level best to murder their own hope and we're at the very nadir now, heading for catastrophe.' He spoke in a grey, undimensional voice that was in keeping with the immobile features of his face: dry, mordant and rather pale, the ghost of an ironic smile. I found his manner attractive, more English than American, even though he was born in Chicago some sixty years ago. He added with alarming lucidity: 'I've seen an awful lot of corpses in my life as a doctor and I am not a man who is given to exaggerating the horrors of this country.'

Dr Hodges explained that he had admitted four girls to his hospital that morning who had been run over by a mayor hurtling along the road towards Dondon in the east. 'They may or may not live. But they are fortunate to find a bed in the hospital. It's now so crowded that I have to turn away a hundred and fifty people every day, at least five of whom will certainly die.' He told me how the terrified mayor had abandoned his car (and $18,000 in the glove compartment) to a crowd of villagers that emerged from the forests brandishing rocks and machetes. They failed to find the mayor and stole his money instead, setting fire to the car with gasoline and smashing every window. 'This is something new in Haiti.' Dr Hodges spoke in a restrained voice still, but with growing indignation. 'There was never this anarchy before! Stoning people to death is now a tremendously popular sport . . .'

I listened to him with deep, though somewhat embarrassed, fascination: my rucksack, trailing behind me like a burden, proclaimed me as an intruder; Dr Hodges must have remarked my awkward expression, for his manner changed in the wink of an eye. 'Navidad you said? Well, you've certainly come to the right person,' assuming a tone of easy banter. 'Sorry about the cold reception but for all I know you could have been a Tonton Macoute. Tell me, have you eaten and do you have anywhere to stay?'

I shook my head in answer to both these questions.

'Then we shall find a bed for the night and give you supper. Just put your bag down there,' he added, 'and follow me.'

Dr Hodges introduced me to the people seated round the dining table: his wife, Joanna; his son, Paul; his daughter, Barbara; and five adopted Haitian children. 'This is Mr Thomson, who, as you will gather from his accent, comes from England,' gesturing me to a chair, 'and who, to judge by the colour of his skin, has been out in the sun for longer than is probably good for him.'

The room filled with laughter.

Conversation was erudite, almost encyclopaedic; in the course of eating, Dr Hodges spoke passionately, all in one breath, about Tennyson, Spengler, Milton, Mark Twain and the King James Bible. 'The great Scottish economist Adam Smith maintained that the discovery of the New World was one of the most important events recorded in the history of mankind. Would you agree, Mr Thomson?'

I countered with the liberal argument that the year 1492 might almost stand as a hieroglyph for rape and spoliation, the genocide of aboriginal peoples, the importation from Europe of syphilis, colonial domination by the white man . . .

'You speak,' Dr Hodges said with slow thoughtfulness, 'like one who has read his Rousseau – the Noble Savage and so forth. In the sixteenth century Montaigne voiced the fear that the white man's contagion would greatly hasten the ruin of the New World. I believe he was wrong, that we should celebrate the five-hundredth anniversary of Columbus's discovery of America with quite as much jubilation as we did the quatercentennial in 1892. Why? Because only the most romantic could claim that Indian tribes of the New World ever lived in a state of prelapsarian grace, untainted by cannibalism, war, religious superstition and cruelty, so artless, happy and free.'

Dr Hodges went on in a louder tone. 'Besides, the extent to which these tribes were exterminated may well have been exaggerated. Even today in Haiti one can detect evidence of Indian blood in the people, particularly in Gonaïves, which derives from the Taino word *gonaibo*. One of my adopted sons is from Gonaïves.' He motioned across the table to a boy with a thin aquiline nose, lofty brow and narrow dark face with a chiselled delicacy of feature. 'Perhaps you will notice how the eyes are distinctly Indian, tilting upwards at the temples?'

One could hardly fail to notice.

'But to return to your argument, Mr Thomson. There are those who would say that the beneficial results of Christianity, of Western civilization, were well worth any loss of Indians who inhabited the forests, the mountains and the plains . . .'

One could detect in this brave utilitarianism the voice of Dr Hodges the Baptist missionary; tomorrow I would visit his archaeological museum at Limbé, over whose entrance hangs the sign: 'Man Was Made in the Image of God'. While I was surprised that the Haitians had not already sacked this building of its valuable relics (Taino-Arawak flint-heads, clay griddles for cooking, grinding stones, projectile points; a porcelain faience from eighteenth-century Rouen; fragments of Venetian glass excavated at Puerto Reale), I was more surprised to note what Dr Hodges had written in his guide for visitors: 'The first goal of Spanish expansion into Hispaniola was to evangelize the pagan peoples . . .' Surely, in the words of the royal order issued to Columbus by Ferdinand and Isabella, it was to *'discover and acquire'*? Gold was the first ambition, religious indoctrination the second.

Dr Hodges had laboured for many years in the spiritual instruction of people whom he probably regarded as heathen. But he went no further, I believe, than to catechize the inhabitants of Limbé with recited passages of scripture: an intelligent man, he understood that Voodoo was at the very root of life in Haiti, the salt of existence. Pastor Moore and Father Aragon, on the other hand, could manage only a blind hatred of Voodoo and had created a climate of fear (the most important weapon in the missionary armoury) among the Tortugans, subjecting the islanders to all manner of tired dogmatic insistencies, enforced prayer and even the destruction of their Voodoo temples. The one was a Baptist, the other a Catholic, but they were united in fanaticism by their narrow minds.

Dr Hodges was able at least to articulate a valid perspective, albeit a Western one, on Voodoo – and did not simply dismiss the religion without regard. 'As with any animist cult, evil is always considered as a force over which humans have no control,' he continued at dinner. 'It is something that comes from the outside, from the bad spirits. Consequently, the Christian concept that man himself has the choice between good and bad, the right to decide his own destiny, does not exist in Haiti. Which is probably why Haitians are prone to be so self-pitying, and never accountable for their own actions: I hate to think how many times I have heard the words "It's not my fault", "I didn't do it", "I don't have it". I would go further and say that these three expressions are absolutely essential for an understanding of Haiti.'

Paul Hodges interposed: 'My father's right, you know. Voodoo is everywhere. I remember talking to a Breton priest in Limbé one day and he told me: "We don't come here to convert the Haitians; the Haitians are here to convert *us*." But I guess that's always been the case. In fact, Haiti is probably one of the most stable countries in the world because nothing has changed here for the two hundred years since independence.'

Everyone laughed. Then Paul's sister, Barbara, told an extraordinary story about a husband and wife who came to the hospital one day with their ailing young boy disguised as a girl: ears pierced with rings, hair plaited into tiny ropes, a frothy dress. 'Four baby boys had already died,' said Barbara, 'so the parents decided to fool the evil spirits by pretending that their last male child was actually a girl.'

Dr Hodges rose from the table. 'Well, that's enough of Voodoo for one night. I must be up at first dawn tomorrow, so I'll take my leave. Good night, Mr Thomson, and sleep well if you can.'

At breakfast early next day, Dr Hodges was presented by his wife with a small model of the *Santa Maria*; the ship was mounted on a globe which opened to reveal a clockwork musical box, tinkling to a sea-shanty tune.

'Isn't that a marvel!' Dr Hodges exclaimed; and then, in a hoarse undertone: 'Perhaps there's hope for the world after all.'

He looked at me with bleared eyes: 'It's my birthday, by the way, Mr Thomson.'

'Oh! Many happy returns.'

Spread on the table in front of Dr Hodges were various maps and diagrams (many adapted from aerial views) of excavations conducted at En Bas Saline. They showed cross-sections of archaeological trenching with vertical and horizontal profiles of soil strata – layers of silt, charcoal and sand, reddish discolorations of rock, seams of decomposing humus – marked off in measurements analysed by computer.

'The University of Florida is convinced that Navidad lies somewhere within the boundaries of these excavations.' Dr Hodges drew the point of a pencil north to south along the dotted line of a pit survey. 'The evidence is not abundant, but neither is it inconclusive. We found an immense deposit of charred wood and waste materials, possibly from the fortress burned by the Indians; we discovered evidence of a pallisade or a moat, pieces of ordnance from late fifteenth-century or early sixteenth-century Spain. And we may have located one of Columbus's men: no head was discovered, although the skeleton was found in circumstances that would suggest a European burial . . .'

'And do you believe,' I asked Dr Hodges, 'that this is the site of Navidad?'

'So far we have conducted only preliminary soundings,' he said evasively. 'We had to suspend excavations in 1988 owing to the political situation – riots, the people in a state of enraged revolt, the usual sort of thing.'

'But do you believe that –'

'I believe that Navidad lies a few thousand feet to the north of En Bas Saline, closer to the coast. Whatever, it is almost certain that Gaucanagarí's village and Navidad are one and the same; and it's just as certain that the site lies within the bounds of the current archaeological zone, or a four-thousand-foot radius of it.'

I asked Dr Hodges if he would reveal the location of this new site. He said: 'It's near the town of Limonade, at a place called Bord de Mer. You'll find the remains of a French fort there, known to the locals as Caille Brûlée, Burned House, which conceal the foundations of Navidad. That, at any rate, is my opinion.' Dr Hodges may well be right: it was at Bord de Mer that he discovered a large wooden stake which was carbon-dated for *1440 plus or minus seventy years*. It is certainly possible that this timber was salvaged from the providential shipwreck on the Day of Nativity, 1492.

'In more salubrious times I would happily drive you to Bord de Mer.' Dr Hodges shook my hand. 'But Haiti's too dangerous at the moment and I'm horribly overburdened with work at the hospital. I hope you will forgive me.'

I thanked him for his time.

'It was a pleasure. Very few Englishmen ever come my way.'

I left Limbé in profound admiration for Dr William Hodges, this Schliemann of the Antilles.

His devotion to the history of Haiti, his proud intellect, inspired a sense of wonder and it was a privilege – a high favour – to have been in his company.

A week passed before I arrived at Bord de Mer, myself in search of Navidad. It was a Godforsaken place: shop signs smeared with soot, potholes the size of small fishponds, a caw-caw-caw of ravens and other dungheap birds. Everything that moved on legs emerged from huts to stare at me – reddish brown oxen, naked children with the pot-bellies of malnutrition, a mangy old nag which a woman whacked and goaded with a guava switch. But there was a healthy boil of life, at least, in the *marchandes* haggling over pyramids of rice, the clickety-clack of foot-treadled sewing machines, and the boys who approached with startling fleetness to beg for money.

One of them yelled, 'Five dollars!' and added a long while after, 'Please?'

'OK, OK! But I'm looking for Caille Brûlée. Ruins. Dr Hodges.'

'Ah! Meester Columbus!' He put himself in step beside me. 'This way, *blanc.*'

We came to the Atlantic Ocean – a wonderful malachite-green – where villagers had cultivated the adjacent land with corn, papayas, plantain and manioc; out to sea, fishermen swept their paddles right and left over the edges of pirogues, trawling for clams and conches much as their Indian ancestors had done.

'Meester Hodges – he come here with Columbus!' The guide led me by the arm to a patch of brownish sand bordered by a lagoon. 'Navidad!' he grandly announced. Little remained of the French fort, which was built in 1690, other than a tumbledown *poudrière* (powder magazine) and a few low walls chiselled with excavation marks or an indentation of pick-axes. Dr Hodges had fashioned a small mound of cement with an archaeologist's cryptic inscription:

800 NORTH; 800 EAST – PLUS 20 METRES. 1986.

The site was snarled in a mass of bayahonda, cacti and mangrove shrub, and shadowed in the distance by the mountainous Chaîne du Nord; Christopher Columbus had given a distance of one and a half leagues from the *Santa Maria* to Guacanagarí's village where he built his fortress; and I was now convinced, beyond rationality, that it was here, at Bord de Mer, that the Europeans had built their first settlement in the New World.

At what price? Walt Whitman imagined Columbus on his death-bed in Valladolid, May 1506, knowing that the end is near, staring into the future:

> 'What do I know of life? what of myself?
> I know not even my own work, past or present;
> Dim, ever-shifting guesses of it spread before me,
> Of newer, better worlds, their mighty parturition
> Mocking, perplexing me . . .'

The Grand Conquistador Christopher Columbus had spoken of spices and cotton, mastic and aloes and 'a thousand other things of value'. Gone, all gone: Haiti is a vast slum floating a few hundred miles off Florida, the poorest nation in the Western Hemisphere. In 1986, by way of demonstration against foreign interference in Haiti, a two-ton statue of Columbus was toppled into the sea at Port-au-Prince. Only the plinth of this stone memorial remains in Place Christophe Colomb, not far from the American embassy.

XX

To the Citadel

'Well, they did for yer right enough, Jonesy, me lad!
Dead as a bloater! Where's yer 'igh an' mighty airs now, yer
bloomin' Majesty? . . . Silver bullets! Gawd blimey, but yer
died in the 'eighth o' style, any'ow!'

Eugene O'Neill, *The Emperor Jones*

SONG OF THE KING OF THE IBOS
'Oh me good friend, Mr Wilberforce, make we free!
God Almighty thank ye! God Almighty thank ye!
Buckra in this country no make we free:
What Negro for to do? Take force by force?'

Matthew Gregory Lewis, *Jamaican Diaries*

Three Haitian women lie buried in the cemetery at Pisa: Athénaïre,
Améthyste* and Queen Marie-Louise. They are the wife and daughters of
King Henri Christophe, who ruled the north of Haiti for fourteen years
before he committed suicide on the night of 8 October 1820. His women
sought refuge abroad: first, with friends of William Wilberforce in
England; later, with Capuchin friars in Italy for whom they embroidered
altar cloths until they died forgotten.

Henri Christophe, a model for Eugene O'Neill's Emperor Jones,
governed on a titanic scale of grandeur and shot himself in the head with
a silver bullet, or so it was whispered. Sadly, his marble statue in Cap-
Haïtien has been decapitated and uniformed police now guard the headless king with thumbs hooked into their cartridge belts, pacing up and
down Place d'Armes. I peered at what remained of the memorial; it was
little more than an inscription beneath an arm raised towards an absent
plumed cocked hat: *'A la Mémoire et à la Gloire de Sa Majesté Henri
Christophe, Le Civilisateur'*.

---

*Améthyste died at the age of fifty-five on 15 October 1831; Athénaïre died at the age
of fifty on 10 September 1839. (Monsieur Jean-Elie Gilles of Jacmel kindly gave me
this information in 2004.)

The civilizer. This is a suitable epithet for Christophe. He proclaimed the dignity of the black races both to themselves and to the rest of the world, and tried to prevent a return to slavery under France. The French were not the only enemy however; mulattoes in the south had broken away from Christophe's rule to form a separate republic under the command of President Alexandre Pétion. Between 1806 and 1820 Haiti was divided into two mutually hostile states – a black monarchy and a mulatto republic. North and south had always been at feud with each other during the War of Independence, but never more so than in the final years. It then seemed that Haiti had found in Christophe a leader of rare genius, under whom it might advance to the Black Renaissance of which the British abolitionists – William Wilberforce, Thomas Clarkson, Archdeacon Wrangham, Zachary Macaulay – had dreamed so long. To his son, Wilberforce wrote: 'In this Haitian instance, we are sowing the seeds of civilisation and knowledge in a society which (may it please God) you will live to see exhibiting the new spectacle of a community of black men, of which the mass will be as well instructed as any nation upon earth.'

Henri Christophe's correspondence with William Wilberforce began in 1814; the letters everywhere abound in truly elevated plans (*'Je suis pénetré, mon cher Wilberforce, des sentiments généreux et philanthropiques que vous m'éxprimez . . .'*), many on the subject of education. Most important for Wilberforce was Christophe's intention to convert Haiti to Protestantism and introduce English as the national language. This was presumably to rid the heritage of Catholic France; Bonaparte had already perverted the ideals of the great revolution with his attempts to reinstate slavery. Henri Christophe had assiduously followed the progress of Napoleon's decline from Moscow to the abdication at Fontainebleau. His fear of the Emperor finally turned to contempt when he learned that he had neither died in battle nor killed himself in defeat. 'If he had to fall, then he should have buried himself in the ruins,' Christophe said. 'I never would have thought he would end his career in a manner so unworthy of a soldier.'

Wilberforce, an evangelist, encouraged Christophe to suppress the Roman Catholic Sunday in favour of a Protestant sabbath of pious inactivity. And in sending him volumes of the *Encyclopaedia Britannica*, he wrote 'you will also do me the honour, I hope, of accepting and placing by their side the History of the Inquisition and that of the Jesuits.' Eventually Catholicism was established as the State religion ('Christophe is not, I fear, governed by religious principles,' Wilberforce complained) but the King was keen to maintain correspondence with the abolitionists, as it was through them that he might obtain the one thing he most desired: British recognition of Haitian independence. Without protection from the Royal Navy his people could have no assurance that their freedom would endure.

Within three years Christophe had established a state printing press, a navy, a judicial system called the Code Henri, and a sovereign court supervised by a Royal Chamber of Public Instruction. It was in education, though, that Christophe excelled. Wilberforce agreed to supply him with seven schoolmasters, a private tutor for the Royal princesses Améthyste and Athénaïre, and seven teachers for a Royal Academy, among them a classical professor, fellows of medicine, surgery and mathematics, and a pharmaceutical chemist. By the end of 1817 four schools had opened in Cap-Haïtien, Port-de-Paix, Saint Marc and Gonaïves respectively, the academy itself being established one year later in Cap-Haïtien to provide secondary education. All teachers came from the British and Foreign School Society in Borough Road, London, which followed the radical system introduced by Sir Joseph Lancaster in 1798, whereby 'one master may conduct a school of 1,000 children with perfect ease'.

The first teacher to arrive in Haiti was a certain T. B. Gulliver, whom Christophe presented with gifts of sheep, coffee and sugar; his colleagues George Sweet and Tom Bosworth, however, were too fond of Haitian rum and, despite ministrations from the King's personal physician, died after attacks of fever and gout. The physician was a Scotsman, Duncan Stewart, also appointed Professor of Anatomy at the Royal Academy and *maréchal de camp* commanding the Haitian Medical Corps. 'The King has given me complete power to order what I think necessary for the dieting, clothing and accommodation of the sick in his hospitals,' Dr Stewart wrote to Thomas Clarkson, the originator of the abolition movement and the man who persuaded Wilberforce to become its spokesman in Parliament. 'I can safely say there is not an hospital in England where the sick are better supplied with all the conveniences and necessaries than the hospitals of Haiti.'

Dr Stewart failed to mention the most interesting of these conveniences, described by an English naval officer as 'a pair of stocks fitted to every bed-place, in which the legs of the occupier are immediately put on the least symptom of insubordination'. Despotism was the corollary of Christophe's attempt to turn Haiti, overnight, into a world power on the European scale, and it brought about his downfall. An early sign that His Highness the President tended towards absolutism came on 30 July 1810 when he announced that the denomination of Cap-Français (now Cap-Haïtien) should be changed to Cap-Henri. The following year, on 28 March, Christophe declared a kingdom with himself as 'King Henri I of Haiti, Sovereign of Ile de la Tortue, Ile de la Gonâve and other adjacent Islands, Destroyer of Tyranny, Regenerator and Benefactor of the Haitian Nation, First Monarch of the New World'. In Napoleonic fashion, Henri himself assumed the crown. He then proposed a toast to 'My dear brother George the Third of Great Britain, whose life I hope the Supreme Arbiter may preserve to be always the constant friend of Haiti.'

Yet for all the grandiloquence, Christophe had a certain taste and style; he was never the figure of buffoonish comicality that Faustin Soulouque became, with his weakness for garish courtly dress. When Eugene O'Neill wrote of his Emperor Jones that 'there is something not altogether ridiculous about his grandeur, for he has a way of carrying it off', he was thinking perhaps of a famous portrait – the only one of Christophe – that hangs in the National Museum at Port-au-Prince. It was executed by the English painter Richard Evans, who had directed the monarch's Academy of Art at Cap-Henri, and shows the King of Haiti as a heavyset man with a powerful, barrel-shaped chest, flat-nosed, with intelligent eyes and Olympian aspect. He is dressed in frank imitation of George III, with a blue cutaway coat, white stockings, cuffs, pumps and knee-breeches, the jaw prominent above a broad-winged collar; in one hand he holds a stout silver-knobbed cane and a bicrone hat with a two-coloured cockade, but there is no other decoration: only the gold star of the Order of Saint-Henri bearing the royal motto 'God, my Cause and my Sword'.

Christophe purchased most of his regalia in London. Indeed, so great was his admiration for England that he ordered his courtiers to roll lead weights into their crinkly hair and wear the straightened strands in a powdered queue, after the Windsor fashion. (He also spelt his first name 'Henry', with the Anglo-Saxon 'y', although this was later dropped as an affectation.) There were English telescopes as well as clothes, imported so that Christophe might catch sight of the expected French invasion, and it was not long before the King was everywhere accompanied by a young page carrying a spy-glass wrapped in a napkin. But stories began to circulate of how these telescopes were used to oversee subjects from afar, how Christophe would send soldiers to beat any man who was not working hard enough, how on one occasion he had trained a gun on an idler and blown off his head at a range of two and a half miles.

As the months went by, Christophe's tyrannies grew more barbarous and, in the tradition of all subsequent Haitian leaders including Papa Doc and Jean-Bertrand Aristide, he began to lose the support of his people and then the army. This came to a crisis when a colonel, suspecting that Christophe had amorous designs on his wife, entered the tyrant's room unannounced and proclaimed: 'Sire, you are known as the father of all the children of Haiti – but I have no desire to be the father of your son.' The colonel then menaced Christophe with the wrath of God, which provoked the startling exclamation: '*He is* God of the Heavens, but I am God of the Earth.'

Not unexpectedly, the King showed signs of increased paranoia; he carried his English telescopes with him to bed and was guarded night and day by a special corps of African police called the Dahomeys, the youngest of whom Christophe dragooned into a cadet *corps d'élite* under the name of the Royal Bonbons – the first, but certainly not the last, precursors of the Tontons Macoute.

The fall of this august sovereign was as tragic as that of Toussaint L'Ouverture. He had effectively raised a republic into a monarchial institution. Englishmen in particular felt a reluctance to address a Haitian as his *Lordship* (Thomas Clarkson remarks on the racial prejudice of even Wilberforce, who shrank from admitting Marie-Louise, Améthyste and Athénaïre into London society). Isolated from his countrymen, half paralysed by a stroke, abandoned by his physician Dr Stewart – Henri Christophe was in a pitiful condition when news reached him one night of sedition in the Place d'Armes. This insurrection had been organized by the mulatto general Jean-Pierre Boyer, who became President of the south on Pétion's death in 1818. 'No King! No Nobility! No Tyranny!' yelled the mutinous subjects. Deafened by the noise outside the palace, Christophe retired to a bedroom and, closing the doors behind him, moved to where he kept a revolver. 'Since the people of Haiti no longer have any faith in me, I know what I have to do.' Then the silver bullet.

Christophe was buried in the Citadel, a massive garrison fortress near Cap-Henri, and Haiti was once more united north and south as the republican Boyer took command of the sovereign state. On 26 December 1820, William Wilberforce wrote to Archdeacon Wrangham: 'Poor Christophe! I cannot help grieving at the idea of his character being left to the dogs and vultures to be devoured.'

Had Christophe survived the mutiny, Haiti might have emerged a very different country. He established an economic stability, and a spirit of education that no longer exists. It is probably true to say that he sought not so much his own aggrandisement as the improvement and prosperity of his subjects, that his sole object was to place their liberty on a sure and permanent foundation. Christophe considered the institution of monarchy as a safe and effectual remedy against invasion from France, and it was created on the very reasonable grounds that royalty should not be the exclusive prerogative of white men. His early distinction as a soldier, his subsequent authority as a King, his desire to bring light and civilization to a people newly emerged from the nightmare of slavery, will mark him as a man of vision. But in the end his faults were too glaring, and the violence of his passions, together with the severity of some of his regulations, could only diminish his popularity.

Wilberforce, on his part, believed that Christophe furnished 'a striking instance of the truth, that by too earnestly pursuing a good cause, you directly defeat it'. It might be more accurate to say that Christophe became a perfect vindication of Lord Acton's dictum about the corrupting tendency of power. Kingship went to his head; he was made delirious by the image of his own majesty, and then there was only the peaceful certitude of death.

Cap-Haïtien was founded in 1670 by Bertrand d'Ogeron, who had been sent by Louis XIV to colonize the buccaneers on Ile de la Tortue. For over a century it was said to be the most attractive city outside France and was often referred to as 'Little Paris'. In 1802, however, the place was put to flames by Henri Christophe. He was then Commander of the North, a capable and fearless general in the War of Independence. Rather than surrender to the armies of Napoleon, he reduced the city to a heap of smouldering debris. Rebuilt as Cap-Henri, it was destroyed in 1842 by an earthquake; and again by a hurricane in 1928.

The city as it stands today could not be described as beautiful. The poverty in the outskirts is appalling – a chaos of tyre cemeteries and shacks fenced by dusty aloe hedges. And everywhere you look, booths made from green boughs and odd pieces of rattan sell meat patties and boiled yam which taste little better (as I now knew from experience) than cotton wool. The taint of dried fish, the effluvia of rotting vegetable matter, is not so apparent as you approach the centre of Cap-Haïtien. There is raffish charm in the heart of this city, even to the advertise-

ments for blue films – *Talk Dirty to Me One More Time, Thai Maid Service*
– outside the cathedral in Place d'Armes.

This cathedral is attractive with its silver domes and stuccoed classical
façade, dazzling white in the sunlight. The square in front is bordered by
steeple-roofed houses of a delicate primrose, fawn-rose and crocus-yellow,
the colours of cassata ice-cream. I was told that they closely resemble the
buildings originally constructed here in the eighteenth century from French
stone brought as ballast in vessels from Nantes, Anjou and Normandy.
They are set four to a block, with a brick or pebble sidewalk in between.
Around Place d'Armes the city has expanded in the form of a grid according to the architectural geometries and stringent harmonies of the
Enlightenment. You cannot easily get lost, thanks to the Americans who
dispensed with the original streets' names – Rue de la Providence, du
Quai, d'Anjou, de Notre-Dame – and replaced them with numbers and
letters, unable as they were to pronounce very much French. All streets
parallel to the ocean are lettered from A to Q; those perpendicular to the
Atlantic are numbered from 0 to 29. The more elderly of the city's sixty-
thousand inhabitants, however, still employ the French designations: they
do not have very fond memories of the Yankee occupation.

By comparison with other Haitian cities, Gonaïves in particular, Cap-
Haïtien has an air of gracious civility, the broad, seaweed-scented streets
divided by formal gardens of royal palms and rhododendrons. In the
dispersing mists of early morning, the city seems suffused with light –
open and spacious, unlike Port-au-Prince, which is closed, suspicious.
There are very few beggars; it is not a good idea, however, to eat at the
Feu Vert along the main maritime boulevard where children rap against
the windows as you raise your knife and fork, holding out their hands
for charity. The one decent hotel in Cap-Haïtien, the Hostellerie du
Roi Christophe, was built by the French in the early eighteenth century
as a government house. It is said to stand on the site of the Auberge de
la Couronne where the young Henri worked as a scullion and later as
a chef with a high white cap (improbably swift progress for a former
slave who was born, as the story goes, in Grenada). They say Christophe
was a master of turtle vol-au-vent and wood pigeon; and when he put
a hand to the mixing bowl, the fragrance of his puff pastry carried as
far as the Rue des Trois Visages, now at the intersection of Rue 6 and
Boulevard E. Pauline Bonaparte herself stayed at this hostelry and something of the grandeur remains: arcades with heavily scrolled armorial
shields of stone, a rambling garden where myna birds twitter among the

patios and flowering vines. The restaurant, all fretwork and mirrors, serves fried frog's legs in Creole sauce.

Cap-Haïtien is considered to be the most African of Haitian cities. The population here is overwhelmingly black – a legacy of King Henri Christophe and the ideological battle he waged against the mestizo-Caribs in the south. Mulattoes were never prevalent in the north, an area which has nevertheless monopolized the great events of Haitian history. It was near Cap-Français that Toussaint L'Ouverture was born in 1743, and where the slaves first rose in rebellion under a Jamaican black of Herculean size named Boukman.

Boukman was the headman of a plantation as well as a *houngan* in the rites of Voodoo. He held a ceremony on the night of 15 August 1791 which united slave leaders and marked the beginning of their revolt against colonial France. Details of the sacrificial rites conducted that night in the forest of Bois Caïman were recorded by a black slave named Ignace who testified before the court of Cap-Français. A French colonist, Monsieur Dalmas, later reported in his memoirs:

An entirely black pig was surrounded with fetishes or offerings the one more whimsical than the other. And the religious ceremonies that the assembled blacks practised in cutting its throat, the avidity with which they drank its blood, the price they paid to possess some of its hairs – in their minds, a kind of talisman – rendered them invulnerable in battle, according to the African belief.

We know from this testimony that the pig was sacrificed during the thunderclaps of a tropical storm: lightning jagged across a sky of sombre clouds, illuminating the mountain peaks by the sea and bringing a torrential shower of rain. Trees writhed and moaned under the repeated assaults of a violent wind; heavy branches, torn away, fell with a crash around the ceremony. When the thunder had died away and a knife was plunged once more into the entrails of the pig, Boukman pronounced that a pact of blood had been sealed between the initiated on this side of the water and the great *loas* of Africa. Here is the rest of his impassioned harangue, echoed by Ignace:

Time of vengeance has come; tomorrow in the night, all whites shall die . . . No more delay, no more fear! We must not leave them any refuge, nor any hope of salvation. All will undergo the same lot; and if some of them avoid our knives, they may not escape the fires that will reduce the plains to cinders.

Boukman exercised an extraordinary power over his adepts; within six weeks a thousand whites had been massacred and hundreds of plantations destroyed. Legend has it that the colonial inhabitants of Cap-Français suspected nothing until a rain of burning cane straw, sweet-smelling, drifted northward over the city, driven on the wind like snow flakes. Soon the horizon was a wall of fire and the revolt had spread to all slaves in the north. Toussaint himself took part in this early rebellion of which Voodoo was the medium – proof perhaps that religion is not always an opium of the people, but a source of inspiration and a prelude to action.

Bois Caïman is situated outside the village of Balan, some five miles west of Cap-Haïtien by the edge of the Baie de l'Acul. I had planned a visit there with Father Jean-Marie Le Ray, a Breton priest who had lived in Haiti since 1930. He was a small hilarious man of eighty-six years, forever amused by the absurdities that prevail in this country, by the lawlessness of the land. *'C'est une bonne blague, hein?'* he would mutter through a stumpy row of yellow teeth. Le Ray looked like a tramp with his filthy trousers held up by a length of string, unshaven, purplish broken capillaries around the nose and that sallow complexion of Europeans who have been in the tropics too long. When not outside in his white pith helmet (repaired round the brim with insulating tape), Le Ray would retreat for prayer in a poky room behind the Justinien Hospital at Cap-Haïtien, where there was less an odour of sanctity than of mould.

It was a real jackdaw's nest of a room, cluttered with such interesting lumber as violins, wooden walking sticks and phalliform African fetishes all hand-carved by the priest himself. There was also a modest collection of Haitian butterflies, many of which had been eaten by bats. 'One cannot keep things too long in this heat.' Le Ray fetched a deep sigh. 'A Sister of Charity once gave me a stuffed wild boar from the Cameroon. Unfortunately the animal disintegrated within a week. The sun is perfectly imbecile, wouldn't you agree?'

The squalor in this room was of a defiant eccentricity. Empty cans of evaporated milk and luncheon meat everywhere bestrewed the floor; icons of Catholic saints hung on the snuff-coloured wall above a truckle bed and there were bobbins of sail twine, inky goose quills, a rusted binnacle lamp and an old canoe in which the priest would hunt for guinea fowl with a twelve-bore manufactured, so he told me, in Bordeaux. There was even a dusty harmonium on which he played the folk songs of Brittany, although he had not returned to his birthplace in sixty years.

'Oh but damn it!' Le Ray would stare at me owlishly from behind broken spectacles. 'I'm condemned to end my days in Haiti.'

For most of his long life in Haiti, Father Jean-Marie Le Ray had tried to eradicate what he called *'idolatrie'*. He took part in the notorious anti-superstitious campaign of 1941 conducted by the Roman Catholic Church with support from the conservative mulatto president Elie Lescot. This spiritual blitzkrieg, called *'l'opération nettoyage'*, was initiated by Monsignor Paul Robert, Bishop of Gonaïves, whose pastoral letters had referred to the 'absolute incompatibility, the irreconcilable opposition, between Christianity and superstition – the collection of religious beliefs and prac-tices that came from Africa'. Within a week, priests were destroying all trace of Voodoo in their respective dioceses. As Father Le Ray remem-bered: 'I used to saddle my horse and ride across country to the temples, set fire to huts and confiscate all idols of gods and devils.'

He showed me a catechism that was used at the time in rural districts around Cap-Haïtien. It was a fearful document:

Who is the principal slave of Satan? – The principal slave of Satan is the *houngan*.

Why do these men give Satan the names of angels, saints, and *loas*? – In order to deceive us more easily.

How do they serve Satan? – In sinning, casting spells, practising black magic, giving food-offerings.

Are we allowed to mingle with the slaves of Satan? – No, because they are evil-doers; like Satan himself they are liars . . .

And so on, for three pages.

'But what was the use?' asked Le Ray with a sort of jocular desper-ation. 'The introduction of a pure form of Christianity in this country was a dream for youthful enthusiasts only,' and he added with feeling: 'We are all of us under the spell of Voodoo.'

I had already suspected that this priest might be in thrall to African animism because his room was also cluttered with relics salvaged from those raids of 1941 – relics that belonged to victims of the campaign. Arranged on a shelf beneath a large label that read *'Mutations'* were pieces of wood carved by *houngans* into images of snarling dogs with human limbs, into women that were hybrid horse or mermaid. And beneath the label *'Palaeontology'* stood fossil animals and plants from pre-Columbian Haiti reputedly endowed with magical properties.

Later, Le Ray asked if he could keep the hat which I had worn at my Bizango ceremony in Saint Marc. It took pride of place on the shelf soon after, marked for posterity with a third label: *'Very Rare Example of Voodoo Headgear'*. This was a strange thing to do for one who had so vehemently believed in the anti-superstitious campaign and certain damnation of heretics. As Blake had said of Milton, Father Le Ray was almost of 'the Devil's party without knowing it'.

There were squalls of rain on the day I visited Bois Caïman and the little wicket-gate of Father Le Ray's enclosure had been loosened from its hinges by the winds of the previous night. I found the old priest cooking a repulsive gruel over a charcoal fire – bits of bread and Spam simmering in evaporated milk.

'Care for some?' he asked casually.

'No thanks. I've already had breakfast.'

Le Ray ventured a slight laugh. 'You don't know what's good for you.'

He ate a bowlful of the mush and shuffled outside, where he blew three sharp trills on a whistle. 'That's to call the *maîtresse de la maison,*' he explained. 'And four short notes like this' – he put his lips to the tin whistle in demonstration – 'is to summon the *petit garçon.*' The priest gave a rheumy cough and laughed. 'It's a good system. They'll come running to me obediently, like dogs wired to a bell.'

Within seconds the maid and young boy materialized apparently out of nowhere, curtseying and giggling.

'Bonjour, citoyens.' Father Le Ray addressed them with a sort of paternal scorn.

'Bonjour, mon père,' they chimed in chorus.

'Have you packed my bag and prepared my thermos?' the priest went on in Creole.

They said yes.

'C'est pas vrai!' Le Ray exclaimed, surprised into the use of his native tongue by what he understood to be a lie. 'You have neither packed my bag nor prepared my thermos, have you?'

They confessed they had not.

'Why not?'

'You never asked us to.'

'Ah yes, right you are,' the priest said wonderingly, as if to himself. 'Well, I'm telling you now! Pack and prepare!'

'Oui, mon père,' and the Haitians skipped away, giggling again.

Back in the room, Le Ray began to charge his briar-root pipe, pressing the tobacco down with a thumb. 'It's always the same with those two. They mock me, like everyone else, and take me for a figure of fun. But what can I do?' he asked wearily behind a cloud of smoke.

We set off in the direction of Balan. Flecks of rain had clouded his spectacles and dampened the pith helmet; there was a growth of white stubble on his chin like kettle fur. Father Le Ray's mongrel (named Peritas after Alexander the Great's favourite dog) accompanied us on the tap-tap – *Le Fruit de Mes Efforts* – to Balan, provoking sniggers of laughter from the passengers.

For twelve years Father Le Ray had been *curé* of Balan; the village today is inhabited mostly by rattan cutters, each of them living under a rough thatch of dried banana leaves. The priest kept a plot of land on the edge of Bois Caïman where he encouraged some fruit and vegetables among the ragged palms rough with spines. 'Time to cultivate my garden,' he said, raking the soil with his hoe. 'Lend me a hand.' After two hours we had sown seeds for mandarin and cherry plants and Father Le Ray made me a present of bread-fruit kernels and cocoa tubers that were later confiscated by customs at the airport in Port-au-Prince. We broke for lunch beneath thickening rain clouds, Le Ray opening a polythene bag full of bread husks, a couple of bananas black with age and, inevitably, slices of Spam. Before we ate, his hand moved to make a sign of the cross in the air and grace was said in Latin: '*Agamus tibi gratias, Domine . . .*'

The massed clouds appeared solid and steady overhead, and the air still, very oppressive. 'Soon it will rain,' the priest said grimly. 'Let's go into the woods in search of Boukman.'

But there were no woods to speak of at Bois Caïman, only deforestation: mountainsides of burned wood, a shameful ravagement.

Le Ray led me to a clearing scattered with the blackened brands of extinct fires. He said they had remained here since last 15 August, the date on which Voodoo priests celebrate the terrible *jacquerie* of Boukman and his revolted slaves. The rain came down, Peritas barking uproariously as his master stood with his arms outstretched in the manner of Christ on the cross. 'You don't seem convinced that I can recite Boukman's prayer by heart.' Le Ray's voice carried loud and clear above the downpour – then he went on in Creole, speaking earnestly: 'But listen . . .'

He began to rant like Lear in the storm, Peritas yapping at his ankles: 'The God who created the sun which gives us light, who raised the sea and speaks in the thunder of the storm, he looks down upon all that the white man has done! The God of the white man ordains only crime, but our God gives blessing. Our God who is good to us cries out for vengeance. He will lead and give us his help. Destroy the cross, that symbol of the God of the whites who has so often caused us to weep, and listen to the voice of liberty, which speaks in the hearts of us all!'

Father Le Ray paused awhile, then said in a shocked voice: 'I suppose they could excommunicate me for that.' Then he went on, musingly: 'No matter. Boukman is a part of our history. Better death than slavery,' he said. 'A very sensible comment. Most sensible . . .'

The light, recovered from the downpour, was now charged with a reddish glow, glimmering slightly. A flock of white rice birds rose from the burnt clearing as we made our way towards the tap-tap for Cap-Haïtien.

Better death than slavery. The nightmare of a second French invasion was expressed in the Fifth Article of the Haitian constitution of May 1805: 'At the first shot from the warning gun, the towns shall be destroyed and the nation shall rise in arms.' Strictures were placed on ownership of land by whites, and foreign merchants were not allowed to stray out of towns towards the mountains which concealed fortifications, food stores and ammunition in readiness for attack. The greatest and most fantastic of defences was the Citadel, built by King Christophe as a 'Palladium of Liberty and Independence' – a fortress more massive than the Tower of London and called the Eighth Wonder of the World.

The Citadel stands on a mountain some three thousand feet above the village of Milot, due south of Cap-Haïtien. Not immediately visible to the eye, obscured by clouds and jungle-grown hills, the fortress is over-whelmed at first by the royal palace of Sans Souci. This was named after Frederick the Great's rococo residence at Potsdam and constructed under the superintendence of Henri Christophe. It was to be the Versailles of the New World, built on a level of grandeur never equalled in the Antilles. From here the King wrote many letters to William Wilberforce, one of which was shown by the abolitionists to Alexander I of Russia. 'A person rising up in the midst of slavery and founding a free Empire is of itself a surprising thing,' the Tsar had remarked to Clarkson. 'But to see him founding it on the pillars of education under Christian auspices is more surprising and truly delightful.'

With its terraced steps mounting like a ziggurat temple, Sans Souci resembles an Aztec or Sumerian ruin, tangled with lianas in the midst of untended fields. Only on approach does the palace emerge in its European design, albeit an anomaly in the Haitian jungle. Many have marvelled that Sans Souci was the work of an uneducated Haitian who dressed as George III. The London *Picture Post* (12 November 1949) carried an article about the palace which stated: 'It must have been very strange to hear orchestras of gourd and marimba beating out the minuet for grandees who had been born to slavery.' At the time, Sans Souci stood as a symbol of black pride and proof that Christophe could vie with the French in more than battle.

According to contemporary reports, Christophe's wife Marie-Louise cared little for the niceties of European etiquette and would rather squat in a corner of the palace boiling root brew on a charcoal brazier; but the King, booted and spurred and resplendent in a tightly buttoned swallow-tailed coat, was a stickler for protocol. We know from Christophe's 1817 *Almanack Royal d'Haïti* that every noble was required to appear at Sans Souci in specially prescribed uniforms, correct and immaculate down to the last button: a white tunic reaching below the knee, white silk hose and red maroquin shoes with square gold buckles, a gold-hilted sword and a round hat; a black coat embroidered with gold and with red facings for princes and dukes; simple coats of blue or red for barons or knights, and plumes of black, red, white and green in descending order of seniority. Leafing through a rare copy of the *Almanack* at the library of St Louis de Gonzague in Port-au-Prince, I was amused by the mention of two particular titles: Comte de Limonade and Duc de la Marmelade.

Within the space of a day at Sans Souci, King Christophe had created an hereditary nobility with four princes, eight dukes, twenty-two counts, thirty-seven barons and fourteen knights. The future president Jean-Pierre Boyer had brought charges of corruption against Christophe yet, once he had overthrown the man, proceeded to impound both the public funds of the old kingdom and as much as he could find of the monarch's private treasure. For twenty-three years, Boyer ruled over a sort of republican monarchy sustained by the bayonet where the army maintained its role as governmental arbiter, quelling opposition with repressive severity. In 1843 Boyer was inevitably accused of corruption and treason. He fled to Jamaica, a presidential route into exile that was later taken by Faustin Soulouque, Boyer's tyrannical successor who remained in power until he was himself arraigned with the crime of taking Haiti to the brink of bankruptcy, and was then toppled in a coup d'état. Such was – indeed still is – the cruel and barren futility of political life in Haiti.

The skeleton of Sans Souci suggests what Haiti might have been before political corruption became so universal as almost to lose its significance. It was built of bricks plastered with yellow stucco, a façade of immense French windows concealing a series of ample apartments that numbered a grand *salon*, an audience chamber, a banqueting hall, library, billiard room, private quarters for the King, Queen, Améthyste and Athénaïre. These rooms, all now dismantled, were paved in marble and panelled with such polished hardwoods – acajou, mahogany – as existed in Haiti before deforestation. Imported from Europe were gilt mirrors, paintings, tapestries and draperies, even a Gobelins tapestry that showed Venus beside the forge of Vulcan. Under the flooring a system of pipes marshalled the waters of a mountain stream to ensure that the palace was kept in a state of refreshing coolness; the water then flowed from the keystone of a marble arch, dropped twenty feet over a bright blue wall and rippled away through ornamental culverts painted a rich Pompeian red. You can still see the remains of these channels and conduits, squared blocks of stone lying in the tall grass of the Queen's pleasure gardens that rose in squares one above another, embowered with tropical trees and planted with an abundant variety of shrubs and flowers. Near by stood the arsenal, barracks for the Palace Guard, a storehouse, the stables and a coach-repair shop where Christophe's own carriage de-luxe, made in England at a cost of £700, lay mouldering until it was removed by President Boyer.

Only the façade and terraces of Sans Souci remain, surrounded by the cow-byres and bamboo huts of Milot. These ruins are nevertheless magnificent, the château rising to four storeys above a sweeping double flight of stairs that converge before the main entrance like a Sicilian palazzo. The steps are flanked at intervals by four stone sentry boxes, green with lichen but still slashed with the original loopholes. A few fragments of marble, all that is left of a grandiose fountain, lie at the entrance where a portico had been graced with a gold sun and the words: *'Je vois tout et tout voit par moi dans l'univers.'* I see all, and all in the universe see by me.

Fallen into desuetude – floors torn up, roofing collapsed, stone gateways crumbling and lizards lounging on toppled pillars – the palace is yet a fabulous outdoor museum. It is the melancholy of Sans Souci, the almost Arcadian setting, that lingers in the memory. Windows are empty spaces like pulled teeth in the wall, gaping above heaps of stone debris, shards of fired clay, pellets of goat or rabbit dung. But they give a spectacular view of rolling jungle; and, on a good day, of the sea that glows green with a strange phosphorescence, streaks of black marking beds of coral. Windows in the south wing look on a fine star-apple tree where Christophe held his morning levees.

The path from Sans Souci to the Citadel climbs steeply to the sky through mangrove forest dotted with lath and plaster dwellings. Slowly the huts of Milot dwindle in size to resemble the bell-tents of a military encampment. Along the trail passed a stream of pack mules and women carrying logwood or stalks of sugar cane. They would sell these wares in Cap-Haïtien and in the late twilight walk home again, wealthier by a handful of gourdes. An old man droving oxen chivvied me in peculiar English: 'Hey boy! You walk Citadel? You crazy! Give me one dollar!'

I replied in French: '*Non, non. Je suis un anglais, pauvre, très pauvre.*'

My money had almost run out now, but I felt little sense of loss at leaving Haiti. The gypsy life of travel from town to town without the comfort of a car, the hardships I endured by horse, boat and bus, the hours of cockroach boredom in bad hotels – all this had become very trying; so my heart was steeled against the sadness of departure, although the smell of Haiti will be unforgettable, and I hope unforgotten. The Citadel itself was now a sort of symbol for my journey's end; in reaching it, I would know that the time had come to leave this place.

The late afternoon sun was hot. There was no hurry in climbing this tough, scorched path but the begging began to irritate. Two boys emerged from a wattle lean-to and tried to offer me a horse, a wretched creature with sores. 'Yo! Yes, you sir. Just twenty dollars for to ride up on Citadel. *Ca va?* We have many friends in America also. You give us visa for Miami and we offer to you one horse for free. OK?'

'Thank you but I don't need a horse.'

'No problem, *blanc*. So we give you ride on horse all the same, anything the Monsieur say he want.'

Again I said that I had no need of a horse.

In the end I was gulled into surrendering most of my carefully calculated minimum of money; it was the only way to lose the boys. *Marchandes* were the next to pester. 'Very good souvenirs of Christophe.' They came running towards me with beads and edible necklaces: 'Only fifty dollars.'

'I'm sorry. No money.'

Then a poor child, worrying at its mother's breasts, began to cry and I felt shame: what good was I doing here, a *blanc* without any money among those who had even less than myself?

The path began to mount through higher altitudes, the air more cold in the twilight. About the middle of the ascent and I was alone. The jungle and trees fell back into their landscape of brown gold and brilliant emerald, creeper and sodden woods subsiding to clumps of mountain plant: blue wisteria, rose-laurel.

Rising like a staircase into continents of cloud, the road vanished to become an ox-cart trail. In the dead calm of evening it felt at last as though departure was imminent. My map of Haiti had regressed to pulp from sweat and rain and salt sea water; I would no longer need it. All that poverty, the awful clamour of life, the hate of race, the hate of blood, my few Creole phrases got by heart: it was all falling away . . .

At a bend of the trail loomed the Citadel. It appeared to me as a mass of titanic stone and the loneliness and sheer vastness of the thing was bewildering. Apparently welded to the landscape, a dream of empire wrought in rock, the fortress was tremendous and appalling: it conjured designs from the imagined architecture of Piranesi. Construction of the Citadel must have been a task to stagger the ambition of a Pharaoh as it towers above the timberline on the Pic de la Ferrière, one of the highest mountains in Haiti. The main bastion projected at a sharp angle like the ram of a gigantic ship and walkways were etched by the sinking sun in black intaglio, a gleam of metal from the lips of cannon squatting four-tiered within the walls.

Another twist in the trail and the Citadel vanished from view like a hallucination; from here it would appear and reappear above the treeline, a beacon to guide my steps. Materials for construction were all dragged by human hands from Milot and beyond, and the royal offices were unsparing in their exaction of labour, imposing regular levies on a peasantry that had been returned to virtual slavery. The King himself was a tireless taskmaster; wagon axles were mortised into the walls and every day several bulls were slaughtered so that their blood could curdle the cement. Often a worker spiralled to earth over the ramparts, carrying his bricks and mortar. It is said that twenty thousand died this way.

The fortress appeared again above the treetops. In the distance overhung by haze it now resembled a crusader castle from Syria or one of those lumbering battlements built by the Angevin kings in Italy – anything but a stronghold erected in the last century.

Work on the Citadel actually began in 1805 on the order of Dessalines. It was the last of a series of fortifications placed strategically from north to south of Haiti, and stood as a defence against the worst that a white man could bring. (Europeans were forbidden to ascend this mountain path, even to approach very near it, during the time it took to build the Citadel.) A good ten years were lavished on its construction and when the fortress was solemnly inaugurated in 1816, Christophe could claim that its bastions were able to garrison fifteen thousand men, that inexhaustible supplies of ammunition lay within the magazines, that the entire civilian population of Cap-Henri would find refuge there during an emergency. The walls are prodigiously thick, some thirty feet in width, and they concealed a hospital, a foundry, a forge; dungeons, treasure chambers, an artilleryman's chapel; kitchens, dormitories, storerooms, bomb proofs and water cisterns. But it is curious to reflect that none of the 365 huge bronze cannon, one for every day of the year, was ever fired. The enemy never came.

I arrived at the Citadel in the last flush of light. There was no one about and the solemnity of the place frightened a little. The fortress had been here, it seemed, since the beginning of remote ages and the Cyclopean walls were partly covered with a red lichen, smooth as brocade. Superstitious Haitians call this the blood of Christophe. A sole cannon lay in the grass beneath the colossal perpendicular bastions: nobody had bothered to move it since the death of the King.

It was surprisingly cold inside and stones were damp with dew. I consulted a plan of the Citadel – reservoir, drawbridge, ventilation shafts – that had been given to me by the Institut de Sauvegarde du Patrimonie National and made my way towards the gunnery room where I was to sleep. ISPAN, the acronym for this Haitian preservation society, had guaranteed a camp bed for the night with the warning that I would probably find the fortress haunted. It is said that Christophe walked round at dawn when construction was under way and set to laying bricks after his workers had departed, returning to Sans Souci in the small hours. The clinking of his spurs on the stairways can still be heard, apparently.

My electric torch showed a baffling maze of corridors and passageways, rooms and ever more rooms honeycombed with oubliettes, tunnels and tiers of galleries. Cylindrical cavities looked down on massive storerooms piled with pyramids of cannonballs, shiny like clusters of black grapes. Floors and walls were of uneven limestone, distempered green and faintly clammy to the touch. A smell of urine hung in the vast silence of these rooms – bats swooped into the sombre brilliance of the night.

We know nothing of the engineers or foremen who built this Haitian Alhambra. Some historians maintain that it was the work of German military engineers who lived on inside the walls, forbidden to leave for fear that they might betray its secrets. No architectural plans survive. Perhaps they will come to light one day in England, given the anglomania of King Henri Christophe. I noted that blocks and construction bricks varied dramatically in size and shape: much of the masonry was salvaged from the demolition of colonial plantations around Cap-Henri – stones of slavery hauled up to Pic de la Ferrière by men and women who had been submitted to another form of slavery. The Citadel is as much a palladium of liberty as a monument to tyranny.

Broad flights of steps ascended to the inner sanctum of the Citadel and a parade ground where, according to legend, Christophe ordered a detachment of soldiers to march clean over the edge as a demonstration of loyalty and discipline. The story is no doubt apocryphal – the King was in need of all the troops he could muster – but it is quite in keeping with the madness of his last days. A plain white stone block in the topmost battlements marks his apparent tomb, adorned only with a tablet that bears the device: *'Je renais de mes cendres'*, I shall rise from my ashes. The King was buried here in quicklime to preserve his corpse from the maddened mobs.

The fifteen or so cannon were not very distinct in the uniform texture of the night, a vague outline of artillery. But close to, my torch shone on dolphin-handled guns of elegant craftsmanship, their metal almost gold in tone. None was cast in Haiti; many were English, engraved with *Dieu et Mon Droit, Honi Soit qui Mal y Pense*; some were French, stamped with lilies and the vapid blazing mask of the Sun King or the arrogant martial 'N' of Napoleon; and others Spanish, bearing the name of the ships for which they were made – *Scipion, Hamilcar, Hannibal.* One, lion-mouthed and more ornate, was adorned with a ducal coronet and a Germanic double-headed eagle, the talons curved round a ribbon with the melancholy legend *Fiel Pero Desdichado*, faithful but unhappy. When I searched months later in London for the identity of this Spanish legend, it emerged that it could only belong to John Churchill, 1st Duke of Marlborough, who was Master-General of Ordnance under George II. The cannon must have been a relic of the ill-fated British expedition to Saint Domingue.

I found my room near the exploded powder magazine. The bed was there all right, facing three more cannon mounted on wooden carriages riddled with worms. (Their wheels still ran on rails to allow for accurate aim.) The room was quite small, faintly illuminated through one window by the June full moon, and cluttered with spirit levels, scrolls or architectural blueprints, drawing boards and the paraphernalia of draughtsmen. ISPAN had been here, busy with restoration. The adjacent chamber was a munitions depot containing ballistics and dangerous fire-power: bombards the size of snowballs, piles of buckshot and musket pellets, rusted trigger-guards, also horses' hooves and bridles. Heaped in one corner were mortar balls, each of them hollow with a hole in the top for gunpowder. I quickly extinguished my cigarette (the projectiles still gave a whiff of saltpetre) and groped for the camp bed where I opened a bottle of Burgundy bought at a supermarket in Cap-Haïtien.

I drank the wine in celebration of my journey's end and sleep overwhelmed.

When Joseph Conrad returned to Marseilles via Port-au-Prince in 1876, barely nineteen, he met a Haitian whom he later immortalized as the brutish Pedro in *Victory*. 'He fixed my conception of blind, furious, unreasoning rage, as manifested in the human animal, to the end of my days.' Conrad's third voyage to the West Indies provided him with material which his imagination was already beginning to ponder, and he never forgot Haiti: 'My eyes were full of tropical splendour, my memory of my own experiences, lawful and lawless, which had their charm and their thrill; for they had startled me a little and amused me considerably.'

In deference to Conrad, I should like to say the same. My memories of Haiti are good and bad, the intensity of experience in this country as exhilarating as it was exhausting. I had found a devil-may-care gaiety among the people, a courage and humour in the face of desperate odds that was like an intoxication of hope. A hope which rose above the evil – Papa Doc, Tontons Macoute, the random violence – to become a celebration of life amid hardship, a remarkable resilience. There was always the dread of officialdom and the nightmarish parody of administration without law, without security, without justice; always men like Pedro with their guns and their corruption, the intimidation and extortion; yet the thousands of Haitians with whom one could talk freely, whom one could trust, they provided humanity and hope for the future.

I shall miss their hospitality, the shelter they offered when it came to rain, a bed at night, a bowl of rice and beans, the measures of rum – all those ordinary lives trapped beneath the crust of dictatorship, beneath the cloak of lawlessness. I shall not miss the tap-taps, the begging, the white missionaries or those uniformed churls who interrupted my journey with demands for bribery, the summary interrogation. But then the horror of Haiti has always been in the army, in simple thieves like Prosper Avril who removed a handsome balance from the Treasury. Duplicity or cunning, together with physical strength, are considered, even more than courage, heroic virtues here; to overcome your adversary is the great affair in life and the pity of Haiti is that it thrives on a survival of the fittest.

Democracy, it has been said, does not arrive overnight for a people snatched from their home in Africa to slave for Europe. Every Haitian, man or woman, would like to survive as a Macoute, for history has blown them to a harsh lee shore: the constitution is made of paper, they say, but the bayonet is made of steel. And the danger of national independence obtained by war is that, after victory, the heroes themselves become the representatives of power: Christophe, Dessalines, Faustin Soulouque, François Duvalier, Aristide – all these men stand as confirmation of Engels's remark that 'A revolution is certainly the most authoritarian thing there is.'

Smaller than Belgium, Haiti may yet be ungovernable. In the bitterness of his heart, Simón Bolívar believed this to be true of all Latin America: 'Those who have worked for her independence have ploughed the sea.' Haiti is a country that was never meant to be, formed in the crucible of French colonialism. Historians in the nineteenth century attributed its political stagnation to a problem of race: Haitians were incapable of government because they were black. The refusal of France to acknowledge Haitian independence until 1825 was largely determined by this prejudice and Great Britain half agreed with the French prime minister Villèle who proclaimed: 'Recognition of a Black Empire founded upon insurrection and upon the Massacre of the White Population would have a most pernicious moral Effect.' The truth is that Haiti was shunned by the West because it had overthrown a white government and become a dangerous symbol of redemption for the whole African race, of racial equality and – most unforgivable – of anti-colonialism. So it became a pariah, excluded from the family of nations and trapped in a time warp where there was no room for progress.

A dream of democracy will survive but after five months in Haiti the immortal legend *L'Union Fait la Force*, watermarked on all its banknotes, appeared to me as a grimly ironic joke. Mulattoes against blacks; the military against democracy; Voodoo against Christianity; people ashamed of their African origin and those many others who were proud of their distant homeland. The country seemed split on every side:

Haitians like to say that they are difficult to understand, but all nations enjoy this vanity. One can only hope that, despite the indignity of their dependence on foreign aid, this proud people will one day enjoy the fruits of independence for which they so courageously fought. As a politician here once told me: *'La maison est à nous, c'est à vous d'en sortir'* – this is our house; it is for you to get out.

Dawn came quickly on the ramparts of the Citadel. A damp wind ripped across the royal battery; it rattled sheets of metal and whistled through the cannon. Soon the sun was up, shining in the morning mist like points of diamond light. As far as the eye could reach there stretched a great antiquity of mountain and forest and sea, luxuriant plains that rolled beneath me towards Le Bonnet-à-l'Evêque, the twin-peaked Bishop's Mitre. The sun coruscated brilliantly in the blue and empty overhead, and I thought: This must be one of the most magnificent scenes in all the world. I could clearly see Ile de la Tortue, even the reflections of its treacherous canal; and away there, beyond a ragged barrier of palms, the village of Bord de Mer where Columbus had built his settlement. Columns of smoke rose like an Indian massacre amid the splendour of tropical vegetation and the eye lost itself in the mountains that rose above mountains thickly carpeted with forest – lost itself in all this marvellous banality of the picturesque.

The silence remained suspended as deep and complete as if never disturbed. Then a rain began to fall, pattering over the strong hot breath of the land; soon it would churn the earth to mud, brown as tobacco juice.

Postscript

Bonjour Blanc: A Journey Through Haiti

In the winter of 2003 I returned to Haiti for the first time in thirteen years. I was curious to see how the country had changed and what had happened to the characters in *Bonjour Blanc.* This time I would not be travelling by tap-tap or fishing boat, but in a rented air-conditioned car.*
A glossy magazine had commissioned me to stay in Haiti's best hotels and report on the country's prospects for tourism. I had arrived at Port-au-Prince in time for Carnival and the touts seemed to be in party mood. At the airport, bunting had been put up for Haiti's approaching independence gala in 2004, a key date in the history of this bedevilled land. The smells I knew so well from the winter of 1990 – jasmine, burning rubbish – hit me forcibly and it was as though I had never been away.

I was booked in for two nights at the Hotel Oloffson. I had not seen the manager, Richard Morse, since I proposed marriage here in 1990 (I went down on *two* knees to Laura after a burst of gunfire startled me). 'Ian, it's been too long', Richard said over drinks. Richard had not only kept the Oloffson open all these years but even managed to attract some business. He is a father now and performs in a Voodoo pop band, named *RAM* after his initials. 'I'm fine', he went on, 'but Haiti's a mess'.

There had been some changes in the old hotel. Morgan Destouches, the barman, had either died or been sacked. And one of the Oloffson guides, my friend Enoch, was surely dead. Enoch had been 'killed' by his girlfriend after she discovered he was married. In a rage she paid a *bokor* – black magician – to cut short his life. Soon afterwards Enoch began sleeping badly and stopped drinking or smoking – a bad sign. He died at the age of forty in 1993 and was buried in his birthplace of Les Cayes.

---

*In 1992 I received a letter from the manager of Haiti's plush Relais de l'Empereur hotel, François Richili, then living in England: 'The only advice I could possibly give you, should you wish to retrace your journey, is: travel on the *roof* of tap-taps. It is cheaper, cooler, less crowded and you get to see a damn sight more; and instead of spending nights in the company of over-zealous missionaries, spend them in the *bordelles*. Every Haitian town, however small, has a brothel. It is in these that you discover the *joie de vivre*, or should I say the lost hopes, of the Haitian. You certainly do not have to indulge in the girls and would, for that matter, be most unwise to.'

Next morning Port-au-Prince looked more delapidated than it had thirteen years ago and the streets round the Oloffson appeared to have degenerated into a slum. After breakfast I went in search of the Café Napoli but, to my disappointment, found that an American takeway ('Big Style') had taken its place. I had met the café's Neapolitan owner, Aïda, on my first night in Port-au-Prince and instantly liked her. Sadly no one knew where Aïda was now. I also tried to find the Roxy nightclub which I had visited that same January night in 1990, only to discover that it had been burned down by a vengeful drug-dealer. All that remained of the building was the scorched sign: 'NO WEAPONS ALLOWED'. Haiti's capacity for violence seemed to be unchanging and limitless, but the people's suffering was worse than before.

When I was last in Haiti in 1990 Jean-Bertrand Aristide was about to become the country's first democratically elected president since Papa Doc in 1957. Having studied Hebrew in Israel as part of his Bible studies, the frail, soft-spoken priest had returned to Haiti in 1982 to wage war on the 'corrupt'. He became a Christ-figure for Haiti's dispossessed and a firebrand in the pulpit. Today, however, Aristide has been corrupted by power and is reduced to a mere autocrat alongside the other emperors, kings and presidents-for-life who have misruled this country since independence in 1804. From the outset Aristide was a demagogue with an impossible task. He earned the disapproval of the Vatican hierarchy by inciting the poor to acts of violence against the wealthy, and unsurprisingly the military did not like him either. Less than a year into office, Aristide was deposed and bundled into a waiting car while bullets strafed the National Palace.

Haiti's president-priest spent three years in exile in Venezuala and America. Bill Clinton, buoyed up by his new 'ethical' foreign policy, meanwhile schemed ways to restore Aristide to power and topple the regime that had overthrown him. In September 1994, America invaded Haiti: Special Forces moved in by sea and air, and journalists made excited comparisons with Vietnam. More than 3,000 Haitians had been killed by the military since the coup, and most of the country's 8 million population hated the junta. Instead of retaliating, the regime's 7,000-strong troops lay about in their string vests playing cards. (This was Nam without the bullets.) Any civilians remotely associated with the junta, however, were slaughtered.

Eventually, in October 1994, Aristide was allowed to re-enter Haiti.

Some say he had changed dramatically during his three-year exile. Dependent on American 'hospitality' and surrounded by White House aides, it seemed his political integrity had been compromised by promises of power and money. Aristide's term had almost expired when he returned to Haiti; in the ensuing elections, closely watched by the world, his associate Réné Préval became president. Yet Aristide had developed a taste for government, and in February 2001 he was returned once more to the National Palace as apparent champion of the poor. Since then, Aristide has been implicated in the grossest human rights abuses, murder and disappearances. Moreover he has created his own private militia known in Creole as the *Chimè*, or Chimeras, similar in kind to the Tontons Macoute under Papa Doc.

These 'personal enforcers' of Aristide are routinely involved in graft. Cocaine smuggling has reportedly tripled in Haiti since the former priest returned in 1994, and the presidential clique has grown fat on the profits. Alix Legros, ex-chief of security at Port-au-Prince airport, was shot at by Aristide's paramilitary for refusing to let through a cocaine shipment and narrowly avoided death. Alix is an art dealer now, and one night in the Oloffson he showed me a photograph he still carries in his wallet of Aristide as a Salesian ordinand from the early 1970s. Alix, like so many Haitians, had once believed 'the Messiah' could redeem this country and its run-down people. But now Aristide rules by decree – without a functioning parliament – and Haiti is on the brink of becoming a Caribbean Sierra Leone, menaced by feuding gangs.

One person I was determined to see on my return was Eleanor Snare. Eleanor was already in poor health when I met her at the Haitian-American Institute in March 1990, and I had said goodbye to her fearing that I would not see her again. Even so, news of her death came as a shock. Eleanor was a remarkable woman and I would always send friends to see her if they happened to be in Haiti. She was sixty-nine when she died in July 2000 of a stroke. I wanted to put flowers on her grave and, hoping to find it, drove up to the mountainside suburb above Port-au-Prince where she had lived since 1969.

Eleanor's was a small, insignificant house off the Route Turin. Her battered silver car which I knew so well stood in the yard covered in dust, and the sight of it tugged at me nostalgically. Eleanor had been cremated at the local Episcopal church and her ashes interred in her garden. I placed the flowers beside her and knocked on the door. I was greeted by Eleanor's elderly housekeeper and two adopted Haitian children, Billiny and Meleine, now teenagers and both of them attractive and intelligent. In the course of my visit they told me some surprising things about Eleanor. In 1950s America she had been known as 'Airman Snare': Eleanor had worked at a US Air Force base in Texas as a photographic technician. On her desk I noticed a framed snapshot of my wedding in 1991. Haiti suddenly seemed a very barren place without Eleanor and I will not forget her. '*Bonjour Blanc* is great!' she had written to me in 1992, adding: 'You rascal! I chuckled over the pages which have my name etched into history!'

Using the Hotel Oloffson as a base, I set out to discover the fate of others in *Bonjour Blanc*. There were some disturbing revelations. The painter Stivenson Magloire had been stoned to death by enemies on 9 October 1994 during the chaos of Clinton's Operation Uphold Democracy. Nobody knows exactly why Stivenson had to die or even who killed him. However, his friends buried him in three sackfuls of wet concrete to prevent *bokors* from putting his remains to evil use. Other characters mentioned in this book were more fortunate to die of natural causes. Dr Louis Mars, the exquisitely-mannered psychiatrist and Voodoo authority, died in 2000 in his late nineties. Gwen Mellon, the American nurse and philanthropist whom I met in remote central Haiti, had also died in 2000, aged eighty-nine. (She was buried in a cardboard box, the way the poorest of the poor are buried in Haiti.) William Hodges, the medical doctor and archaeologist, died in 1995 at his home in Limbé. He had complained to his wife Joanna of chest pains; at about 6 p.m. the next day, 16 September, he summoned his children and grandchildren to his bedside to tell them he was dying. Half an hour later he peacefully closed his eyes. Dr Hodges was seventy-one. A memorial service held for him behind his Arawak Indian museum gathered over 3,500 Haitians: he and his wife had lived in Haiti for forty-five years.

In 1994 news had come to me, I think from Eleanor Snare, that Father Roger Riou, the French priest of Ile de la Tortue, had died suddenly aged eighty-four. His successor on Turtle Island, the unsavoury Father Aragon (not his real name), still runs a Catholic mission in Palmiste village. (I had taken a strong dislike to Aragon, and he to me.) Hérard Simon, the domineering *houngan* whom I encountered in Gonaïves, died in the early 1990s, apparently of natural causes. Other casualties? The cossack officer who lived behind the Hotel Oloffson, Nikolai Ivanovich Roude,[*] is deceased, as is Papa Cadet, the *homme mystique* who had known the great Marcus Garvey. Other deaths occurred closer to home. Gerard Corely Smith, Britain's last Ambassador to Haiti, died in 1997 aged eighty-eight. Sheldon Williams, the Haitian art collector who lived in London's Stoke Newington, died in 1994. He was seventy-five.

Happily, there are many surprising survivors. Max Beauvoir, Haiti's best known Voodoo priest and a former Duvalierist, briefly ran a temple in Washington D.C. before returning to live in Haiti in 2002. Rolf, the German plumber and gift shop owner in *Bonjour Blanc*, has opened a brothel in the Dominican Republic; his long-suffering Haitian wife Charlotte has become a nun. ('And I don't blame her', Richard Morse commented to me tartly.) Serge Beaulieu, the beret-wearing Tonton Macoute, operates a radio station from New York City and has attacked Aristide with a venom which proves that freedom of speech (or something like it) still exists in America. Hubert de Ronceray, the exiled politician whom I interviewed in Miami, is now part of the vicious, far-right opposition to Aristide; naïvely in 1990 I had assumed that he was anti-Duvalierist. Issa El Saïh, the Haitian-Syrian gallery owner who had known both Graham Greene and Charlie Parker, is still going strong at eighty-five.

No one in *Bonjour Blanc* was more stylish or suave than Carlos Jara, the Chilean psychiatrist and art dealer. In his tropical white drill, Carlos was a genuine connoisseur and I liked his generosity. In 1997 he had sent me a Haitian painting on the birth of my daughter, and I owe my slender knowledge of Haitain art to him. Carlos died two years later, in 1999, of heart failure. He had told his young Haitian wife Emeraude that he felt ill and wanted to lie down. Later the Haitian poet Rodney Saint-Éloi, in an extraordinary obituary for *Le Nouvelliste*, defamed Carlos as an 'exploitative' and 'unscrupulous' businessman. The level of hatred directed against Carlos in that paper reminded me once more of the Haitain expression: 'We are rightly called Haitian because we all hate each other'. Carlos had lived in Haiti for over twenty years: 'He was a good man slandered in his grave', said his friend Jørgen Leth, the Danish film-maker and honorary consul in Haiti.

---

[*] 'I used to go and see Nikolai, too', the historian Norman Stone wrote in his review of *Bonjour Blanc* in 1992, 'and he is responsible for my spoken Russian, which I got going in Haiti in the worst days of the Tontons Macoute. How good to learn that he is still going strong.' (Professor Stone had lived in Haiti on and off during the early 1970s.)

In search of further information, I travelled to Jørgen's adopted Jacmel, the beautiful coffee port on Haiti's south coast. Unfortunately the Manoir Alexandra where I had stayed in 1990 was closed indefinitely, so I checked in to the Hotel Florita off Rue du Commerce (formerly it had belonged to the American art collector and poet Selden Rodman, who died in 2002 after a game of tennis, aged ninety-three). I had been stranded in Jacmel during the coup that overthrew General Avril, and knew the town well. I was about to turn out the light in my bedroom when the telephone rang and a German voice said: 'My God! Is it *really* you?'

The next day Gottfried Kraüchi, the Swiss–German director of Jacmel's Collège Suisse, arrived with military punctuality at 8.00 a.m. for breakfast. More than a decade had passed since we played chess at the Manoir Alexandra, but Gottfried's manner had not changed. 'My God! It really *is* you!' he greeted me affably. I was unsure what Gottfried thought of my portrait of him in *Bonjour Blanc*, but apparently he liked it. 'You got me just right!' he said, beaming like a boy. We spoke of old times and the fate of friends and acquaintances. Gottfried's loyalty to Haiti remains deep; in the thirty years he has lived in this country he has returned to his native Switzerland only four times.

I wanted to know what had happened to Jack Carey, the London fireman who had taught at Gottfried's school. 'Fireman Jack? Yah, he died. His heart was too small for his enormous body and he had problems getting uphill.' In April or May 1991, in need of medical attention, Jack had managed to fly home to London, but he died that summer in hospital. Soon afterwards Gottfried received a letter from a man purporting to be Jack's son; he demanded to know if his father had invested any money in the Collège Suisse. Gottfried was astonished to learn that Jack had children. 'Because in Jacmel, as you know, he was the complete bachelor!' I suppose Haiti was Jack's escape from a difficult home life in north London. As he told me in 1990: 'You know it's a funny thing, Mr Thomson, but the stars above Jacmel always seem . . . *brighter* and *nearer* than they do in Enfield'.

Over coffee, Gottfried went on to tell me of the time he was arrested by the Haitian military on subversion charges. In 1993, pupils at the Collège Suisse had staged a sit-in to protest against the overthrow of President Aristide two years earlier. 'Police broke into the school and put me on a lorry for Port-au-Prince'. Their orders were to deport Gottfried back to his native Zurich but, owing to some bureaucratic hitch, he remained in the Port-au-Prince penitentiary. 'I was treated very well there

– in fact it was quite *beautiful*!' Gottfried recalled. His release was arranged in typical fashion by the junta. An army colonel whom Gottfried had taught at the Collège Suisse heard of his captivity, and within two weeks the Swiss troublemaker had returned to Jacmel a local hero.

In Jacmel later that morning on the beach I was amazed to encounter Aublelin Jolicœur, the gossip columnist 'Petit Pierre' from *The Comedians*. 'Aubie!' I called out to him, but he appeared a shadow of his old flamboyant self. Indeed he was in a dressing gown and dishevelled. For almost forty years Jolicœur had enjoyed the fame that Graham Greene's novel had brought him, but now I noted his shaking hands and glazed eye. No one seemed to know whether Jolicœur had depression or Alzheimer's or Parkinson's disease. Yet for all his questionable politics (Jolicœur remains loyal to Papa Doc), he passionately loved Haiti and its people. When 'Petit Pierre' dies, a part of Haiti will die too.

Unfortunately there was not enough time for me to visit Jérémie on the southern peninsula but an aid worker there, Seth Pickens, helped me to establish the fate of various Jérémiens in *Bonjour Blanc*. Saint-Ange Bontemps, feared and villified as a Macoute, had died in 1999. Willy St Elmé, the eccentric 'US president' of Jérémie, disappeared in 1997, presumed dead. Antoine Roumer, the city's 'last mulatto', is still alive at 93; his wife died in 2002. Father Samedi, the former parish priest of Saint-Heleine in Jérémie, has become a courageous scourge of Aristide ('President Aristide, your mouth is full of worms') and indeed repeatedly calls for his resignation. The potential for massacre under Aristide, as he loses control of the country, is now real and frightening, says Samedi. Three years after I last saw Samedi, Jérémie became associated with a dreadful maritime disaster. On 16 February 1993, the *Neptune* capsized on her return journey to Port-au-Prince: 2,000 market women and other countryfolk were drowned. On the ferry's outward voyage to Jérémie I had spoken to the *marchandes* on board and got to know something of their lives. Few of the women said they could swim; there were no lifeboats.

After a week in Haiti my time had almost run out, and I felt the same emotion as thirteen years ago, a mixture of impatience for home and regret at leaving. But there was one last thing I wanted to do. During my initiation into the Voodoo cult of Bizango I had had to swear an oath inviting extreme repercussions if ever I disclosed the secrets of the society, only to reveal quite a few of them in *Bonjour Blanc.** So far there has been no malevolent payback. But I was curious to know what had become of my Bizango hat. In 1990 a French priest in Cap-Haïtien, Father Jean-Marie Le Ray, had asked to keep it for his private 'Voodoo' museum. I could not leave Haiti without knowing whether Father Le Ray was still alive.

Instead of the eight hours my journey north to Cap had taken by tap-tap in 1990, I arrived at the city after a brief twenty-minute flight. From the airport I took a taxi to the Justinien Hospital where Father Le Ray had lived. I was unable to locate the address, so his housekeeper was summoned from the presbytery nearby. '*Père Le Ray?*' she asked in startled tones. He had died in 1997, she said – at the age of ninety-two. The woman agreed to show me inside the priest's old museum, and I found that I had not exaggerated its chaos in *Bonjour Blanc*: Voodoo flags and drums lay higgledy-piggledy on the floor. Looking round, I was delighted to see my hat resting on a shelf with the hand-written label: '*Very Rare Example of Voodoo Headgear*'. I was tempted to take it back to London but, for superstitious reasons, didn't.

Flying back to London from Port-au-Prince in 2003 brought to an end this powerful interlude in my life. Haiti is a country of incredible intensity and extremes – one of the most astonishing places on earth – and writing now, some 3,500 miles away in London, I can see that I must have returned home in 1990 with the air of one bewitched.

Four months before I returned to Haiti, in the winter of 2002, I made my way to a secret address in Queens, New York, where Duvalierist exiles gather to plot the destruction of Aristide and the restoration to power of Baby Doc. I was hoping to secure an interview with Jean-Claude Duvalier, but first I had to be checked out. Dr Franz Bataille ushered me in warily – he edits the pro-Duvalier newspaper *Haiti Observateur*. As he puffed importantly on a cigar, his Haitian girlfriend Micheline Millery emerged with a plate of *grillot* for us and a bottle of Barbancourt rum. She began to speak of the 'golden years' of Haiti under

---

*Bizango membership proved unexpectedly useful to me when a rival Primo Levi biographer became convinced that I was casting Voodoo spells on her. In the London *Guardian* she confessed: 'One morning I caught sight of a small dark object beside my left foot. . . . I knew it was crazy, but the words that kept coming to mind were [Bizango] coffin nails.' The nails turned out to be cheap plastic hair brush teeth; I have Bizango to thank for the misunderstanding.

Baby Doc and added tearfully: 'Jean-Claude is an angel. Haitians would jump for *joy* to have him back'. By now Dr Bataille also had tears in his eyes: he had not set foot in Haiti, he said, since Baby Doc was deposed in 1986.

With a sigh he got up and dialled a long number. I watched as he bowed to the phone. '*Bonjour Monsieur le Président, comment allez-vous?*' (I could feel the tension in the room.) 'Yes, we have Mr Thomson here. I'll pass him over to you.' Taking the phone, I repeated Dr Bataille's fawning words to Baby Doc: 'Good morning Mister President, how are you?' The president spoke so slowly in reply that I thought he must be drugged or ill. After more suitably ingratiating remarks from me, the ex-dictator agreed to be interviewed for the London *Sunday Telegraph* but asked me to contact him in his Paris exile once I had returned home. Back in Stoke Newington, I telephoned Baby Doc on 5 November, Guy Fawkes Day, and this proved to be a mistake. The instant *Monsieur le Président* picked up the telephone, a neighbour let off fireworks beneath my window. There was a long silence as I spoke above a background detonation of rockets. No reply was forthcoming. And in increasingly ridiculous French I tried to explain to Baby Doc the significance of the 1605 Gunpowder Plot. But Baby Doc wasn't listening any more. The phone went dead, and I never got the interview.

Ian Thomson
October 2003.

Envoi

Early on the morning of Sunday, 29 February 2004, President Jean-Bertrand Aristide fled Haiti into exile. The country's future is uncertain.

I.T., 29.ii.04

YOU ARE INVITED TO CELEBRATE THE DEPARTURE TO HAITI
OF IAN THOMSON AT "ANDREW EDMUNDS", 46 LEXINGTON ST. W1.
ON FRIDAY 26th JANUARY 1990 FROM 6·30 p.m. ONWARDS.
VOUS ME DEMANDEZ "OU EST CET HOMME BLANC QUI S'APPELLE IAN THOMSON?" JE RÉPLIQUE "IL EST UN ZOMBIE MAINTENANT"...
WINE AND/OR CHICKEN'S BLOOD WILL BE SERVED...
BE THERE OR PAPA SAMEDI'LL GETCHA!
TU ME SURPREND!
MERDE!
PAPA DOC
TOUSSANT LOUVERTURE
BABY DOC
GRAHAM GREENE
THE COMEDIANS

Acknowledgements

In writing this book, I am indebted to numerous accounts of Haitian politics and history. *Haiti: The Duvaliers and their Legacy* by Elizabeth Abbott (McGraw-Hill, 1988); *The Life of Toussaint L'Ouverture* by the Rev. J. R. Beard (Ingram and Cooke, 1853); *The Overthrow of Colonial Slavery 1776–1848* by Robin Blackburn (Verso, 1988); *Christophe: King of Haiti* by Hubert Cole (Eyre & Spottiswoode, 1967); *Papa Doc: Haiti and its Dictator* by Bernard Diederich and Al Burt (The Bodley Head, 1969); *Papa Doc, Baby Doc: Haiti and the Duvaliers* by James Ferguson (Basil Blackwell, 1987); *The Black Jacobins* by C. L. R. James (Allison & Busby, 1989); *The Haitian People* by James Leyburn (Yale University Press, 1941); *Haiti and the United States 1714–1938* by Ludwell Lee Montague (Duke University Press, 1940); *From Dessalines to Duvalier* by David Nicholls (Cambridge University Press, 1979); *The Rainy Season: Haiti Since Duvalier* by Amy Wilentz (Jonathan Cape, 1989).

For those interested in the Polish community of Haiti, I would suggest *Poland's Caribbean Tragedy* by Jan Pachonski and Revel Wilson (Columbia University Press, 1986). Kirkpatrick Sale's *The Conquest of Paradise* (Hodder & Stoughton, 1990) is recommended as a reference to the history of Christopher Columbus and Hispaniola.

Among travel books on Haiti, the following have been of help and inspiration: *The Traveller's Tree* by Patrick Leigh Fermor (Penguin Books, 1984); *Notes on Haiti, Made During a Residence in that Republic* by Charles Mackenzie (Henry Colburn and Richard Bentley, 1830); *The Present State of Hayti* by James Franklin (John Murray, 1828).

Literature on Voodoo is very extensive; for cannibalism see *The English in the West Indies* by James Anthony Froude (Longmans, 1888), an historian much beloved of V. S. Naipaul; and *Hayti, or the Black Republic* by the biting and very sarcastic Sir Spencer St John (London, 1889). Also rather sensationalist, but greatly entertaining: *The Magic Island* by W. B. Seabrook (George G. Harrap & Co, 1929). I have drawn extensively from the essential references on this religion. These are: *Divine Horsemen: The Living Gods of Haiti* by Maya Deren (Thames & Hudson, 1953); *Life in a*

Haitian Valley by Melville Herskovits (Alfred A Knopf, 1937); *Dieu Dans le Vaudou Haïtien* by Laënnec Hurbon (Henri Deschamps, 1987); *Voodoo Gods* by Zora Hurston (J. M. Dent, 1939); *The Invisibles* by Francis Huxley (Rupert Hart-Davis, 1966); and the classic *Le Vaudou Haïtien* by Alfred Métraux (Gallimard, 1958).

In addition, I would like to express admiration for two studies by Wade Davis on the zombi: *The Serpent and the Rainbow* (Collins, 1986) and *Passage of Darkness: the Ethnobiology of the Haitian Zombi* (University of North Carolina Press, 1988). These are models of research and exposition, the latter more serious, and I have plundered them both. The chapter on secret societies in *Voodoo and Politics in Haiti* by Michel S. Laguerre (Macmillan Press, 1989) was also useful.

Finally, I recommend *Mémoires d'un Leader du Tiers Monde* by Papa Doc (Hachette, 1969) as essential reading for those who wish to further their knowledge about the cruel and absurd doctor.

I should like to thank many people in Haiti, Great Britain, the United States and France: Margot Ammidown and Michael Carlbach for their information on Little Haiti, and their cocktails on Palm Beach; the former British ambassador to Haiti, Gerard Corley Smith, for afternoon tea at the Travellers'; Father Roger Riou for lunch in Rogny, and the books he gave me on Caribbean buccaneers; the Reverend David Nicholls, Vicar of Littlemore, Oxford, who kindly provided me with telephone numbers for Port-au-Prince; Will Ellsworth-Jones and Dr Ginette Theano, who did the same; Caroleen Conquest; Norman Lewis; Christopher Pillitz; Christopher Hawtree, John Letts, Robert O'Brien, Cecilia Robustelli, Susan Robinson, Martin Rowson, Mark Thompson and Sheldon Williams for all manner of help and strange information; Charles Spragge for his law reports on Baby Doc. Édouard Duval-Carrié at the Musée des Arts Africains et Océaniens (Paris) furnished me with an introduction to other Haitian artists.

The staff of the British Museum Reading Room and the London Library were helpful as ever, as were the archivists at the Press Association (Fleet Street) and the Central Science Reference Library in Holborn. I am particularly indebted to the French priests who facilitated my research at the Bibliothèque St Louis de Gonzague, Port-au-Prince, and who gave me much encouragement in writing this book. I am equally grateful to the many people in Haiti who said *yes* when it would have been just as easy to say *no*, for their thousand hospitalities: Dr William Hodges, Dr

Carlos Jara, Dr Louis Mars, Enoch and Milford at the Hotel Oloffson, also the barman Morgan Destouches for his legendary rum punches. I feel especially impelled to thank Eleanor Snare at the Institut Haïtiano-Americain, who sustained me with words of comfort and cups of coffee, and who generously allowed me to consult her private library. Other characters in this book are identified by pseudonyms, and perhaps they will know who they are.

I also wish to record my profound gratitude and appreciation to Euan Cameron for reading the manuscript. Any mistakes, etc., etc., are entirely my fault. Thanks, above all, to Laura Fleminger, who lived so patiently with another's obsession and became my best critic.

October 2003. Many friends and colleagues helped me with the new edition of this book and also provided information for the postscript. My sincere thanks to: Jørgen Leth (for his candlelit hospitality in Jacmel and use of the word 'fantastic'), Greg Chamberlain, Bernard Diederich, Sarah Miller of *Condé Nast Traveller*, Caroline Michel, my agent Pat Kavanagh, Lucy Plaskett (with grateful affection, and thanks for the memorable night out with Jørgen), Rachel Cugnoni, Ali Reynolds and Audrey Fitt at Vintage books, Euan Cameron (Graham Greene's acquaintance and later *Bonjour Blanc*'s midwife), Dr Robert Bricston, Cameron Brohman and Sarah Davies (who suggested the Haitian cookbook *Foodoo*), Leah Gordon and Charles Arthur of the Haiti Support Group in London, Consuelo and Professor Anthony Maingot, Alix 'Loulou' Legros, Joanna Hodges, Seth Pickens, Dr Georges Michel, Gottfried Kräuchi, the divine Noelle Théard, Andy Kershaw (and the memory of our first encounter in 'Grumbles' in 1992), Sir Richard Auguste Morse, Esq, of the popular Haitian music combo *RAM* (with belated apologies for the ganja reference). And finally dear Laura again as always.

Index